University of California Publications

LINGUISTICS
Volume 126

Reconstructing Proto-Afroasiatic (Proto-Afrasian)

Vowels, Tone, Consonants, and Vocabulary

Christopher Ehret

University of California Press

RECONSTRUCTING PROTO-AFROASIATIC (PROTO-AFRASIAN)

Reconstructing Proto-Afroasiatic (Proto-Afrasian)

Vowels, Tone, Consonants, and Vocabulary

Christopher Ehret

UNIVERSITY OF CALIFORNIA PRESS
Berkeley • Los Angeles • London

UNIVERSITY OF CALIFORNIA PUBLICATIONS IN LINGUISTICS

Volume 126

UNIVERSITY OF CALIFORNIA PRESS
BERKELEY AND LOS ANGELES, CALIFORNIA

UNIVERSITY OF CALIFORNIA PRESS, LTD.
LONDON, ENGLAND

Library of Congress Cataloging-in-Publication Data

Ehret, Christopher.
Reconstructing Proto-Afroasiatic (Proto-Afrasian): vowels, tone, consonants, and vocabulary / Christopher Ehret.
p. cm. — (University of California publications in linguistics; v. 126)
Includes bibliographical references (p.) and index.
ISBN 0-520-09799-8 (alk. paper)
1. Proto-Afroasiatic language. 2. Reconstruction (Linguistics).
I. Title. II. Series.
PJ992.E35 1995
492—dc20 95-13152
CIP

The paper used in this publication meets the minimum requirements of American National Standard for Information Sciences—Permanence of Paper for Printed Library Materials, ANSI Z39.48-1984.

To Pat

Contents

Tables

Acknowledgments

This work is the culmination of one of several paths my research interests have led me along over the past two and a half decades, and a large number of people have contributed in substantial and important ways to the growth of my knowledge and understanding at different stages of the journey.

The first steps on this particular path were my field studies of the Southern Cushitic languages, undertaken at a variety of times in the later 1960's and in the 1970's. Among the various speakers of those languages, Afraim Hayuma, Damas Dinya, and Aloisi Pius Kidara were especially helpful teachers and deserve special thanks for the time and effort they shared with me. I owe a great deal as well to Edward Elderkin, whose knowledge and gracious sharing of his own field research on the Dahalo language were essential to my development of an adequate historical-comparative reconstruction of the Southern Cushitic group.

At the end of the 1970's and in the early 1980's, the establishment for a time of a close academic relationship between my institution, the University of California at Los Angeles, and the national university in Somalia had the unplanned consequence of turning my attention toward the study of the Soomaali language subgroup. I owe special thanks to Hussein Adam, who helped set up my first work on this topic in 1979; to my colleague Edward A. Alpers, who took time out from his own researches to assist me; to Ali Hersi, then head of the Somali Academy, whose efforts on my behalf provided me a place to stay and a place to work during my major field studies in 1982; and to Adan Maxamed Isaaq, whose unparalleled cultural knowledge and lively participation in the process of field collection, contributed immeasurably to the effectiveness of the work. Above all, I owe a debt of gratitude to Mahamed Nuuh Ali, who on many occasions between 1982 and 1985 discussed and studied with me the materials thus collected, gathered his own additional evidence on the topic, and made extensive use of these data in writing his doctoral dissertation on the history of the eastern Horn of Africa.

Over the years a number of scholars have been continuing sources of valued criticism, advice, correction, and apt example for me in pursuing work on Afrasian languages. These include most notably David Appleyard, Dick Hayward, Edward Elderkin, Bernd Heine, Phil Jaggar, Derek Nurse, Russ Schuh, and above all Robert Hetzron. Many others have contributed significantly to the growth of my knowledge and understanding along the way, among them Linda Arvanitis, Giorgio Banti, Lionel Bender, Hal Fleming, Gene Gragg, Carlton Hodge, Grover Hudson, Marcello Lamberti, Ed

Meltzer, Paul Newman, Gerard Philippson, Joseph Pia, Mauro Tosco, and Rainer Voigt. Needless to say, none of these scholars are to blame for any errors that remain in the work. Finally, I owe special thanks to the copy editor of this volume, Orin Gensler, whose editing skills and knowledge of Afrasian and especially Semitic helped me to make this work much better that it could otherwise have been, and to the series editor, Rose Anne White, whose patient efforts and expertise oversaw the publication process from beginning to end. I know that I have surely missed mentioning others who truly deserve inclusion here, and to them I apologize most deeply.

Several different granting agencies funded different phases of the research that has gone into this historical-comparative reconstruction of this family. My initial field studies of the later 1960's, which included firsthand work on the Southern Cushitic languages, was supported by a Foreign Area Fellowship of the Social Science Research Council. In the 1970's my researches were variously helped along by a Ford Foundation grant and by several smaller Faculty Senate grants of the University of California. The major work in Somalia in 1982 I pursued under a Fulbright research fellowship, while other Faculty Senate grants provided me subsequent support that contributed to the finishing stages of the Afrasian reconstruction.

Abbreviations

A.	Arabic
adj.	adjective
ampl.	amplificative extension
and.	andative extension
anim.	animate
Append.	Appendix
Arb.	Arbore (South Lowland Eastern Cushitic language)
assim.	assimilation, assimilated
attrib.	attributive
BA	Boreafrican (see Chapter 6 for this subgroup)
BB	Bauchi-Bade (branch of West Chadic)
BM	Biu-Mandara (grouping of Chadic languages)
C	consonant
C.	Coptic
C_s	consonant suffix
caus.	causative extension
CCh	Central Chadic (of Jungraithmayr and Shimizu)
Ch.	Chadic
comp.	complementive extension; complement (noun suffix)
conc.	concisive extension
concom.	concomitant (prefix)
cont.	continuant
Cush.	Cushitic
demons.	demonstrative
denom.	denominative
deverb.	deverbative
dial.	dialect, dialectal
diffus.	diffusive extension
dimin.	diminuative
dissim.	dissimilation, dissimilated
dur.	durative extension
EC	Eastern Cushitic
ECh	Eastern Chadic (of Jungraithmayr and Shimizu)
Eg.	Egyptian
ER	East Rift (Southern Cushitic subgroup)
Eryth.	primary branch of Afroasiatic (see Chapter 6)
ESA	Epigraphic South Arabian

ext.	extension
extend.	extendative extension
fem.	feminine
fin.	finitive extension
foc.	focative extension
fort.	fortative extension
freq.	frequentative
H.	Harsūsi (Modern South Arabian language)
HEC	Highland Eastern Cushitic
incep.	inceptive
inchoat.	inchoative extension
imper.	imperative
intens.	intensive extension
intr.	intransitive
iter.	iterative
J	Jungraithmayr and Shimizu 1981
Ji.	Jibbāli (Modern South Arabian language)
LE	Late Egyptian
M.	Mehri (Modern South Arabian language)
masc.	masculine
ME	Middle Egyptian
modif.	modifier
MSA	Modern South Arabian (subgroup of Semitic)
m.v.	middle voice extension
N	Newman 1977; Newman and Ma 1966
NE	North Erythraean (see Chapter 6 for this group)
n.	noun
n. comp.	noun complement deverbative suffix
NAgaw	North branch of Agaw (branch of Cushitic)
Ng.	Ngizim (Chadic language)
NOm	North branch of Omotic
nom.	nominalizing; nominal
NSom	North Soomaali dialects
obstr.	obstruent
PAA	proto-Afroasiatic (proto-Afrasian)
PBA	proto-Boreafrasian (see BA above and Chapter 6)
PC	proto-Cushitic
PCh	proto-Chadic
PEC	proto-Eastern Cushitic
PEth	proto-Ethiopic (South Semitic subgroup)
pl.	plural
PLEC	proto-Lowland Eastern Cushitic
PO	proto-Omotic
pPS	pre-proto-Semitic
PR	proto-Rift (branch of Southern Cushitic)
precip.	precipitive extension

pfxd.	prefixed
pron.	pronoun, pronominal
PS	proto-Semitic
PSC	proto-Southern Cushitic
PSom	proto-Soomaali (South Lowland East Cushitic subgroup)
PSom-II	proto-Soomaali-II (second stage of Soomaali differentiation into separate languages)
PSom-III	proto-Soomaali-III (third stage of Soomaali differentiation into separate languages)
redup.	reduplicated, reduplication
ref.	referential, reference
S.	Soqotri (Modern South Arabian language)
SC	Southern Cushitic
Sem.	Semitic
sing.	singular
SLEC	South Lowland Eastern Cushitic
Som.	standard Soomaali
SOm	South branch of Omotic
stat.	stative
suff.	suffix
tr.	transitive
TV	terminal vowel
V	vowel
v.	verb
ven.	venitive extension
WCh	West Chadic (of Jungraithmayr and Shimizu)
WOT	Western Omo-Tana (South Lowland Eastern Cushitic subgroup)
WR	West Rift (Southern Cushitic subgroup)
YD	Yaaku-Dullay (branch of Eastern Cushitic)

Notes on Transcription

b' Voiced labial implosive.

c (1) In proto-Semitic (PS) reconstruction, denotes a proposed dental affricate [ts];
(2) in Soomaali (Cushitic) orthography, represents the pharyngeal voiced consonant [ʕ];
(3) in Afar (Cushitic) orthography, denotes the pharyngeal fricative [ħ];
(4) everywhere else, normally reflects a palatal or prepalatal affricate [č].

d' Voiced alveolar implosive.

dh In Soomaali orthography, denotes, depending on the particular dialect, either an apical voiced alveolar stop or a voiced alveolar implosive stop (elsewhere given as *d'*).

dl (1) In Ngizim (Chadic), represents a voiced lateral fricztive [ɮ];
(2) elsewhere, denotes a voiced lateral affricate.

g' Voiced velar implosive.

j' Voiced palatal or prepalatal implosive.

q (1) In Afar orthography, represents the pharyngeal voiced consonant [ʕ];
(2) in Dullay and Yaaku (Cushitic), denotes a voiceless ingressive uvular stop;
(3) elsewhere, has its usual uvular voiceless stop value [q]

sh Voiceless (pre)palatal fricative [š] (used in Soomaali, Sidamo [Cushitic], and Ngizim orthographies)

tl (1) In proto-Cushitic reconstruction, denotes an ejective lateral affricate [tl'];
(2) in Ngizim, represents the voiceless lateral fricative [ɬ];
(3) elsewhere, reflects a voiceless, non-ejective lateral affricate.

x (1) In Afar orthography, denotes an apical voiced alveolar stop (equivalent to Northern Soomaali *dh*);
(2) in Soomaali orthography, represents the pharyngeal voiceless fricative [ħ];
(3) elsewhere, has its usual voiceless velar fricative value.

zh Voiced (pre)palatal fricative [ž] (in Ngizim orthography)

Notes on Alphabetization

The alphabetic sequence of consonants followed in this work is as shown:

b, c, c', d, dl, dz, f, g, g^w, ɣ, ɣ^w, h, ħ, j, k, k^w, k', $k^{w\prime}$, l, ɬ, m, n, ɲ, ŋ, ŋ^w, p, p', r, s, s', š, t, t', tl', ts, w, x, x^w, y, z, ʔ, ʕ.

For further commentary on the marking and ordering conventions and on the notations used for the data presented here, see first two sections of Chapter 4.

1

INTRODUCTION

The Afroasiatic (Afrasian)[1] language family has a history of scholarly acceptance almost as long as that of Indo-European, despite being a family of much greater internal diversity and historical time depth (Ehret 1979; Fleming 1977). Its comparative study has had many distinguished contributors, most notably in the past half-century Marcel Cohen (1947) and I. M. Diakonov (1965, 1988). But a full, systematic phonological reconstruction of proto-Afroasiatic (Proto-Afrasian, PAA), with detailed substantiation and applying the normal canons of the historical-comparative method, has yet to appear. It is that deficiency which the present study seeks to remedy.

This work provides therefore a comprehensive, systematic reconstruction of the family, concrete and specific in both evidence and argument. It proposes a full vowel and consonant reconstruction, along with a provisional reckoning of tone, and substantiates in detail each aspect of the reconstruction in an extensive comparative vocabulary of more than 1000 roots based on data from the Semitic, Egyptian, Cushitic, Chadic, and Omotic divisions of the family. (Data from the sixth recognized division of Afroasiatic, Berber, proved of less immediate usefulness, for reasons discussed in Chapter 2.) Two requirements were rigorously imposed in the building up of this data base: (1) regularity of sound correspondences had to hold without exception for each segment (and suprasegmental, where known) of each root being compared; and (2) only minimal semantic differences, or else meaning differences clearly explainable on substantive morphological grounds, were allowed in roots being considered for possible cognation.

A historical-comparative reconstruction of proto-Afroasiatic faces several potentially daunting obstacles. One of these is the great number of triconsonantal roots in Semitic that must be compared with the more commonly found biconsonantal stems of other subgroups of the family. A second is the lack of rigor with which the semantic dimension of reconstruction, in Semitic as much as in wider familial comparisons, has often previously been treated. A

[1]The author's own preference is "Afrasian," as proposed and used by I. M. Diakonov and his colleagues (hence the notation in parentheses), and he intends in future publications to use that term exclusively. But in deference to wide Anglophone usage, the term "Afroasiatic" is still applied to the family in most instances in this work. Afrasian has a primary virtue of being a simpler formation. In English this formation has the effect also of deemphasizing the Asian element in the name; apparently in Russian it does this even more effectively. And this point is a very important one, because Afrasian is primarily an African language family, and the great majority of its history has been played out in Africa.

third potential source of difficulty is the immense variety and time-depth of the relationships among the languages that make up the Afroasiatic family.

With respect to triconsonantal roots in Semitic, a comprehensive and systemic, but certain to be controversial, explanation of the third consonants — as lexicalized pre-proto-Semitic suffixal morphemes — has now been put forward (Ehret 1989). This scheme, and the linguistic procedures by which it was built up, provide one of the key steps in the Afroasiatic root and affix reconstructions carried out in this book. It has been applied here without apology because, quite simply, it works. The comparative materials from Egyptian, Cushitic, Chadic, and Omotic provide further point-for-point confirmations of the specific meanings and functions of the great majority of the affixes proposed for pre-proto-Semitic. The validity of the scheme is resubstantiated time and again, throughout the long vocabulary of proto-Afroasiatic roots by its explanatory power — its ability to account reasonably, economically, and aptly, in *more than 2400 separate instances* (indexed in Tables 2 and 3 in Chapter 3) for the individual variations of meaning that are found amongst the several thousand cited reflexes of those roots (Chapter 5 and Appendixes 1-3).

The procedures involved in this internal reconstruction of third-consonant meanings have consequences for the second problem as well, that of semantic comparison. Specifically, the analytical groupings of roots distinguished by this approach reveal more sharply than ever before the pervasive polysemy and homonomy of a large proportion of Semitic verb roots. From the semantic patternings within these groupings, it becomes clear that in pre-proto-Semitic, because of the loss of stem vowel distinctions in verbs, a great many previously distinct roots had fallen together. A very large number of homonyms, in other words, were created in proto-Semitic by prior developments in verb morphology (Ehret 1989: 186-201). The recurrent polysemy of Semitic verbs can thus be laid to lexical polyphylesis, that is, to the derivation of a very great portion of seemingly single roots in proto-Semitic from two or more pre-proto-Semitic roots. Once this historical factor is recognized, the semantics of Semitic roots become much less confusing — the supposedly figurative development of opposed meanings for single roots, for example, probably received its initial impetus from the falling together of earlier Afroasiatic roots of disparate connotation — and the comparativist is thus able to begin confidently to identify the different clusters of meaning, and thus distinguish the separate source roots, that underlie so many ostensibly single roots.

The making of over-imaginative semantic connections among Cushitic, Chadic, Omotic, and Egyptian roots is easily enough avoided through the stricture, applied in this work, of accepting only relatively obvious, unexceptionable meaning resemblances between prospective cognates, and by explicitly identifying, whenever they appear, any meaning-modifying affixes. Maintaining the same degree of rigor with Semitic comparisons requires the additional step of sorting out the semantic confusions that pre-proto-Semitic root history itself created, quite apart from any later interventions of scholarly inventiveness. From a traditionalist viewpoint, it might seem necessary first to work meticulously through all the arrays of Semitic roots that have been proposed over the years. But in fact the task can be accomplished much more economically, and indeed *much more effectively*, by simply applying the techniques of internal reconstruction developed for the determinations of third-consonant meanings. The reconstructions of pre-proto-Semitic biconsonantal roots produced in Ehret 1989 form a sizeable body of stems already sorted out semantically. By the same procedures, a large additional body of such roots can and has been identified in the present work (for all of which see the many Semitic entries in the 1000-plus vocabulary of proto-Afroasiatic roots in Chapter 5, and also the additional demonstrations in Appendix 1 of this monograph).

Even more important, this approach allows us to go a step farther back in time in generating our comparative data: by this means we recover earlier, pre-proto-Semitic root shapes, closer in time and appearance to their proto-Afroasiatic etymons. Seen in this light, a detailed reconsideration of past Semitic etymological work takes on a different aspect; instead of a prerequisite it becomes a subsequent task, more effectively pursued once there exists the external evaluatory apparatus that only the systematic reconstruction of Afroasiatic phonology can provide. It not only appears an unnecessary sidetrack, given the existence of a procedure fully capable on its own of revealing root forms and meanings of a stage preceding proto-Semitic, but it would commit us to data less ancient and less archaic of aspect than best suit our historical-comparative purposes. Quite deliberately, then, this work selects its Semitic attestations principally (although not entirely) from either reconstructed pre-proto-Semitic forms or particular Arabic or Modern South Arabian root attestations from which such forms can explicitly be derived.

These latter considerations bring us to the final problem, that of sure and effective historical linguistic reconstruction in a family considerably more ancient than Indo-European. The key elements for success are reasonably early historical-comparative reconstructions of at least some of the branches of such a family and, where this may be lacking, solid collections of data from phonologically conservative individual languages. Contrary to received opinion, detailed reconstruction of every subgroup of a family is not at all necessary to overall reconstruction, provided that the family has numerous member languages, some of them very accurately and extensively recorded, and that there exist among these languages a number of major branchings and that for at least a few of these branchings good reconstructions are available.

The resources at hand for Afroasiatic reconstruction more than meet these requirements. The proto-Semitic consonant correspondences have, of course, long been known. Detailed reconstructions with extensive supporting data now exist for the Southern and Eastern branches of Cushitic (Ehret 1980 for Southern Cushitic; Sasse 1979, Arvanites 1990, and Ehret 1991 for Eastern Cushitic) and for Cushitic as a whole (Ehret 1987), while a less extensive reconstruction has been made of the Agaw subbranch of Cushitic (Appleyard 1984 and n.d.). A considerable body of Chadic roots also exists (Newman

1977; Jungraithmayr and Shimizu 1981; Jungraithmayr's expected revision of Chadic was not available at press time) and can, with careful reanalysis, be put to effective use in overall Afroasiatic reconstruction. In the case of Egyptian, which may always have been a single language, although at times dialectally diverse, it is important to use a consistent but sufficiently large body of relatively early occurrence, and for that reason attestations are taken mostly from Middle Egyptian (Faulkner 1964) and only rarely from Late Egyptian (Lesko 1982-90). Finally, a provisional reconstruction of Omotic consonants and vowels is offered in the present work (Chapters 2 and 4, q.v.; cf. also Bender 1988). Whenever possible, the particular attestations for a proto-Afroasiatic root (in Chapter 5) are drawn from these various reconstructions. Of course, in the case of Semitic, for the reasons noted above, an important source is reconstructions of the pre-proto-Semitic forms. Berber data figures in the outlining of proto-Afroasiatic vowel history, but otherwise is little drawn on here (for reasons, as noted above, that are described in Chapter 2).

In addition, from each major branching of Afroasiatic one or more very well recorded languages, usually ones with important archaic features in their phonologies, have been chosen for special representation among the data cited for their branch. From Semitic were selected Arabic, which retains all the standardly accepted proto-Semitic consonant distinctions except one (though often not with their original pronunciations) and is exceedingly thoroughly recorded, and the Modern South Arabian languages, usually Jibbāli and Harsūsi, which are particularly important for their retention of lateral values for the old Semitic (and Afroasiatic) lateral obstruents, and for a number of other phonetic archaisms. From Cushitic a variety of individual languages provided valuable information, especially Soomaali, for which a very large and reliable dictionary exists. As for the Chadic branch, Ngizim data proves especially useful because of its preservation in many cases of the probable proto-Chadic vowel system. The reconstructed roots of proto-Southern Cushitic (Ehret 1980) and lexemes from Ngizim in Chadic, Awngi in Agaw, Arbore in Eastern Cushitic, and Mocha, Bench, and Yem in Omotic jointly offer crucial evidence for the provisional reconstruction of proto-Afroasiatic tone. Other individual Cushitic and Omotic languages are cited from time to time in instances where they may happen to preserve old roots as yet unrecorded for other languages of their branch.

There is, finally, another obstacle of a different kind facing those who attempt the historical-comparative reconstruction of Afroasiatic, potentially much more daunting than all of the practical obstacles put together, and that is the immense wealth of previous literature on the family and the enormous accumulation of specialized knowledge to be found among the thousands of publications on the family, and above all on its Semitic branch. So particular and so varied are the expertises and specialities involved that almost nothing can be said that will not be opposed, often with great vigor and warmth of feeling, by someone in this vast field. This reservoir of accumulated knowledge, moreover, has over the decades generated all sorts of historical hypotheses, some widely held and others idiosyncratic, some explicit and consciously adhered to and others implicit and perhaps not even recognized as such by their adherents. The scholar who reconstructs proto-Afroasiatic must thus be prepared to face, along with much substantive and justified criticism, the magnification of individual mistakes into fundamental flaws, the assertion of *a priori* views as though they were factual counterevidence, and sweeping dismissals of the work based on agendas sometimes hidden even from those who hold them.

The central point to be made here is that we must not allow previous views to impose themselves on the structuring of the data or on our responses to the conclusions that emerge from the analysis. That a particular Semitic root may have been proposed in a past work (for example, in Cohen 1947) as cognate with a particular word found in some Cushitic languages does not mean its automatic acceptance as a proto-Afroasiatic root today. Now that we actually possess relatively full reconstructions of proto-Cushitic and of the Eastern and Southern branches of Cushitic, and partial reconstructions of the Chadic branch — *major* additional bodies of evidence not available even twenty years ago — we must ask all over again, "Do these formerly accepted items actually show fully regular sound correspondences? Can their points of dissimilarity be explained by defensible morphological arguments? Do the semantics still seem plausible?" Inevitably, many of the lexical connections posited in the past and often widely accepted today prove wanting in the face of these criteria, while others not previously considered or not known at all turn out to work quite well.

Nor can we afford to let the great imbalance of interest among Afroasiaticists in favor of Semitic, and secondarily toward Egyptian, preshape our historical views. The Cushitic, Chadic, and Omotic divisions of the family are not pale reflections of Semitic. Each is an equally important, separate source of comparative evidence, and their contributions, combined with those of Semitic and Egyptian, depict a proto-Afroasiatic language only distantly similar in structure to its Semitic daughter tongues or to Egyptian.

It must be reiterated that the reconstruction of Afroasiatic proposed here follows throughout the established techniques and approaches of the historical-comparative method. It is systematic, comprehensive, and rigorous, with unyielding phonological and demanding semantic requirements for cognation. It is detailed and thorough in its etymological analysis, providing at the minimum a parenthetical explanation of almost every morphological modification of each cognate form and an explicit justification of any less-than-transparent semantic connection. Its citations from individual languages, where they appear in the data, are also given parenthetical phonological derivations from their proximate proto-language whenever that is needed; and such derivation in each case rests on established reconstructions of the correspondences involved. The reconstruction may bypass areas and resources of concern to other scholars, but only when its own routes of inference and substantiation seem more direct and effective than those not taken, and every bit as sound. It uses a body of evidence which is, for Semitic, still controversial, but does so precisely because the validity of that evidence appears strongly corroborated by the wider Afroasiatic comparisons presented here. Its conclusions may often surprise, and some of its consonant correspondences may be unexpected. But its arguments and conclusions rest on sound method and solid and detailed evidence.

2

PRELIMINARY CONSIDERATIONS IN AFROASIATIC (AFRASIAN) RECONSTRUCTION

BASES FOR RECONSTRUCTION

Two recent works (both mentioned in Chapter 1) contribute especially to making the systematic reconstruction of proto-Afroasiatic (Proto-Afrasian; PAA) an eminently feasible enterprise. The first is a comparative-historical reconstruction of proto-Cushitic (PC), and the second, an internal reconstruction of the origins of the third consonants (C_3) of Semitic triliteral roots (Ehret 1987, 1989). The earlier of these studies (1987) permits the establishment, on a reliable basis, of regular sound correspondences between proto-Semitic (PS), proto-Cushitic (PC), and the third well studied division of Afroasiatic, Egyptian (Eg.). The comparison among these three lies at the heart of the present effort. The second study (1989) allows for the first time an effective morphological analysis of Semitic triconsonantal roots and in consequence the identification of a great number of underlying pre-Semitic biliteral stems with which to compare the biliteral roots of Cushitic and Egyptian.

The internal reconstruction developed for Semitic C_3 meanings turns out, moreover, to explain equally well the third consonants of the less numerous Cushitic and Egyptian trilieral roots. The comparative evidence thus confirms conclusions reached previously from Semitic evidence alone, and demonstrates that the morphological processes from which the third consonants derived were productive at very early stages in the history of the Afroasiatic languages (see the text and tabulation of comparative data in Chapter 5 for extensive exemplification of these features). Prefixation, in contrast, was not a common derivational process in very early Afroasiatic; it became predominant only later, in the Boreafrasian subgroup (for which see the subclassification of Afroasiatic presented in Chapter 6).

A point already brought out in relation to Semitic — that, more often than not, the particular PS root shapes tend to appear polysemic by reason of their polyphyletic origins — requires iteration here. Because of the Semitic verbal system's capture of the vowel realizations in PS verb roots, a great many instances were created of formal homonymy between what were once separate PAA roots. Identical in their PAA consonants, such roots were distinguished originally by different stem vowels and prosody — features that have since been lost. A second and lesser, but still important contribution to Semitic homonymy has come from the falling together in PS of several pairs of PAA consonants. The failure to recognize the pervasive polyphylesis of PS roots has led to much imaginative but specious explanation of divergent meanings for root shapes having identical PS consonants but distinct PAA provenances. The West Semitic root *ɬʕr "barley" need no longer, for example, be explained by assuming barley to be the "hairy grain" (e.g., Diakonov 1981); it and homonymous proto-Semitic *ɬʕr "hair," as the evidence for PAA roots #887 and 889 in Chapter 5 shows, can be derived much more straightforwardly from distinct Afroasiatic roots.

The polyphylesis of such roots has not contributed merely to scholarly confusions. Undoubtedly it has also significantly influenced the actual semantic evolution of Semitic languages — by allowing or encouraging the emergence of semantic usages which combine or blur originally distinct meanings, by building metaphorical linkages which might not otherwise have been chanced upon; and by the development of opposing meanings for a seemingly unitary verb root. (The origin of such oppositions in distinct underlying roots is apparent in a number of the examples given in Ehret 1989, although not explicitly commented upon there.) Once the multiple origins of PS roots and the morphological provenience of third root-consonants are recognized, a great many clearly comparable Afroasiatic roots emerge for the first time into view.

Besides Cushitic, Egyptian, and Semitic, two other major divisions of the Afroasiatic family, Chadic and Omotic, also contribute in significant ways to the overall reconstruction of proto-Afroasiatic (PAA) — among others, to our understanding of PAA tone and vowels. Berber, the sixth recognized division of the family, plays a lesser, but not entirely insignificant, role in the work undertaken here. Because these three language groups tend to be less well studied, they offer data that, in several respects, require further interpretation and explanation before the details of PAA reconstruction can be laid out.

CHADIC EVIDENCE

Proto-Chadic (PCh) root reconstructions have been offered by P. Newman (1977, and earlier, Newman and Ma 1966) and, in considerably larger numbers, by H. Jungraithmayr and K. Shimizu (1981). Newman (1977) provides both consonants and vowels in his reconstructed PCh roots; Jungraithmayr and Shimizu frequently offer only consonants. Newman's consonants are certainly too few to account for the full range of Chadic sound correspondences, notably those involving the laterals and sibilants. His reconstruction of the PCh vowels, however, seems very probably to be correct in most cases, since they appear to produce regular correspondences (somewhat obscured at times by apparent ablaut effects) with the proto-Cushitic vowels.

Jungraithmayr and Shimizu's reconstructions account for the range of PCh consonants far better than Newman's, as the comparative data presented in Chapter 5 show, although they embody a major problem of their own. Certain kinds of distinct PCh consonants have fallen together with other consonants in so many of the modern Chadic languages that the diagnostic evidence for distinguishing among them has been maintained in relatively few languages. From the comparative PAA evidence, it would appear that, instead of explicitly noting alternative possible reconstructions when relevant diagnostic examples are lacking, Jungraithmayr and Shimizu have simply chosen to group such cases with legitimate examples of one of the possible alternative consonants. For example, they postulate on a quite solid basis three PCh laterals in addition to *l, denominating them as *ɬ$_1$ (or simply *ɬ), *ɬ$_2$, and *ɬ$_3$. The latter two each show a consistent and distinct four-way set of correspondences with particular Egyptian, PS, and PC consonants. Their *ɬ (*ɬ$_1$), in contrast, seems to be the catch-all member of the lateral set. It normally participates in a third four-way match-up with particular Egyptian, PS, and PC consonants, confirming its status as a valid additional PCh lateral. But *ɬ is also capable, in the Jungraithmayr and Shimizu, lists of having the same extra-Chadic correspondences as their *ɬ$_2$ — such instances presumably being cases of actual *ɬ$_2$ in which evidence to distinguish *ɬ and *ɬ$_2$ was lacking in some way (for particular cases see section on PAA laterals in Chapter 5).

Similarly, their *s (*s$_1$) seems to be the catch-all representative of a sibilant set composed of PCh *s, *s$_2$, *s$_3$, and *s' (see sections on PAA dental and alveolar-palatals in Chapter 5). It should be noted here that the distinctive outcome on which a separate *s$_2$ is based appears in only one section of one sub-branch of one branch of Chadic, and its occurrence even there may have an extremely restricted environment — seemingly found word-initial only where the second consonant is a voiced labial (*b or *w), and non-initial only after a preceding *g. Its manifestations are thus probably the regular reflexes of PCh *s or *s$_3$ in a restricted pair of environments in one particular subgrouping of Chadic, and no distinctive *s$_2$ should therefore be reconstructed for the PCh language.

OMOTIC CONSONANT RECONSTRUCTIONS

The Omotic languages emerge from the available comparative data as definitely Afroasiatic. The demonstrations in Fleming (1969, 1974) and Bender (1975) that Omotic forms a division of the family quite distinct from Cushitic seem fully convincing (contra Zaborski 1986), and the evidence discussed in Chapter 5 below further validates its distinctiveness not only from Cushitic but from the other subdivisions of the family.

A provisional partial reconstruction of Omotic is formulated here, in order to facilitate the inclusion of Omotic evidence among the comparative data. The observed consonant correspondence patterns across the group are noted in Table 1 following. For a majority of the known languages of the group, the correspondences are those that are overtly apparent in the comparative wordlists of Bender 1971. But in several instances these data can be confirmed or expanded upon by other materials (*inter alia*, Mocha evidence from

Leslau 1959, Koyra collections in Hayward 1982, other Ometo data from Hayward 1987, and especially high quality sets of data for Yem, Bench, and Ari in Hayward 1990). Bender (1988) provides additional comparative Omotic material independently supporting a reconstruction of PO consonants differing only slightly from that offered here.

There remain many gaps in the correspondence sets, and some patterns are as yet known from only a single kind of word environment. If no environment is specified in Table 1, then the reflexes cited here for a PO consonant can be considered to be general ones. In the table the proposed PO consonant reconstructions and supporting data are listed in the same order as the order of presentation of the PAA consonants from which they derive in the comparative Afroasiatic materials of Chapter 5. Here and in subsequent tables the sign Ø represents a zero-reflex of a proto-consonant. Blanks in the table indicate a lack as yet of relevant comparanda from the language group in question. Three languages, Wolayta, Male, and Zayse were chosen to represent the Ometo subgroup, and two languages, Kafa and Mocha, to exemplify the Gonga subgroup. These subgroups together with Yem, Bench, and Maji constitute the North Omotic branch. Dime and Ari represent the two subgroups of South Omotic.

Table 1. Provisional Omotic Consonant Reconstructions

PO	Wolayta	Male	Zayse	Yem	Kafa	Mocha	Bench	Maji	Dime	Ari
*b /#_	b	b	b	b	b	b	b	b	b	b
/V_V	w	w	w	w	b, w/_ -#	w	b	b		b
*p /#_	f	p	p	f	p	p	p		f	f
/V_	f	f	p	f	f	p	p	p	f	f
*p'	p'	p'	'p	b		b, p/V_	p'	b		p'~ɓ /V_
*d /#_	d	d	d	d	d	d	d		d	d
/V_	d		d	d	d	d	d		d	d
*t	t	t	t	t	t	t	t	t	t	t
*z /#_	z	z	z	z	y	y	z		z	z
/V_		d		d	y	y	z		d, z	d, z
/Vy_	z	ts	ts	z	y	jj	z	d		
*zz					jj	jj				
*s	s	s	s	s	š	š, s /V_	s	s	s	s

Table 1. Provisional Omotic Consonant Reconstructions (continued)

PO	Wolayta	Male	Zayse	Yem	Kafa	Mocha	Bench	Maji	Dime	Ari
*ts'	t'	ts'	s'		č'	č	ts'	ž/V_	ts'	ts'
*g	g	g	g	g	g	g	g	g	g	g
*k	k	k	k	k	k	k	k	k	k	k
*x_1 /#_	k	k	k	k	k	k	k	k		
/V_		k				k				g
*x_2 /#_	h	h	h	k	k	k	k	k		g
/V_V	Ø	g	Ø	Ø	Ø	Ø	Ø	Ø		g
	k/_-#		g/V_#,				k/			
			/n_							
*k' /#_	k'	k'	k'	k	k'	q[k']	k'	k'	g'	q
*ž /#_			ž		š	š	ž̧, ž/_e	č~ts		ž
/V_			ž	s	č	s /_-#	ž		ž	ž
*č /V_	č	č	č	ʔy	č	č	ts	č	ts	ts
*ts /V_	s	s	ts	s	š	š	ts			ts
						s/_-#		č/i_	š/i_	
*tsts /V_	t	ts	ts							
*$\check{s}_3$ /#_	s	š	š	š	š	š	ş̌	č(?)		
/V_V			š				č	č		
/V_-#	š	š	š	š	č	s	ş̌		č	č
š ($\check{s}_1$)	š	š	š	š	š	š	š	š	š	š
*$\check{s}_2$ /V_	š	š	č	š	š	š, čč	č	č	čč	z
*s' /#_		č'				č'	ts'	ts'		
/V_		s	s, č		č'	č'	ts'	ts'	ts	ts
*č'	č'	č'	č'	č	č'	č'	č'	č'	č'	č'
							ç̌'/_u			
*m	m	m	m	m	m	m	m	m	m	m
*n	n	n	n	n	n	n	n	n	n	n

Table 1. Provisional Omotic Consonant Reconstructions (continued)

PO	Wolayta	Male	Zayse	Yem	Kafa	Mocha	Bench	Maji	Dime	Ari
*ɲ	n	n	n	n	n	n	ɲ			
*ʔ /V_	ʔ	ʔ	(ʔ)	(ʔ)	ʔ	ʔ	Ø	Ø	ʔ	ʔ
*h_1 /#_	h	h	h	h,Ø		h,Ø	h,Ø	h		Ø
*h_2 /#_	h	w	w	w	w	w	Ø	h		
*l /#_VC	l	l	l	n	d	d	d	l		l
/#_Vb					n	n				
/#_VN	n	l	n	n			n			
/V_	l	l	l	l	l	l	l	l		l
*d' /#_	t'	d'	d'	t	t'	t'	t'	t'		d'
/V_	d'	d'	d'	r	t'	t'	t'			d'
*r /V_	r	r	r	r, ll	r	r	r	r	r	r
*w /#_	w	w	w	w	w	w	w	w	w	w
*y	y	y	y	y	y	y	y	y	y	y

THE EVIDENTIAL POSITION OF BERBER

Evidence drawn from the Berber subgroup of Afroasiatic plays a much more minor part in the present work. It can be and is used here to further our understanding of vowel history in the family (see Chapter 4). Certain lexical innovations of the Berber group can already be recognized also, as developments shared with certain other divisions of Afroasiatic and therefore of value in the subclassification of the family (as noted in Chapter 6).

For two interconnected reasons, however, Berber attestations have been left out of the direct comparative tabulations of PAA roots in Chapter 5. In the first place, proto-Berber greatly reduced its range of consonant distinctions via its apparent merging of many of the original PAA consonants and its resulting loss of key Afroasiatic phonological distinctions, most notably in the lateral, pharyngeal, and ejective categories. Such a contraction of the inherited consonant system is bound to have added considerably to the difficulties of identifying the particular Afroasiatic sources of many Berber roots. On top of this, the kind of extensive reconstruction of proto-Berber lexicon that might help in sorting through alternative possible etymologies is not yet available.

Reliance on Berber consonant data is thus at this stage in the development of PAA reconstruction as likely to obscure as to clarify the process of discovery.

In contrast, Cushitic and Semitic and also Middle Egyptian, except for its collapsing of the PAA sibilants and certain ejectives, have each retained a significant proportion of the key complexities of PAA consonantism. Proto-Chadic and proto-Omotic were clearly of similar rententiveness, although the reconstructions of these two are less advanced than those of PC and PS. Each provides the range and variety of consonantal distinctions from which an effective discrimination of valid from invalid etymological connections can usually quickly be made and on which an overall PAA phonological reconstruction can effectively be built.

RECONSTRUCTING PROTO-AFROASIATIC

In the next three chapters the reconstruction of PAA is set forth. The effort differs from other works of similar intent in presenting systematically and in detail, here and now, the specific comparative evidence for each of its phonological and root reconstructions. From these extensive data, contained principally in the very long Chapter 5, it proceeds to establish vowels and prosody — both actually argued for in Chapter 4 — as well as the consonants of PAA, which form the organizing focus of Chapter 5. The evidence in that chapter shows that many previous conjectures regarding the consonant system of PAA are indeed solid postulations, e.g., the distinct sets of velars and labial velars, the four distinct oral labials, and the several laterals. Diakonov's (1988) list of "Common Afrasian" consonants is largely congruent with the PAA inventory required by the data presented here, although he also includes at least four for which the writer can find no basis: *x̣ and *x̣^{w} plus four non-glottalic dental affricates where only two can be solidly demonstrated.

The Omotic data do offer one consonant, however, that might someday be found to fit in with one of Diakanov's additional consonants. The correspondence set represented as *h$_2$ in Table 1 just might support *h^w, since its reflexes, known so far only in word-initial position, are variously /h/ and /w/ across the Omotic branch. In the four roots noted in Appendix 3 (#1012-1015) for which an Omotic reflex containing *h$_2$ can be cited, this sound corresponds to *h in most of the rest of the Afroasiatic, but possibly to *w in Chadic, again best favoring an original PAA pronunciation [hw]. But only those four cases can currently be given tentative identification, and so for now the existence of a PAA *h^w must remain a conjecture for future investigation.

At the same time, the data presented here confute various other conjectures and proposals about PAA. Notably, the word and stem ("root") structures posited by Diakonov (1988) *may* be valid as secondary developments within the Boreafrasian subgroup of the family (see Chapter 5 below on subclassification), but *cannot* be projected back to PAA (see Chapter 3 for the simpler stem structures which *can* in fact be postulated for PAA). Syllabic "sonants" similarly may have emerged in conjunction with the development of the Boreafrasian stage, and independently in a couple of instances elsewhere in the family, but have no place in the comparative picture for earlier PAA (again see Chapter 3). Finally, while a considerable degree of congruence may obtain between the consonant inventory established here and previously published conjectural or comparatively-based inventories, the actual reflexes of the particular consonants can often be quite different from those previously suggested, as for instance in Bomhard's (1988) work and, one may suspect, sometimes even in Diakonov. The most striking such case is that of the Egyptian palatals *ḏ*, *ṯ*, and *š*, which can be shown consistently and resoundingly to derive *not* from the PAA palatals, or normally even from palatalized dentals or velars, but from the lateral obstruents of PAA. Chapter 5 presents more than 130 PAA roots containing these three laterals and cites around 25-30 Egyptian examples of each of the three correspondences.

A historical connection between lateral and palatal obstruents is neither surprising nor unprecedented in the world's languages. Such a link is clearly attested even in Semitic, notably by Arabic /š/ from PS *ɬ. But the lack of previous recognition of the correct Egyptian correspondences in this instance does underscore a point which comes forth very strongly from the data of the succeeding chapters. Bending of sound correspondence rules, assumptions of "unstable" consonants, over-imaginative stretching of semantic resemblances, and other ad hoc measures need not and should not be invoked any longer in PAA reconstruction. The comparative-historical method, rigorously applied, works very well indeed for Afroasiatic once sufficient data and some of the key intermediate levels of reconstruction are available to the comparativist.

3

DERIVATIONAL MORPHOLOGY IN AFROASIATIC (AFRASIAN) RECONSTRUCTION

STEM, WORD, AND SYLLABLE STRUCTURE IN *PAA*

The laying out of the comparative Afroasiatic data, undertaken in Chapter 5, shows that just two fundamental stem shapes can be reconstructed for proto-Afroasiatic, CVC and C(V), the latter having the possible alternative shape VC in verb roots. To the stem could be added any of a number of nominalizing suffixes of the form -(V)C- or any of a great variety of verb extensions of the shape -(V)C-. The evidence makes it probable that the underlying form of such suffixes was usually -C-, with the surfacing of a preceding vowel depending on, and its particular realization in different Afroasiatic subgroups predictable from, the syllable structure rules of the particular groups. (The particular outcomes of such processes will not be further argued here, but will be left to future studies.) Afroasiatic roots containing such suffixes are therefore given in Chapter 5 in the form $*C_1VC_2C_S$, where C_S represents the suffix. Two exceptions would have been the nominal suffixes in *w and *y, which probably did have fixed vowel accompaniments and -VC shapes (see suffixes #1 and 2 below).

The Omotic, Cushitic, and Chadic evidence conjoin in requiring the existence in PAA of an additional element in word formation, a terminal vowel (TV) in nouns and modifiers, the original function and meaning of which remain obscure. TVs have been subjected to comparative-historical investigation in only two groups of Afroasiatic languages. In Omotic they have no reconstructible function beyond their necessary attachment to singular noun stems in semantically unpredictable fashion. With the exception of Kafa, in which two TVs, *-o* and *-e* , have been grammaticalized respectively as masculine and feminine markers, they carry no grammatical or recognizable semantic load (Hayward 1987). In proto-Southern Cushitic, pairs of TVs formed a variety of singular-plural markers. Particular paired sets tended to go with either masculine or feminine nouns, but an individual TV on a singular noun generally gave no indication of the grammatical gender of that noun (Ehret 1980: 49-50).

From these indicators it seems reasonable to conclude that TVs are fossils of a nominal morphology productive in pre-proto-Afroasiatic and predating the rise of grammatical gender in the family. Having lost their original grammatical function, they have been reanalyzed as markers of the singular or sometimes, as in the case of Southern Cushitic, of the plural in nominals. In the Boreafrasian subgroup (Semitic, Egyptian, and Berber: see Chapter 6 for this classification), the TVs have generally been dropped entirely, leaving most nouns and adjectives as consonant-final words.

The existence of TVs at early stages of Afroasiatic evolution obviates the need to reconstruct any syllabic consonants for PAA. The usual word structure of nouns and adjectives would have been $*C_1(VC_2)(C_S)V_{tv}$, in which the only possible syllable structures are CVC and CV and never just C. The presence of syllabic C in Boreafrasian languages can be understood as the natural outcome of vowel loss, whether word-internal or word-final, within that particular subgroup (as is also separately the case in a few modern Omotic languages, notably Bench and Maji, where the same kind of sound change has independently been at work).

NOMINAL SUFFIXATION IN *PAA*

At least ten and possibly thirteen nominalizing suffixes can be reconstructed for very early Afroasiatic. They occur in Semitic, Egyptian, and Cushitic with the same or easily relatable meanings and functions, and most of them can also be observed in the Chadic and Omotic data presented in Chapter 5 below.

1. *w (*-aw-) deverbative complement and result suffix.

This suffix, found in all divisions of Afroasiatic, seems most often to form deverbal result, complement, and attribute nouns. It is not unreasonable to consider *w as having originally been a deverbative complement and result marker, and its attributive application to have arisen secondarily. An original shape *-aw- for this suffix is indicated by its attestations in Cushitic, Chadic, and Omotic.

2. *y (*-ay-, *-iy-) attributive deverbative and attributive noun suffix.
2a. *y (*-ay-, *-iy-) adjective-forming suffix.

This suffix can operate as a noun-forming deverbative in Semitic, Egyptian, Chadic, and Cushitic instances, but is also often added to nominals to form attributives — names of things having the attribute(s) of, or associated by location or resemblance with, the item named by the stem to which *y is affixed. It appears as an adjective-forming suffix in all the divisions of the family (see citations listed in Table 3, item 2a). Evidence from Chadic and Semitic as well as Cushitic requires *-ay- as one shape of this affix, while an alternative form *-iy- can be found in Omotic and Cushitic reflexes and in Semitic cases (i.e., Arabic *nisba -īy-*). In West Semitic a relatively rare prefixed version, *y-, of this affixal pair is also present (Moscati 1964: 80).

3. *t associative noun suffix.

A noun formative in *t is well attested all across the Afroasiatic family. Its original function may no longer be clearly specifiable. It appears to have been especially productive in Egyptian, as a variety of entries in the comparative lists show, forming noun instruments, attributives, and complements from verbs as well as deriving nouns from other nouns of related or associatable meanings. This latter function has also been observed in Cushitic derivations (Ehret 1980: 53-54), and hence the formative is called an "associative" marker here. The suffix apparently remains productive in many Afroasiatic languages today. Semitic *-ūt/*-īt forming abstract nouns is presumably a direct reflex of it, and it is the probable source, although shifted to prefixed position, of the Semitic *t- verbal noun marker. It is *not* to be confused with the widely found *t feminine marker of Afroasiatic.

A distinct Afroasiatic suffix in *t, a nominal plural marker, may be reflected in the Egyptian cases where *t indicates a collectivity, such as a flock or a crew (e.g., #322, 367, and 470), and in the *-Vt- plurals of Southern Cushitic (Ehret 1980: 54-55) and Eastern Cushitic (e.g., Afar entry in #579).

4. *t adjective suffix.

An adjective suffix in *t, often still productive, is prominent in Cushitic (Ehret 1980, 1987) and is more weakly attested in Egyptian, Semitic, and apparently Omotic.

5. *m attributive noun suffix.
5a. *m adjective-forming suffix.

A deverbative suffix in *m, forming attribute and result nouns, must also be posited. It is common in Semitic in the C_3 position and is well attested also for Egyptian, Cushitic, Chadic, and Omotic. In a few instances in Cushitic (see #635 in Appendix 2) and Chadic (see #30, 228, and 295) and in at least one Semitic case (Ehret 1989: Table 34a, Arabic "sword"), this suffix acquired an instrumental connotation; but the bulk of the examples are clearly interpretable as attribute, or sometimes possibly result or complement, formations. The use of *m as an adjective formative in a number of cases in Semitic, Omotic, and Chadic argues for it having had an originally attributive connotation. The *mV- instrument-agent prefix of Semitic, Egyptian, and Chadic is argued below (this chapter) to have had an origin quite distinct from that of this suffixed *m deverbative.

6. *n attributive (?) noun suffix.
6a. *n adjective suffix.

Another nasal, *n, also functioned at times as an attributive suffix, but its scope more closely paralleled that of the *y attributive (q.v.). Like *y, it appears frequently to have produced adjectives from verbs or nouns. It is known from all branches of the family. Its Semitic reflex appears to have been *-ān.

7. *l attributive and complement deverbative suffix.
7a. *l adjective suffix.

A noun-deriving suffix in *l turns up widely in Afroasiatic with a variety of effects. In pre-proto-Semitic (pPS) it can be proposed to have been a noun-patient and noun-complement formative (Ehret 1989: Table 13a). Examples of the suffix in Egyptian seem often to go with attributive nouns or noun-complements, while a similar function may existed in Chadic (e.g., Chadic entries in roots #654, 864, and 909) and in Cushitic. In Cushitic, *l became especially prominent as a suffix in animal names, probably because such names not infrequently derive from roots descriptive of the animals' attributes, i.e., their appearance or behavior. Like *y and *n, *l became important as an adjective-forming suffix, with a variety of proposed examples of this usage attributable to Semitic, Egyptian, and Cushitic (see Table 3, item 7a below). At least one example of *l as an adjective formative also appears in the Omotic evidence (root #546).

8. *r instrument and complement deverbative suffix.

Noun suffixes in *r are common in the comparative data, but their reconstructed meaning is unclear. For pPS, *r has been suggested to have been a noun-complement marker (Ehret 1989: Table 11a); but in Egyptian PAA *r (> Eg. *3* /_#) seems fairly commonly to have marked instrument or means (e.g., roots #170, 546, and 713). In still other cases *r appears to have carried little or no semantic load even when quite clearly suffixal in origin (e.g., entry for Yem [Omotic] in root #11). A possible early noun singular marker in *r known from Cushitic (Ehret 1987: 9) may have been at times conflated with the *r deverbative and thus contributed to its semantic opacity.

9. *r adjective suffix.

In Cushitic, Egyptian, and pPS (Ehret 1989: Table 11b), a probably distinct *r suffix (realized in PSC as *-ar-) forming modifiers, usually from verbs, can also be identified (see Table 3, item 9). A couple of instances of this suffix from Chadic (#268 and #497) and one from Omotic (#262) can also be cited.

10. *b animate noun and deverbative noun suffix.

A suffix in *b, used to derive from verb roots nouns that name animals and parts of the body, is strongly attested in Cushitic (Ehret 1987) and in Semitic (cf. Diakanoff [Diakonov] 1965) and is evident in several instances from Egyptian and from Omotic.

Three further nominal derivational suffixes can be given a more provisional reconstruction.

11. *s deverbative complement suffix.

The case for this suffix seems relatively strong, and is supported by a number of plausible occurrences in the comparative data of Chapter 5 and also Appendix 1. The known examples are limited to Chadic, Semitic, and Egyptian, especially the latter two (Table 1, item 11 lists the proposed instances).

The two other possible formatives —

12. *ŋ attributive noun suffix; and
13. *ʔ adjective deverbative suffix —

are both best known from Cushitic examples of derived adjectivals or adverbials. The first of these two suffixes, in *ŋ, was productive in Southern Cushitic (Ehret 1980: 59-60); it also appears in at least one Chadic citation in the comparative data (root #641), where it forms an attribute noun, and is tentatively proposed in one early Afroasiatic root (#916). The second suffix, in *ʔ, also can be identified in Southern Cushitic and possibly elsewhere in the Cushitic branch of the family (Ehret 1980: 60; Ehret 1987: 9). Several probable cases of *ʔ as an adjective formative appear to be present in the Semitic evidence as well (cf. also possible examples in Ehret 1989, e.g., in Table 38, no. 44), and several Egyptian adjectivals may also contain it (see Table 3, item 13 below for particular citations).

With the exception of *w and *y, these suffixes cannot as yet be assigned an original vowel component, and in fact are probably best considered to have been composed simply of a consonant, with any vowel accompaniments arising later in different branches of the family, as a consequence of language-specific syllable structure rules. Analogy effects may then account for the particular vowel components chosen to satisfy such rules, as for instance can be seen in the development in Southern Cushitic of adjective suffixes in *-at-/*-it- and *-ar-/*-ir- (Ehret 1980: 54-58), which follow the pattern of the PAA adjectival marking *-ay-/*-iy-.

Table 2 (beginning on the next page) lists the more than 800 occurrences of these thirteen nominal-deriving suffixes that are cited in the extensive etymological dictionary of Chapter 5, thus enabling the reader quickly to locate for critical examination the attestations of each particular suffix. (The table also includes citations for two additional nominalizing processes, via prefixation and by stem-internal change, which are dealt with later in this chapter.)

Table 2: Attestations of Nominal Affixes

affix	Semitic	Egyptian	Cushitic	Chadic	Omotic
1 *w deverbative complement and result suffix	#103, 105, 220, 243, 293, 369, 669, 836, 837?; Appendix 1: #312, 334, 372, 613, 841?	#5, 20, 27, 38, 93, 97, 160, 198, 211, 237, 273, 279, 288, 307, 336, 356, 357, 367, 377, 379, 393, 401, 403, 405, 407, 408, 426, 434, 436, 460, 503, 538, 555, 562, 569, 595, 625, 643, 646, 675, 686, 702, 716, 745, 750, 773, 775, 777, 779, 788, 790, 817, 836, 837, 862, 878, 879, 899, 932, 939, 942, 950, 976, 986, 992, 1003	#637, 860	#93, 160, 273, 429, 565, 644, 675, 889, 933	#437, 794, 806, 1008
2. *y attributive noun and attributive deverbative suffix	#218, 239, 293, 407, 503, 551, 596, 862?, 975, 989	#52, 86, 112, 118, 140, 249, 261, 290, 292, 322, 357, 365, 368, 396, 403, 407 460, 535, 574, 585,	#264, 280, 365, 407, 587, 606, 652, 967	#46, 219, 238, 354, 365, 449, 513, 572, 606, 768,	#146, 569, 976

Table 2: Attestations of Nominal Affixes (continued)

affix	Semitic	Egyptian	Cushitic	Chadic	Omotic
		599, 596, 599, 614, 650, 753, 756, 827, 996, 975, 1003		804, 837, 914, 967, 985?	
2a. *y adjective suffix	#105, 181, 371	#309, 396, 655, 697	#437, 652	#804	#437, 506, 983
3. *t associative noun suffix	#91, 218, 350, 370, 374, 383, 399, 699, 837, 867	#32, 36, 39, 73, 85, 106, 146, 187, 218, 244, 249, 286, 290, 291, 292, 301, 330, 336, 337, 350, 352, 356, 365, 374, 375, 392, 399, 403, 424, 426, 434, 474, 482, 495, 496, 501, 517, 520, 532, 547, 555, 557, 580, 581, 588, 593, 596, 603, 611, 618, 619, 627, 643, 644, 657, 662, 670, 671, 675, 689, 709, 720, 744, 748, 752, 753, 754, 756, 762, 765, 779, 780, 798,	#181, 478, 752; Appendix 2: #971	#187, 216, 252, 399, 567, 579, 589, 768 986	#235, 251, 301, 399, 427?, 436, 469, 488, 526, 640, 740, 759 785, 926

Table 2: Attestations of Nominal Affixes (continued)

affix	Semitic	Egyptian	Cushitic	Chadic	Omotic
		801, 802, 804, 808, 837, 855, 864, 878, 880, 886, 890, 894, 958, 914, 926, 941, 953, 958, 964, 971, 975, 976, 986, 987, 1003, 1006, 1008			
4. *t adjective suffix	#374, 709, 748, 831, 872; Appendix 1: #697	#353, 374, 831	(PSC *-at-: productive)		#160, 275, 427?, 495, 777
5. *m attributive noun suffix	#115?, 234, 237, 244, 345, 374, 427, 429, 482, 541, 669, 712, 845, 875, 958, 964, 968; Appendix 1: #79?, 285, 418, 474, 615; Appendix 3: #1015?	#307?, 529, 333, 471, 682?, 998, 1006	#123, 292, 318, 481, 532, 653?, 761, 1001?; Appendix 2: 634	#30, 155, 288, 295, 470, 471, 478, 481, 520, 695, 884, 962	#160, 260, 328, 483, 520, 540, 700, 913-915; Appendix 3: #1015
5a. *m adjective suffix	#63, 97, 556, 626, 863, 986; Appendix 1: #868	#382, 872	Appendix 2: #635	#335, 556	#265, 269, 556, 556, 563; Appendix 3: #1019

Table 2: Attestations of Nominal Affixes (continued)

affix	Semitic	Egyptian	Cushitic	Chadic	Omotic
6. *n attributive (?) noun suffixe	#26, 154, 238, 259, 282, 289, 399, 424, 466, 513, 520, 599, 702, 763, 809, 827, 837, 840, 958, 999; Appendix 1: #155?, 754, 821?, 948	#2, 38, 120, 243, 259, 424, 483, 568, 598, 786, 897, 1001	#120, 143, 478?, 483, 512, 528, 653?, 654, 985, 1001?	#143, 179, 471, 482, 483, 485, 504, 615, 709, 768, 810, 841, 845, 927, 938	#64, 119, 122, 145, 251, 480, 543, 569, 915, 927, 927, 942
6a. *n adjective suffix	#29, 102, 439, 505?, 558, 698; Appendix 1: #155?, 256	#367, 454, 893	#102, 439, 714	#326, 439, 505?	#246, 262, 427, 508, 756, 781
7. *l attributive and complement deverbative suffix	#76, 98?, 257, 263, 264, 341, 358, 464, 469, 475, 515, 794, 877, 935; Appendix 1: #280, 334, 436, 507, 540, 683, 754, 799, 902?, 981	#39, 73?, 102, 260, 261, 348, 373, 521, 631?, 657, 745?, 862?, 963, 977, 981, 1000	#11, 188, 447, 653, 700, 963, 1000?	#94, 160, 190?, 329, 346, 654, 864, 909, 977	

Table 2: Attestations of Nominal Affixes (continued)

affix	Semitic	Egyptian	Cushitic	Chadic	Omotic
7a. *l adjective suffix	#148, 190, 227, 234, 350, 415, 497, 617, 707, 859, 903; Appendix 1: #262, 401, 697, 861, 897; Appendix 3: #1017, 1022	#102, 401, 776, 905?, 951?, 999	#11, 125, 654, 655, 698, 776, 893		#546
8. *r instrument and comple-deverbative suffix	#9, 11, 17, 24, 25, 47, 73, 94, 96, 100, 121, 146, 204?, 268, 353, 392, 447, 482, 485, 641, 741, 871, 872, 876?, 887, 892, 899, 914, 996; Appendix 1: #5, 89, 155, 163, 280, 721, 753, 841, 913	#11, 170, 221, 240, 265?, 278, 360, 434, 498, 546, 601, 631?, 673?, 713, 766, 798, 853, 862?, 928, 953, 990,	#25, 79, 119, 374, 493, 540, 641, 653, 654, 687?, 960, 981, 1005; Appendix 2: #958, 971	#88, 153, 213, 506, 540, 641	#11, 97, 182, 811, 950
9. *r adjective suffix	#365, 366, 497, 567, 629, 679, 742, 749, 763,	#265?, 748, 758?, 816?, 905?, 951	#639, 650	#268, 497	#262

Table 2: Attestations of Nominal Affixes (continued)

affix	Semitic	Egyptian	Cushitic	Chadic	Omotic
	785, 920, 963; Appendix 1: #262, 334, 337, 615?, 868, 897				
10. *b animate deverbative suffix	#144, 366, 422, 504, 706, 900?, 984, 1000; Appendix 1: #337	#275, 308, 742, 983	#144, 221, 301, 308, 401, 460, 687		#144, 301, 426
11. *s deverbative complement suffix	#34, 121, 252, 618, 946, 966; Appendix 1: #240, 402	#136, 337, 338, 358		#121, 433,	
12. *ŋ attributive noun suffix	#916	#916	#79, 916	#641	
13. *ʔ adjective deverbative suffix	#86, 120, 877; Appendix 1: #221, 256?	#11, 160, 265?, 314, 758?, 816?	#105	#395 (n.)	#806

Table 2: Attestations of Nominal Affixes (continued)

(items dealt with below in this chapter)

affix	Semitic	Egyptian	Cushitic	Chadic	Omotic
14. *a- attributive deverbative prefix	#525, 596, 611, 749	#23, 85, 616, 827?	#265, 317, 438, 596, 613, 1011	#449, 569, 827	#438, 569, 621, 807
14a. *i- attributive deverbative prefix		#93, 140, 159, 282, 470, 568, 582, 621	#224, 637, 875	#93	
15. noun derivation from verb by stem-vowel lengthening		#595	#64, 121, 124, 161?, 203, 234?, 245?, 246, 340?, 341?, 367, 378?, 415?, 418, 517?, 546, 595, 610, 643?, 665, 671, 686?, 760, 766?, 787?, 807?, 814?, 919?, 928, 938; Appendix 2: #402	#337?, 352 919?	#22, 27?, 52, 85, 101, 148, 196, 251, 257, 265, 271?, 281, 305, 316, 339, 381?, 447, 493, 519, 558, 584, 590, 610, 619, 636, 663, 667, 851, 859, 868, 904, 928, 952; Appendix 3: #1014

A number of suffixes that are not derivational in function are certainly of ancient standing in the family. Unlike the derivational suffixes, most of these *have* previously been recognized by scholars. They include the well-known feminine marker in *t found in Semitic, Egyptian, Cushitic, Chadic, and Berber, and possibly in Omotic in some rare instances (Bender 1989); plurals in *w in Egyptian and Southern Cushitic (Ehret 1980: 61); plurals in *t, probably reconstructible as *-at-, seen in Semitic, Egyptian (as the collective in *t), Cushitic, and Omotic; plurals in *n, probably reconstructible as *-en- (Greenberg 1963), as in Cushitic (PSC *-en-: Ehret 1980: 56), Omotic (Fleming 1974), Chadic, and Berber; plurals in *m, probably reconstructible as *-eem-, seen in Cushitic (PSC *-eema, correcting Ehret 1980: 53) and in Semitic, and noun pluralization by a suffix of the form *-(a)C(u), where C reduplicates the final consonant of the singular noun (Greenberg 1963). This last process is known from Chadic and Cushitic (cf. Ehret 1980: 66) and seems present also in the derivation of the PAA "we" (see root #725). Except for some Egyptian plurals in *w* (and duals in *wy*) and feminines and collectives in *t*, these markers do not figure, however, in the comparative data below and thus do not require further attention here.

VERB EXTENSIONS IN EARLY AFROASIATIC

The most startling aspect of PAA derivational morphology — startling, and for that reason sure to be controversial, yet by all appearances well-grounded — is the array of proposed verb extensions productive at early stages in the history of the family. Internal reconstruction in Semitic indicates that almost every PAA consonant could act as an extension in pre-proto-Semitic (Ehret 1989). This scheme, developed in a Semitic context, is reconfirmed in detail by its point-for-point applicability to the Egyptian, Cushitic, and Chadic data wherever the corresponding third consonants turn up in these groups. A number of PS consonants can be shown to have had two distinct extensional meanings, but all such cases can be demonstrated to have collapsed two separate earlier PAA consonants (see Chapter 5 for this demonstration, and the listing of extensions in Table 3 for particular instances).

The extensions generally are preserved in Semitic and Egyptian only in lexicalized form, although the *s causative retained its productivity, resituated as a prefix, and the *y and probably *w inchoative/denominatives (extensions #3 and 4 below) were productive suffixes in Egyptian. Similarly, the *n non-finitive and *t durative (#17 and 25 below) appear to have continued in use in Semitic, both taking on intransitive implications and both, like *s causative, shifted to prefixal position. The Ngizim data and various other Chadic evidence presented in Chapter 5 suggest, on the other hand, that a rather larger proportion of the extensions remained productive for a long time in Chadic. One set of indicators of relatively recent productivity in Ngizim or pre-Ngizim are the cases of stem-vowel lengthening in Chadic *CV verb roots (< PAA *CVC$_2$, where C$_2$ was a consonant of the pharyngeal-glottal set widely lost in

Chadic) with the addition of an extension — long vowels not normally being present in Ngizim except in such cases (e.g., Ngizim entries in #157 and 299 in Chapter 5, among others). Another kind of indicator is the coexistence in Ngizim of several differently extended forms of the same root (e.g., #594, which attests to the recent or current productivity of six different extensions).

Cushitic holds a position intermediate between Semitic-Egyptian and Chadic in its retention of productivity in these old extensions. The two inchoative/denominatives in *y and *w have continued widely to be productive in the Cushitic branch, along with *m stative/intransitive, *s causative, and *t durative (see below extensions #34, 37, and 25 respectively). In addition, Eastern Cushitic preserves active use of the *dl (> PEC *d') middle voice extension (#1 below), while some Agaw languages until recently probably had a productive reflex of the PAA *n non-finitive (#17 below).

About twenty of the extensions can be identified in the available Chadic data, and at least 28 in Cushitic roots. Omotic attestations of the extensions are harder to discover. The paucity of examples is surely in part an artifact of the lesser availability of Omotic data, but may also reflect the actual historical absence of many of the extensions. The general Afroasiatic causative in *s is well attested in the Omotic branch, as are *t durative and *dl (PO *t') middle voice, but thus far less than fifteen of the 37 proposed extensions are even tentatively inferable for Omotic. The Omotic grouping, it is argued in Chapter 6, may have split off from the ancestor language of the rest of Afroasiatic while this extensive body of verb extensions was still being elaborated and, as a result, may never have included many of these affixes.

The widespread lexicalization of the proposed extensions, above all in Semitic, has a particular consequence for the analysis of the extensions' meanings: the original connotation of a given extension cannot be expected still to be overtly apparent *in each individual case*. Once an affix has become lexicalized, the subsequent semantic history of the root to which it has become attached is no longer governed by the former meaning of the affix, and future meaning shifts thus might well take directions that would tend to obscure that meaning. Most such semantic shifts retain something of the characteristics of the action previously denoted by the word concerned. "To cut into pieces" easily yields "to slice," still an action involving repetitive movement; if the original sense "to cut into pieces" had been derived via the addition of a no longer productive iterative extension, its iterative implication would remain clearly discernable. Still later, however, the sense "to slice" for the verb might evolve to "to slash." The fact that the affix originally connoted repeated action would now be obscured. But while some of the individual lexicalizations of any particular extension may become analytically opaque in this way, the overall ensemble of cases normally brings out with fair clarity the original implications of the extension.

The verb extensions identifiable for early Afroasiatic, some no longer productive anywhere, have been numbered here according to the sequence established in Ehret 1989. For the consonantal sound correspondences involved, the reader must look ahead to Chapter 5.

1. *dl middle voice: pPS *ḍ = Eg. *ḏ* = PC *dl = PCh *ɮ = PO *d'.

The evidence is consistent across the board in indicating *dl to have been a middle voice extension. Throughout, its occurrences tend to involve the reflexive/benefactive nuances of classical "middle voice" constructions or the factitive/inchoative and reflexive/autobenefactive senses visible in its modern-day productive Eastern Cushitic reflexes (Hayward 1977). It appears probably to have been productive in early Chadic, and may possibly still be so in some Chadic groups today. It is also clearly productive today (or has been in the recent past) in some Omotic languages, such as the Gonga subgroup (which includes Mocha, a language repeatedly cited in the data of Chapter 5).

2. *h amplificative: pPS *h = Eg. *h* = PC *h.

This extension in *h indicated, apparently, an action carried out to a fuller extent than the action of the verb root to which it was attached.

3. *w inchoative/denominative: pPS *w = Eg. *w* = PC *-Vw- = PCh *-aw- = PO *w; and
4. *y inchoative/denominative: pPS *y = Eg. *i* = PC *-ey-, *-ay- = PCh *-iy-, *-ay-.

In pPS both the *w and *y extensions often appeared in verbs that can be explained as subsequently having been shifted from intransitive to transitive application, in which case the presence of *w or *y came to have a pluractional effect on the verb meaning (Ehret 1989). The same effect can be noted in Egyptian in a large number of the instances of its *i* extension (< PAA *y), but not usually for *w. Both extensions remain widely productive in Cushitic in their reconstructible usages.

5. *ɣ^{w} complementive: pPS *ɣ = Eg. *ḫ* = PC *ɣ^{w} = PO *x$_1$ (?).

The extension in *ɣ^{w} can denote an action reciprocal or reversive toward that of the verb stem to which it attaches, or in some way apposite to or consequent upon that action, hence its appelation "complementive."

6. *k$^{w'}$ andative: pPS *ḳ = Eg. *ḳ*.

The attribution of andative semantics ("action toward") to PAA *k$^{w'}$ in C$_3$ position is made by process of elimination. Non-labial PAA *k' can be directly established by positive evidence to be the etymon of an intensive extension (see extension #31 below); thus the pPS *ḳ andative must be connected to the only other PAA consonant, *k$^{w'}$, to have produced *ḳ as its outcome in pPS and Egyptian (Ehret 1989). Because of the lack so far of attested

Cushitic or Omotic instances of PAA *kʷ' in C_3 position, this postulation cannot yet be directly confirmed.

7. *ʕ partive: pPS *ʕ = Eg. *ᶜ* = PC *ʕ.

This extension in *ʕ in all three divisions of Afroasiatic for which examples can be cited primarily imputes to the verb the sense "action-away-from," in contrast to the nuance "action-to(ward)" of the andative (#6 above). In the pPS reconstruction of Ehret 1989, it should be noted, the *ʕ extension was given the less appropriate name "sunderative." Because action-away-from is at the same time action-toward somewhere else, the partive has also come to attach to verbs whose current meanings have a more straightforward andative connotation.

8. *ɬ venitive: pPS *ɬ = Eg. *š* = PC *ɬ.

The venitive, denoting action toward speaker or subject, seems to have been applied especially frequently to verbs of rubbing, scratching, and the like, actions in which the hand or instrument has its primary effect when it is drawn back toward the actor.

9. *tl' focative: pPS *ṣ = Eg. *ṯ* = PC *tl ([tl']).

The affix tl' imputes to an action a narrower scope or focus than was present in the action denoted by the simple verb root it is attached to. This connotation seems clear in Semitic and Egyptian, although more Cushitic data are needed to safely posit the same meaning can be assumed in that branch.

10. *ts diffusive: pPS *θ = Eg. *s* = PCh *s; and
11. *r diffusive: pPS *r = Eg. *3* = PC *r = PCh *r = PO *r.

The two "diffusive" extensions imply an action broad in its focus or uneven or irregular in its unfolding. Whether the first of these two existed in Cushitic, and what meaning it might have had there, cannot yet be determined because no examples of PAA *ts (PC *ts) in C_3 position have been identified thus far. The latter of the two, *r diffusive, seems sometimes to have gained a durative connotation (e.g., Omotic entry in #169).

12. *kʷ finitive: pPS *k = Eg. *k* = PC *kʷ; and
13. *l finitive: pPS *l = Eg. *r* = PC *l = PCh *l.

The finitive extensions turn an unbounded action into a bounded one, with a distinct end-point implied, e.g., changing "to cut" into "to cut off."

14. *p' finitive fortative: pPS *b = Eg. *p* = PCh *ɓ = PO *p'; and
15. *g finitive fortative: pPS *g = Eg. *g* = PC *g.

The binary term "finitive fortative" defines two extensions that amplify or moderately intensify the action of verbs to which they attach, as well as impute boundedness to that action. The first of these is reconstructed above as PAA *p'. One means of arriving at this conclusion is, as for #6 above, via a process of elimination: PAA *b is already demonstrated as the source of the extendative extension of #18 below, and PAA *p' is the one other consonant to have fallen together with *b in pPS. But the clinching evidence comes from Chadic data, where the PAA shape *p' (> PCh *ɓ) for the extension is clear. A number of examples in the Ngizim dictionary (Schuh 1981) — among others, *gə̀rà ɓ-* "to be terrified," *r̃áa ɓ-* "to knock down" (root #937 in Chapter 5), and *r̃úgɓ-* "to break in pieces" — suggest that it may have remained productive down to recent times in that language, at least in its fortative function. The two known Cushitic cases of PAA *p' in C_3 position are of unclear implication and their connection to the present item is uncertain (Ehret 1987: #112, 388). The second of the two finitive fortative extensions, in *g, may also not be securely attributable to Cushitic (see root #712 in Chapter 5 for a proposed Southern Cushitic example, however).

16. *ŝ non-finitive: pPS *c = Eg. *s* = PCh *s; and
17. *n non-finitive: pPS *n = Eg. *n* = PC *n = PCh *n.

These two extensions, in *ŝ and *n, can have the connotation either of unboundedness of an action (hence "non-finitive") or of inceptivity of the action involved. The extension in *n has an inceptive effect especially commonly, and that may thus have been its original meaning. Once again, no Cushitic examples are known for one of the pair of extensions, namely *ŝ, and so its presence in PC cannot yet be averred; but *n was once very productive in the Agaw branch of Cushitic (Ehret 1987: 9). In Semitic the verbal prefix *n-, conveying a passive or reflexive meaning, would seem a probable reflex of PAA *n. For a discussion of how an intransitive sense can be taken on by an extension of unbounded or extended action, see root #34 below. A parallel shift in connotation also can be argued for the Semitic *t- verb extension (#25 below).

18. *b extendative: pPS *b = Eg. *b* = PC *b = PCh *b = PO *b (?); and
19. *c' extendative: pPS *ẹ = Eg. *s* = PC *c' = PCh *s' (?).

The extensions in *b and *c' imply an open-ended action, usually of some duration. They often specifically remove a connotation of finitive action from the verb root to which they are affixed, in direct contrast to the effect of the two non-finitives (#16 and #17), which commonly impart non-boundedness to a verb whose action need not specifically have been finitive before.

20. *f iterative: pPS *p = Eg. *f* = PC *f = PCh *f (?) = PO *p; and
21. *ḫ iterative: pPS *ḫ = Eg. *ḫ* = PC *ḫ.

The most usual implication of the iteratives in all the language groups is one of repetitive action, although the sense of present-day verbs containing the extensions may be more durative than iterative. The Chadic reflex of the latter of these two extensions may be the Chadic *-a inceptive, but this remains to be demonstrated.

22. *g^w durative: pPS *g = Eg. *g* (?) = PC *g^w;
23. *k durative: pPS *k = Eg. *k* = PC *k = PCh *k = PO *k;
24. *d durative: pPS *d = Eg. *d* = PCh *d = PO *d; and
25. *t durative: pPS *t = Eg. *t* = PC *t = PCh *t = PO *t.

Four extensions, in *g^w, *k, *d, and *t, consistently connote some sort of ongoing or inherently durational activity. The two most surely describable as duratives are *g^w and *k. The next-to-last extension, in *d, so frequently has a stative implication, particularly in pPS examples but also in other branches, that it may originally have been a stative rather than a durative marker (it may well be the source of the Ngizim *da-* stative prefix, described in Schuh 1981). The last of the four, *t, is still vigorously productive in most of the Southern Cushitic languages (Ehret 1980 calls it a "continuative" extension) and probably remains so in a variety of other Cushitic tongues. From the beginning it may have had a subsidiary function as a detransifier, as examples from several of the divisions of Afroasiatic indicate; Omotic cases are especially prominent, e.g., Bench reflex in #302, among others. In the Boreafrasian subgroup (for Afroasiatic subclassification, see Chapter 6), this application may early have become its principal one: in its Semitic form the extension in *t, moved to prefixal position, came to produce reflexive, passive, and reciprocal senses (for discussion of how an extension of extended action might recurrently evolve into an intransitive, see affix #34 below) while in Egyptian it gave rise to a suffixed passive *t(i) / t(w)*.

26. *ʔ concisive: pPS *ʔ = Eg. *3* = PC *ʔ = PO *ʔ; and
27. *x precipitive: pPS *x = Eg. *ẖ* = PC *x = PCh x (?).

The concisive and precipitive extensions, each in a different way, impose a counter-durative connotation on verb roots to which they attach. The concisive imparts a more restricted scope of action than is implied by the underlying simple verb; the precipitive, at least in its pre-proto-Semitic manifestation, implies in addition an abruptness of action.

28. *p intensive (of manner): pPS *p = Eg. *p* = PC *p;
29. *z intensive (of manner): pPS *z = Eg. *z* (> *s*) = PC *z = PCh *ɗ;
30. *ɣ intensive (of effect): pPS *ɣ = Eg. *ḫ* ; = PC *ɣ (?) = PCh *x (?) = PO *x_1 (?);
31. *k' intensive (of effect): pPS *ḳ = Eg. *ḳ* = PC *k' = PO *k'.

The four intensive extensions divide up according to the focus of the intensification of action they impart to the verb. The intensives of manner, *p and *z, indicate how the action is carried out; for example, the addition of either could change the meaning of a verb from "to beat" to "to beat violently." In contrast, addition of an intensive of effect, either *ɣ or *k', would tend to shift attention to the object of the beating; "to beat" might thus become "to beat to pieces" or "to smash."

32. *t' durative intensive: pPS *ṭ = Eg. *s* (?) = PO *ts'.

The extension in *t' adds both duration and intensity to the action of the verb stem it attaches to. With the addition of this extension, a verb meaning "to strike," for instance, could take on the meaning "to beat violently," changing a single blow into repeated blows strongly delivered. The extension is clearly present in the Semitic materials (Ehret 1989), but its existence outside Semitic remains to be satisfactorily established.

33. *s' (or *s ?) fortative: pPS *s = Eg. *s* = PC *ts' = PCh *s' (?).

The term "fortative" is used here to indicate an extension which imparts a lesser degree of intensification to an action than a true intensive extension would. The fortative extension can be suggested to have been PAA *s' because PAA *s is already accounted for by the PAA causative in *s, noted below (#37). But the Egyptian and PS reflexes allow either PAA *s or *s' as the proto-segment.

34. *m extendative (?): pPS *m = Eg. *m* = PC *m (*-am- ?) = PCh *m = PO *m.

The pPS manifestation of this extension was characterized in Ehret 1989 as a fortative, like the *s' (or *s ?) extension (#33). But re-examination of its effects on Semitic verbs suggests that it might better be understood in many of its occurrences as having originally been an extendative marker. In Egyptian examples, too, *m* is most often interpretable as having an extendative effect. The Cushitic reflexes, on the other hand, consistently give it an intransitive connotation. Hayward (1984b) reconstructs it for proto-Eastern Cushitic (PEC) as *-am- neuter-passive, while its Southern Cushitic form has been called a stative/intransitive marker (Ehret 1980). Its cognate in Agaw, *-ŋ- (regular PC *m > Agaw *ŋ in this environment), acts as a reciprocal and reflexive extension. In some Omotic languages, it can also have a stative effect (e.g., Yem verb in #592 in Chapter 5).

Possibly these divergent usages reflect two extensions of distinct origin. But if they are indeed facets of one and the same extension, as is argued here, one can plausibly posit that the original application of the suffix was as an extendative of some sort. An extended action is in effect a greater amount of the action, thus yielding for the *m extension the fortative implication that appears sometimes in pPS and more rarely in Egyptian. In intransitive contexts, on the other hand, an extended action can translate into an ongoing condition or state. If the extension then undergoes a usage shift by which it ceases to apply to transitive verbs, condition or state may be left as its primary connotation, thus yielding the characteristically detransitizing connotations of the *m extension found in the various subbranches of Cushitic. Exactly this kind of relation can be understood to explain the dual durative and intransitive functions of the extentions in *n (#17 above) and *t (#25 above).

Widely in Cushitic, *m continues to be a productive element in verb derivational morphology.

35. *dz extendative fortative: pPS *ð = Eg. *z* (> *s*) = PCh *z; and
36. *x^w extendative fortative: pPS *x = Eg. *ẖ* = PC *x^w.

The two extendative fortatives provide another pair one member of which is not yet known from Cushitic examples and may therefore not have been present in the Cushitic proto-history. The two tend to impart both a strengthening and an unboundedness to the action denoted by a verb; in PC, for example, a PAA root meaning probably "to bite" took on the meaning "to gnaw" by addition of the *x^w extension (see root #737).

37. *s causative: pPS *s = Eg. *s* = PC *s = PCh *s (s_3 ?) = PO *s.

The causative in *s continues to be productive in many of the languages of the Afroasiatic family today, although in the Boreafrasian division of the family it long ago became a prefixed rather than suffixed marker. Several examples of lexicalized suffixed *s causative can be proposed, however, among the Semitic and Egyptian attestations in Chapter 5.

Table 3, which begins on the page opposite, lists the more than 1600 instances of these extensions that are cited in the etymologies of Chapter 5 and Appendixes 1-3. As with Table 2, the purpose is again to facilitate the reader's critical examination of the etymological analyses of the 1011 PAA roots offered in that chapter.

Table 3: Attestations of Verb Extensions

extension	Semitic	Egyptian	Cushitic	Chadic	Omotic
1. *dl middle voice	#83, 297, 362, 379, 640, 644, 693, 748, 765; Appendix 1: #5, 20, 52, 131, 681, 744, 778	#43, 53, 81, 139, 484, 644, 662, 686, 926, 927, 942	#50, 687, 753, 957, 970	#565	#113, 204, 224, 271, 378, Appendix 3: #1014
2. *h amplificative	#201, 294, 577, 581, 708, 968, 971; Appendix 1: #14, 79, 273, 280, 321, 540, 654, 681, 863, 926	#581, 893	#50, 346, 523, 581, 667, 997		
3. *w inchoative/ denominative (> durative)	#46, 66, 103, 137, 158, 180, 232, 246, 254, 270, 273, 276, 328, 345, 367, 369, 371, 379, 421, 426, 472, 486, 498, 530, 569,	#205, 228, 368, 540, 598, 600, 619, 631, 676, 709, 752, 756, 801, 863, 921, 1007	#573, 600, 791, 837, 919; Appendix 2: #61, 999	#13, 96, 205, 238, 273, 481, 527, 600	#386

Table 3: Attestations of Verb Extensions (continued)

extension	Semitic	Egyptian	Cushitic	Chadic	Omotic
	569, 600, 631, 638, 663, 671, 678, 665, 702, 719, 745, 794, 837?, 854, 863, 881, 911, 918; Appendix 1: #113, 131, 221, 245, 289, 298, 508, 537, 841?, 897; Appendix 3: #1019				
4. *y inchoative/ denominative (> durative)	#46, 69, 184, 243, 264, 272, 316, 328, 333, 345, 363, 382, 407, 419, 426, 437, 467, 472, 476, 539, 545, 546, 569, 631, 732, 769, 772, 823, 832, 833, 862?, 925, 973, 988; Appendix 1: #113,	#20, 45, 51, 53, 60 69, 95, 125, 139, 172, 183, 185, 188, 214, 220, 237, 238, 261, 280, 286, 290, 292, 294, 319, 357, 363, 372, 377, 382, 407, 421, 434, 437, 491, 494, 502, 507, 518, 538, 560, 562, 569, 572, 581, 583, 590, 611, 626, 627,	#280, 319, 382, 407, 458, 720, 833	#43, 122, 160, 180, 207, 214, 372, 463, 482, 624, 644, 836, 933	#5, 131?, 275, 382, 386, 873

extension	Semitic	Egyptian	Cushitic	Chadic	Omotic
	418, 579, 620, 721, 931, 982	636, 646, 649, 654, 681, 692, 708, 719, 734, 739, 741, 753, 757, 760, 761, 765, 793, 799, 802, 805, 808, 810, 817, 824, 830, 833, 836, 843, 856, 858, 860, 880, 885, 886, 909, 918, 926, 954, 957, 958, 969, 975, 987, 1003, 1007			
5. *ɣʷ complementive	#85, 516; Appendix 1: #20, 945	#41, 50, 349, 590, 640, 665, 690, 810?, 950?, 984	#202, 259, 690		#690
6. *kʷ' andative	#32, 74, 211, 370, 407, 478, 496, 881, 975; Appendix 1: #14, 240, 474, 579, 819, 954	#762			
7. *ʕ partive (> andative)	#18, 27, 30, 102, 172, 213, 214,	#358, 362, 433, 604, 605, 645, 833, 880,	#18, 50, 110, 171, 196, 243, 440,		

Table 3: Attestations of Verb Extensions (continued)

extension	Semitic	Egyptian	Cushitic	Chadic	Omotic
	219, 226, 287, 335, 412, 440, 452, 477, 513, 514, 534, 573, 589, 590, 820, 844, 909, 910; Appendix 1: #113, 114, 145, 250, 280, 289, 295, 312, 335, 400, 402, 431, 436, 493, 508, 540, 579, 620, 821, 839, 842, 868, 902, 913, 915, 954, 984; Appendix 3: #1020	933, 961	563, 635, 734, 817, 821, 838, 839, 929		
8. *ɬ venitive	#83, 107, 421, 435, 612, 615, 649, 651, 656, 692, 693, 746; 800; Appendix 1: #113, 145, 321, 404, 604, 632,	#85, 89, 113, 297, 369, 378, 379, 977	#723		

Table 3: Attestations of Verb Extensions (continued)

extension	Semitic	Egyptian	Cushitic	Chadic	Omotic
	645, 695, 696, 753, 754, 770				
9. *tl' focative	#130, 270, 315, 447, 452, 831, 950; Appendix 1: #20, 695, 744, 747, 754, 947	#113, 183, 187, 481, 481, 589, 687, 788, 952	#82, 589, 592		#452
10. ts diffusive	#40, 335, 382, 580, 612, 936; Appendix 1: #285, 337, 620, 632, 645	#126, 227?, 328, 349, 614, 833?, 965		#398?, 595	
11. *r diffusive	#6, 39?, 40, 70, 108, 164, 189, 191, 192, 201, 204, 215, 219, 225, 238, 248, 274, 275, 290, 314, 351, 373, 387, 451, 453, 481, 494, 509, 512, 543, 560,	#5, 126, 278, 386, 400, 420, 586, 611, 651, 663, 673?, 681, 744, 815, 841, 879, 957, 960, 982, 990, 1004	#193, 213, 510, 651, 653, 687?, 773, 970	#60, 191, 208, 214, 333, 458, 512	#39, 169, 199, 770 988, 989

Table 3: Attestations of Verb Extensions (continued)

extension	Semitic	Egyptian	Cushitic	Chadic	Omotic
	652, 653, 673, 678?, 687, 743, 845, 862, 865, 876, 912, 914, 916, 986, 987; Appendix 1: #114, 117, 145, 155?, 163, 240, 298, 349, 390, 508, 604, 615?, 632, 645, 683, 744, 747, 878, 902, 915				
12. $*k^w$ finitive	#92, 111, 149, 518; Appendix 1: #113, 117, 221	#516	#175, 339, 516, 647, 685		
13. *l finitive (> fortative in Eg.)	#98?, 216, 266, 407?, 531, 543, 583, 666, 678, 987; Appendix 1: #116, 131, 157, 245, 285, 321, 372, 431, 616,	#57, 74, 194, 225, 235, 349, 367, 407?, 478, 499, 534, 552, 745?, 818, 850, 903, 921, 987, 989	#407?	#107, 156, 190	

Table 3: Attestations of Verb Extensions (continued)

extension	Semitic	Egyptian	Cushitic	Chadic	Omotic
	632, 665, 758, 761, 863; Appendix 3: #1023				
14. *p' finitive fortative	#163, 208, 214 293, 368, 376, 403, 542, 563, 649, 652, 688, 743, 856, 870, 890, 932, 988; Appendix 1: #312, 384, 402, 566, 665, 721, 913, 931	#149, 336, 376, 634?, 817,		#341, 376, 402, 937	#425?
15. *g finitive fortative	#207, 208, 478, 516, 688, 722, 784?; Appendix 1: #117, 155, 285, 400, 695, 878, 947, 948	#22	#712	#594, 653, 840, 927	
16. *š non-finitive	#15, 42?, 50, 134, 151, 595, 660, 802?; Appendix 1:	#833?, 942		#142?, 398?	

Table 3: Attestations of Verb Extensions (continued)

extension	Semitic	Egyptian	Cushitic	Chadic	Omotic
	14?, 131, 133?, 256?, 537, 761, 775?, 947?, 954?				
17. *n non-finitive	#184, 186, 214, 242, 361, 406, 488, 509, 567, 582, 667, 684, 773, 818, 884, 956, 977, 983?; Appendix 1: #20, 52, 810, 821?, 841, 842	#6, 8, 46, 70, 110, 129, 166, 168, 189, 191, 234, 270, 415, 463, 477, 540, 576, 667, 864, 893, 900, 912, 933, 950, 952, 983?	#96, 357, 478?, 916, 997, 983?	#96, 175, 243, 476, 477, 567, 653, 840, 926, 983?	#132, 660, 983?
18. *b extendative (> stative)	#206, 207, 269, 300, 346, 389, 484, 511, 531, 533, 634, 653, 654, 666, 729, 742, 774, 777, 789, 791, 801, 814, 846, 900?, 946, 952, 969, 976, 978; Appendix 1: #20, 131,	#163, 239, 295, 303, 338, 361, 368, 474, 519, 544, 565, 630, 750, 762, 791, 800, 827, 870, 955, 956, 989	#202, 557, 782, 916?, 975, 1002	#269, 369, 469, 544	#425?, 486

Table 3: Attestations of Verb Extensions (continued)

extension	Semitic	Egyptian	Cushitic	Chadic	Omotic
	245, 250, 285, 334, 337, 372, 431, 632, 645, 654, 695, 775, 819, 863, 868, 902, 915, 984; Appendix 3: #1016				
19. *c' extendative	#587, 656, 818, 999	#49, 653, 936?, 960	#49, 222, 421, 753	#49	#421?
20. *f iterative	#127, 191, 202, 258, 340, 387, 394, 396, 412, 452, 510, 527, 529, 539, 562, 619, 630, 648, 694?, 763, 771, 794, 830, 957; Appendix 1: #256, 334, 390, 404, 540, 613, 861, 931; Appendix 3: #1023	#331, 370, 486, 537, 539, 671, 906, 988	#328, 336, 376, 687, 694?, 753	#302, 687	#194, 696

Table 3: Attestations of Verb Extensions (continued)

extension	Semitic	Egyptian	Cushitic	Chadic	Omotic
21. *ḫ iterative	#44, 84, 90, 92, 104, 236, 332, 420, 592, 622, 895, 910, 912, 914, 934, 942; Appendix 1: #14, 88, 89, 256, 273, 334, 436, 474, 507, 540, 620, 645, 821, 926, 945; Appendix 3: #1020	#39, 115, 268, 298, 435, 576, 579, 583, 587, 633, 701, 808, 834, 931, 955, 975	20, 50, 81, 251, 273, 349, 587, 967	[-*a* incep.: #55, 108, 175, 191, 271, 369, 654, 687, 852, 942]	
22. *g^w durative	#129, 364, 532, 575?, 627, 756, 784?, 833; Appendix 1: #131, 139, 262, 334, 400, 625, 665, 753, 770, 775, 799, 931	#116, 756, 833	#833		#20, 150?

extension	Semitic	Egyptian	Cushitic	Chadic	Omotic
23. *k durative	#80, 532, 581, 637, 751, 983; Appendix 1: #20, 537, 615, 753, 758; Appendix 3: #1014	#21, 555, 751; Appendix 3: #1014	#14, 740, 751, 824, 976	#42, 252, 316, 401, 662?, 741, 909, 926, 980	#22, 401, 543, 596?
24. *d durative (> stative)	#43, 54, 82, 191, 200, 228, 330, 391, 416, 486, 521, 542, 618, 682, 687, 711, 816, 825, 907, 923, 939, 967, 980; Appendix 1: #20, 171, 285, 443, 493, 604, 613, 634, 683, 695, 697, 758, 863, 926	#62, 337, 364, 379, 420, 442, 592, 635, 687, 709, 744, 755, 890, 929, 942, 950, 1008	#687, 935, 964	#346, 373, 401, 417, 480, 687, 842, 856, 972	#136, 199, 377, 974
25. *t durative (> intransitive)	#58, 66, 214, 315, 319, 480, 486, 500, 517, 600, 644, 748?, 783, 805, 906, 938;	#212, 219, 406, 582, 600, 754, 756, 811, 933	#94, 238, 441, 566, 570, 594, 607, 659, 678, 722, 926; Appendix 2: #857, 1009	#5, 14, 42, 49, 50, 84, 217, 299, 316, 404, 472, 484,	#38, 43, 302, 335, 477, 493, 527, 540, 579, 585, 692,

Table 3: Attestations of Verb Extensions (continued)

extension	Semitic	Egyptian	Cushitic	Chadic	Omotic
	Appendix 1: #5, 52, 113, 326, 349, 402, 620, 695, 770, 778			576, 589, 594, 600, 782, 811, 851, 873, 987	926
26. *ʔ concisive	#167, 199, 294, 339, 342, 433, 440, 507, 773, 802, 852, 854, 971; Appendix 1: #14, 88, 131, 256?, 289, 334, 537, 654, 744, 915, 945, 981; Appendix 3: #1019	#78, 433, 532, 584, 590, 602, 706, 714, 854, 914	#212, 442, 448, 842		#199?, 377
27. *x precipitive	#828, 955?; Appendix 1: #113, 196	#218	#232	#476?, 594?	
28. *p intensive (of manner)	#171, 391, 421, 499, 516, 524, 529?, 639, 869; Appendix 1: #285, 295, 418, 566,	#251, 297, 329, 401, 538, 634?, 648, 660, 676,764, 786, 965; Appendix 3: #1024	#303, 880	#458, 823	#138

Table 3: Attestations of Verb Extensions (continued)

extension	Semitic	Egyptian	Cushitic	Chadic	Omotic
	625, 654, 758; Appendix 3: #1025				
29. *z intensive (of manner)	#4, 153, 319, 338, 398, 442, 582, 646, 815, 848, 850, 869, 965; Appendix 1: #14, 131, 285, 321, 681, 697, 761, 878	#190?, 710, 817?	#258, 710	#42, 44, 63, 76, 168, 226, 364, 401, 425, 436, 477, 496, 527, 594, 688, 750, 821, 848, 849, 873, 986	
30. *ɣ intensive (of effect)	#41, 55; Appendix 1: #114, 273, 507, 540, 915	#62, 810?		#481	
31. *k' intensive (of effect)	#23, 44, 110, 124, 182, 226, 361, 526, 606, 617, 660, 730, 667, 730, 734, 796, 866, 884, 895, 907, 910, 969,	#23, 48, 388, 705, 730, 770, 796, 873	#20, 23, 94, 547, 573, 576, 647, 730, 753, 981, 1001		#23

Table 3: Attestations of Verb Extensions (continued)

extension	Semitic	Egyptian	Cushitic	Chadic	Omotic
	Appendix 1: #20, 113, 114, 117, 123, 139, 157, 196, 256, 402, 443, 537, 540, 842, 984				
32. *ṭ' durative intensive	#116, 183, 233, 427, 441, 480, 502, 506, 524, 528, 535, 619, 634, 661, 824, 825, 984; Appendix 1: #123, 493, 625, 654, 747, 778, 841, 913, 926	#747?	#450		#69, 421?, 695
33. *s' fortative	#42?, 281, 291?, 335?, 738, 802?, 840?; Appendix 1: #14, 131?, 155, 157, 250, 349, 400, 615, 775?, 926, 954?	#42?, 167, 352?, 433?, 437?, 603?, 614?, 747?, 822?, 833?, 936?	#304	#157	

Table 3: Attestations of Verb Extensions (continued)

extension	Semitic	Egyptian	Cushitic	Chadic	Omotic
34. *m extendative (?) (> stative in Cushitic)	#21, 73, 99, 112, 115?, 129, 132, 152, 195, 213, 307, 313, 348, 417, 436, 440, 442, 446, 484, 486, 490, 491, 530, 545, 660, 674, 700, 701, 736, 737, 740, 826, 907, 962, 979; Appendix 1: #88, 114, 131, 155, 196, 250, 285, 295, 298 334, 349, 357, 390, 404, 493, 566, 620, 778, 799, 913, 945; Appendix 3: #1014, 1015?, 1021	#165, 233, 307?, 315, 338, 401, 552, 645, 660, 773, 795, 819, 861, 872, 897, 898, 962, 966, 986; Appendix 3: #1014	#678, 682, 842, 942	#62, 103, 196, 243, 330, 457, 478, 537, 544, 594	#592, 804
35. *dz extendative fortative	#57; Appendix 1: #357, 863	#190?, 817?, 980		#134, 558	

Table 3: Attestations of Verb Extensions (continued)

extension	Semitic	Egyptian	Cushitic	Chadic	Omotic
36. $*x^w$ extendative fortative	#54, 83, 136, 224, 592, 601?, 829?, 908, 978; Appendix 1: #540, 613	#277, 601?, 728	#601?, 728, 737		
37. *s causative	#87?, 147, 291?, 755, 853, 984; Appendix 1: #133?, 245, 285	#8, 426, 579 (pfxd.), 620 (pfxd.), 629?, 750 (pfxd.), 878, 908, 984	#11, 56, 58, 102, 180, 206, 463, 528, 611, 683, 769, 883, 973, 984, 996, 997	#87?, 147, 192, 984	#20, 129, 131, 361, 426, 447, 569, 942; Appendix 3: #1015
38. *-u- transitive infix	#137?, 292?, 866	#292?, 997, 866	#50, 137?, 202, 292?, 315, 649, 788, 866, 995, 997	#14, 41, 50, 84, 163, 252, 866, 918, 927, 932	#150, 497, 587, 777, 927, 995
39 . *in- concomitive prefix			#617; attested for PC and probably still productive in some SC and Agaw languages	#4, 17, 33, 35, 51, 56, 168, 208, 366	

PREFIXES, INFIXES, AND REDUPLICATION IN *PAA*

Just one derivational prefix is certainly traceable at present to PAA. Its usual shape was *a-, and affixed to verb roots it produced noun attributives derived from those verbs. At least two PAA noun roots contain it (#438 and 569) and a third (#65) probably has it as well. It is separately attested for Omotic, where it derives an old Omotic root for "tongue" from a verb "to lap" (root #808) and contributes to the Kafa word for "man" (#621). It can be observed in both Cushitic examples (e.g., the PSC entry in root #317 and the PC root for "breast," #613) and remnant Egyptian occurrences (#23, 85, and 616), and it is noted by Schuh (1981) as a no longer productive prefix in Ngizim (Chadic). It is also the visible deriving prefix of the PCh noun for "tongue," which is built on a different PAA root for "to lick" or "to lap" (#827) from that seen in the Omotic example just mentioned.

The shape *ʔa- found in some Semitic reflexes (e.g., the noun "nose" in #611) and in one PSC case (#317) can be understood as separate analogy shifts to bring the morpheme into conformity with the usual consonant-initial pattern of Afroasiatic words. But the outcomes in other instances favor its reconstruction as originally a vowel alone. One such example is provided by PSC *agad- "man" (q.v. under root #265). The Egyptian cases indicate that *a- yielded a reduced central vowel there (> Coptic ɛ; for word-initial PAA *a > Coptic ɛ, see Chapter 4 and root #924 in Chapter 5), or else became Ø (at least before PAA *l: see root #827; had the prefix been *ʔa-, the Egyptian reflex of "tongue" in this item would have produced ME **3ns* rather than *ns*.

A probable allomorph of *a-, of the shape *i-, appears in several derived nouns in Cushitic and Egyptian (see roots #224, 637, and 875 for PC examples and #140, 282, 568, and 621, among others, for Eg. instances). Its conditioning environment may originally have been that of a high stem-vowel in the stem to which it was attached. If so, its development should probably be traced to the period immediately after the proposed split of Omotic from the common ancestor of the rest of the family, because the use of *a- before stem vowel *i is clearly attested in Omotic (see root #808 in Chapter 5). Egyptian instances of this allomorph seem usually to have been brought into comformity with the more general consonant-initial pattern by treating it as *y (Eg. *i*), although it may have alternatively have been deleted before a voiceless sibilant (cf. root #483). Semitic, in addition to the prefixes in *a- (written as *ʔa-) and *i- (*ʔi-), has innovated a third shape *u- (*ʔu-).

A second derivational prefix, an *in- concomitive applied usually to verbs but sometimes to nouns, can be proposed, on the basis of evidence from Cushitic and Chadic, to have arisen very early in Afroasiatic linguistic history. Its reconstructibility outside Cushitic remains to be systematically established; nevertheless, the Chadic data (e.g., the paired items cited under root #33 of Chapter 5), seem to require it, in the reduced shape *N-, in the prehistory of that branch also. In Egyptian and Semitic, any earlier word-initial *N- in preconsonantal position, because of syllabic structure rules, would necessarily have gone to zero (see example of PAA "kidney" in root #343), deleting most surface attestations of such a prefix in those subgroups. A fuller discussion of this prefix's proposed connotation and uses is presented in the penultimate section of Chapter 5.

One other Afroasiatic derivational prefix, an agent and instrument formative in *m, has long been recognized by scholars. Though common in Semitic, Berber, Egyptian, and a variety of Chadic languages, it should not be reconstructed for PC, since its Cushitic occurrences are only in languages where its presence is certain or highly likely to be accounted for by Semitic influence. It should therefore be understood as an innovation of later provenance than PAA, specifically emerging in the common ancestor tongue of the Chadic and Boreafrasian languages (see Chapter 6 for further discussion of Afroasiatic subclassification).

Prefixal in position at a stage in Afroasiatic history when nominalizing morphology was predominantly suffixal — i.e., before the splitting off of the Boreafrasian subgroup, in which prefixation became characteristic (see Chapter 6 on this matter) — the *m- agent-instrument marker cannot plausibly be derived from a pre-existing suffix. Rather, the usual historical linguistic pattern in such cases is for the prefix in question to have derived from a previously independent free morpheme whose normal syntactical position would have immediately preceded the kind of word to which it later attached as a prefix. Just such a likely source for the *m- agent-instrument prefix does indeed exist, namely, the old PAA indefinite third person pronoun *m- (root #568). The prefix thus plausibly began as a syntactically independent, syntactically preverbal pronominal denoting "that which, one who" performs the action of the following verb.

Two stem-internal processes of derivation can also be proposed for PAA. One of these, forming nouns from verbs by lengthening the stem vowel, can be strongly established with a high degree of confidence. Although possibly no longer productive anywhere in Cushitic, it can be identified in a fairly large number of Cushitic root reconstructions (Ehret 1987 and roots from Chapter 5, listed in Table 2, #15, above); and the comparative data presented here show it also to have long been a productive process in Omotic for deriving not only nouns but adjectives (again see Table 2, #15). Chadic cases can be proposed as well (e.g., root #352), along with one clear instance in Egyptian, but the possibility of its former productivity in the ancestry of Berber and Semitic remains to be explored.

A second process, forming a transitive from an intransitive verb by replacing a stem vowel *a or *i by an infix *-u-, is widely but sporadically indicated in the family. Three examples in early Cushitic have previously been proposed (Ehret 1987), and a considerable number of other cases from outside Cushitic appear in the data of Chapter 5: notable examples are the transitive forms of old Afroasiatic verbs seen in roots #50, 866, 927, 995, and 997 and a number of similar instances in Omotic (e.g., Mocha entry in #497) and in Chadic (e.g., Ngizim citations in #84 and 163). The Mocha case, because it retains the marker as *u, implies the productivity of the infix at a time postdating the early Omotic shift of PAA short *u in CuC stems to *o. The formation of transitive verbs in Ngizim by the substitution of ə for stem a, with accompanying tone reversal, occurs in a number of instances in that language (for an especially clear example, see root #932); and since PAA *u is one of the sources of Ngizim ə, these examples thus probably show the affix to have been preserved and to have been productive at a relatively recent date in Chadic. At least one early Afroasiatic example of the *-u- infix (#866), if rightly identified, also overtly shows the accompanying stem tone reversal, suggesting this effect to have been an old feature of this marker, not limited just to Chadic (see Table 3, affix #38, for a fuller listing of examples of *-u- transitive appearing in Chapter 5).

Still another root-modifying process, the reduplication and partial reduplication of stems as an intensifier of the verbal action, probably goes back to PAA. Partial reduplication of the form $*C_1VC_2 > C_1VC_2(V)C_2$ occurs in Egyptian, Omotic, and Cushitic (see Ehret 1987: 10). The gemination of verb-stem-final consonants in a number of proto-Eastern Cushitic (PEC) verb roots appearing in Chapter 5 is surely a version of this kind of reduplication; it occurs consistently with verbs that convey a durational or repetitive action. Examples can be noted under roots #127, 152, 155, 257, 471, 476, 553, 789, 907, 911, and 957, among others.

An alternative form of reduplication, $*C_1VC_2 > C_1VC_1VC_2$, is known from Chadic (see roots #41 and 233 for examples) and Cushitic, most notably Southern Cushitic (Ehret 1980: 66-67). This second kind of partial reduplication appears most often to have had a frequentative implication. In Semitic it became a semantically neutral means of creating canonical triliteral stem shapes out of earlier biconsonantal verb stems (Ehret 1989).

Full reduplication of CVC stems also occurs widely in Afroasiatic, having most often an intensive and less commonly a frequentative effect in Semitic (Ehret 1989), an intensive or frequentative sense in the few cases known from Egyptian and Cushitic, and a frequentative meaning in Chadic (e.g., root #404). Rich exemplification of the several kinds of reduplication can be found among the data of Chapter 5.

A final issue requiring mention is the matter of subordinate morphophonemic gemination. Its occurrences in the data of Chapter 5 include cases in Eastern Cushitic, and sometimes in other Cushitic languages, of doubling of a stem-final C upon addition of certain verbal or nominal affixes (see roots #70, 101, 122, 188, 242, 439, 517, 573, 629, 707, 713, 735, 791, 838, 839, 844, 893, 906, and 981). Similar instances appear in the Semitic data (e.g., #120, 785, 836, and 872) and in Omotic (e.g., #169, 194, and 355 among others); and the recurrence of certain patterns — for example, stem-final consonant gemination with addition of a suffix in *r or *l (e.g., in Semitic in #262, in Cushitic in #893, and in Omotic in #170) — suggests that very old Afroasiatic rules lie behind these outcomes. The derivation of nouns from verbs seemingly by gemination of the stem-final consonant, seen in Egyptian, Cushitic, and Omotic (e.g., among others, the Egyptian nouns in #682, 747, and 752; the Cushitic nouns in #242, 278 and 908; and the Omotic nouns in #904 and 920), may be the relict of another such underlying rule. Still another form of subordinate gemination appears in the numerous examples of Mocha verb-stem-final CC; these probably most often reflect surface realizations of underlying non-geminate consonants, a process whose governing conditions remain to be studied. Not essential to the etymological reckoning of PAA roots, the fuller explicating of these epiphenomena, even if sometimes reflective of quite old synchronic processes, can safely be left to future study.

4

VOWELS AND TONE IN EARLY AFROASIATIC (AFRASIAN)

THE *PAA* VOWELS

With the structural issues necessary to the interpretation of the comparative data now dealt with, we can move on to the task of identifying the elements of the phonological system of proto-Afroasiatic (proto-Afrasian).

On present evidence, a PAA vowel system of five different vowel qualities, each occurring both long and short, must be postulated: *a, *aa, *e, *ee, *i, *ii, *o, *oo, *u, and *uu. There is one factor which somewhat complicates the reconstruction of the vowels: in a number of instances, early ablaut effects of verb conjugational marking on stem vowel quality can be invoked to explain the reconstructibility of alternate stem vowels in roots. This phenomenon has been encountered most significantly in the reconstruction of Cushitic verb roots (Sasse 1979; Ehret 1987) and may indeed have been particularly characteristic of the development of proto-Cushitic. But it can also appear in Omotic (e.g., root #51, among others, and the South Omotic entries in roots #676 and 928) and may account for some of the instances in Chadic where Newman (1977) or Jungraithmayr and Shimizu (1981) felt unable to decide on stem vowel reconstructions. Once these probable instances of ablaut are taken into account, however, clear regular vowel correspondence patterns can be discerned among the three branches, Cushitic, Chadic, and Omotic, that have best maintained the stem vowels in a form accessible to the investigation here.

Egyptian and Berber also preserved stem vowels, as did PS in its nominals. These three divisions of Afroasiatic, along with Chadic, have all greatly reduced the inherited PAA system, and much of the clarifying of their histories of vocalic sound change must be left to future work. Nevertheless, a first approximation of those histories can be laid out even now, and that matter is taken up later in this chapter.

In contrast to the balanced five-vowel system postulated for PAA, the Omotic sound-shift rules (see below, this chapter) imply an alternative, unbalanced array of shorter and longer vowels for the ancestor language of at least one of its two primary branches, North Omotic. Five long vowels *a:, *e:, *i:, *o:, and *u:, but only three short vowels, *a, *e, and *o — with the realization of *e as *[i] or [e] and of *o as [u] or [o] governed by definable consonantal environments — appear sufficient to explain the great majority of the modern North Omotic vowels (see below).

Might this system be projected back to PAA? The Cushitic and Chadic correspondences do not allow this interpretation. To be sure, recontructed PAA *a and *aa (as noted already for Southern Cushitic in Ehret 1980) are at least twice as common as the combined instances of *e/*ee and *i/*ii and of *o/*oo and *u/*uu, and this situation might lead scholars used to the traditional three vowels of Semitic reconstruction to suggest a derivation of *i/*ii and *e/*ee, and of *o/*oo and *u/*uu, by split from earlier single front and back vowels respectively. Consistent plausible conditioning environments for such splits are not at all apparent, however, in the overall data (for which see Chapter 5). Thus the overabundance of *a and *aa might just as well be explained by an alternative history, according to which a seven-vowel system, of *a, *ɛ, *e, *i, *ɔ, *o, and *u, once existed in pre-PAA, with *ɛ and *ɔ then falling together with *a in the PAA language to create the surfeit of PAA *a and *aa. Just such a history can be traced elsewhere among African languages, in particular in certain subgroups of the Nilo-Saharan family (Ehret MS). In any case, by neither hypothesis can the unbalanced patterning of long and short vowels found in proto-North-Omotic be understood to explain the observed vowel correspondence patterns of Afroasiatic. Nor does this evidence suggest an original two-tier system, like that proposed by Joseph Pia (1984).

The underlying pre-proto-North Omotic system of three short and five long vowels can thus best be understood as a specifically Omotic development, realized by the falling together of the respective pairs of PAA short front and back vowels. The drift toward similar eight-vowel systems discernable in some Cushitic languages, notably Afar and Soomaali of the Lowland Eastern Cushitic group — a drift which is, in the writer's view, the source of the vowel alternations and mergers that Pia (1984) attributes to a two-tier vowel system — may in turn reflect substratum effects of an earlier Omotic presence across the northern and eastern parts of the Ethiopian plateau, and not just in the southwest portions to which Omotic languages are restricted today. Such a presence is, in any case, distinctly indicated by the existence of Omotic loanwords in Agaw and in Lowland Eastern Cushitic (see, for example, roots #587 and 696 in Chapter 5). (The two-tier concept is adopted in modified form, however, as a way of looking at the contraction, discussed below, of the PAA vowel system in Chadic, Egyptian, Berber, and Semitic.)

In Table 4, in which the vowel correspondences of Cushitic, Chadic, and Omotic are laid out, the Cushitic long vowels, following established convention, are represented as VV; the same convention has been extended to PAA. In works on Omotic, however, a different representation of long vowels, as V: or V˙, has commonly been used and so appears as such in the table. The Omotic vowel reconstructions presented here are those inferable for the much more diverse and better-known North Omotic branch.

Table 4: Afroasiatic (Afrasian) Vowel Correspondences

PAA	PC	PCh	North Omotic
*a	*a	*a	*a
*aa	*aa	*a	*a:
*e	*e	*a	*e (> *i in several environments)
*ee	*ee	*ə	*e:
*i	*i	*ə	*e (> *i in several environments)
*ii	*ii	*i	*i:
*o	*o	*a	*o (> *u /_[+labial])
*oo	*oo	*ə	*o:
*u	*u	*ə	*o (> *u /_[+labial])
*uu	*uu	*u	*u:

OMOTIC VOWEL REFLEXES

For Omotic the falling together of the respective pairs of PAA front and back vowels, as discussed above and as depicted in Table 4, cannot yet be traced with certainty before proto-North Omotic. Its sister branch, South Omotic, seems on present evidence not have shared in this particular vocalic development, although it must be noted that the South Omotic languages are still too poorly known phonologically for this conclusion to be asserted categorically.

Even in the present state of our knowledge, however, several vowel shifts do seem traceable to the proto-Omotic (PO) language or even to pre-proto-Omotic (pre-PO). One very early shift fronted PAA *a and *aa in the environment of a following pharyngeal:

PO #1. PAA *a(a) > PO *e(:) /_C- (C = PAA *ʕ or *ḥ).

This sound change necessarily preceded a general PO consonantal shift,

#2. [+pharyngeal] > [-pharyngeal],

which removed PAA *ʕ and *ḫ from the consonant inventory of PO by collapsing them with, respectively, *ʔ and *h.

A third very early vocalic sound change began the removal of labiovelars from PO:

#3. PAA $*C^{w}a$ > *Co /#_C_2 (C_2 = *l, *dl, and *ts, in the examples so far noted).

It must be placed earlier in the evolution of proto-Omotic than still another consonant shift apparently general to the Omotic group,

#4. PAA $*C^{w}$ > PO *C /#_V, V ≠ i(:),

which removed the conditioning environment of #3 by collapsing the word-initial PAA labiovelars with their equivalent simple velars in PO.

The disposition of $*C^{w}i$ /#_ within this set of developments remains to be fully worked out. Its known modern North Omotic reflexes — *Ci in Gonga and *Cu in most other North Omotic tongues (roots #305, 347, 375, 377, 382, and 445) — indicate that it maintained a distinctive outcome in proto-North Omotic vis-a-vis other initial sequences of $*C^{w}V$-. One possibility is that $*C^{w}$ /#_i was not affected by PO rule #4 and that it was repeatedly and universally simplified to *Cu or *Ci in different North Omotic subgroups at a much later period. The alternative solution is that $*C^{w}i$ produced some intermediate outcome, possibly a rounded high central vowel ($*C^{w}i$ > *Cɨ, as proposed in Ehret 1980 for the same environment in PSC).

One proto-Omotic sound shift must have preceded the disappearance of $*C^{w}i$,

#5. PAA *š̌ > PO $*\check{s}_2$ /i, y_.

The reason for this ordering is that the loss of $C^{w}i$ sometimes changed PAA *i to Omotic /u/ and would thus have removed the environment in which PO $*\check{s}_2$ apparently was created. For more on this shift, see the section on PAA alveolar and palatals in Chapter 5.

Still another PO shift eliminated nasal clusters in which the oral element was a voiceless obstruent, at the same time reflecting this loss in compensatory lengthening of the preceding stem vowel:

#6. PAA *VNC > PO *V:C (C = [-voice])

(e.g., in roots #324 and 365).

Also following #6 came another shift — on present evidence marking the start of the separate emergence of the proto-North-Omotic (NOm) language — by which PAA short *o and *u, and short *e and *i, fell together:

#7. PAA *u > NO *o, PAA *i > NO *e, except /#(ʔ)_V-.

The NOm short vowels represented as *e and *i were most commonly realized as *[e] and *[e], but they also apparently developed the respective allophones *[i] and *[u] in various restricted environments:

#7a. */e/ -> *[i] /#N_C (N = nasal);
#7b. */e/ -> *[i] /#l_$C_{[+labial/+voice]}$ (PO *l < PAA *l and *ɬ);
#7c. */e/ -> *[i] /#b, p_r;
#7d. */e/ -> *[i] /#S_K (S = PO *s, *s', or *š; K = PO *k, *k^{w}, or *ʔ);
#7e. */o/ -> *[u] /#C_$C_{[+labial]}$;
#7f. */o/ -> *[u], */e/ -> [i] /#(ʔ)_C;
#7g. */o/ -> *[u], */e/ -> [i] /#k, x, k'_C (C = PO *t, *t', *s');
#7h. */o/ -> *[u], */e/ -> [i] /#(ʔ)_C- (but not /#(ʔ)_CC-); and
#7i. */o/ -> *[u], */e/ -> [i] /#$C_{[+labial]}$_C_2 (C_2 = ts, č').

In at least one case of stem-final C^{w}, preceding PAA *i also yielded NO *u (#170); whether this was another allophonic outcome of shift #7 or was the consequence of an earlier rule shifting pre-NO *i > *u in some, as yet undefined set of C^{w} environments.

In addition, some PAA *a went to NO *o before a [+labial] consonant, at least in a restricted and as yet only partially defined environment of a PO dental or palatal consonant (see #169, 193, and 463):

#8. *a > *o /#C_1_$C_{[+labial]}$- (observed for C_1 = PAA *t, *z, or *j).

Three subsequent sound shifts in the evolution of proto-North-Omotic then rephonemicized these originally allophonic distinctions:

#9. *C^{w} > C (deleting all remaining labiovelars);

#10. *e(:) > i(:) /#S_C (S = sibilant; C = *d, *n, or *r); and

#11. *V: > V /#C[+velar, -voice]_C, where root had PAA falling word-tone (see discussion of tone below, this chapter);

along with a fourth shift apparently restricted to the Ometo subgroup,

#12. *u > *o, *i > *e /#(ʔ)_$C_{[-continuant, -voice]}$.

North Omotic data also indicate an apparent stem-vowel lengthening in one restricted environment (see roots #4, 148, 273, and 842):

#13. *u > *u: /#C_P (C = voiced oral stop, P = voiceless labial).

Another sound change, probably morphophonemic in inspiration and possibly still synchronically productive in some languages, may well be of wide Omotic occurrence, although the examples so far encountered come principally from Gonga and Ometo:

#14. *V: > V /#C_C- + -(V)C- suffix.

This rule is in fact probably of ancient proto-Afroasiatic provenance since it can be observed in early Afroasiatic formations (e.g., the root pair #709, 710) and is postulated for proto-Southern Cushitic (Ehret 1980: 70, 71).

VOWELS IN CHADIC AND BOREAFRASIAN

The proto-Chadic vowel correspondences can be explained by a brief sequence of shifts that yield Newman's four-vowel system of PCh, *a, *ə, *i, and *u. Note that the first three of these shifts are identified as North Erythraean (PNE) rules, the reasons for which will become clear shortly. A sound shift, represented formally as

PNE #1. *Vy, *Vw > *VV /#C__C,

is proposed to have intitiated this set of changes (see section on the glides in Chapter 5 for more on this sound shift). Its particular outcomes remain to be fully sorted out. PAA *ay in such environments, at least, apparently became *ee, and PAA *ey probably became *ii, and so both were subsequently further affected by the PNE shifts #2 and 3. The first of these,

#2. PAA *ee > pre-PNE *i, *oo > pre-PNE *u,

raised and shortened long mid vowels; it was followed by

#3. pre-PNE *o, *e, *a (< PAA *o, *e, *a) > PNE *ä,
pre-PNE *u, *i (created by #2) > PNE *ə.

centralizing all short vowels and, in consequence, resituating the formerly distinctive long vowels *ii and *uu in the slots in the vocalic system vacated by short *i and *u. A fourth sound shift,

PCh #1. PNE *a [aa], *ä > PCh *a,

then eliminated the last remaining environment of distinctive vowel length in PCh.

What has been treated to this point as simply Chadic vowel history was in all probability, however, a history of wider inclusiveness than Chadic alone. Sound shifts #1-3 appear to have been the common heritage of a North

Erythraean branch of the family, consisting of Chadic, Berber, Semitic, and Egyptian (for which see Chapter 6) — hence the denoting of rules #1-3 as "PNE." The Berber and Semitic vowel systems can each be seen to have passed through a stage in which the PAA system was contracted in a fashion parallel to that described for Chadic — into two vocalic tiers (to use a term coined in Pia 1984, although somewhat differently applied here). The central tier comprised one or both of two central vowels, high central *ə (realized probably as [ɨ] or [ʌ]) and low central *ä; the peripheral tier consisted of three vowels, *i, *u, and *a, or, if *a had fallen together with *ä, of two vowels, *i and *u. The vowels of the central set would have been articulated with shorter length than those of the peripheral set, but vowel quantity as a formal phonemic distinction would have been lost. Much the same history seems implied for the Egyptian vowels.

In the case of Berber, Prasse (1975) reconstructs on solid grounds a proto-Berber system composed of the full two tiers, five vowels in all — *ə and *ä, and *i, *u, and *a — the first two being shorter in quantity than the latter three. He goes on to conjecture that a pre-proto-Berber system with three vowels *i, *u, and *a, occurring both long and short, lies behind the proto-Berber array. But that conjecture is not directly implied by the Berber material itself, and reflects the influence of the usual attribution by scholars of such a three-vowel system to proto-Semitic.

Ironically, from the work of Diakonov (1970, 1975), it appears that Semitic vocalic history itself requires revision. Diakonov shows that just two vowels, *ə and *a, are enough to account for most stem vowel realizations in Semitic nominal roots of *CVC(C) shape. Apparently,

PS #1. PNE *i, *u, *ə > PS *ə;
PNE *a, *ä > PS *a /#C_C(C).

The two vowels, *u and *i, remained distinct only in verbal and other morphological operators and in word-final position in adverbials of the shape CV (e.g., roots #209, 310, and 803). Vowel length in Semitic is not required at the phonemic level in this PS reconstruction, and its latter-day occurrence in Semitic languages was in all probability generated anew by morphophonemic and word-structure requirements in PS and its various descendant languages. Diakonov's arguments thus leave us with a four-vowel array in PS, *ə, *a, *i, and *u.

The earliest Egyptian vowel system is normally represented as comprising *a, *i, and *u. The original Egyptian vocalism showed, in other words, reductions in the vowel-quality distinctions similar to those in the PCh, Berber, and PS and, as well, the same loss of phonemic vowel quantity (phonemic vowel length did, however, re-evolve in the language, through processes of consonantal merger and loss, by or before the Late Egyptian period). The indications therefore are that the proto-history of the Egyptian vowel system should fit quite well within the broad scheme of North Erythraean vocalic history outlined here.

BOREAFRASIAN VOCALIC HISTORY

Like all good hypotheses, this proposition provides a set of testable predictions. In the case of Semitic, the posited PNE sound shifts #2-3, together with PS shift #1, predict that in nominals PAA short *i and *u and long *ii, *uu, *ee, and *oo should all be realized as Diakonov's PS *ə, and PAA short *o, *e, and *a and long *aa, as his PS *a. In Arabic in particular (following Diakonov 1975), PS *ə should surface as *u* in the environment /_C[+labial] and often in the environment /C[+velar]_ but usually as *i* elsewhere, while PS *a should appear as *i* /C_CVC, where V is long, and as *a* in other /C_C(C) environments.

An examination of the Semitic (especially Arabic) vowel reflexes found in old Afroasiatic nouns or adjective roots and in very early derived nominals, as presented in Chapter 5, *consistently* bears out these expectations. PS *ə can be seen in these data to derive specifically from

PAA *i (roots #25, 230, 247, 255, 364, 445, 505, 513, 555, 556, 563, 564, 618, 621, 726, 809, 827, 836, 917, 935, and 985);
PAA *u (#133, 146, 366, 669, and 707);
PAA *u or *i (#220);
PAA *ii (#59 and 641);
PAA *uu (#282, 323, 501, and 515);
PAA *ay (> *ə /#C_C by PNE rules #1-3: roots #833 (2nd entry) and 984);
PAA *ee (#254);
PAA *oo (#422); and
PAA *oo or *ee (#28).

PS *a, for its part, is amply attested as deriving variously from

PAA *a (#47, 102, 140, 144, 154, 181, 201, 257, 259, 260, 262, 263, 264, 285, 324, 341, 374, 358, 383, 388, 399, 447, 477, 503, 520, 663, 706, 718, 724, 725, 727, 749, 864, 877, 891, 1000, and 1002);
PAA *aa (#26, 792, 958, and 974);
PAA *a or *aa (#887);
PAA *o (roots #29, 105, 243, 244, 318, 327, 550, 806, and 888);
PAA *e (#82, 247, 289, 529, and 558); and
PAA *o, *e, *a, or *aa (889).

Three modifications of Diakonov's specifications can be proposed from these examples. First off, in a restricted environment additional to those he cites — /#C_{n,r}, where C is a voiceless dental obstruent in Arabic (see #254, 255, and 501) — PS *ə yields Arabic *u* rather than *i*. Secondly, PS *a gives Arabic *i* in /#C_NC_r# word shapes (as in #47). Thirdly, the realization of PS *ə as *[u] (Arabic *u*) or *[i] (Arabic *i*) has no consistent relation to whether or not that velar derives from a PAA labiovelar or simple velar (cf. #317, 364, 366, and 422 versus 396 and 445). What does govern the appearance of these two alternative outcomes remains unclear (the two South Semitic instances cited here of [i] for *ə, in #396 and 445, both are followed in the same word by a voiceless fricative). These reflexes indicate that the labiovelar distinction was already lost in PS and must therefore have been recreated in Ethiopic Semitic by processes particular to that subgroup.

It appears also that two of the noun roots for which Diakonov reconstructs PS stem *a are better posited, on the basis of wider Afroasiatic comparisons and their specific Arabic vowel reflexes, as containing PS *ə or, alternatively, as preserving earlier *a/*ə stem-vowel alternances (#827 and 935). This latter suggestion points up a further consideration for PS vowel reconstruction — that seemingly irregular stem-vowel correspondences in nominals may not always trace back to intra-Semitic borrowing, but may at times reflect the PS retention of older Afroasiatic stem-vowel alternances. Some instances in a single language of alternative vowel realizations for the same noun may also derive from such phenomena (e.g., the two Arabic vowel reflexes in #121, which correspond to the respective alternate vowels reconstructed for the PAA etymon in question).

This reconstruction can similarly be tested against the Egyptian evidence as preserved in the Coptic reflexes of PAA roots. If, as is commonly presumed, Old Egyptian indeed had three vowels /a/, /i/, and /u/, the PNE set of sound shifts #2-3 predict that Eg. /a/ should have merged PAA *a, *aa, *e, and *o, and that Eg. /i/ should derive from PAA *ii and Eg. /u/ from PAA *uu. The hypothesis does not overtly predict the outcome for the posited North Erythraean high central vowel *ə, derived from the merger of PAA *i, *u, *oo, and *ee; but in fact, as will emerge below, it clearly fell together with Eg. /i/.

Between Old Egyptian and Coptic times, a complex history of vowel sound change took shape. Early Eg. /a/ evolved usually into Coptic *o* in closed syllables and *ō* in open syllables. Following a nasal consonant in an open syllable, however, Eg. /a/ yielded Coptic *ū*. Eg. /u/, like /a/, produced *o* in closed syllables, but its reflex in open syllables was long *ē*. More rarely, Eg. /u/ could also have a Coptic reflex transcribed as *ī*. Eg. /i/, for its part, developed into Coptic *a* in closed syllables, into *ī* in most open syllables, and into *ē* in open syllables where the following consonants were *tn* or *ty*. A fourth direction of change, the deletion of Eg. /i/ altogether, took place in the environment /#C_C_2, where C_2 was a voiced continuant. Coptic short central *ε* also generally derives from earlier Eg. /i/. (See Vycichl 1990 for these various patterns; the data used here is drawn from the Sahidic dialect of Coptic, unless otherwise noted).

The Coptic vocalic system thus reflects a very long history of complex vocalic change. Nevertheless, even with the complexity of this history, the Coptic and the earlier Egyptian reflexes visibly confirm the predictions already generated by the examination of Chadic and Semitic.

Firstly, early Egyptian /a/ — yielding Coptic *o* in closed syllables, *ō* in open syllables, and *ū* following a nasal — combines, as the hypothesis predicts and the roots in Chapter 5 attest, the following reconstructed PAA vowels:

PAA *a (roots #48, 50, 69, 93, 110, 139, 145, 164, 167, 170 (v.), 198, 205, 229, 249, 279, 294, 297, 316, 330, 336, 352, 361, 367, 384, 381, 398, 401, 408, 442, 448, 460, 483, 498, 539, 552, 569, 587, 589, 590 (first alternant), 591, 621, 679, 685, 691, 703, 725, 734, 741, 747-749, 751 (first alternant), 754, 786, 788, 804, 810, 822, 837, 853, 864, 884, 885, 924, 926, 927, 933, 952, 955, 956, 965, 970, 982, 1002, 1004, and 1008);
PAA *aa (roots #78, 267, 379, 478, 491, 521, 600, 627 (second alternant), 637, 831, 862, 958, 962, and 1003);
PAA *a or *aa (roots #814 and 989);
PAA *e (roots #250, 793, and 890 (first alternant));
PAA *e or *a (root #42);
PAA *o (roots #435, 619, 629, 631, and 850); and
PAA *o or *e (roots #168 and 178)

In the rarer instances where PAA *a was word-initial and not preceded by any other consonant, even *ʔ, it yielded the reduced Coptic vowel *ε* (roots #23, 85, 616, and 924)

The second early Egyptian vowel phoneme, /u/ — realized in Coptic as *o* in closed syllables and as *ē*, or in some instances by the grapheme for *ī*, in open syllables — derives generally from PAA *uu (as shown by roots #282, 323, 546, 553, 595, 697, 713, and 930). Interestingly, in one restricted environment in Coptic, /#{h,x,p}_(y,t)#, Old Eg. /a/ and /i/ also regularly produced *ē* (#51, 374, 382, 399, and 757).

The third vowel, early Egyptian /i/ — changed in Coptic to *a* in closed syllables, to *ī* in most open syllables, to *ē* in open syllables before *tn* or *ty*, to Ø preceding a voiced continuant, and to a reduced central vowel *ε* in certain other contexts — combined the rest of the reconstructed PAA vowels:

PAA *i (roots #23, 85, 106, 187, 240?, 280, 301, 396, 405, 470, 479, 485, 538, 581, 611, 621, 683, 689, 698, 720, 725, 751 (second alternant), 808, 827, 918, 939, and 969);
PAA *u (roots #36, 146, 162, 240?, 265, 319, 330?, 366, 484, 546, 590 (second alternant), 810, and 866);
PAA *i or *u (roots #220, 419, and possibly 1015);
PAA *ii (roots #59, 268, 369, 382, 553, 627 (first alternant), 709, 873, and 944);
PAA *i. *ee, or *ii (root #616);
PAA *ay (> *ə /#C_C by PNE rules #1-3: roots #260, 309, 983, and 984);

PAA *ey (probably > *i by PNE rules #1-3: root #433, first entry, and root #565);
PAA *ee (roots #95, 537, 778 (second alternant), and 950); and
PAA *oo (roots #122, 355, 393, 500, 599, and 799).

Overall, these data show us that the derivation of the presumed Old Egyptian vowels /a/, /i/, and /u/ from the five vowels posited for the North Erythraean stage can be explained by a single rule change. This shift collapsed the high and low central vowels with equivalent members of the peripheral tier:

Eg. #1. PNE *ə > Old Eg. /i/,
PNE *ä > Old Eg. /a/.

Curiously, a reversal of the usual Coptic reflexes of Old Eg. /a/ and /i/ turns up in two kinds of consonantal environments. Most notably, Old Eg. /i/, when it occurs before a reconstructed laryngeal in the same word, often yields the usual Coptic reflexes of Old Eg. /a/ (notably, roots #275, 433 (second entry), 701, 800, 819, 834, 870, and 922). An opposite shift affected Old Eg. /a/, with such /a/ — again in the environment of a following laryngeal — producing the Coptic reflexes expected of Old Eg. /i/ (roots #357, 372, 373, 626, 659, 660, 817, 839, 858, 887, 888, 890 (second entry), 922, 948, 961, 990, and 1007, and possibly 627). The full environment of this dual sound shift has not been definitively established. In general, however, it appears to have switched vowel realizations of Old Eg. /a/ and /i/ before a laryngeal in C_2 or C_3 position, as long as the preceding word-initial consonant was not a PAA labial, dental, or alveolar-palatal obstruent. This vowel switch also seems not to have operated in triconsonantal words of the LE shape C_1_C[+laryngeal]C, in which C_1 was *w*, *y*, or a velar obstruent (see roots #297, 336, 398, 435, 873, 962, 989, and 1008).

The switching of the reflexes of /a/ with those of /i/ appears, too, in two other, rather different and more restricted contexts. The first of these is the Coptic environment /#[-contin./+velar]_r; examples include the Coptic reflexes of roots #285, 301, 329, 330, and 419). The second kind of environment in which the vowel reflexes are reversed consists of both /#(_)C_a(_)C_b and /#C_b_C_a, where C_a was a dental obstruent (cases of ME *s* or *d* are known) and C_b was a non-dental voiceless stop, Old Eg. /a/ again produced the expected reflexes of /i/, while Old Eg. /i/ and /u/ yielded the usual reflexes of /a/ (see roots #53, 251, 412, 426, 428, 620, and 705).

The shared Chadic and Boreafrasian vocalic history, proposed here initially on the basis of the Chadic data, thus proves out very well indeed for Semitic and for Egyptian as well for Chadic. Its applicability to Berber remains to be similarly tested, but the close structural fit of the proto-Berber vowel system with the expectations of this history gives us every reason to think that the Berber data too will turn out be well accounted for by this scheme.

To sum up, the systemic distribution of vowels in Chadic, Berber, and Semitic, and Egyptian indicate their having shared in a common proto-period, characterized by the contraction of the PAA system — which had five vowels occurring both long and short, in effect, a ten-vowel system — into a differently distributed set of five vowels, consisting of a peripheral tier (*i, *u, and *a) and a central tier (*ə and *ä). Seen in this light, the sequence of vowel sound shifts #1-3 emerge as rules of a wider proto-North Erythraean provenance (for this subgroup, see Chapter 6), able to explain the initial stages in the evolution of the vowel systems of proto-Berber, proto-Semitic, and Egyptian, as well as that of proto-Chadic.

In PCh an additional sound-shift (PCh #1) would have collapsed *ä with *a to produce a four-vowel system, composed of two peripheral vowels, *i and *u, and two central vowels, *ə and *a; alternatively the proto-Chadic vowels could be considered to consist of three peripheral vowels, *i, *u, and *a, and one central vowel, *ə.

In the proto-history of Semitic, a sweeping reduction of vowel distinctions apparently collapsed North Erythraean *u and *i with *ə, and *ä with *z (as per PS rule #1 above). This merger presumably took place in all CVC(C) stems, but its consequences in verb stems are no longer apparent — stem vowels in verbs having been deleted by the developments of PS verb conjugational history. In morphological contexts, i.e., outside of C_C(C) stem environments, *i and *u apparently did not fall together with *ə and so remained distinct PS vowels.

In the evolution of Egyptian, a less extensive merger of the North Erythraean vowels can be proposed from the evidence. The reflexes, it seems, of two members of the central tier, *ə and *ä, fell together respectively with those of the peripheral vowels *i and *a, creating a three-vowel array in Old Egyptian.

The proto-Berber system revealed in Prasse (1975) suggests that there, in contrast, the five vowels created by PNE rules #1-3 simply persisted, with PAA short *a being realized as a reduced central vowel *ä, and PAA *aa, in the guise of proto-Berber *a, filling the low-vowel slot of the peripheral tier. The assumption that a still earlier three-vowel array underlies that system would seem to be an unexamined transference to Berber of earlier ideas about proto-Semitic vowels, themselves in apparent need of revision. The investigation of the Berber correspondences of the reconstructed PAA vowels will thus provide a further testing ground for the propositions presented here.

We can now expand the charting of Afroasiatic vowel sound correspondences, presented above in Table 4, by integrating into a revised Table 5 the findings on North Erythraean vocalic history that emerge from the Semitic and Egyptian data:

Table 5: Afroasiatic (Afrasian) Vowel Correspondences Revisited

PAA	PC	PNE	PCh	pre-Eg.	PS (in nouns)	NOm
*a	*a	*ä	*a	*a	*a	*a
*aa	*aa	*a	*a	*a	*a	*a:
*e	*e	*ä	*a	*a	*a	*e (> *i in several environments)
*ee	*ee	*ə	*ə	*i	*ə	*e:
*i	*i	*ə	*ə	*i	*ə	*e (> *i in several environments)
*ii	*ii	*i	*i	*i	*ə	*i:
*o	*o	*ä	*a	*a	*a	*o (> *u /_[+labial])
*oo	*oo	*ə	*ə	*i	*ə	*o:
*u	*u	*ə	*ə	*i	*ə	*o (> *u /_[+labial])
*uu	*uu	*u	*u	*u	*ə	*u:

TONE IN *PAA*

Phonemic tone is a widespread feature of Afroasiatic, appearing regularly in the languages of the Omotic, Chadic, and Southern and Eastern Cushitic divisions of the family. Only the Boreafrasian subgroup (Semitic, Berber, and Egyptian; see Chapter 6 for Afroasiatic subclassification) has entirely deleted tone. Tonal reconstructions have been produced previously for only one division of the Afroasiatic family, Southern Cushitic; proto-Southern Cushitic (PSC) had what has been depicted as three phonemic word-tones: falling, rising, and level (Ehret 1980). A provisional reconstruction of the PAA system can nevertheless be proposed by comparing the PSC patterns with those recorded for the Chadic language Ngizim and for the Omotic languages Mocha, Yem, and Bench, data from which are used extensively in

Chapter 5 to supplement the relatively sparse comparative evidence from their respective branches.

Ngizim has just two tones, high (/ˊ/ and low (/ˋ/), as do many of the Chadic languages; and if PCh had the same system, then Ngizim may well largely conserve the tonal situation of PCh. An alternative possibility, however, is that PCh had three tonemes.

Mocha, on the other hand, is given five separate prosodic markings by Leslau (1959). One, described as "secondary stress" ([ˌ]), occurs only in a few polysyllabic words and participates in no minimal pairs in the available data. It surely represents a conditioned development of original low tone ([ˋ]) and can safely be ignored here. Leslau's "main stress" ([']) and "low level tone" ([ˍ]) are in complementary distribution, the first appearing only on short-vowel syllables and the second only with long vowels. His high tone ([ˊ]) appears nearly always on nouns; and in fact internal reconstruction in Mocha supports the proposition that at least some [ˊ] were in origin the realization of the complementary pair, ['] and [ˍ], in simple noun derivations from CVC- verb stems (e.g., root #842 in the comparative data of Chapter 5, and *tu̱:c'-* "to take a handful" versus *tú:c'c'o* "handful," among other examples in Leslau 1959). Still, by no means all cases of [ˊ] can be explained by such secondary developments. This high tone sign also occurs on terminal vowels where the CVC- stem to which it is attached is unmarked; in these cases the comparative evidence suggests the unmarked stem to have had original low tone. One is thus left with certainly two, and probably three, underlying Mocha prosodic phonemes:

a. /¯/ -> ['] /V ("main" stress),
-> [ˍ] /V: ("low level tone"), and

b. /ˋ/ -> [ˋ], along with

c. /ˊ/ (sometimes deriving, however, < ['] ~ [ˍ]).

Yem and Bench each have prosodic systems that probably reflect an earlier three-tone system, of high, mid, and low. In Yem the reconstructible root tone was usually retained in words of underlying *CVCC, *CCVC, and *VC root shapes. In CVCV words built on *CVC root shapes, however, a number of tone shifts, not yet fully understood, took place. Generally speaking, in such roots a reconstructible low tone changed in Yem to mid tone and, except where the second consonant (C_2) was a sibilant, the high and mid tones became low tone. But in words having a sibilant in C_2 position, it seems rather that the reconstructible mid and low tones both went to high.

In Bench the three-tone system has been expanded to one consisting of five level tones and one rising tone, largely through the reduction of bisyllabic stems (Wedekind 1985, 1990). In simple *CVC verb roots the original three tones — high, mid, and low — are, in general, maintained. They are realized, however, as respectively mid, low-mid, and low tones (coexisting with the derived high and very-high tones), and are represented in the published Bench materials by the respective superscript numbers ^{3}, ^{2}, and ^{1} (Wedekind 1990; Breeze 1990). The high and very-high tones of Bench, marked by ^{4} and ^{5}, and the rising tone, denoted by $^{2\text{-}3}$, normally reflect the former attachment of segmental morphemes, sometimes still present on the surface (e.g., Bench *sums*^{4} "to name, call out," which adds the PAA causative in *s as a denominative to *sum*^{1} "name"), but often no longer visible at the segmental level (e.g., Bench *k'og* ^{3} "cold" versus *k'og* ^{4} "to be cold"). In verbs the high tone (^{4}) may derive from original low, mid, or high tone, but in nouns it seems generally to reflect reconstructed high tone. The very-high tone of Bench (^{5}) is quite rare. In nouns of surface CVC shape, at least, its occurrence can signal the loss of a former medial consonant in a word that originally carried PO high tone (e.g., root #235); it also can occur in CVC nominals derived from verbs (see root #101), again possibly but not certainly where the PO tone was high. The sliding tone ($^{2\text{-}3}$) in Bench occurs almost entirely in CVC nominals for which an earlier CVCV shape, with high or sometimes mid tone on the first syllable, can be posited.

The usual tonal correspondences among the three North Omotic (NOm) languages, Mocha, Yem, and Bench, appear to be the following:

(1) NOm *´ (high) = Mocha ['] ~ [̠] = Yem /`/ = Bench ^{3} (/´/);
(2) NOm *` (low) = Mocha /`/ = Yem /¯/ = Bench ^{1} (/`/).
(3) NOm *- (mid) = Mocha /´/ = Yem /`/ = Bench ^{2} (/¯/);

As noted, Yem has /´/ for NOm *` and *¯, where C_2 is a sibilant, and apparently preserves the North Omotic values in underlying triconsonantal stems.

The reconstructed North Omotic tones in turn show regular correspondences with the PSC and Ngizim (Ng.) tones:

(1) PSC * ^ (falling word-tone) = Ng. /´/ = NOm *´ (high);
(2) PSC * ˇ (rising word-tone) = Ng. /`/ = NOm *` (low); and
(3) PSC * ` (level word-tone) = Ng. /`/ = NOm *- (mid).

(In Ehret 1980, it should be noted, a different representations, /+/, /¯/, and /`/, were used for the respective PSC falling, level, and rising word-tones.) One notable, and seemingly regular although uncommon, exception to these patterns has been encountered in the Mocha data in the comparative lists of Chapter 5 (#304, 335, and 339):

Mocha ['] /#{g,k}oC-# (C = *s* or *t*) = NOm *` = PSC *ˇ = Ng. /`/.

Ngizim, for its part, regularly shifts high tone to low upon addition of an extension of the shape -C or -*a* to a CVC- verb stem; and some nouns may also be derived by tone shift from verbs (cf. root #880 for an example of noun derivation by tone-raising). The language appears also to reverse tone in transitive verbs derived from CVC- intransitive stems by substitution of /ə/ for the stem vowel /a/ (e.g., roots #163 and 932, among others). But otherwise Ngizim consistently shows the correspondences noted.

On the basis of the three correspondence patterns, PAA is proposed here to have had definitely two reconstructible tone phonemes,

1. PAA *^ = PSC *+ = Ng. /´/ = NOm /´/, and
2. PAA *ˇ = PSC *¯ = Ng. /`/ = NOm /`/,

and probably a third,

3. PAA *- = PSC *- = Ng. /`/ = NOm /¯/.

The reconstruction of the PAA etymons of the three correspondence sets as respectively falling, rising, and level word-tone in PAA would yield a neat phonetic accounting for the third pattern, but would also make the PAA reconstruction perhaps suspiciously parallel to that postulated by the writer for PSC (Ehret 1980). An alternative possibility is a system of high, low, and mid tones for the respective PAA markings *^, *ˇ and *¯, with the syllable rather than the word as the tonemic environment (as can be argued to be the case in Omotic). A third alternative, that distinctions of *stress* underlie the tonal correspondences presented above, is possible but — in view of the weight of the evidence from all over the family, viz. Omotic, Cushitic, and Chadic (see discussion of subclassification in Chapter 6) — much less probable than some kind of tonal system in PAA.

Diagnostic evidence for tone in Cushitic generally comes from Southern Cushitic, but in a number of cases the Eastern Cushitic language Arbore (Hayward 1984a) and the Agaw language Awngi (Hetzron 1978) provide the necessary indications. The following regular correspondences of Arbore (Arb.) and Awngi (Aw.) to Southern Cushitic word-tone have been noted:

a. PSC *^ = Arb. CVCv́, CVVC = Aw. CVCv́, VCV, CVCCVCVCv́;
b. PSC *ˇ = Arb. Cv́CV, Cv́v́C = Aw. Cv́Cv́(C), Cv́C, VCv́;

and probably

c. PSC *¯ = Aw. CVCVC,

where sequences of C and V (or v) represent Arbore and Awngi word and verb-stem shapes. The Arbore and Awngi tone patterns seen in (a), (b), and (c) thus correspond to PAA (1) *^, (2) *ˇ, and (3) *¯ respectively.

The data drawn from Southern Cushitic, along with Arbore and Awngi, from Ngizim, and from Mocha, Yem, and Bench have made it possible for a considerable fraction of the Afroasiatic roots presented in Chapter 5 to be marked for tone. For many others, however, such marking cannot yet be ventured, and these have been left with tone not indicated.

5

PROTO-AFROASIATIC (PROTO-AFRASIAN) CONSONANT RECONSTRUCTIONS

PRESENTING THE DATA FOR *PAA* RECONSTRUCTION

About forty consonant phonemes can be firmly attributed to the proto-Afroasiatic (proto-Afrasian) language. And it is the presentation of these consonants that brings this study around finally to the main body of primary evidence: the comparative listing of Afroasiatic roots and their reflexes, referred to repeatedly in previous chapters, on which PAA reconstruction as a whole rests. The consonants come to the fore at this point because the fundamental data — the more than 1000 reconstructed roots presented in this chapter — are grouped for discussion according to their first stem consonants.

The order of presentation will follow two patterns. The obstruents, with the exception of the three laterals, are treated in sets defined by shared *point* of articulation. The comparative data for such consonants are therefore grouped into sets of roots beginning respectively in labial, dental, alveolar-palatal, velar, labiovelar, and pharyngeal-glottal obstruents. Within each of these sets, the listing starts with voiced-stop-initial roots and moves on to roots beginning in, successively, the equivalent voiceless stop, voiced fricative (where present), voiceless fricative, and ejective. The pharyngeal-glottal set differs in having PAA *h rather than an ejective as its glottalic member.

The sonorants, and also the non-sonorant laterals, are grouped instead by *manner* of articulation: there are thus three further sets of roots beginning respectively in nasals, liquids (the laterals and *r), and the glides *w and *y. Within the nasal set, roots are subgrouped by point of articulation, beginning with the labial *m and moving back through the mouth. The liquid set, in contrast, is arranged much like the obstruents, with the voiced member *l opening the set and the voiced lateral affricate, the voiceless lateral fricative, and the equivalent ejective lateral following; PAA *r rounds out the set. This method of grouping the evidence for the Afroasiatic consonants is heuristically important because a great many of the consonant sound shifts in the family have taken place within such sets, and the majority of the numerous consonant co-occurrence constraints have operated within the same confines.

The actual order in which the eight consonant sets (the velars and labiovelars are combined as one for heuristic purposes) are discussed is somewhat different from the order in which they have just been defined. The PAA labial, dental, velar, and labiovelar consonants form natural groups of clearly parallel composition, with equivalent stops, fricatives, and ejectives occurring in each. The alveolar-palatal set, in contrast, may eventually come to be seen as a grouping of convenience. Its voiced and voiceless non-continuants seem better reconstructible as affricates than as stops. The alveolar-palatals will thus be discussed immediately following the four well-defined obstruent sets, but before the presentation of the set of nasals, because each of the points of obstruent articulation (including the palatal) can be matched up with either definitely or provisionally with a PAA nasal stop. The presentation proceeds thereafter to the pharyngeal-glottal (laryngeal), liquid, and glide sets, each of which lacks a corresponding nasal.

Within each main group of roots — those beginning with the same PAA consonant — the reconstructions are ordered according to their second root consonant, alphabetized as follows: *b, *c, *c', *d, *dl, *dz, *f, *g, *g^{w}, *ɣ, *ɣ^{w}, *h, *ḩ, *j, *k, *k^{w}, *k', *k^{w}', *l, *ɬ, *m, *n, *ɲ, *ŋ, *ŋ^{w}, *p, *p', *r, *s, *s', *š, *t, *t', *tl', *ts, *w, *x, *x^{w}, *y, *z, *ʔ, and *ʕ. If two roots have identical consonants, they are ordered according to the usual alphabetic sequence of their vowels. If they differ only in vowel quantity, the root with a long vowel is put after the root containing the short one.

Because of the overwhelming evidence that Egyptian and Semitic (along with Berber) form a single subgroup of Afroasiatic, called here North-Afroasiatic (see Chapter 6 below), a cognate was normally allowed into the comparative data *only* if the root could be found in Cushitic, Chadic, or Omotic, as well as in Egyptian and/or Semitic. A very, very few items having just Semitic and Egyptian attestations do appear, however, because they provide essential illustration of a rare correspondence or a point in need of clarification (e.g., the actually quite restricted distribution of a root for "two" that has commonly been presumed to be PAA: see root #503 versus #505 and 877). Roots so far known only from Cushitic and Omotic have also only rarely been used here, since the ancient long-term geographical proximity of these two divisions of the family increases the possibility of undetected word-borrowing in such cases.

The primary aim in selecting among the welter of possible sources of data was to obtain high-quality evidence from as far back in time as possible for each major subgroup or, failing that, for individual languages that have been well recorded and are especially conservative in phonology — thus the importance of the works by Jungraithmayr and Shimizu (1981) and Newman (1977) on Chadic reconstruction; by Sasse (1979) on proto-Eastern Cushitic, as revised and added to by Arvanites (1990) and Ehret (1991); by Appleyard (1984; n.d.) on Agaw reconstruction (as supplemented in Ehret 1987); and by the writer on Southern Cushitic and proto-Cushitic reconstruction (Ehret 1980, 1987). The provisional and partial reconstructions of Omotic consonants arrived at in Chapter 2 (Table 1), and of vowels in Chapter 4, above similarly provide a comparative perspective on the data cited from languages of that branch.

The longest timeline for Semitic comes from the pre-proto-Semitic biconsonantal roots reconstructed in Ehret (1989), supplemented by those to be found in Appendix 1 of the present work. Many of the classically accepted PS triliteral roots are thus only implicitly present in the comparative data that follow, because they are themselves subsumable as derivatives of the pPS biconsonantals that are directly cited here or indirectly implied in the citations of Arabic words. Of major importance as a second and direct source of Semitic data is Arabic, which has maintained all but one of the PS consonant distinctions, although changing many of the individual consonant articulations. Definitions of Arabic words are commonly cited here from Steingass 1884, not because his is a particularly good dictionary but because his meticulously detailed glosses are especially useful in the comparative semantic analysis. A third source of value here, because of the conservatism of its rendering of a number of key PS phonemes, is Modern South Arabian (especially Johnstone 1977, 1981).

The views of Alice Faber (1985) on PS sibilant realizations are followed in the representation here of the PS and pPS roots. The only two significant departures from convention are the substitution of *c ([ts]) for traditional PS *s, and of *s for traditional PS *š. The validity of using *s in place *š is nicely backed up by the wider Afroasiatic comparisons, from which it is clear that PS *s (erstwhile *š) is the regular PS reflex of PAA *s. In addition, the now standard recognition that the conventional PS *ś was a lateral fricative is given overt expression here by representing it as PS *ɬ.

Egyptian materials are drawn principally from the dictionary of R. O. Faulkner (1964), supplemented by data from Late Egyptian (Lesko 1982-90). The Coptic evidence, useful in establishing vowel correspondences, is taken in all but one instance from the Sahidic dialect (Vycichl 1983; Czerny 1976).

PRESENTING THE ARGUMENTS AND SUPPORTING EVIDENCE

In order to encompass within a single volume the amount of argumentation and supporting information required in a reconstruction of this scale, it was necesssary to develop a shorthand format for presenting the historical-comparative evidence. This format includes a regular sequence of laying out the different kinds of data and supporting materials, and the use of a variety of signs and abbreviations to convey concisely the particular bits of evidence and argument needed for interpreting each data set.

A first set of conventions used here governs the transcription of data:

1. Reconstructed Afroasiatic roots normally appear in either of two forms in the tabulations of this chapter: (a) in the case of verb stems, as *-CVC(C)-, *-VC-, or *-CV-, with the initial and terminal hyphens indicating the points of attachment of conjugational and derivational affixes; and (b) as *CVC(C)- or sometimes *VC- or *C- in nominals, where the hyphen denotes the point of attachment of the PAA suffixed TVs (terminal vowels) as proposed in Chapter 3 above. A few pronominals and markers of position (notably roots #1, 2, 118, 181, 209, 210, 309-311, 470, 482, 568, 571, 608, 609, 803, 924, and 949) manifest the shapes *C-, *-C-, or *CV, presumably reflecting their different syntactical or morphological positioning from those of the verbs and the

more common nominals, as well as their sometimes variable vowel components.

1.1. Two subsidiary conventions followed in the root reconstructions require mention here. One has to do with interpreting the instances where alternate shapes are given for a particular root. If such alternants are linked by the conjunction "or," the evidence is considered insufficient to decide which one is correct. If, on the other hand, the alternant forms are separated by a slash (/), then they represent alternate pronunciations that may have existed in the proto-language.

1.2. The second convention involves tonal representations. In general, tone when known is marked on the first vowel of a reconstructed root; in the case of long vowels represented as VV, the tone mark will reside above the first V.

2. For each comparative-historical data set, the reconstructed root and its meaning are presented in the lefthand column, with, successively, the Semitic, Egyptian, Cushitic, Chadic, and Omotic attestations of the root in the next five columns. Reconstructed roots are usually shown in the Cushitic and Omotic branches as stems of the shapes *CVC(V)C)-, *C-, and *VC-, and also, in the case of verbs, sometimes as CV-, where the hyphen denotes the stem-final point of attachment of any applicable suffixes. Verb stems cited from particular Cushitic, Chadic, and Omotic languages are given the same kind of representation.

2.1. A few verbs in their Cushitic reconstructed forms appear with hyphens both preceding and following the stem; in these instances, the roots are known, unlike most Cushitic verbs, to have been prefix- rather suffix-conjugating. For one particular Eastern Cushitic language, Yaaku, all verbs have conventionally been represented in this fashion and appear so in the data cited from it.

2.2. A rather different use of the hyphen appears in the Chadic reconstructions of Jungraithmayr and Shimizu (1981). In their Chadic root representations, such marking forms part of the root itself, in general denoting a consonant of undetermined reconstruction. Usually such consonants can be derived from one of the PAA laryngeals, *ʕ, *ʔ, *ḥ, or *h, but in some root-initial instances they indicate the presence of the Afroasiatic attributive prefixes *a-/*i- (as in the their reconstruction of PCh "four" in #94).

The morphological composition of an attestation and its semantic explanation, if not self-evident, are laid out parenthetically, directly following the citation of the reflex (or root) and its meaning. Where further information on the phonological derivation of an entry is needed, this too is presented within the parentheses. Cushitic correspondences are taken from Sasse (1979), Appleyard (1984; n.d.), and Ehret (1980, 1987, 1991); for Omotic correspondence patterns, see Table 1, Chapter 2. If no such further information is proffered, the particular cited form, whether an attested word or a reconstructed root, should be understood to preserve the same realization of its segments as that reconstructed for its PC, PCh, PS, or PO etymon (as described in Chapter 4 for the vowels and in Chapter 5 for the consonants).

A second set of conventions is followed in communicating the etymological information about particular reflexes and their roots:

3. Within the parentheses that follow the root or word and its gloss, the first item of information offered — provided more than a simple stem is involved — is an abbreviated morphological analysis of that root or word, following the format: prefix (if any) + stem + suffix(es). The nominal affixes and verb extensions are given in their reconstructed PAA shapes, for the patterns of which see Chapter 3 above, and the name of each affix is abbreviated as indicated in the list of Abbreviations. For example, the finitive fortative verb extension in *p' is represented as "*p' fin. fort.," and the non-finitive extension in *n as "*n non-fin." To cite a particular case, proto-Eastern Cushitic (PEC) *bakkal- "morning star" in root #12 is followed by the notation "(stem + *l n. suff...)," indicating that the PEC root is composed of a PAA stem, in this case *-bâk-, plus a named nominal suffix, here of the shape *-l- (gemination in this instance is a secondary morphophonemic consequence). The lack of any further identification of this suffix means that its function and form are as discussed in Chapter 3.

3.1. In a few instances (nearly all from Egyptian), where a very common suffix is self-evidently present, the morphological explanation has been left out as superfluous. These cases typically involve occurrences of stem plus PAA *y inchoative/denominative (Egyptian *i* or *y*), PAA *t noun suffix, PAA *w deverbative, or Egyptian *w* plural, *wy* dual, or *t* feminine markers.

3.2. Nominals derived from verbs by stem-vowel lengthening are depile depicted differently, by the expression, "n. (or adj.) < v. by V > VV (or V:)." Also, in a scattering of cases, verbs seem to have been derived from nominals directly, without overt extensional marking, by simply applying the conjugational system to the stem of the word. Outside of Semitic, examples of this kind are relatively rare. They are identified by the notation "(v. < n.)" or "(v. < adj.)." Here as elsewhere in the text and in the tabling of data, the sign "<" denotes "derives from," while ">" signals the opposite derivational connection, "becomes" or "yields."

4. Next, if needed, comes a short semantic explanation, introduced either by the word "semantics" or the expression "i.e." For instance, the PEC root *biš- "body," entered under PAA root #25, *biš- "skin," is followed by the notation "(semantics: "skin" > "body")." Here the sign ">" ("yields") indicates that a meaning shift from earlier "skin" to "body" accounts for the Eastern Cushitic meaning; no morphological addition to the stem appears in this case, and thus only the semantic change needs to be mentioned.

4.1. The expression "i.e." has a particular signification when used in a semantic explanation: in instances where a word or root has developed a range of meanings, it directs attention to the specific part of the gloss that supports the morphological argument contained within the parentheses. For example, in root #57, PAA *-pax- "to bend," the Egyptian entry — *pḫr* "to turn, turn about; revolve; surround, enclose" (stem + *l fin., i.e., surround, enclose) — has such a range of meanings. But it is the last of these, "surround, enclose," that preserves the finitive sense which the parenthesized morphological information, "stem + *l fin.," would lead us to expect. The use of "i.e." specifically singles out that meaning from among the several glosses and identifies it as the bearer of the connotation imparted by its given affix.

5. Usually last within the parenthesis, and again only when needed, comes the phonological derivation. Most often, this information identifies an earlier consonant or vowel reconstruction that gave rise, by regular sound changes within the relevant branch of the family, to the particular segment or segments in question. Either of two formats is followed in transmitting the phonological information:

5.1. If the attested segment collapses two or more proto-segments, then the identified proto-segment is said to yield the attested reflex, and the statement of this proposition conforms to the format, "X > Y." For instance, Eastern Cushitic *beel- "to lose," a reflex of PAA *-pêel- (root #44), carries the parenthetical comment, "PC *p > PEC *b," thus implying that at least one other PC consonant (in this case PC *b) can also have PEC *b as its outcome.

5.2. If, however, the attested segment has only a single possible source, then an opposite format is used, "Y < X." Once again drawing on an Eastern Cushitic example, we may cite from PAA *-p'ac'- "to cut off" (root #100) the PEC entry *b'ac'-, to which the following notation is appended: "(PEC *b' < PC *p')." This abbreviated commentary declares that PEC *b' derives regularly from proto-Cushitic (PC) *p', and implies as well that only PC *p' can yield PEC *b'. No further comment is necessary because the regular correspondence of PC *p' to PAA *p' is established in the portion of Chapter 5 that immediately precedes the presentation of the labial consonant data, of which root #100 is a part. (A tabular summary of such information for all the consonants is contained in Table 8 at the end of the chapter.)

6. Most of the conventions followed in representing the governing environments of particular phonological outcomes need no further explanation. But two particular notations may cause some confusion and so are worth special mention. First, the notation /_-# signifies a stem-final as opposed to a word-final environment, indicated by /_#. Second, the notation /C can be taken to mean "in the environment of a proximate consonant in the same word, whether following or preceding the sound in question."

7. Sometimes, too, a particular language's reflex of a reconstructed root may be cited within the parentheses, usually because that reflex provides information not otherwise available regarding tone or, in the case of Ngizim (Chadic), vowel realization. In addition, in a number of Omotic and a few Chadic and Eastern Cushitic entries, two or more cognate forms from different languages or subgroups have been included in the parenthesized part of the entry in order to substantiate a root not previously reconstructed for the particular Afroasiatic branch in question.

8. Not explicitly commented on in the parenthetical data are two kinds of gemination: (1) verb-stem-finally in Eastern Cushitic, connoting durational action; and (2) as a morphophonemic concomitant of certain suffixation processes in Eastern Cushitic and other divisions of the family. For discussion of these two processes, see the concluding section of Chapter 3.

THE *PAA* LABIAL OBSTRUENTS

In labial position proto-Afroasiatic (proto-Afrasian), like its daughter languages proto-Chadic (Newman and Maa 1966) and proto-Cushitic (Ehret 1987), must be postulated to have had four obstruents. The demonstration of PAA *b, *p, and *f is straightforward. One-to-one correspondences of PC *b, Egyptian *b*, and PCh *b are amply attested. Similarly, PC *p matches up with Egyptian *p* and PCh *p, and PC *f with Egyptian *f* and PCh *f. (Curiously, Jungraithmayr and Shimizu seem not to have recognized this last pattern, found both in Newman's data and in the evidence of Ngizim separately presented here, and offer only *p for both our *p and our *f.)

The fourth PAA labial was the least common in occurrence and is therefore less strongly attested than any of the other three. The wider systemic patterning of the PAA inventory and the actual reflexes of this consonant make a clear case, however, for reconstructing it as an ejective *p'. Its PC realization was apparently *p' (Ehret 1987), while its PCh reflex was the voiced counterpart of [p'], the implosive *ɓ. In Egyptian, PAA *p' yielded *p*, except in environment /#dlV_, where instead it seems to have produced *b* (roots #853 and 854).

In Semitic, normally reconstructed with just two labial obstruents *b and *p, the PAA consonants *p and *f fell together as PS *p while PAA *b and *p' both yielded PS *b. For proto-Omotic three labials were preserved: PAA *b as PO *b, PAA *p' as PO *p', and PAA *p and *f collapsing to PO *p.

Consonant co-occurrence constraints are prominently visible in the occurrence patterns of the PAA labials. The oldest and most widely found of these, forbidding non-identical labials (other than *w) from occupying the two consonant slots of a biconsonantal stem, goes back at least to the common point of ancestry of all the Afroasiatic divisions except probably Omotic. The evidence is as yet insufficient to fully prove the case for the archaic character of Omotic in this matter. But there is one strong datum, root #3, in its favor. This example supports the conclusion that the constraint came into being after the splitting off of the pre-Omotic ancestry from the rest of Afroasiatic, and indicates that its effect in the common ancestor language of the rest of the family would have been to shift the second of two unlike labials to identity with the first (in root #3, PAA *p or *f > *b /#bV_). Where two non-identical labials other than *w compose the first two consonants of a word in Cushitic, Egyptian, Chadic, or Semitic, one must thus postulate the loss of a former intermediate non-labial consonant, the addition of a labial-consonant prefix (e.g., the instrument-agent prefix in *m) to an already labial-initial stem, or a borrowed or onomatopoetic origin for the word. As part of a more general development, proto-Semitic extended its labial co-occurrence constraint to forbid even instances of *identical* labials in the first two consonants of a root.

In its more general form, this pPS or PS co-occurence constraint apparently forbade any and all sequences of the same consonant in C_1 and C_2 position in PS (noted as pPS/PS rule #8 in Appendix 4). Only two simple verbs with identical C_1 and C_2 appear in Steingass's dictionary of Arabic, *hahh* "to stammer" and *zazz* "to touch lightly on the neck," the first transparently onomatopoetic and the second perhaps arguably of such an origin; and only a handful of nouns have this shape. What became in Semitic of PAA $*C_1VC_2$- sequences where $C_1 = C_2$ is a matter for future investigation. Among the five Afroasiatic roots here reconstructed with identical C_1 and C_2 (#354, 355, 489, 708, and 911), just two have identified Semitic reflexes (#708 and 911), each showing a different kind of dissimilation of the consecutive root consonants.

A rather different constraint in Egyptian greatly reduced the frequency of [f] in the language by blocking its occurrence as an initial consonant when the following stem consonant was Eg. *r* or one of the voiceless fricatives *s, h*, *ḫ*, or *ẖ*. (Curiously, however, a new *f* apparently deriving from earlier *p appears in the case of the alternate Egyptian forms *fsi* ~*psi* "to cook," root #53.) In such instances PAA *f was replaced with [p] (roots #74, 76, 85, 86, and 89). That this shift is specifically counter-indicated for Eg. *ẖ* (root #72) is further demonstration of the originally voiced pronunciation of *ẖ* (and its derivation from PAA *ɣ and $*ɣ^w$, as shown below in the section on velar consonants):

Eg. #9. PAA *f > Eg. *p* /#_VC[+continuant, -voice] and /#_Vr.

(Egyptian sound shift rules #2 and 4-8 are given below in the section on PAA dental obstruents below, while rule #3 appears in the section on the velar and labiovelar obstruents.) A further shift collapsing PAA *p' with *p,

#10. PAA *p' > Eg. *p*,

may have preceded a sound change,

#11. *p > Eg. *b* /#dl_ (= Eg. /#*ḏ* _).

But as yet the only known examples of the shift to *b* involve PAA *p' and not *p (roots #853 and 854)

One notable but as yet rarely attested labial sound shift marks off the Cushitic division of the family. In one environment PAA *b did not yield PC *b, but rather *m:

PC #1. PAA *b > PC *m /#_Vn.

The rule thus appears to be a PC phonological innovation (see roots #18 and 19). The same assimilatory sound shift developed independently in certain Chadic languages and apparently in the Gonga subgroup of Omotic (see Mocha entry in root #32), but is not a general feature of either of those divisions of the family.

*PAA Labial Obstruents: *b*

PAA *ƃ	SEMITIC	EGYPTIAN	CUSHITIC	CHADIC	OMOTIC
1. *ƃǔ "place"	MSA *b- "in, with, by"	*bw* "place"	*ƃǔ "ground"		
2. *ƃa "not be there"		*bw* negative (*baw ?); LE *bn* "not, without, there is not"	*ƃa- "to not have"	*ƃa negative marker (N)	NOm *ƃa "no" (Bender 1988: *ɓa)
3. *ƃôf- or *ƃôp- "upper chest"		*bbwy* "collarbones"; *bbwt* "region of throat"	*ƃôb- "armpit"		NOm *bu:p- "chest" (Maji "liver")
4. *-ƃoɣ- "to hit"	A. *baɣz* "to beat, kick" (stem + *z intens. of manner)		*ƃoɣ- or *poɣ- "to hit"	WCh, CCh *mƃg "to beat" (J: *N- concom. + stem)	NOm: Zayse *buk-* "to thresh" (*o > *u shift is unexplained: /_*ɣ, not /_*$ɣ^w$, is indicated)

	SEMITIC	EGYPTIAN	CUSHITIC	CHADIC	OMOTIC
5. *-bâh- "to go secretively"	pPS *bh "to sneak up on and surprise" (Append. 1)	*bh3* "to flee" (stem + *r diffus.); *bh3w* "fugitive" (v. + *w n. suff.)	*bâh- "wild animal"; PSC *bah- "to be stealthy"	Ng. *báatâ* "lurking nearby, following secretly" (stem + *t dur.)	NOm *ɓay- "to disappear" (stem + *y inchoat.; Bench *bay-k'* 3)
6. *-ɓâḫ- "to strike with a blade or point"	A. *baḫr* "to split wide" (stem + *r diffus.)	*bḫn* "to cut off (limbs)" (stem + *n non-fin., i.e., strike *and* penetrate through)	PSC *ɓaḫ- "to kill"	Ng. *vá-* "to shoot"	
7. *ɓaaḫ- "voice"		*bḫn* "to bark, bay, bellow; revile" (stem + *n non-fin. as denom.)	PSC *ɓaaḫ- "shout, cry, yell" (n.)	*ɓa "mouth" (N)	

	SEMITIC	EGYPTIAN	CUSHITIC	CHADIC	OMOTIC
8. *-ɓoḩ- "to go away"		*bḩn* "to drive off (foes)" (stem + *n non-fin.); *bḩs* "to hunt" (stem + *s caus., i.e. "to chase")	*ɓoḩ- "to depart"		
9. *-ɓôoḩ- "to flow"	A. *baḩr* "river, sea" (stem + *r n. suff.)		*ɓôoḩ- "to spill (intr.)"		
10. *b-j(r)- "seed"	*bðr "seed; to sow" (A. *biðār*)			*bz(r) "seed" (J: *bzr, *bdr, *bz(n))	

	SEMITIC	EGYPTIAN	CUSHITIC	CHADIC	OMOTIC
11. *-ɓâk- "to burn, shine; to dawn" (Sem., Eg. **innovation**: n. "morning" by addition of *r n. suff.)	A. *bakar* "morning" (stem + *r n. suff.)	*bk3* "the morrow" (stem + *r n. suff.); LE *bk3* "to be bright" (stem + *ʔ adj. suff., v. < earlier adj.?)	SC: Dahalo *ɓakkeeð-* "to kindle" (ð < PC *s caus.; ɓ < PSC *ɓ); PEC *ɓakkal- "morning star" (stem + *l n. suff.); HEC: Sidamo *bakkal-* "to become yellow" (stem + probably *l adj. suff., v. < earlier adj.)	*ɓ-kə "to roast, burn" (N) (Ng. ɓák-); rare ECh, CCh *ɓg "morning" (J)	NOm *ɓak- "star" (Yem *bà:kūrā̄*, stem + *r n. suff.; N. Mao *ɓage*)
12. *-ɓŏkʷ- "to leak, seep, run out"	A. *bakk* "to vomit"		*ɓŏkʷ- or *p̣ŏkʷ- "mist, drizzle"		Ometo: Koyra *buk-* "to rain"

	SEMITIC	EGYPTIAN	CUSHITIC	CHADIC	OMOTIC
13. *-ɓâl- "to wet"	A. *ball* "to wet, sprinkle"		PEC *ɓal- "wet"	*ɓl "to vomit" (J) (Ng. *ɓánúw* -, stem + *w in-choat. > dur.?)	NOm: Bench *bal* ^{3} "menses"
14. *-ɓâl- "to move (intr.)"	pPS *ɓl "to proceed, move along" (Append.1)		PSC *ɓâlak- "to move house" (stem + *k dur.)	Ng. *ɓànt* - "to pass by" (stem + *t dur. with *-u- tr. infix > Ng. /ə/)	
15. *-ɓel- "to break (tr.)"	*ɓlc "to pluck (figs, etc.)" (stem + *š non-fin.)		*ɓel- "to break"		
16. *ɓiil- "tip"		LE *br* "tip (?); tuft (?)"	*biil- "ear of grain"		
17. *ɓŭɬ- "skin"	*ɓɬr "flesh" (stem + *r n. suff.)		PSC *ɓŭɬa "skin, hide"	BB *^{m}ɓɬ "hair" (J; *N-concom.+ stem; i.e., fur < hide; PCh *$ɬ_2$ >BB *ɬ)	

	SEMITIC	EGYPTIAN	CUSHITIC	CHADIC	OMOTIC
18. *-ɓîn-/*-ɓân- "to beget"	A. *ibn* "son" (*ɓən); *bint* "daughter"	*bnn* "to beget"	PSC *mânaʕ- "baby" (stem + *ʕ part.; i.e., < give birth)	WCh, CCh *ɓan "father" (J)	
19. *-ɓĭn- "to build, create; house"	*ɓnn "to build"		*mĭn-/*măn- "house"; Beja *man-* "to create"	*ɓən- "house" (N); *ɓn "to build" (J)	Dime *bin-* "to build, create"
20. *-ɓâr- "to leak, seep; bleed" (additional Cushitic alternants *-ɓîr- and *-ɓûr-)	pPS *ɓr "to be moist" (Append.1)	*b3iw* "damp" (stem + *y inchoat. + *w n. suff.; possible alternative attribution: see #36)	EC: Afar *baraaraco* "sound of falling rain" (redup. stem as intens. + *ħ iter.: *c* = [ħ]); Agaw *ɓər "blood"; Beja *bire* "rain"; PEC *ɓurk'- "to spring, well up" (stem + *k' intens. of effect)	*ɓarə "blood" (N)	SOm: Ari *bɛrrgi* "rainy season" (stem + $*g^w$ dur.); NOm: Bench *bars* 3 "to pour" (stem + *s caus.)

	SEMITIC	EGYPTIAN	CUSHITIC	CHADIC	OMOTIC
21. *-ɓêr- "to hold"	A. *barm* "to fix, make firm" (stem + *m extend.)	LE *brk* "to offer, present; serve" (stem + *k dur.)	*ɓer- "to grasp"	*ɓarə "to give" (N) (Ng.*ɓár* -) (J: *ɓr)	
22. *-ɓir- "to burn brightly"	pPS *ɓr "to be light, bright" (Ehret 1989)	LE *brg* "to light up" (stem + *g fin. fort.)	EC: Jiiddu *ɓir* "lightning"; Soomaali *ɓir* "to glitter"		NOm: Shinasha *bi:ro* "red" (adj. < v. by V > V:); Bench *bars* [2-3] "fireplace" (stem + Omotic *ts n. suff.); SOm: Ari *burk*- "to boil" (stem + *k dur.)
23. *-ɓǐrk'-/*-ɓǎrk'- "to flash" (root #22 + *k' intens. of effect)	*brḳ "to lighten; lightning"	*brḳ* "to shine, glitter, flash" (C. *ɛbrēčɛ* ; probable *a- attrib. n. pref. + stem ("flash") + *y denom. rederiving v. sense)	*ɓǎrk'-/*ɓǐrk'- "to flash"		Mocha *p'arìq*- "to lighten" (PO *ɓ > Mocha *p* /_VC',V= short)

	SEMITIC	EGYPTIAN	CUSHITIC	CHADIC	OMOTIC
24. *bǎs'- "to start off, begin"	A. *basr* "first beginning; to begin, commence" (stem + *r n. suff.; v. < n.)	*bs* "to introduce, initiate, install, bring in, enter"	*bǎts'- "front" (see Append.2 ; with #26 below corrects Ehret 1980: 133)		
25. *biš- "skin"; *bĭšr- "hull, shell" (stem + *r n. suff.; SC semantics: early beads were made of shell)	*bcr "unripe fruit" (2nd PAA stem)		PEC *biš- "body" (semantics: "skin" > "body"); SC: Ma'a *m-bišálo* "bead" (PSC *r > Ma'a *l* /a_o#; semantics: anciently, beads from ostrich eggshell)		SOm: Dime *biččo* "skin"
26. *-bǎat'- "to be in front, go in front"	A. *baṭn* "belly" (stem + *n n. suff.: i.e., front of body)		PSC *bǎat'- or *p'ǎat'- "to go first" (see #24 above)		NOm: Zayse *baats'á* "chin, beard" (semantics: face > chin)

	SEMITIC	EGYPTIAN	CUSHITIC	CHADIC	OMOTIC
27. *-ɓatl'- "to move away, move apart"	A. *baṣʕ* "to gather, take to oneself" (stem + *ʕ part., i.e., move stuff *away from* somewhere else)	*bṯ* "to abandon, forsake; run"	*ɓatl- "to spread open, be cleared"		SOm. Ari *bəd'-* "to go"
28. *-bĕets-/*-bŏots- "bright, lit up"	A. *biθa* "ashes"	*bsw* "flame" (stem + *w n. suff.)	PSC *bĕets- or *bĕets'- "sunlight"		Ometo *bo:ts- "white" (Zayse *bóots*)
29. *-ɓox- "to swell"	A. *baxn* "tall, long" (stem + *n adj. suff.)	*bḫbḫ* "pride (?)" (as bad quality; re-dup. as intens.)	PEC *ɓoox-/ *ɓoxx- "to swell"	some WCh *ɓok- "big"	
30. *-ɓoox- "to cut into, dig into (with sharp tool)"	A. *baxx* "to gouge eye"; *baxʕ* "to cut throat" (stem + *ʕ part.)			*ɓkm "knife" (J; stem + *m n. suff.)	*book- or *$boox_2$- "to dig" (NOm: Zayse *book-*; SOm: Ari *book-*)

	SEMITIC	EGYPTIAN	CUSHITIC	CHADIC	OMOTIC
31. *-ɓĕxʷ-/*-ɓŏxʷ- "to spill out in drops, sprinkle"	A. *baxx* "to sprinkle; drizzle"		PEC *ɓex- "to pour, spill (intr.)"		NOm *ɓuk- "to sow" (i.e., to scatter seed; Yem *būk* ; PO $*x_2$ > NOm *k)
32. *ɓāayn- "grindstone"		*bnbn* "sacred stone"; *bnwt* "grinding stone"		*ɓəna "grinding stone" (N)(Ng. *vənyí*)	Mocha *má:no* "upper stone of mill" (assim., *ɓ > m /#_Vn-)
33. *-ɓeez- "to emerge; reveal"	A. *bazq* "to rise (sun)" (stem + *kʷ' and.)	*bs* "to reveal" (presumed earlier *bz*)	*ɓeez- "to be uncovered" (PSC to appear, emerge)	*ɓɗ "to show" (J); some WCh *ᵐɓɗ "to look for" (J: stem + *N- concom. + stem)	
34. *-ɓaʔ- "to be ruined"	A. *baʔs* "calamity, misfortune" (stem + *s deverb. comp.)	*bȝ* "to destroy, devastate"	PEC *ɓaʔ- "to become destroyed"		

	SEMITIC	EGYPTIAN	CUSHITIC	CHADIC	OMOTIC
35. *-ɓiʔ- "to go"	*ɓʔ "to come"		*ɓaʔ-/*ɓiʔ- "to go"	*mɓ- "to go (away)" (J: *N- con-com. + stem)	NW Ometo *ɓe- "to go"
36. *-ɓûʔ- "to flow"		*ɓ3ɓ3t* "inshore eddy (?)" (redup. stem as freq. + *t n. suff.; C. *ɓεɓε* "to bub-ble, well up")	PSC *ɓûʔ- "to pour"		
37. *-ɓaʕ- "to increase"	A. *ɓaʕɓaʕ* "prime of youth"	*ɓ ᶜḫ* "abundance" (stem + ḫ iter.)	SC: PR *ɓaʕ- "to excel, exceed"		
38. *-ɓaʕ- "to sit"		LE *ɓ ᶜnw* "mounting" (stem + *n, *w n. suff., i.e., what a statue, etc., sits on)	*ɓaʕ- "to lie down" (semantics: sit down > go down > lie)		NOm *ɓe(t)- "to sit" (stem + *t dur.)

	SEMITIC	EGYPTIAN	CUSHITIC	CHADIC	OMOTIC
39. *-ɓăaʕ- "to flow heavily; to defecate"	pPS *ɓʕ "to pour out" (Ehret 1989); A. *baʕr* "to drop globular dung (animals)" (stem + *r diffus.)	*bᶜbᶜt* "stream" (redup. as freq. + *t n. suff.); *bᶜḫ* "inundated land" (stem + *ḫ iter., i.e., land flooded *each* year); LE *bᶜr* "fountain" (stem + *l n. suff.)	PSC *ɓaaʕ- "to defecate"	Ng. *bà* - "to excrete (shit)"	NOm: Yem *bèʔr* - "to filter beer" (stem + *r diffus.)
40. *-ɓuʕ- "to pick, pluck"	A. *baʕθar* "to take out and examine" (stem + *r and *ts diffus.)		PSC *ɓuʕ- "to harvest"		

PAA *p	SEMITIC	EGYPTIAN	CUSHITIC	CHADIC	OMOTIC
41. *-pac- or *-pats- "to scatter (intr.)"	A. *faθɣ* "to shatter" (stem + *ɣ intens. of effect)	*psḫ* "to disarray; be strewn" (stem + probably *ɣʷ comp.)	SC: WR *pas- "to scatter" (WR *s < PC *s, *ts, or *ts' /_-#) (corrects Ehret 1980: 161)	Ng.*pə̀ps-* "to render in small pieces" (redup. for intens./freq., with *-u- tr. infix > Ng. /ə/)	
42. *-pâḫ- or *-pêḫ- "to take into the mouth"	A. *faḥs* "to take out of hand with the tongue or lips" (stem + *š non-fin. or *s' fort.; semantics unclear)	C. *pōhs* "to bite" (stem + *s' fort.?; alternative derivation by metathesis of #115 below is ruled out by V correspondences)	PSC *pâḫ- or *pêḫ- "to eat" (of people)	Ng.*páaɗ-* "to suck" (stem + *z intens. of manner); *páatk-* "to lick" (stem + *t, *k dur.)	

	SEMITIC	EGYPTIAN	CUSHITIC	CHADIC	OMOTIC
43. *-păḫ- or *-pĕḫ- "to break off"	A. *faḫd* "to break (anything soft)" (stem + *d dur.)	*pḫḏ* "to cut up, cut open; burst open" (stem + *dl m.v., i.e., burst open)	PSC *păḫ- or *pĕḫ- "to break into pieces"	*py "to break" (J; stem + *y inchoat.)	NOm: Bench *pet*[1] "to tear apart" (stem + *t dur.)
44. *-pêel- "to take out, take away"	A. *falqaḫ* "to eat or drink all in vessel" (stem + *k' intens. of effect + *ḫ iter., i.e., *completely* remove contents of vessel)		PEC *beel- "to lose" (PC *p > PEC *b); SC: Ma'a *-pwí1-ija* "to circumcise" (< *pêel- + Ma'a *-ija* caus., i.e., *remove* foreskin)	Ng. *pə̀lɗ-* "to draw out, e.g. knife from sheath" (stem + *z intens. of manner, i.e., taking out from single narrow spot, perhaps quickly)	
45. *-pil- or *-piil- "to drive, chase"	pPS *pl "to put to flight; flee, run away" (Ehret 1989)	*pri* "to go/come out; escape; burst forth" (stem + *y inchoat. > intr.; C. *pεīrε*)	SC: Kw'adza *pil-* "to drive away" (corrects Ehret 1980: 144)		

	SEMITIC	EGYPTIAN	CUSHITIC	CHADIC	OMOTIC
46. *-piɬ- "to split apart, lay open"	*pɬ "ax"; *pɬy/*pɬw "to extend" (stem + *y/*w inchoat.); pPS *pɬ "to spread apart" (Ehret 1989)	*pšš* "to straddle; spread (oneself); spread out" (redup. as freq. > dur.) *pšn* "to separate combatants)" (stem + *n non-fin.; homographic outcome with #110)	PSC *piɬ- "to lay open"	*pɬ₂ "to break" (J); Ng. *pə̀tlàyù* "flower" (stem + *y deverb.; semantics: < opening up of a flower in blooming)	
47. *pand- "peak"	A. *fand, find* "mountain, mountain tract" *findîr* "crag" (stem + *r n. suff.)		SC: PR *pand- "prominence, projection"		

	SEMITIC	EGYPTIAN	CUSHITIC	CHADIC	OMOTIC
48. *-păŋ^{w}- "to clear away, remove, empty out"	A. *fann* "to throw away, reject"	*pnḳ* "to bail out (boat); expend (provisions); to exhaust [LE]" (stem + *k intens. of effect; C. *pōnk*)	*păŋ^{w}- "to lay open, make bare"		
49. *-pŭnc'- "to pluck out, pull out" (root of #48 + *c' extend.; *u < *i /#-p_ŋ^{w}C-#?)		*pns* "to pull out (hair); cut off (a joint)"	PSC *pŭnt^{y}'- "to pluck out, remove (from body)"	Ng. *pə́st*- "to strip edges of palm mid-rib" (stem + *t dur.)	
50. *-pār-/-pīr- "to separate (intr.)"; *-pur- "to take apart" (intr. stem + *-u- tr. infix)	*prc "to divide" (stem + *š non-fin.)	*prḫ* "to open (flower); spread" (stem + *ɣ^{w} comp.; C. *porš*)	*părḥ- "to come apart" (stem + *ḥ iter. > extend.); PSC *păreh- "calabash sherd" (stem + *h *h ampl.);	*pərə "to untie" (N); Ng. *pə̀r̃t*- "to undo, take apart" (stem + *t dur.)	NOm: Bench *pir-k'* 2 "to open" (R. Hayward 1994 derives *k'* here from old past stem marker; for other ex-

	SEMITIC	EGYPTIAN	CUSHITIC	CHADIC	OMOTIC
			SC: WR *puruʕ- "to strip off" (stem + *ʕ part.); SC: Iraqw *paratl-* "to separate" (stem + *dl m.v.; PC *dl > PSC *tl)		amples, see #6 and 461)
51. *-pîr- "to fly"	*pr(r) "to flee"	*p3* "to fly" (C. *pēi*); *pri* "to go up. ascend" (stem + *y inchoat. > dur.)	*pâr-/*pîr-/*pûr- "to fly, jump"	*pərə "to fly, jump" (N) (J: *pir, *par; *mbr "to jump" (J; *N- concom. + stem)	*par-/*pir- "to fly" (NOm: Ometo *pir-; Yem *fìll-* "to jump"; SOm: Dime *far-*)
52. *-poor- or *-pur- "to speak"	pPS *pr "to speak" (Append. 1)	LE *pry* "utterance" (stem + *y deverb.)		*p-rə "to say" (N)	NOm: Sheko *fo:ri* "neck" (n. < v. by V > V:; recurrent African semantics: speak > > voice > neck)

	SEMITIC	EGYPTIAN	CUSHITIC	CHADIC	OMOTIC
53. *-pas'- or *-pac- or *-pats- "to light up"		*psi, fsi* "to cook" (stem + *y inchoat. > dur.; C. *pīsɛ*); *psḏ* "to shine" stem + *dl m.v. > intr.)	SC: PR *pas- or *pats- "daylight" (PC *ts' and *ts > PR *s /V_)	rare WCh, CCh *ps "to roast" (J); some WCh *ps "sky" (J)	
54. *-pooš- "to be worn out, disabled"	A. *fasx* "to grow disabled, worn" (stem + $*x^w$ extend. fort.); MSA *fsd "to spoil" (stem + *d dur.; MSA *s < PS *c)		EC: Soomaali *boos* "ruined thing, enervated person" (PC *p > EC *ɓ)	Ng. *pə̀s-* "(machine, animal) to be worn out"	
55. *-put- "to step along"	A. *fatɣ* "to tread to pieces" (stem + *ɣ intens. of effect)	*ptpt* "to tread, trample" (redup. stem as intens.)		*pəta "to go out" (N; stem + *-a incep.)	Ometo: Koyra *pot-* "to cross"

	SEMITIC	EGYPTIAN	CUSHITIC	CHADIC	OMOTIC
56. *-patl'- or *-paatl'- "to separate (intr.)"	pPS *pṣ "to separate"		SC: Alagwa *pa*ɬ*is*- "to separate" (stem + *s caus.; PC *tl > SC *ɬ /pV_)	*mbɬ "to untie" (J; *N- concom. + stem, i.e., a kind of separating)	
57. *-pax- "to bend"	MSA *pxð "thigh" (stem + *dz extend. fort.; semantics: to bend *large* limb of body)	*pḫr* "to turn, turn about; revolve; surround, enclose" (stem + *l fin., i.e., surround, enclose)	PEC *ɓax- "bow (n.)" (PC *p > PEC *b)		
58. *-pax- or *-paax- "to scrape off, scrape out"	A. *faxt* "to dig, dig out" (stem + *t dur.)		SC: Alagwa *paxus*- "to peel, skin" (stem + *s caus.)	Ng. *pápk* - "to scrape (bark), shave (wood)" (stem with redup. as freq.)	

	SEMITIC	EGYPTIAN	CUSHITIC	CHADIC	OMOTIC
59. *piiz- "limb" (Berber, Eg. **innovation**: "knee"; Berber *afud < *puuz)	H. *fedfîd* "centipede" (redup. as augmentative, i.e., creature of many legs)	*pd* "knee" (C. *pat*)	*piz- or *piiz- "limb"		
60. *-păʔ-/*-pŭʔ- "to spit out, make spurt"		LE *p3y* "to spurt" (stem + *y inchoat. > intr.)	PSC *pâʔa- or *pâʕa- "spit, sputum"	Ng. *pùur-* "to spit out in spray" (stem + *r diffus.)	
61. *-pâʔr- "to dig up"	A. *faʔr* "to dig out; bury in the ground"		*paʔr- or *ɓaʔr- "field, cultivated ground" (Append.2)	Ng. *páar-* "to make holes with planting hoe to drop seeds in"	
62. *-piiʔ- "to turn round (intr.)"		*p3ḫd* "to be turned upside down; be turned over" (stem + *ɣ intens. of effect + *d dur. > stat.)		Ng. *pìim-* "to look around at" (i.e., turn in someone's direction; stem + *m extend.)	

	SEMITIC	EGYPTIAN	CUSHITIC	CHADIC	OMOTIC
63. *-piʕ-/*-puʕ- "to be raised, stick up"	A. *faʕm* "fleshy, muscular" (stem + *m adj. suff.)		*piʕ- "to swell (of bud, fruit, flesh, etc.)"	Ng.*pùuɗ-* "to bank up, hoe up to make hills" (stem + *z intens. of manner)	
64. *-pûʕ- "to spill out (intr.)"		LE $p^{c}p^{c}$ "to drop (calf); deliver (baby)" (redup. stem as intens.)	PSC *pûuʕ- or *pûuʔ- "excrement" (n. < v. by V > VV)	*pə "to pour" (N)	Mocha *po:no* "waterfall" (stem + *n n. suff.; PO *ʔ > Ø /V_VC)

PAA *f

	SEMITIC	EGYPTIAN	CUSHITIC	CHADIC	OMOTIC
65. *âf- "mouth"	*-p- "mouth" (Ethiopic *ʔaf-: possible loan < Cush.?)		*ʔâf- "mouth"		SOm *ap- "mouth" (Ari *afá*; [NOm: Yem *āāfā* "language": probable loan < EC language]

	SEMITIC	EGYPTIAN	CUSHITIC	CHADIC	OMOTIC
66. *-fi- "to go out"	A. *faut* "to pass, pass by" (stem + *w inchoat. + *t dur.)		*fi- "to go out"		
67. *-fic'- "to scrape"	A. *faẓîẓ* "harsh, rough, blunt"		*fic'- "to rub, wipe"		Mocha *'p'ič'*- "to rake" (PO *p, *b > p' /_V(CV)C', V = short; see #24 above)
68. *-fiic'- "to press out fluid"	A. *faẓẓ* "to press water out of camel's stomach"				Mocha *pi̱:č'*- "to squeeze, wring clothes"
69. *-fad- "to draw out, pull out"	MSA *fdy "to recover, get back" (stem + *y inchoat. > dur., i.e., to take out and retain)	*fdi* "to pluck, pull up, uproot, pull out, remove" (stem * *y inchoat. > dur.; C. *fōtε*)	PSC *fad- "to go out, go away" (Dahalo "to take out, draw out")		Mocha *p'äričʼ*- "to be uprooted" (stem + *t' dur. intens.; see #67 for *p > *p'*)

	SEMITIC	EGYPTIAN	CUSHITIC	CHADIC	OMOTIC
70. *-fug- "to drain out"	A. *fajr* "to drain, drain off" (stem + *r diffus.)	*fgn* "to defecate" (stem + *n non-fin.)	EC: Harso *fukko* "(urinary) bladder" (PC *g > Harso *k*)	CCh *pg "to pour" (J)	[SOm: Ari *pug* "bladder": probable loan < Dullay (EC)]
71. *-fôɣ- "to spread apart (intr.)"	pPS *pɣ "to spread" (Ehret 1989)		PLEC *fog- "far" (PC *ɣ > PLEC *g)	Ng. *fák* "at a great distance"	
72. *-fŏɣ- or *-fŭɣ- "to cast off, cast out"		*fḫ* "to loose, release, cast off, get rid of"			Mocha *pòk-* "to throw away"
73. *-fuɣ- "to inhale"	A. *faɣm* "to kiss one's wife; suck its dam" (stem + *m extend.); MSA *fɣr "hollow of throat" (stem + *r n. suff.)		PEC *fug'- "to inhale, exhale" (Dullay "to blow"; PEC *g' < PC *ɣ)	WCh *pk "to blow" (J; for other WCh *k < PAA *ɣ see roots #71, #378, and 381)	[Mocha *pùg-*, Yem *fùg-* "to blow," etc.: loans < Dullay (EC)? (expected *pok-; also failed tone correspondence)]

	SEMITIC	EGYPTIAN	CUSHITIC	CHADIC	OMOTIC
74. *-faah- "to flow out"	A. *fahq* "to be full" (stem + *$k^{w'}$ and.; i.e, flow *into* rather than out of)	LE *phrt* "pond (?)" (stem + *l fin.; semantics: > stop flowing + *t n. suff.)	EC: Dullay *faah- "to bleed"		
75. *-fâaḫ- "to blow (with the mouth)"	A. *faḫḫ* "to hiss"; *faḫfaḫ* "to be hoarse, snore" (redup. stem > intens.)		PSC *fâaḫ- "to blow (with mouth)"		
76. *-fiiḫ- "to penetrate"	MSA *fḫl "penis" (A. *faḫl* "stallion" (stem + *l n. suff.)	*pḫ* "to spear" (LE "to penetrate")		Ng. *fìiɗ*- "to poke in ribs" (stem + *z intens. of man- ner)	
77. *-fâk- "to be finished, come to an end, be used up"	A. *fakk* "to be infirm and decrepit"	*fk* "to be empty; be wasted (through op- pression)"	PSC *fâk- "to come to an end"		

	SEMITIC	EGYPTIAN	CUSHITIC	CHADIC	OMOTIC
78. *-faak'- "to break off, cut apart"	pPS *pḳ "to break or cut open" (Ehret 1989)	*fḳ3* "to pick; to fall out" (stem + *ʔ concis.; C. *fōčɛ*)	*faak'-/*fiik'- "to cut apart, break open"		
79. *-fuk'- or *-fuuk'- "to be wise, intelligent"	pPS *pḳ "to be wise, intelligent" (Append.1)		SC: Iraqw *fuqraŋ* "intelligence, ability, skill" (stem + *r and SC *ŋ n. suff.; PC *VV > Iraqw V)		
80. *-fǎl-/*-fǔl- "to accomplish"	Ji. *fɔlɔk* "to be clever at" (*flk, stem + *k dur., i.e., be able to accomplish again and again)		PSC *fǎl- "to do"; [PLEC *fa(a)l- "to do" may conflate this root with borrowings of PS *pʕl, for which see #98]		Ometo *pol-* "to be accomplished"; Mocha *pàll-* "to create"

	SEMITIC	EGYPTIAN	CUSHITIC	CHADIC	OMOTIC
81. *-fĭl- "to cut hole or cavity in"	pPS *pl "to slit, nick" (Ehret 1989)	*fnḍ* "nose, nostril" (stem + *dl m.v., i.e., to form a hole)	*ful-/*fil- "to pierce, bore hole"	ECh *pl "to hollow out" (J)	NOm: Bench *pel* 1 "hole"
82. *-feŋ- "to set apart, move apart (tr.)"	A. *fann* "species, kind, category; way, manner"; *fand* "branch; class, category" (stem + *d dur. > stative, i.e. be separate)		*fenḫ- "to spread apart (intr.)" (stem + *ḫ iter.); PEC *finj'- "to scatter (intr.)" (stem + *tl' foc.; PC *tl > PEC *j'; *e > *i /_nC, [C = palatal]?)		Ometo: Gamo *penge* "door" (semantics: move apart > open > door)
83. *-fôoŋ- or *-fôon- "to be frail"	A. *fanan* "to dwindle away; be perishable, mortal; be infirm, decrepit; run	*fn* "to be weak, faint"	SC: Dahalo *fóófoone* "light(weight)" (redup. stem; PC *n and ŋ > Dahalo *n*)		

	SEMITIC	EGYPTIAN	CUSHITIC	CHADIC	OMOTIC
	short, be used up; perish, die"; *fanšax* "to be weary; very old" (stem + *ɬ ven. + $*x^w$ extend. fort.)				
84. *-făr- "to call out"	*prḫ "to rejoice" (stem + *ḫ iter., i.e., rejoicing is marked by repeated happy calling); A. *farfar* "to cry out at" (redup. stem as as intens.)		*făr- "to call out" (Ehret 1980: 322)	Ng. *fə̀r̃fə̀r̃t-* "to backbite, abuse someone not present" (redup. stem as intens., with *-u- tr. infix > Ng. ə + *t dur.)	

	SEMITIC	EGYPTIAN	CUSHITIC	CHADIC	OMOTIC
85. *-fir- "to flower, bear fruit"	MSA *frɣ "to ripen, bloom" (stem + *ɣʷ comp.)	*prt* "fruit, seed" (stem + *t n. suff.; C.*ɛbra*, probable *a- n. attrib. pref. + stem); LE *prš* "to unfold, bloom, open up, flower" (stem + *ɬ ven.)	*fir- "to flower, bear fruit"	WCh *pr "grass" (J)	Ometo: Koyra *fi:re* "flower" (n.< v. by V > V:)
86. *-foor- "to defeat, be victorious over"	MSA *frʔ "brave" (stem + *ʔ adj. suff.)	*pry* "hero, champion; ferocious bull" (stem + *y deverb.)	EC: Soomaali *foor* "to beat someone at games"		
87. *-f-s- "to take apart" (root #66 + *s caus.?)	pPS *ps "to move apart" (Ehret 1989)			*faṣə "to break" (N)	

	SEMITIC	EGYPTIAN	CUSHITIC	CHADIC	OMOTIC
88. *-fât'- "to excrete"	pPS *pṭ "to excrete" (Append.1)		PSC *fât'a "fresh dung, mud"	*ps'r "urine" (J; stem + *r n. suff.)	
89. *-feet'-/*-foot'- "to separate (tr.)"	pPS *pṭ "to break apart" (Append. 1)		PEC *feet'-/ *foot'- "to separate"		
90. *-fit'- "to scrape repeatedly"	A. *faṭḥ* "to plane" (stem + *ḥ iter.)		*fit'- "to scrape repeatedly" (EC "to comb")		[Mocha *'pič'*- "to comb": loan < EC (expected *'p'ec'-)
91. *-fox- or *-fox^w- "hole, breach"	A. *faxt* "hole, breach; to pierce, break through" (stem + *t n. suff.; v. < n.)		SC: WR *fox- "hole, opening" (PC *x^w > SC *x /V$_{[+round]}$_)		

	SEMITIC	EGYPTIAN	CUSHITIC	CHADIC	OMOTIC
92. *-fayt- "to remove, take off"	*ptḫ "to open" (stem + *ḫ iter. > dur.); MSA *ftk "to come out, take out" (stem + *k^w fin.)	*ftt* "to obliterate (inscription)" (stem partially redup. as intens.)	EC: Soomaali *feyd* "to uncover" (PEC *t > Soomaali *d* /V_)	Ng. *fə̀t-* "to extract, pull thing out, pluck feathers, etc."	Ometo: Malo *pett-* "to sweep" (i.e., remove dust, rubbish, clean off floor)
93. *fâzw- "four" (stem + *w n. suff.); *ifz- "having four parts" (*i- attrib. pref. + stem)		*fdw* "four" (C. *ftou*); *ifd* "to quadruple; rectangular"; *ifdt* "quartet" (stem + *t coll. suff.)	[Beja *faḍig* and PLEC *ʔafar- "four" are **not** cognate with this root **nor** with each other: Beja *ḍ* < PAA *dl, PLEC *r < PC *r]	*f^{w}aɗə "four" (N) (Ng. *fúɗú* ; J. *-pɗ(w/y); 1st PAA root form occurs in WCh, most CCh; 2nd root shape, in some CCh, as per J)	

	SEMITIC	EGYPTIAN	CUSHITIC	CHADIC	OMOTIC
94. *-fĭz- "to swell, rise up"	A. *fizr* "swelling in the hypochondria" (stem + *r n. suff.); MSA *fz(z) "to spring up"		PSC *fĭḍak'- "penis" (stem + *k' intens. of effect; semantics: erection of penis; corrects Ehret 1980: 149)	WCh *pɗʸl "fat" (J; stem + *l n. suff.)	
95. *-feeʔ- "pick up"		*f3i* "to raise, lift up; carry, support" (stem + *y as dur., i.e., carry; C. *fî*)	SC: Asa *feʔet-* "to bring" (stem + *t dur.; PSC *VV > Asa V)		
96. *-fîʔ-/*-fâʔ- "to smell"	A. *faʔr* "musk" (stem + *r n. suff.)		*fiʔ- or *fiʕ- "to smell"`	Ng. *fáun-* "to smell at, sniff at" (stem + *w as dur. + *n non-fin.)	

	SEMITIC	EGYPTIAN	CUSHITIC	CHADIC	OMOTIC
97. *-fūʔ- "to grow, become large"	A. *faʔam* "fat" (stem + *m adj. suff.)	*f3w* "magnificence, splendour; magnificent" stem + *w de-verb.)	EC: Dullay *fuʔ- "to grow (of plants)"		NOm: Yem *fūʔrā* "flower" (stem + *r n. suff.; semantics: to grow > to bloom; *u* for expected *o, however; possible loan < Cushsitic?)
98. *-fiiʕ- "to make, do"	*pʕl "to do" (stem + *l fin.; or else + *l n. suff., i.e., "deed," with v. < n.)		EC: Soomaali *fiic* "good, of good quality" (i.e., accomplished, done well; *c* = [ʕ]); [PLEC *fa(a)l-, PSC *fal- "to do" seems a chance resemblance to PS *pʕl; see #80]	some WCh *piʔ "to make (do)" (J)	

	SEMITIC	EGYPTIAN	CUSHITIC	CHADIC	OMOTIC
99. *-fuuʕ- "to stop up, close up hole"	A. *faʕm* "to fill, fill up" (stem + *m extend.)		PSC *fuʕ- or *fuuʕ- "to cover with earth"	*fu "to close/cover" (N)	

PAA *p'

	SEMITIC	EGYPTIAN	CUSHITIC	CHADIC	OMOTIC
100. *-p'ac'- "to cut off"	A. *baẓr* "clitoris" (stem + *r n. suff.; v. *baẓar* "to circumcise (girl)," i.e., perform clitoridectomy, < n.)		PEC *b'ac'- "to cut off" (PC *p' > PEC *b')		
101. *-p'ûc'- "to increase (intr.)" (Sem., Cush. **innovation**: "increase" > "grow fat, thicken")	A. *baẓẓ* "to grow fat"		EC: Afar *buxxe* "penis" (PC *c' > Afar *x* [d'], PC *p' > Afar *b*)		NOm: Bench *p'uč'*^{5} "many, much" (< pre-Bench *p'u:c', n. < v. by V > V:)

		SEMITIC	EGYPTIAN	CUSHITIC	CHADIC	OMOTIC
102.	*-p'âd- "to increase (in size)"	A. *badin* "fat and strong" (stem + *n adj. suff.); *badaʕ* "to grow fat" (stem + *ʕ part.; semantics: grow *out*ward)	LE *pdr* "fat" (stem + *l n./adj. suff.)	EC: PSom *ɓadan "many, much" (stem + *n adj. suff.); Soomaali *badi* "to make numerous; increase" (< *ɓadiš-, stem + *s caus.; PC *p' > Som.*b*)		NOm *p'ad- "long" (Bench *p'ad*³); [SOm: Ari *bed-* "to become much, many": loan < EC (expected *b'ad-)]
103.	*-p'ad-/*-p'id- "to become lost, useless, non-functioning"	A. *badd* "to injure"; *badw* "desert" (stem + *w denom.)		PEC *ɓ'ad- "to disappear, become lost, useless, non-functioning" (PC *p' > PEC *ɓ')	Ng. *ɓədàm-* "to be impossible to, not be able to be; fall short in, fail to" (stem + *m extend.)	

		SEMITIC	EGYPTIAN	CUSHITIC	CHADIC	OMOTIC
104.	*-p'ăd-/*-p'ˇd- "to break off"	A. *badd* "to separate, remove, keep separate"; *badḫ* "to cut down" (stem + *ḫ iter., i.e. cut-down requires repeated strokes of ax)			Ng. *ɓə̀d-* "to pinch off a bit, break off a bit"	Gonga *ɓad- "to split wood" (Mocha *bàd-*; PO *p' > Gonga *b)
105.	*-p'oh- "to be wide"	A. *bahw* "large, extensive" (stem + *w deverb.); *bahbahiyy* "great, tall, strong" (redup. stem + *y adj. suff.)		PEC *ɓ'ohaʔ- "wide" (stem + *ʔ adj. suff.; PEC *b' < PC *p')		

	SEMITIC	EGYPTIAN	CUSHITIC	CHADIC	OMOTIC
106. *p'ĭḫ- "flank"		*pḫwy* "hindquarters" (C. *pahu*); LE *pḫt* "buttocks" (stem + *t n. suff.)	*p'ĭḫ- or *ɓĭḫ- "side"		
107. *-p'ăk- "to break up (tr.)"	A. *bakk* "to tear, break into pieces"; *bakš* "to loosen the tether of a camel" (stem + *ɬ ven.)		EC: YD *ɓ'ak- "to break by striking" (YD *ɓ' < PC *p')	*ɓak(l) "to break" (J; stem + *l fin.)	Mocha *bàg-* "to pound, crush" (in mortar) (PO *p' > Mocha *b* /#_)
108. *-p'ak'-/*-p'ik'- "to split (tr.)"	A. *baqq* "to split"; *baqr* "to split, cleave" (stem + *r diffus.)		PEC *ɓ'ak'- "to split" (PEC *ɓ' < PC *p')	Ng. *ɓìy(a)-* "to gut an animal by slitting open stomach" (stem + *-a incep., i.e., 1st cut in gutting is to slit stomach)	

	SEMITIC	EGYPTIAN	CUSHITIC	CHADIC	OMOTIC
109. *p'ul- "shell"			PEC *ɓ'ulɓ'ul- "shell" (Yaaku *bolboli* "egg"; Soomaali *bulbul* "thick hair": redup. stem; PEC *ɓ' < PC *p')	*ɓul "tortoise" (J)	[Ometo *p'ul- "egg": loan < EC (expected *p'ol-)]
110. *-p'aɬ- "to break by hitting"	A. *bašq* "to beat with a stick" (stem + *k' intens. of effect)	*pšn* "to split (heads); fracture (bones)"; separate (combatants); slice (bread)" (stem + *n non-fin.; C. *pōš*, *pōšε* "to divide, split, break"; V correspondence disallows deriving C. word < #89; but 1st sense shows shows influence of #89 on #110)	EC: Afar *baluq-* "to be chipped, chip off" (stem + *ʕ part.; PC *p' > Afar b; Afar *q* = [ʕ])	*ɓaɬə "to break" (N) (Ng.*ɓáɓtl-* "to hatch out of egg": redup. as freq.; semantics: descriptive of chick's efforts at breaking out of egg)	

	SEMITIC	EGYPTIAN	CUSHITIC	CHADIC	OMOTIC
111. *-p'ûɬ- "to deceive"	A. *bašk* "to lie; lie" (stem + *k^w fin.; semantics: lie is a single act, deception is an ongoing process)		PSC *p'ûɬ- "to fool (some-one)"		
112. *-p'ăar- "to twist (tr.), especially rope"	A. *barm* "to twist a rope tight" (stem + *m extend. > fort.) (*burm* "rope": n.< v.)	LE *pry* "bandages, strips, rope" (stem + *y deverb.)	PSC *p'ăar- "to make rope, string"		
113. *-p'ŭr- "to rend, split up"	pPS *ƀr "to cut" (Ap-pend.1)	LE *prš* "to rend, tear, break open" (stem + *ɬ ven.); LE *prṯ* "to break" (stem + *tl' foc.)	EC: Soomaali *burbur* "to break, frag-ment" (redup. stem as intens.; *p' > Som.*b*)	Ng. *ɓə̀r-* "to separate into parts; divide up"	Mocha *bòrit'-* "to lose teeth, be chipped" (stem + *dl m.v.; PO *p' > Mocha *b* /#_)

		SEMITIC	EGYPTIAN	CUSHITIC	CHADIC	OMOTIC
114.	*-p'is'k'- "spit, saliva"	A. *basq* "to spit" (A. *bazq* and *baṣq* "to spit" < distinct pPS roots, *bz "to secrete," *bṣ "to exude," for which see Append.1)		*p'its'ak'- "saliva"		
115.	*-p'îiz- "to bite"	A. *bazm* "to bite with the fore-teeth" (stem + *m extend. as fort. or *m n. suff. with v. < n.)	*pzḫ* "to bite, sting" (stem + *ḫ iter.)			Mocha *bi̱:jj-* "to pain, be painful" ("bite" >"hurt" is common African semantics; PO *p' > Mocha *b*)
116.	*-p'uʔ- or *-p'uuʔ- "to stop (intr.)"	A. *baʔaṭ* "to lie on one's side" (stem + *t' dur. intens., i.e., to stop and lie down as well)	*p3g* "to squat (?)" (stem + $*g^w$ dur.)	SC: PR *p'uʔ- "to cease" (PR *V < PSC *V or *VV)		

	SEMITIC	EGYPTIAN	CUSHITIC	CHADIC	OMOTIC
117. *-p'uʕ- "to cut into"	pPS *ɓʕ "to cut with a blade" (Ap-pend.1)		PSC *p'uʕ- "to drill hole"		

THE *PAA* DENTAL OBSTRUENTS

Proto-Afroasiatic (proto-Afrasian) had six stops and fricatives of dental articulation, *d, *t, *z, *s, and *t'. The stops *d and *t represent uncomplicated reconstructions, their usual outcomes being either dental or alveolar *d* and *t* respectively, across the family. They were most probably dental in PAA because the likeliest PAA homeland, northeastern Africa (Ehret 1979), is an area of consistently dental *d* and *t*. PAA *s similarly offers no problems, yielding [s] in almost all members of the family.

The postulated voiced PAA fricative *z became PS *z, PC *z, and apparently PO *z in most environments (see Omotic consonant correspondences in Table 1, Chapter 2); hence its postulation as PAA *z. In early Egyptian it usually yielded *z*, which had devoiced to [s] by Middle Egyptian times; in PS its reflex was also *z in most instances. In one restricted environment, however — in noun-stem-final position — PAA *z fell together with *d in Egyptian, Semitic, and Berber (see roots #59, 93, 289, 707, 944, and 985). Clearly counterindicated elsewhere in Afroasiatic, this shift thus provides an strong criterion of the validity of the Boreafrican subgroup of the family, discussed in Chapter 6. It can be represented as follows:

PBA #8. PAA *z > PBA *d /_-# (noun-stem-final).

Curiously, the proto-Chadic reflex of PAA *z was the implosive stop *ɗ, apparently in all environments. Future discussion of the precise articulation of PAA *z may therefore be non-trivial and quite interesting.

Of the two ejectives among the dental set, PAA *s' is only relatively rarely preserved as a distinct consonant in the modern Afroasiatic languages. Its PC reflex has been reconstructed as *ts'. In Chadic it was one of the sources of Jungraithmayr and Shimizu's *s'; and while in Omotic it appears to have produced a distinct set of correspondences (see Table 1), the best PO representation of which is probably *s'. In Semitic and Egyptian it fell together with the reflexes of PAA *s, as part of a shared sequence of two sound shifts further attesting to a common, intermediate proto-Boreafrican (PBA) ancestor language for those two branches. The shared changes involved a shift of PAA *h > *ḥ /_Vs, in which s derived from either (and only) from PAA *s or *s' (roots #791-793, 797 below), thus requiring the ordering,

PBA #1. PAA *s', *s > PBA *s, followed by

#2. PAA *h > PBA *ḥ /#_Vs.

These changes attested in both Egyptian and Semitic and only in those two. (This phonological history may once also have been evident in pre-proto-Berber, by reason of Berber's shared Boreafrican ancestry with Semitic and Egyptian, argued in Chapter 6. But the loss of both the ejective and pharyngeal distinctions in proto-Berber would probably have removed all surface evidence of the two sound shifts. Only if there turn out to have been pre-proto-Berber vowel shifts generated by the now lost pharyngeal environment would their existence in Berber proto-history be detectable.)

A third shift, generalizing the pharyngealization of *h to all environments involving any following dental fricative, took place in Egyptian but not in Semitic (roots #798, 799):

Eg. #2. PAA *h > ḥ /_Vz,

(The difficulties in determining whether or not this rule affected pre-proto-Berber will be the same as those for PBA shifts #1 and 2.)

The ejective reconstructed as PAA *t' was probably, like PAA *d and *t, dental in its point of articulation, and for the same reasons. It yielded PC *t' ([t̪']) and PS *ṭ, which itself was probably realized phonetically as [t̪']. The proto-Omotic reflex appears most likely to have been the affricate *ts' (see Table 1). The Chadic reflexes of PAA *t' and *s', as well as *c' (for which see the section on alveolar-palatals below), and of the PAA non-ejective sibilants are obscured in Newman's reconstruction of the PCh sibilants. Newman offers just two consonants, *s and *ş, whereas Jungraithmayr and Shimizu (1981) postulate four, $*s_1$ (normally represented as simple *s), $*s_2$, $*s_3$, and *s' (written *sʔ by them). A comparison of the two sets shows clearly that Jungraithmayr and Shimizu's $*s_3$ corresponds to Newman's *ş and is in fact the PCh reflex of PAA *s. Their $*s_2$, as was argued in Chapter 2, can probably be disregarded as a development out of PCh $*s_3$, restricted to one subgrouping of West Chadic. Newman's *s therefore subsumes Jungraithmayr and Shimizu's remaining sibilants, *s ($*s_1$) and *s'. PAA *t', *s', and *c' fall together as PCh *s' in the Jungraithmayr-Shimizu scheme; hence they all yield *s in Newman's renditions. Unfortunately, Jungraithmayr and Shimizu include in their list of reconstructions involving *s ($*s_1$) all those roots for which they lacked the diagnostic indications of exactly which sibilant to use, but for which their *s was one possible source. This approach means that some cases of actual PCh $*s_3$, and also of *s' — and thus of PAA *t', *s' and *c' — are to be found among their roots in *s, and not just among the examples they present as involving PCh *s'.

In Egyptian an extensive collapsing of the PAA sibilant phonemes took place. PAA *t' had apparently spirantized even before this wide-ranging change began; it therefore became /s/ in Egyptian, as did PAA *s', *s, *š, *c, and the ejective *c'. By devoicing, PAA *z and *j also became one with /s/ by Middle Egyptian times. The probable order of the changes involved, which were subsequent to the shared Egyptian and Semitic pharyngealization shifts noted above as PBA shifts #1 and #2, was the following (for Eg. shift #3, which logically preceded #4-8, see the section on PAA velar obstruents):

Eg. #4. PAA *t' > pre-Eg. *ts';

Eg. #5. PAA *c > pre-Eg. *ts,
PAA *c' > pre-Eg. *ts',
PAA *j > pre-Eg. *dz (presuming *c = [č], *j = [ǰ]), and
PAA *š > Eg. *s*;

#6. pre-Eg. *ts' > pre-Eg. *ts (de-glottalization);

#7. pre-Eg. *ts > Old Eg., ME *s*,
pre-Eg. *dz > Old Eg. *z* (de-affrication); and finally

#8. Old Egyptian *z* > ME *s*,

the latest of the shifts, postdating the beginning of written documentation of ancient Egyptian. The sibilantization process must have begun after the pharyngeal shift of PBA #2 above, because PAA *h in the environment of Eg. /s/ deriving from PAA *c or *t' did not undergo this shift to *ḥ (see #795).

The possibly equally late Egyptian shift,

#9. PAA *f > Eg. *p* /#_VC[+continuant/-voice] and /#_Vr,

noted above in the discussion of the PAA labial obstruents, must also be dated after #6, since all Eg. *s*, whatever their source, cannot normally co-occur with *f*. It may be a shift as recent in history as sound change #8 because a single case of alternant word-shapes, ***ps* /*fs*** "to cook" (see root #53 below), can still be found in ME writing (Faulkner 1964).

The dental correspondences can be summarized as follows:

Table 6: Afroasiatic (Afrasian) Dental Correspondences

PAA	PS	Eg.	PC	PCh	PO
*d	*d	d	*d	*d	*d
*t	*t	t	*t	*t	*t
*z	*z	z	*z	*ɗ	*z
*s	*s	s	*s	J: *s3/s N: *ṣ	*s
*t'	*ṭ (*t')	s	*t'	J: *s'/s N: *s	*ts'

A consonant co-occurrence constraint of far-reaching scope affected the distribution of the dentals in Semitic and Egyptian. Arabic (per Steingass

1978 [1884]) shows no root sequences of *td, *tt, *ts (< PAA *tVs, *tVs', and *tVš), *tz, *tẓ (< *tVc'), *tð (< *tVj), *tṣ (< *tVtl'), or *tḍ (< *tVdl). The regularly corresponding equivalent sequences in Egyptian *td*, *tt*, *tz* (= Arabic *tz, tð*), *ts* (= Arabic *ts, tẓ*), *tṯ* (= Arabic *tṣ*), and *tḏ* (= Arabic *tḍ*) — are likewise missing from that language (as attested in Faulkner 1964). This constraint seems probably to have affected Berber as well. But several such sequences, forbidden in Egyptian and Semitic, certainly *are* attested in both Cushitic and Chadic, notably *tVt, *tVs, *tVz, *tVj, and *tVtl' (Ehret 1980 and 1987; Jungraithmayr and Shimizu 1981). The evidence is not yet sufficient to determine fully the situation of PO, but at least some of the sequences are clearly present in Omotic, too. The constraint against the co-occurrence of PAA *t with a range of other dental obstruents, including the two laterals *tl' and *dl, thus shows itself to have been a shared innovation of Egyptian and Semitic and presumably also Berber, but was not present in the prehistory of Cushitic, Chadic, or Omotic. Because the specific effects of this constraint are not yet known, it can be given only a generalized formulation:

PBA #3. PAA *t > ? /#_VC̣ (C = dental obstruent).

A second fundamental constraint disallowed virtually all sibilant sequences in Semitic and, from all appearances, ruled out the equivalent pairings of consonants in Egyptian. From Arabic and other Semitic evidence, it can be concluded that it was forbidden in proto-Semitic roots to have both C_1 and C_2 selected from the set {θ, z, s, c, ð, θ̣}, i.e., for C_1C_2 to both be fricatives (or affricates) derived from the PAA dental and alveolar-palatal serices. Specifically, the sequences *θθ, *θz, *θs, *θc, *θð, *θθ̣, *sθ, *sz, *ss, *sc, *sð, *sθ̣, *zθ, *zs, *zc, *zð, *zθ̣, *cθ, *cz, *cs, *cc, *cð, *cθ̣, *θ̣θ, *θ̣z, *θ̣s, *θ̣c, *θ̣ð, *θ̣θ̣, *ðθ, *ðz, *ðs, *ðc, *ðð, and *ðθ̣ were lacking in PS. A single instance of *zz appears in Steingass (1978: 455); but its inconsistency with the rest of the sibilant patterns and its violation of the more general Arabic prohibition on identical root consonants in C_1 and C_2 position presumably make it a later development, and indicate that *zz, too, should have been missing from PS. These sequences would correspond regularly to the much-reduced Egyptian set *ss* (= PS *θθ, *θs, *θc, *θθ̣, *sθ, *ss, *sc, *sθ̣, *cθ, *cs, *cc, *cθ̣, *θ̣θ, *θ̣s, *θ̣c, and *θ̣θ̣); *sz* (= PS *θz, *θð, *sz, *sð, *cz, *cð, *θ̣z, and *θ̣ð); *zs* (= PS *zθ, *ðθ, *zs, *ðs, *zc, *ðc, *zθ̣, and *ðθ̣); and *zz* (= PS *zz, *zð, *ðz, and ðð). Of these four possible sequences, only *ss* actually occurs as a word in Middle Egyptian (Faulkner 1964), and indeed there are only three or four instances of word-initial *ss* in which the first *s* is not certainly or probably the prefixed Eg. *s causative. Except for those rare exceptions, the evidence thus confirms, point for point, the common possession by Egyptian and Semitic of the sweeping prohibition against consecutive root sibilants. Moreover, the sibilant distributions in Berber languages suggest that the same constraint manifested itself in the proto-history of that group as well. In contrast, the clear reconstructibility of such stem-consonant pairings as PAA *s and *z, *c' and *c', and *c' and *z in Cushitic (Ehret 1980, 1987; Sasse 1979), and of *sVd, *s_3Vɗ (< PAA *sVz), *sVs, and *ɗVs (< PAA *zVs) in Chadic (Jungraithmayr and Shimizu 1981) tells us that once again we are dealing with a shared innovation of Egyptian and Semitic and apparently also Berber, not found in the other branches.

As for the rare Egyptian cases of root *ss*, a probable explanation is close at hand. Eg. *ss* can in principle derive from PAA stem sequences that combine a sibilant with PAA *t', a consonant which remained non-sibilant *ţ in PS and therefore was not subject to the sibilant constraint. At least three PAA stem consonant sequences that would yield *ss* in Egyptian — *t'Vs', *t'Vc or *t'Vts, and *šVt' or *šVt' — are currently known from Semitic languages (as respectively PS *ţs, *ţθ, and *sţ or *cţ ; see roots #232, 257, and 525 for examples).

The specific consequences of the development of these constraints in Semitic and Egyptian remain to be properly investigated. At least two particular outcomes of the sibilant constraint do appear in the data below, however: in Semitic, PAA *sVz dissimilated to PS *sd (root #236), while PAA *zVts/c produced *dVts/c in both Egyptian and Semitic (#203). As with PBA #3 above, the statement of the governing rule remains unclear. Both the cited examples changed PAA *z to *d, preserving the other sibilant whether it preceded or followed *z in the word. A least for instances of PAA *z, the rule may have been

PBA #4. PAA *z > *d /$C_{[+sibilant]}$ in the same word.

What became of sibilant combinations not involving *z remains to be discovered, however.

PS alone seems to have extended the sibilant constraint to cases of PAA *tl', concurrent (as might be expected from the phonetic relations involved) with the pPS shift of that consonant from an originally lateral affricate articulation (see discussion in section on laterals below) to the sibilant in PS reconstructed as *ş. Interestingly, the constraint was maintained in that new context by blocking the normal shift of PAA *tl' to PS *ş and substituting an allowed co-occurent lateral, *ɬ, in place of expected *ş:

PS #2. PAA *tl' > PS *ɬ /$C_{[+sibilant]}$ in same root.

(See roots #918 and 920 for a pan-Afroasiatic demonstration that the extended constraint is limited to Semitic.)

Note that, because Old Egyptian *z* was becoming *s* by or before Middle Egyptian times, a number of instances of apparent PAA *z (and *j) are represented in Egyptian in the known record only as *s*, not as the expected *z*. One example of this has already appeared in the data above (root #33), and several more such cases appear in subsequent materials.

	SEMITIC	EGYPTIAN	CUSHITIC	CHADIC	OMOTIC
PAA *d					
118. *-d- (*ada ?) "here/there"	A. *da* "this"	*dy* "here, there"	PSC *(y)ad- "here/there" (Iraqw *da* "that referred to")		
119. *dâb-/*dîb- "back; to come or be behind"	[for A. *dubr* "backside," see #146]		PEC *dab-/*dib-/ *dub- "tail"; EC: Soomaali *dabar* "back" (stem + *r n. suff.)	*dab "back" (J)	SOm: Kara *dibini* "tail" (stem + *n n. suff.); NOm: Bench *dab* 3 "to follow"
120. *dab(n)- "hair"	A. *dabbaʔ* "hairy" (stem + *ʔ adj. suff.)	*dbnt* "lock of hair" (stem + *t coll. suff.)	PEC *dabn- "feather; hair"		

	SEMITIC	EGYPTIAN	CUSHITIC	CHADIC	OMOTIC
121. *-dăb-/*-dĭb- "to have honey"	A. *dabr*, *dibr* "swarm of bees" (stem + *r n. suff.); *dbs "honey" (stem + *s deverb. comp.) (A.*dibs*)		PSC *ḍăaba "honeycomb" (PSC *ḍ < PC *d /#_; n. < v. by V > VV)	Ng.*də̀bə̀s* "thickness, viscosity" (as of honey) (stem + *s deverb. comp.)	
122. *-doob- "to stick up"		*db* "horn; wing (of army)" (C. *tap*)	EC: Soomaali *doobbo* "long, pointed horn"	Ng.*də̀b-* "to erect"; *də̀bày-* "to become fat" (stem + *y inchoat.)	SOm: Banna *do:bana* "tail" (stem + *n n. suff.; influenced by, but not cognate with Kara word #119 above)
123. *-dac- "to flow"	pPS *dθ "to spill down" (Append.1)		EC: Soomaali *dashuun* "sweat; to sweat" (stem + *m n. suff.; v. < n.; Som. *sh* [š] < PEC *c)	some ECh *ds "fish" (J; semantics: earlier "flow" > "float," hence "swim" > "fish")	NOm: Zayse *dás* "diarrhea" (PO $*š_3$ > Zayse *s* /C[dental]V_)

	SEMITIC	EGYPTIAN	CUSHITIC	CHADIC	OMOTIC
124. *-dif-/*-daf-/ *-duf- "to leak, seep, run"	A. *dafq* "to pour out; be poured out; flow over" (stem + *k' intens. of effect)	*dfdf* "to drip" (redup. stem as freq.)	EC: Soomaali *dįįf, dųųf* "snot, nose mucus" (presumed n. < v. by V > VV)	Ng. *ndáfâk*, pl. *ndáfáfin* "cold, stuffiness, phlegm" (*in- concom. + stem; see also #798 for *-k* sing. suff. of n. for a liquid)	
125. *-dug- "to obscure, block from view"	pPS *dg "to cover, put in darkness" (Ehret 1989)	*dgi* "to hide"	EC: Soomaali *dugul* "dark; black" (stem + *l adj. suff.; < EC *dukl-: *k > Som.*g* /V_)		Mocha *dogo* "blind"; *dò:g-* "to disappear" (V-length unexplained)
126. *-dag^{w}- "to walk about"	A. *dajj* "to walk along"	*dg3*, *dgs* "to walk" (stem + *r diffus.; stem + probably *ts diffus.)	PSC *ḍak^{w}- "to be going" (PC *d > PSC *ḍ /#_)		

	SEMITIC	EGYPTIAN	CUSHITIC	CHADIC	OMOTIC
127. *-dîɣ- "to take away"	A. *daɣf* "to take much of a thing" (stem + *f iter.)		*dîɣɣ- "to remove, take away, send away"		
128. *-diɣʷ- "to tell"	A. *daɣdaɣ* "to state a thing unintelligibly; taunt; gibe" (redup. stem as intens.)		*diɣʷ- "to tell"		
129. *-dâh- "to move (intr.)"	A. *dahm* "to come unexpectedly" (stem + *m extend. as fort.); *dahmaj* "to walk swiftly with short steps" (stem + *m as fort. + *gʷ dur.)	LE *dhn* "to convey" (stem + *n non-fin.)	*dâh- "to travel"	*d- "to go" (N) (Ng. *dá-*)	SOm: Ari *dáhis-* "to chase" (stem + *s caus.)

	SEMITIC	EGYPTIAN	CUSHITIC	CHADIC	OMOTIC
130. *-dâḫ- "to strike"	A. *daḫṣ* "to beat the ground with the feet" (stem + *tl' foc.)		PSC *ḍâḫ- "to knock" (PSC *ḍ < PC *d /#_)		
131. *-dĕeḫ-/*-dŏoḫ- "to lie flat, be low"	pPS *dḫ "to lie prone" (Append.1)	LE *dḫ* "to be low"	EC: Soomaali *dooxo* "valley, plain" (*x* = [ḫ]; semantics: low-lying area)		SOm *de:s- "to kill" (stem + *s caus.); NOm: Yem *dí́*, *dūū* "to sit and rest" (stem + conjugational suff.)
132. *-dîk- "to pound"	A. *dakk* "to grind, pound, pulverize, crumble; beat flat"; *dakm* "to knock on the chest; knock one hard thing against		EC: Soomaali *dig* "pulse" (of blood)	*dək- "to pound (in mortar)" (N)	NOm: Bench *dekn* 2,3 "to hit" (stem + *n non-fin.)

	SEMITIC	EGYPTIAN	CUSHITIC	CHADIC	OMOTIC
	another; pound" (stem + *m extend.)				
133. *duk^{w}- or *duuk^{w}- "heap"	pPS *dk "heap (A. *dukk* "low hill; to heap up" (Ap-pend.1)		SC: PR *duk^{w}a "rubbish heap" (PC *d > PSC *ḍ > PR *d)		
134. *-dôk'- "to insert, stick into"	A. *duqūs* "to travel through; pene-trate into the ground" (stem + *š non-fin.)		PSC *ḍôk'- "to plant, fix in place" (PC *d > PSC *ḍ /#_)	Ng. *dә́gz*- "to fuck (vul-gar)" (stem + *dz extend. fort.)	
135. *-duk'- or *-duk^{w}'- "to break to pieces by hitting"	*dḳḳ "to pound, break up by pounding"	*dḳ* "flour"; LE *dḳ* "to hack up"	PSC *ḍuk'- "to be broken to pieces" (PSC *ḍ < PC *d /#_)		

	SEMITIC	EGYPTIAN	CUSHITIC	CHADIC	OMOTIC
136. *-dîl- "to increase, grow large"	A. *dalax* "to be fat" (stem + *xʷ extend. fort.)	*dns* "heavy; over-burdened; weighty" (stem + *s deverb. comp.)	PSC *dîl- or *ḍîl- "elder, senior person" (PSC *ḍ < PC *d /#_, PSC *d < PC *z /#_)		SOm: Dime *dildo* "many" (stem + *d dur. > stative, "be increased"?)
137. *-dul- "to raise, put above" (#136 + *-u- tr. infix?)	MSA *dlw "to pull up by rope; remove" (stem + *w in-choat. > dur., i.e., pull up)		EC: Soomaali *dul* "top part of something"	some ECh *dl "to carry" (J)	
138. *-duɬ-/*-diɬ- "to beat"	A. *dašš* "to pound, grind"		*daɬ-/*diɬ- "to beat"		NOm: Zayse *dúlp-* "to punch" (stem + *p in-tense. of man-ner)

	SEMITIC	EGYPTIAN	CUSHITIC	CHADIC	OMOTIC
139. *-dăm- "to press together"	pPS *dm "to join two things by inserting one in the other" (Append.1)	*dmi* "to touch, be joined, cleave"; (C. *tōōmɛ*); *dmḏ* "to assemble; associate; join; accumulate; compile" (stem + *dl m.v.)	*dăm- or *zăm- "to squeeze, press"		
140. *dîm-/*dâm- "blood"	*dm (*dam) "blood"	*idmi* "red linen" (*i- attrib. n. pref. + stem of shape *dim- + *y n. suff.)	*dîm-/*dâm- "red"	WCh *d-m- "blood" (N)	Gonga *dam- "blood" (Mocha *'damo*) (contra Leslau, loan < Sem. seems implausible in this case)
141. *-dîm-/*-dûm- "to leak out" (probable source of #140)	A. *damʕ* "to water, run (eyes)" (stem + + *ʕ part., i.e., fluid runs *out of* eyes)		*dim- "to leak out" (Ehret 1980: 325)		NOm: Yem *dùmà* "damp area"

		SEMITIC	EGYPTIAN	CUSHITIC	CHADIC	OMOTIC
142.	*-dûm- "to proclaim, speak forcefully"	A. *damdam* "to address angrily, inveight against" (redup. stem as intens.)	*dm* "to pronounce, proclaim (name); mention (name)"	EC: Soomaali *dundun* "argument" (redup. stem as freq.; *m > *n* /_# in Som.)	Ng. *də́mâ* "oath"; CCh *dms "to sing" (J; stem + *š non-fin.?)	
143.	*dumn- "cloud" (root #141 + *n n. suff.; PC variant *damn-)	[PEth *dämän "cloud": loan < Agaw]		*dumn-/*damn- "cloud"	Ng. *də̀mán* "rainy season"	[Ometo: Dacho *damäna* "cloud": EC loan; Shinasha *dawɨna* "cloud": Awngi (Agaw) loan]
144.	*danb- "hindquarters"	*dnb (*danb) "tail"		*danb- "hindquarters"		NOm: Kafa *dambo* "back"
145.	*-dap- "to touch, feel, put the fingers on"	pPS *dp "to touch; to put hands on" (Append.1)	*dp* "to taste, experience" (semantics: as in English *taste*; C. *tōp*)			NOm *dap-/dip- "nail, claw" (Yem *dìfnà*; Male *dapo*)

		SEMITIC	EGYPTIAN	CUSHITIC	CHADIC	OMOTIC
146.	*dup'- "lower back"	A. *dubr* "back, back-side; buttocks" (stem + *r n. suff.)	*dpt* "loins" (C. *tpɛ*)			Ometo: Koyra *dup'iya* "tail" (stem + *y n. suff.)
147.	*-dup's- "to put behind" (#146 + *s caus. as deverb.)	A. *tadbis* "to conceal; be concealed"			Ng. *də́ɓs-* "to hide"	
148.	*-dip'-/*-dup'- "to rise, swell"	A. *dabīl* "fat" (stem + *l adj. suff.)		*dip'-/*dup'- "to rise"		Ometo: Male *dɛ:p'i* "big" (adj. < v. by V > V:); Ometo: Kullo *du:p-* "to jump"
149.	*-dâr- "to grasp, grip, carry in the hands"	A. *darak* "to seize, take hold of" (stem + $*k^w$ fin.)	*drp* "to offer; pre-sent; make offerings" (stem + *p' fin. fort.)	PSC *ḍâr- "to handle" (PC *d > PSC *ḍ /#_)		

	SEMITIC	EGYPTIAN	CUSHITIC	CHADIC	OMOTIC
150. *-dăr- "to enlarge, increase"	A. *darr* "to abound, yield in abundance"		PSC *ḍar- "to increase, enlarge, add to" (PC *d > PSC *ḍ /#_)		N. Ometo *dar- "big"; Bench *dorg* 1 "fat, strong" (stem with *-u- tr. + *g^w dur. > stat.)
151. *-dir- "to step"	pPS *dr "to step" (Ehret 1989); *drc "to trample" (stem + *š non-fin.)		PSC *ḍir- "to pass (by)" (PC *d > PSC *ḍ /#_)	ECh *dr "thigh" (J)	SOm: Banna *rro* "foot" (< presumed *dVro, with V-deletion)
152. *-dăas'-/*-dŭus'- "to put over, put on top of, cover over"	A. *dass* "to hide one thing beneath another"		PEC *daacc-/ *duucc- "to put over, put above" (PC *ts' > PEC *c)	Ng. *dùs* "densely wooded area of brush" (semantics: area densely cloaked with vegetation)	[Mocha *dà:s*- "to cover, veil": loan (expected *dà:č'-; PO *s' > Mocha *č'*)

	SEMITIC	EGYPTIAN	CUSHITIC	CHADIC	OMOTIC
153. *-daw- "to walk"	MSA *dwz "to tread, tramp on" (stem + *z intens. of manner)		EC: Soomaali *daw* "road, way, path"	WCh, CCh *dw "to go" (J); some ECh *dwr "shoe"(J; stem + *r n. suff.)	
154. *-dax- "to burn low, smolder"	A. *daxan* "smoke" (stem + *n n. suff.)		PSC *ḍax- or *ḍak- "to dry over a fire" (PC *d > PSC *ḍ /#_)		
155. *-dax- "to cover up, conceal from view" (Ng. < alternate shape *-dix- or *-dux-)	pPS *dx "to cover over, conceal from view" (Append. 1)		PEC *dax-, *daxx- "to cover up, conceal"	*d-k- "to darken" (J: *dk "black"; Ng. *dəkəmá* "west": stem + *m n. suff.)	
156. *-dŭux- "to close, shut"			PSC *ḍŭux- "to shut, close, stop up" (PC *d > PSC *ḍ /#_)	*dk(l) "to close" (J; stem + *l fin.)	*du:k- "to bury" (NOm: Mocha *dù:k-* ; SOm: Ari *du:ki* "grave")

	SEMITIC	EGYPTIAN	CUSHITIC	CHADIC	OMOTIC
157. *-dăʕ- "to insert"	pPS *dʕ "to put into, stick into" (Append.1)	*d3* "to copulate"	*dăʕ- "to enter; to insert"	Ng. *dáas-* "to stop up, plug up" (stem + *s' fort.; PC *s' > Ng. *s*)	
158. *-daʕ- "to call"	A. *daʕw* "to call aloud; call upon; call to" (stem + *w inchoat. > dur.); *daʕdaʕ* "to call to be on one's guard" (redup. stem as intens.)		*daʕ- "to speak (forcefully?)"		

PAA *t

	SEMITIC	EGYPTIAN	CUSHITIC	CHADIC	OMOTIC
159. *-iit- "to eat" (Ch., Eg., Sem. **innovation**: *-VC- v. stems > *-CV-)	MSA *twy/*tyw "to eat" (stem + *w inchoat. > dur.)	*t* "bread; loaf"; *it* "barley; corn" (*i- attrib. pref. + stem, i.e., stuff for bread)	EC: HEC *iit- "to eat"	*ti "to eat" (N) (Ng.*tà*- ; J: *twy)	
160. *-tâ- "to be hot"		*t3* "hot" (stem + *ʔ adj. suff.); *t3w* "heat" (above stem + *w n. suff.)		some ECh *tw "sun; fire" (J; stem + *w de-verb.); some WCh *tyl "sun" (J; stem + *y inchoat. + *l n. suff.)	NOm *tam- "fire" (stem + *m n. suff.; Bench *tam*[3]); NOm: Mao *tant- "red" (n. "fire" + *t adj. suff.)
161. *-tĭb- or *-tĭib- "to rise, grow"	A. *tabtab* "to grow old" (redup. stem, as intens.?)	*tbtb* "to hoist" (re-dup. as freq. > dur.; shift: intr. > tr.)	PSC *tĭib- "large male animal" (n. < v. by V > VV?)		

	SEMITIC	EGYPTIAN	CUSHITIC	CHADIC	OMOTIC
162. *-tuf- "to spit"	*tf(f) "to spit"	*tf* "to spit" (C. *taf*)	*tuf- "to spit"	*təfə "to spit" (N)	
163. *-tăɣ- "to perish, be extinguished"	A. *taɣab* "to perish" (stem + *p' fin. fort.)			Ng.*tə́k-* "to kill; put out fire" (tr. by *-u- infix, > Ng. /ə/ and tone shift)	Mocha *tàk-* "to extinguish fire"
164. *-taɣ-/*-tuɣ- "to splash, splatter"	A. *tuɣūr* "to pour down, rain abundantly" (stem + *r diffus.)	*tḫb* "to immerse; irrigate" (stem + b extend.; C. *tōhb*)	[EC: Soomaali *tog* "annual stream": loan < unidentifed language (expected *tug)]	Ng. *tə́k-* "to rain, beat down; splash"	Mocha *tàk-* "to sprinkle" (expected high tone?)
165. *-tah- "to tap"		*thm* "to knock" (stem + *m extend.)	*tah- "to tap"		

	SEMITIC	EGYPTIAN	CUSHITIC	CHADIC	OMOTIC
166. *-taḫ- "to reach"		*tḫn* "to meet" (stem + *n non-fin.)	*taḫ- "to reach"		
167. *-tāk-/*-tūk- "to stick (in), prick"	A. *takk* "to cut"; *itkaʔ* "to pierce with sword" (stem + *ʔ concis.)	*tks* "to pierce" (stem + *s' fort.; C.*tōks*)	PSC *tāankaʔ- "stinging fly" (stem + SC *ʔ n. suff.; Ehret 1980: 169 has incorrect *ʕ; PC *k > PSC *nk /tV_V, *a > PSC *aa /#C_Caʕ/ʔ-: see also #563)		NOm *tok- "to plant" (Mocha *'tok-*, Bench *tok*², Malo *tokk-*, etc.)
168. *-tĕk-/*-tŏk- "to tread"	A. *takk* "to tread under the feet, crush by stamping"	*tkn* "to approach, draw near; be near" (stem + *n non-fin.; C. *tōhn*)	EC: Northern Soomaali *teg "to go, walk" (PEC *k > Som *g* /_#)	Ng.*tákɗ-* "to step on; press down on" (stem + *z intens. of manner); *ⁿdk "to go" (J; *N- concom. + stem)	NOm *tok- "foot"; Bench *tok*¹ "to stamp"

	SEMITIC	EGYPTIAN	CUSHITIC	CHADIC	OMOTIC
169. *-tăk^{w}- "to descend, go down"	A. *itkaʔ* "to throw down" (stem + *ʔ concis.)		*tăk^{w}-/*tĭk^{w}- "to descend"		Mocha *tòkkar-* "to fall asleep" (stem + *r diffus. > dur.; semantics: "go down" > "lie down" > "sleep"
170. *-tik^{w}-/*-tak^{w}- "to light"		*tk3* "torch; to illumine" (stem + *r n. suff.; v. < n.; C. *tōk* "to light")	*tak^{w}-/*tik^{w}- "to heat"		Mocha *túkko* "day"
171. *-tĕl- "to fall down"	A. *tall* "to fall down; throw someone down"; *talaf* "to perish" (stem + *p intens. of manner)		PSC *telaʕ- "dying person" (stem + *ʕ part.; semantics: be falling > be dying)		

	SEMITIC	EGYPTIAN	CUSHITIC	CHADIC	OMOTIC
172. *-tŭul- "to rise; to form a heap, mound"	A. *tall* "small hill"; *talʕ* "to spread; rise; stretch forth the hand; hill" (stem + *ʕ part.)	LE *tri* "to respect, esteem" (stem + *y inchoat., i.e., risen in one's estimation > tr. use)	PEC *tuul- "to rise; hill, heap"	ECh *tlŋ "to hang" (J; stem + possible *ŋ ext. of uncertain meaning)	Mocha *tu:lló* "heap"; Yem *túul-* "to heap up"
173. *-tum- "to beat"			PEC *tum- "to pound, beat"	WCh, ECh *tm "to beat" (J)	
174. *-tar- "to increase"	A. *tarr* "to be full in flesh and bones"		PSC *tar- "to increase"		

	SEMITIC	EGYPTIAN	CUSHITIC	CHADIC	OMOTIC
175. *-tār- "to start off"	pPS *tr "to depart, leave" (Ehret 1989)	LE *trr* "to race" (stem with redup. as intens.)	*tar-/*tir- "to start up"; PSC *torik- "to move suddenly" (< pre-PSC *tark^w-, stem + *k^w fin.; PC *k^w > PSC *k /i_)	Ng. *tàra-* "to approach" (stem + *-a incep.); *tàr̃n-* "to head for, start out for" (stem + *n non-fin. as incep.)	Mocha *'tär-* "to go"
176. *-tăr- "to shake (intr.)"	A. *tartar* "to move, shake; be shaken, tremble" (redup. stem as freq.)		PSC *tărar- "to tremble, shake" (partially redup. stem as freq.)		
177. *-tăar- "to cut into"	A. *tarr* "to be cut off; cut off"		PSC *tâar- "to spear, pierce with a weapon"	some CCh, ECh *tr (?) "to hollow out" (J)	

*PAA Dental Obstruents: *t*

	SEMITIC	EGYPTIAN	CUSHITIC	CHADIC	OMOTIC
178. *tĕr-/*tŏr- "earth"		*t3* "earth, land, ground" (C. *to*)	*tĕr- "dust"	some WCh *tr "fields, bush" (J: semantics: land > country)	NOm *tor- "earth" (Bench *tor*^{1} "down")
179. *tĭr- "liver"			*tĭr- "liver"	*trn "liver" (J; stem + *n n. suff.)	SOm: Ari *tirá* "liver" (possible loan < EC); [NOm: Ometo *tir- "liver": loan < EC; expected *ter-]
180. *-taʕ- "to become weak"	pPS *tʕ "to become weak" (Ehret 1989)		PSC *taʕas- "to subdue" (stem + *s caus.)		

PAA *z	SEMITIC	EGYPTIAN	CUSHITIC	CHADIC	OMOTIC
181. *za "something" (indefinite pron.)	A. *ziyy, zayy* "outer aspect, shape, form; as, how" (stem + *y adj. suff.)		EC: Soomaali-II *zat "person" (stem + *t n. suff.)	*ɗ- "this, that, the" (N)	
182. *-zâb- "to grasp, take hold of"	A. *zabq* "to pluck the beard" (stem + *k' intens. of effect)		*zâb- "to grasp"	WCh, ECh *ɗb "granary" (J; semantics: grain *holder*)	Gonga *yabaro "finger" (stem + *r n. suff.; Mocha *yaba'ro*)
183. *-zab- "to call"	A. *zabṭ* "to quack" (stem + *t' dur. intens.)	*zbṯ* "to laugh; laughter, mirth" (stem + tl' foc.)	EC: Soomaali *dabuub* "conversation" (redup. as freq.; PEC *z > Som. *d*)	WCh, CCh *dab "to call" (J)	

	SEMITIC	EGYPTIAN	CUSHITIC	CHADIC	OMOTIC
184. *-zăab- "to take"	A. *zaby* "to take up, carry" (stem + *y inchoat. > dur.)	*zbi* "to send; conduct; go, travel" (structure as in Sem.)			Mocha *yà:b-* "to pull, lead by the hand" (influenced by #182 ?)
185. *-zaab- "to look"	MSA *zbn "to protect" (stem + *n non-fin.; semantics: to watch over)	*zbi* "to watch over" (stem + *y inchoat. > dur.)	PSC *daab- "to look" (PSC *d < PC *z/#_)		
186. *-zaf- "to walk, travel"	A. *zafn* "to kick, tread; dance" (stem + *n non-fin.)		*zaf- or *daf- "to pass"	*ɗap "to follow" (J)	

	SEMITIC	EGYPTIAN	CUSHITIC	CHADIC	OMOTIC
187. *-zif- "to break up (by hitting)"		*zf* "to cut up, cut off"; *sfsf* "to break (?)" (redup. stem); *zfṯ* "to slaughter" (stem + *tl' foc.); *zft* "sword, knife" (stem + *t n. suff.; C. *sēfɛ*)	*zaf-/*zif- "to pound"	WCh, CCh *ɗəft- "flour" (WCh: Diri *ɗəpti* "flour"; CCh: Gongola-Higi *ɗəf(t)- "porridge"; stem + *t n. suff.; writer's reconstruction; semantics: flour is grain crushed by pounding in mortar)	
188. *-zag- or *-zaɣ- "to strike repeatedly"		*zḫi* "to hit, smite" (stem + *y in-choat. > dur.; PAA *g and *ɣ > Eg. *ḫ* /z_)	EC: Soomaali *dagaal* "fight; to fight" (stem + *l n. suff.; v. < n.; PEC *z > Som. *d*; PC *g and *ɣ > Som. *g*)	CCh, some WCh *ɗg "to pound (in mortar)" (J has *g for PAA *g and *ɣ)	

	SEMITIC	EGYPTIAN	CUSHITIC	CHADIC	OMOTIC
189. *-zăg^{w}-/*-zĭg^{w}- "to stay in place, not move"	A. *zajr* "to forbid, prevent" (stem + *r diffus.)	*zḫn* "to occupy a place" (stem + *n non-fin.)	EC: Afar *digga* "firmness, permanence" (PEC *z > Afar *d*)	*ɗəg^{w} "to sit down" (J)	Gonga *yàg- "to last"
190. *-zaɣ- "to move about quickly"	A. *zuɣlūl* "agile, nimble, quick" (stem + *l adj. suff. with redup.)	*zḫz* "to run; hurry; flee" (stem + *z intens. of manner or *dz extend. fort.)	EC: Soomaali *dag* "to do quickly with little effort" (PEC *z > Som.*d* ; PC *ɣ > Som. *g*)	some WCh *ɗgl "to dance, play" (J; stem + *l fin. or *l n. suff., with n. < earlier v.?)	
191. *-zŏoɣ- "to move (tr.), make move, convey" (Eg., Sem. shared **innovation**: "move, take" > "take hold of")	A. *zaɣr* "to snatch with violence" (stem + *r diffus.); *zaɣd* "to press skin bag until butter comes out" (stem + *d dur.); MSA *zɣf "to take away" (stem + *f iter.)	*zḫn* "to embrace" (stem + *n non-fin.)	PSC *doox- "to take away" (PSC *d < PC *z; PC *ɣ > PSC *x)	WCh, ECh *ɗgr "to carry" (J; stem + *r diffus.); Ng.*ɗə̀g-* "to follow; come after"; *ɗə̀ga-* "to travel along (road)" (stem + *-a incep.)	Mocha *yò:k-* "to chase"

	SEMITIC	EGYPTIAN	CUSHITIC	CHADIC	OMOTIC
192. *-zaaḫ- "to flow out"	A. *zaḫr* "to give birth" (stem + *r diffus.)		*zaaḫ- "to become wet"	Ng *ɗáas-* "to pour through narrow opening" (stem + *s caus.)	
193. *-zâk^w- "to turn (intr.)"	A. *zakīk* "to circle round a hen"		*zâk^{w}r- "to turn round" (stem + *r diffus.)		Mocha *'yok-* "to spin"
194. *-zâk'- "to raise, make rise" (Cush., Ch., Eg., Sem. shared **innovation**: "raise" > "lift, pick up"; probable further Ch., Eg., Sem. **innovation**: "lift" > "carry"	pPS *zḳ "to carry" (Ehret 1989)	*sḳr* "to offer, present; grasp (hand)" (stem + *l fin.; presumed Old Eg. *z*; semantics: carry *to* someone, i.e., offer, present)	PSC *dâk'- or *dâak'- "to lift up" (PSC *d < PC *z /#_)	*ɗk "to carry" (J; *k' > PCh *k /ɗV_-#: see also #195 following)	Gonga *yak'k'ap- "to be pregnant" (stem + *f iter. > dur.; semantics: make rise > continue swelling [descriptive of pregnancy]; PO *z > Gonga *y)

		SEMITIC	EGYPTIAN	CUSHITIC	CHADIC	OMOTIC
195.	*-zaak'- "to eat up"	A. *zaqq* "to feed the young ones"; *zaqm* "to swallow at one gulp" (stem +*m extend. as fort.)		*zaak'- "to eat up"	CCh *ɗk "to swallow" (J; *k' > *k: see also #194)	
196.	*-zǎl- "to cut (into, off)"	pPS *zl "to cut" (Append.1)		*zalaaʕ- or *dalaaʕ- "to gash, notch" (stem + *ʕ part., i.e., cut apart)	Ng. *ɗálm*- "to pluck peanuts from dried vines" (stem + *m extend., i.e., break off repeatedly"	Ometo: Zayse *za:lé* "tusk" (semantics: tusk is used to pierce; n. < v. by V > V:)
197.	*-zoɬ- or *-zooɬ- "to scrape (surface of)"	A. *dašš* "to pound, grind" (i.e., to grind < scrape)	*zš* "to write" (semantics: scratch > write, as commonly in other languages, e.g., English *write*)	SC: WR *doɬ- "to cultivate" (WR *o < PSC *o or *oo; PC *z > PSC *d; semantics: < hoeing to clear ground)	Core WCh *ɗs "to grind" (J; PCh $*ɬ_2$ > Core WCh *s)	

	SEMITIC	EGYPTIAN	CUSHITIC	CHADIC	OMOTIC
198. *-zanf- "to seep out"		*znfw* "blood" (stem + *w deverb.; C. *snof*)	*zanf- or *danf- "to seep out"		
199. *-zîn- "to lie still"	A. *zanʔ* "to stick to a place; adhere to the ground" (stem + *ʔ con-cis.)			some CCh (also ECh?) *ɗn "to sleep" (J)	NOm *zí n- "to lie" (NW Ometo *zinʔ- "to sleep": stem + *ʔ concis.?; Mocha *yḭ:n-* "to spend the day"); Mocha *yìndar*- "to doze" (stem + *d dur. + *r dif-fus.)
200. *-zaŋ-/*-ziŋ- "to shine"	A. *zand* "to strike fire; materials to strike fire with" (stem + *d dur.)		PEC *ziŋ-/*zaŋ- "to light up (intr.)"	WCh *ɗng, *ɗŋ "sky" (J)	

	SEMITIC	EGYPTIAN	CUSHITIC	CHADIC	OMOTIC
201. *-zaŋ- "to watch, observe"	A. *zann* "to have an opinion, judge"; *zanhar* "to look sharply at with protruding eyes" (stem + *h ampl. + *r diffus.)		EC: Soomaali *dan* "interest"; *danee* "to be interested in" (PEC *z > Som.*d* ; PC *ŋ > PEC *n /_-#)	some WCh *ɗŋ "to see" (J)	Ometo: Male *zəg-* "to see"
202. *-zaar- "to move along"	A. *zarîf* "to walk slowly" (stem + *f iter.)		*-zruɣ- "to shift, move (tr.)" (stem + *-u- tr. infix + *$ɣ^w$ comp.); PEC *zaarɓ- "to pass" (stem + *b extend.)	*ɗr "path(way)" (J)	

	SEMITIC	EGYPTIAN	CUSHITIC	CHADIC	OMOTIC
203. *-zots- or *-zoc- "to stick out, stick up, form a point"	A. *daθθ* "to push forth leaves" (PAA *z > *d because of Sem., Eg. co-occurrence constraint against consecutive sibilants in same root)	*ds* "knife, flint" (PAA *z > *d: see A. entry)	EC: Soomaali *doosh* "point securing sail to prow; forward part of triangular sail; prow" (PEC *z > Som.*d*, *c > *sh* [š]; n.< v. by V > VV)	some WCh *ɗs- "mountain" (J); some WCh *ɗs(-k) "sky" (J; stem + uncertain suff.)	[NOm: Zayse *dóts* "point": loan < EC language (expected *zots- or *zos-)]
204. *-zaax- "to become drenched"	A. *zaxx* "to emit urine"; *zaxr* "to flow over; inundation" (stem + *r n. suff. or *r diffus.)		PEC *zaax- "to swim"		Ometo: Basketo *zak* "cold" (semantics: see #458); [S.Ometo *dakad'- "to swim": stem + *dl m.v.; loan < EC]
205. *-zâʔ- or *-zâʕ- "to look at"		*z3w* "to guard; ward off; heed" (stem + *w inchoat. > dur.; C. *so*)	PSC *dâʔ- or *dâʕ- "to look at" (PSC *d < PC *z /#_)		

	SEMITIC	EGYPTIAN	CUSHITIC	CHADIC	OMOTIC
206. *-zăʕ- "to be held, be grasped"	A. *zaʕb* "to carry a full skin bag; walk under a heavy burden" (stem + *b extend.)	*z3* "cattle-hobble"	PSC *dăʕas- "to catch hold of" (stem + *s caus.; PSC *d < PC *z /#_)	Ng. *ɗáaw-* "to put, place" (stem + *w inchoat.; but semantics unclear)	
207. *-zâaʕ- "to flee"	A. *zaʕb* "to push away, drive away, chase" (stem + *b extend.); *zaʕj* "to drive away, push away" (stem + *g fin. fort.)		PSC *daaʕ- "to flee" (PSC *d < PC *z /#_)	Ng. *ɗáy-* "to get lost, disappear from view, go astray" (stem + *y inchoat.)	

	SEMITIC	EGYPTIAN	CUSHITIC	CHADIC	OMOTIC
208. *-zaaʕ- "to rend, tear"	A. *zaʕj* "to snatch violently from, tear out" (stem *g fin. fort.); *zaʕb* "to cut or break off" (stem + *p' fin. fort.)		PSC *daaʕ- "to rend, tear" (PSC *d < PC *z /#_)	Ng. *ɗáar-* "to cut into long strips" (stem + *r diffus.); *ⁿd- "to cut" (J: *N-concom. + stem)	

PAA *s

	SEMITIC	EGYPTIAN	CUSHITIC	CHADIC	OMOTIC
209. *si, *isi "he/she/it" (unmarked for gender) (Eg., Sem., Cush. shared **innovations:** *su, *usu "he"; *si, *isi "she": see Chap. 6)	MSA *-š "him; his"; MSA *šʔ "he" (MSA *š < PS *s); MSA *-s "her"; MSA *sʔ "she" (normally MSA *s < PS *c < PAA *š; but here palatalization of *s)	*sw* "he, him"; *sy* "she, her"; *nts* "she" (indep. pron. base *nt*- + root)	*ʔusu "he"; *ʔisi "she"	*sV "he" (after Kraft 1974)	*is- "he" (Bender 1988) (Ometo: Koyra *ʔesa* "he," *ʔiso* "she")

		SEMITIC	EGYPTIAN	CUSHITIC	CHADIC	OMOTIC
210.	*su, *usu "they" (Eg., Sem., Cush. shared **innovation**: *ʔisin-/*ʔusun- "they" (originally fem./masc.), #209 + Afroasiatic pl. in *n, as also in #323)	MSA *šm "they (masc.)"; MSA *sn "they (fem.)" (see #209 for why /s/ appears instead of expected *š)	*sn* "they, them, their" (suff. and dependent pron.); *ntsn* "they" (indep. pron. base *nt*- + root)	EC: YD *ʔisin-/ *ʔusun- "they"	WCh *sun "they" (after Kraft 1974); BM *-sV (*-si?) "they" (Shryock 1990)	Ometo: Koyra *ʔuso* "they"
211.	*-sĭf-/*-sŭf- "to put together"	Ji. *šfɔḳ* "to get married" (stem + *k^w' and.; semantics: be joined *to* spouse in marriage; Ji. *š* < PS *s)	*sf* "to mix"; *sfw* "muddle" (stem + *w deverb.)	*suf- "to join (tr.)" (corrects Ehret 1987)		NOm *sip- "to plait, sew" (Bench *sip*-[1]; Mocha *šìpp*-)
212.	*-saɣ- "to plait, weave"		*sḫt* "to weave" (stem + *t dur.)	*saɣʔ- or *saʔɣ- "to weave" (stem + *ʔ concis.)		

	SEMITIC	EGYPTIAN	CUSHITIC	CHADIC	OMOTIC
213. *-săk-/*-sŭk- "to walk"	A. *sakaʕ* "to depart, go away" (stem + *ʕ part.); *sakm* "to walk wearily with short steps" (stem + *m extend.)		*sŭkur- "to move (intr.)" (stem + *r diffus.)	*skr "leg" (J; stem + *r n. suff.)	NOm: Maji *sak-* "to pass by"
214. *-suk- "to stay"	*skn "to reside" (stem + *n non-fin.); *skb "to lie down" (stem + *p' fin. fort.); A. *sakt* "to be silent; subside; die" (stem + *t dur.); *sakaʕ* "to sleep, fall asleep" (stem +		*suk- "to sit" (corrects Ehret 1980: 328)	*sk(r) "to sit down" (J; stem + *r diffus.); Ng. *sə̀kòokùy-* "to pass time" (stem, with redup.?, + *y inchoat.> dur.)	Majoid *sok- "to sleep"

	SEMITIC	EGYPTIAN	CUSHITIC	CHADIC	OMOTIC
	*ʕ part., i.e., depart, of consciousness)				
215. *-sŭk'-/*-săk'- "to excrete, secrete"	A. *saqq* "to drop excrement"; *sḳr "to provide water" (stem + *r diffus.)		*săk'-/*sŭk'- "to secrete, bleed"		
216. *-s^kʷ'- "to rub" (possible V reconstructions: *a, *aa, *e, or *o)	A. *saql* "to smooth, polish" (stem + *l fin.; semantics: rubbing makes smooth)			Ng. *sákwtù* "massage" (stem + *t n. suff.)	
217. *-sîl- "to pull off, draw off"	pPS *sl "to draw out or off" (Ehret 1989)		PSC *sîl- "to strip bare, make empty"	Ng. *sə̀lt-* "to undress" (stem + *t dur; contra source proposed in Schuh 1981)	

		SEMITIC	EGYPTIAN	CUSHITIC	CHADIC	OMOTIC
218.	*-sil- "to run out (of fluid)"	*sly(t) "placenta, after-birth" (stem + *y deverb. + *t n. or coll. suff.)	*snẖt* "phlegm" (stem + *x precip., i.e., *cough* up phlegm, + *t n. suff.)	*sil- "to trickle"		
219.	*-sim- "to pay attention to, take note of" (Sem., Eg., Ch. **innovation**: added sense, "to listen to")	A. *samm* "to examine closely"; *smʕ "to hear" (stem + *ʕ part.; semantics unclear); *smr "to guard" (stem + *r diffus.; semantics: guarding involves looking all around)	*smt* "to hear" (stem + *t dur.)		*ṣəmi "ear" (N; stem + *y deverb.) (J: *s_3m-)	Majoid: Nao *sem-* "to see"

	SEMITIC	EGYPTIAN	CUSHITIC	CHADIC	OMOTIC
220. *sŭm-/*sĭm- "name"	*smw (*səm-) "name" (stem + *w n. suff.)	*smi* "to report, announce" (stem + *y denom.; C. *smmɛ* "to accuse")	*sĭm-/*sŭm- "name" (Agaw: Awngi *sə́m*)	*ṣəm "name" (N) (J: *s_3m)	NOm *sum(ts)- "name" (stem + Omotic *ts n. suff.; Bench *sum* [1])
221. *sŭm- "above, up; crown of head"	pPS *sm "above; high" (Append.1)	*sm3* "scalp" (stem + *r n. suff.)	PSC *sŭmɓa "peak, top, especially of head" (stem + *b anim. suff.)		
222. *-sîn-/*-sûn- "to pour out"	A. *sann* "to pour water slowly over"		sînc'- "to urinate" (stem + *c' extend.); PEC *sun(u)n- "nose-bleeding"	some WCh *sn "to pour" (J)	

	SEMITIC	EGYPTIAN	CUSHITIC	CHADIC	OMOTIC
223. *sĭn-/*săn- "tip, point, projecting part" (Ch., Sem., Berber **innovation:** specialized meaning "tooth"; but note presence of that meaning isolated in single Omotic language)	*snn (*sinn) "tooth"; A. *sann* "to sharpen; provide lance with iron point"; *sinān* "point of tool"	*sn* "harpoon"	PEC *san- "nose; tip" (EC languages show confusion of this root with #224 and 500, which see)	*ṣan(-) "tooth" (N) (J: *s_3n)	NOm *sin- "face" (Yem *sìnà*); Bench *san* [2-3] "tooth" (apparent isolated occurrence, not in other Omotic; rising tone implies stem + lost derivational morphol.: thus separately derived in Bench?)
224. *-sĭiŋʷ- "to smell (tr.)"	A. *sanax* "to be rancid and smell bad" (stem + *xʷ extend. fort.)		*ĭsŋʷ- "nose" (*i- attrib. + stem); PEC *siin- "to sniff" (Afar "to sniff"; Som. "snot"; etc.); [EC: Dullay *sind'- "nose": loan < Omotic]		NOm *sind'- "nose" (stem + *dl m.v.; Bench *sint* '1; separate derivation of n. < v. root, distinct from PC *isŋʷ-)

	SEMITIC	EGYPTIAN	CUSHITIC	CHADIC	OMOTIC
225. *-sap- "to come near" (**innovation**: Sem., Ch. "to come so close as to brush against")	A. *saff* "to skim the the ground (in flying)"; *spr "to travel" (stem + *r diffus.)	*spr* "to arrive, reach" (stem + *l fin.)	SC: Iraqw *sap-* "to draw nearer"	some WCh *sp "to brush" (J: "sweep"; Ng. *sásp-* "to brush off": stem with re-dup. as freq.)	
226. *-sap- or *-saap- "to hit repeated-ly"	A. *safʕ* "to box the the ears, beat" (stem + *ʕ part.; i.e., cuffing ears knocks head *aside*); A. *safq* "to box on the ears" (stem + *k' intens. of effect)		SC: Burunge *sap-* "to forge (iron)"	Ng. *sàpɗ-* "to do first pounding (of grain)" (stem + *z intens. of manner)	

	SEMITIC	EGYPTIAN	CUSHITIC	CHADIC	OMOTIC
227. *-sop- "to be(come) bent over"	*spp "to crawl, bend over"; *spl "low" (stem + *l adj. suff.)	*sps* "to be tousled (?)" (stem + probably *ts diffus.)	SC: Iraqw *sop-* "to limp"		
228. *-sar- "to cut"	A. *sar d* "to pierce, bore through" (stem + *d dur., i.e., "to bore")	LE *s3w* "to break; split; cut off" (stem + *w inchoat.; semantics unclear: perhaps originally > intr., then > tr. again?)	PSC *sar- "to cut with repeated knife strokes"	WCh *srm "knife" (J; stem + *m n. suff.)	
229. *sâr- "back"	[MSA *sr "behind, after": loan (expected *šr)]	*s3* "back" (C. *soī*)	*sâr- "back"		

	SEMITIC	EGYPTIAN	CUSHITIC	CHADIC	OMOTIC
230. *săr-/*sĭr- "root"	*srs (*sərs) "root" (stem + *s n. suff. elsewhere used as deverb comp.?);	*s3* "root"	*săr-/*sĭr- "root" (Beja *sare* "artery"; Agaw *sər "root": Awngi *sə́r*)		NOm: Maji *saru* "hair"
231. *saraar-/*siraar- "muscle, sinew"	*srr (*sərr) "umbilical cord; muscle"		EC: PSom *saraar "muscles of back" (influence < #230?)		
232. *-săt'-/*-sŭt'- "to bite into"	A. *saṭw* "to taste of a dish" (stem + *w inchoat.)		EC: Afar *suxuk-* "to swallow without chewing" (stem + *x precip.; PEC *x > Afar *k*, *t' > Afar *x* [d'])		NOm *sats'- "to bite" (Bench *sats'*1)

		SEMITIC	EGYPTIAN	CUSHITIC	CHADIC	OMOTIC
233.	*-sâx- "to scrape"	*sxṭ "to flay" (stem + *t' dur. intens.)	*sẖm* "to comb (flax)" (stem + *m extend.)	*sax- "to scrape"	Ng. *sásk-* "to scrape or cut off in small pieces" (redup. as freq.)	
234.	*-sīx- or *-sīix- "to fall into ruin, become rubbish"	A. *saxxal* "mean, vile" (stem + *l adj. suff.); *saxīma-t* "dirt, filth" (stem + *m n. suff.)	*sẖn* "to demolish" (stem + *n non-fin.)	*sīix- "remains" (n. < v. by V > VV, if root was *sīx-)		
235.	*-sôx- "to run out (fluid)"	pPS *sx "to run out (fluid)" (Ehret 1989)	*sẖr* "to milk" (stem + *l fin. > fort.)	*sox- "to wet"	*sk "to pour" (J)	Ometo-Bench *sux$_2$ut(s)- "blood" (< *sox$_2$ut(s), stem + *t n. suff.; Bench *sut* 5)

	SEMITIC	EGYPTIAN	CUSHITIC	CHADIC	OMOTIC
236. *-sâaz- "to wait"	A. *sadaḫ* "to stay, abide" (stem + *ḫ iter.)		*sâaz- "to wait"		
237. *-siʔ- "to not want" (Eg., Sem. **innovation**: "not want" > "not need," hence "be sated")	A. *saʔāma-t* "satiety, disgust" (stem + *m n. suff.)	*s3i* "to be sated, satisfied" stem + *y inchoat.); *s3w* "satiety" (stem + *w deverb.)	SC: WR *siʔ- "to obstruct, not allow"	*ṣə "to dislike, not want" (N)	
238. *-soʔ- "to be still"	*sʔr "to remain" (stem + *r diffus.); *sʔn "peace" (stem + *n n. suff.)	*s3i* "to linger, await" (stem + *y inchoat. > dur.)	SC: Alagwa *soʔit-* "to squat" (stem + *t dur.)	Ng. *sáuyâ* "laziness" (stem + *w inchoat. + *y deverb.)	

	SEMITIC	EGYPTIAN	CUSHITIC	CHADIC	OMOTIC
239. *-sâʕ- "to do, accomplish"	A. *saʕy* "endeavor, effort, exertion; to perform; take pains and care in; etc." (stem + *y deverb.; v. > n.)	*s* ^{c}*b* "to be equipped" (as with weapons) (stem + *b extend. > stat.)	PSC *sâʕ- "to do"		

PAA *t'

	SEMITIC	EGYPTIAN	CUSHITIC	CHADIC	OMOTIC
240. *-t'ab-/*-t'ib- "to shut"	pPS *ţb "to cover" (Append.1)	*sb3* "door" (stem + *r n. suff.; C. *sbε* < alternate shape *-t'ub- or *-t'ib-)	*t'abab- "to plug, stop up" (redup. stem as intens.)		
241. *-t'ib- "to perform ritual"	A. *ţabb* "to heal, cure"		PEC *t'ib- "to perform ritual"		

	SEMITIC	EGYPTIAN	CUSHITIC	CHADIC	OMOTIC
242. *-t'ŏg^w- "to burn (tr.)"	A. *ṭajn* "to fry in a pan" (stem + *n non-fin.)		SC: Dahalo *t'ògg^wa* "smoke"		NOm *ts'ug- "to burn (tr.)"
243. *-t'ôɣ- "to rise"	A. *ṭaɣw* "high place; mountain summit" (stem + *w deverb.); *ṭaɣy* "to swell, rise" (stem + *y inchoat.)	*sḫn* "swelling (?)" (stem + *n n. suff.)	PSC *t'ôxooʕ- "to pick up" (stem + *ʕ part.; PC *ɣ > PSC *x)	CCh *s'gn "to dance" (J; stem + *n non-fin.); Ng. *sákə́m-* "to mount, ride (animal)" (stem + *m extend.)	
244. *-t'ôɣ- or *-t'ôɣ^w- "to be wet"	A. *ṭaɣam* "sea; mass of water" (stem + *m n. suff.)	*sḫt* "marshland" (stem + *t n. suff.)	PSC *t'ôx- "cold" (PC *ɣ and *ɣ^w > PSC *x /o_; semanics: see #458)		
245. *-t'êh- or *-t'êeh- "to approach"	pPS *ṭh "to come" (Append.1)		PSC *t'ěeh- "near" (adj. < v. by V > VV?)		

		SEMITIC	EGYPTIAN	CUSHITIC	CHADIC	OMOTIC
246.	*-t'ih-/*-t'ah- "to burn up"	A. *ṭahw* "to cook by boiling or roasting" (stem + *w inchoat. > dur.)		EC: Yaaku *t'eeho* "charcoal" (PC *i > Yaaku *e*; n. < v. by V > VV)		*ts'ahn- "black" (NOm: Maji *ts'ahiniz-; SOm: Dime *ts'a:no*; stem + *n adj. suff.)
247.	*t'îḫ- "body hair"	A. *ṭiḫṭiḫa-t* "hair" (redup. stem)		PSC *t'îḫ- "body hair, fur" (corrects Ehret 1980: 175)		
248.	*-t'iḫ- "to gasp"	A. *ṭaḫr* "to take a deep breath" (stem + *r diffus.)		SC: PR *ts'iḫ- "to gasp" (PC *t' > PR *ts')		
249.	*-t'ĭḫ-/*t'ăḫ- "to understand, be knowledge-able"		*sḫ* "council; coun-sel" (C. *sōh*); *sḫy* "man of good counsel" (stem + *y n. suff.)	*t'ăḫ-/*t'ĭḫ- "to be aware of, acquainted with"	Ng. *sà-* "to experience, undergo"	

	SEMITIC	EGYPTIAN	CUSHITIC	CHADIC	OMOTIC
250. *-t'eɬ- "to observe"	pPS *ṭl "to observe" (Append.1)	*sr* "to foretell; make known; show" (C. *sōr*)		some CCh *s'n "to hear" (J; PCh *l > CCh *n; see also #559 below)	NOm *ts'il- "to see" (Zaysse *ts'el-* ; Shinasha *ts'il-*)
251. *-t'îɬ-/*-t'ûɬ- "to glow"		*sšp* "to be white, be bright; make bright; lighten (darkness)" (stem + *p intens. of manner; C. *šōp*)	PLEC *t'ilḫ-/ *t'ulḫ- "coals" (stem + *ḫ iter.; PC *ɬ > PEC *l)		NOm: Ometo *ts'olint- "star" (stem + *n and *t n. suff.); NOm: Gonga *č'e:ll- "red" (Mocha *č'é:llo* ; n. < v. by V > V:; PO *ts' > Gonga *č')

	SEMITIC	EGYPTIAN	CUSHITIC	CHADIC	OMOTIC
252. *-t'ȃp- "to rise"	pPS *ṭp "to rise, swell" (Ehret 1989); *ṭps "to be fat" (stem + *s de-verb. comp., > adj. "fat," converted to v. "be fat")			Ng. *sáptó* "pile of grass, cornstalks, etc." (stem + *t n. suff.); *sə̀pk-* "to hitch child up on back" (caus. by *-u- infix > Ng. ə, plus *k dur.)	Gonga *č'ap- "to jump" (Mocha *'č 'äp-* ; PO *ts' > Gonga *č')
253. *-t'-p'- "to stamp"	pPS *ṭɓ "to hit, strike" (Ehret 1989)			some CCh *s'ɓ "to pound in mortar" (J)	
254. *t'eer- "long"	A. *ṭurṭur* "long and thin"; (redup. stem as intens.?); *ṭuruww* "to come from afar" (stem + *w denom.)		PEC *t'eer- "long"		*ts'eer- "deep" (Fleming 1974)

	SEMITIC	EGYPTIAN	CUSHITIC	CHADIC	OMOTIC
255. *t'îr- "strand"	A. *ṭurr* "hair hanging in front"		*t'îr- "strand"		NOm: Shinasha *ts'i:ra* "hair"
256. *-t'ur- "to be dirty"	pPS *ṭr "to be dirty" (Append.1)		PEC *t'ur- "to be dirty"		
257. *-t'as'-/*-t'is'- "to seep"	A. *ṭasl* "running water" (stem + *l n. suff.)		PEC *t'acc- "to seep" (PC *ts' > PEC *c)		Mocha *č'e:č'č'o* "marsh" (n. < v. by V > V:)
258. *-t'aaw- "to look at"	Ji. *ṭɔ̄f* (*ṭwf) "to scout; to visit" (stem + *f iter., i.e., "to scout," an action involving repeated or extended looking)		PSC *t'aawar- or *t'aawad- "to look over carefully" (stem + *z intens. of manner; PSC *d /V_-# < PC *z)		

		SEMITIC	EGYPTIAN	CUSHITIC	CHADIC	OMOTIC
259.	*-t'ay-/*-t'iy- "to be moist" (Eg., Sem. shared **innovation**: n. for "clay")	*ṭyn (*ṭayn) "clay" (stem + *n n. suff.)	*sin* "clay" (stem + *n n. suff.)	PEC *t'iyaag'- "to bleed; blood" (stem + $*\gamma^w$ comp.; PC $*\gamma^w$ > PEC *g')	Ng. *shìshìy* - "to melt" (redup. stem as freq.; PCh *s' apparently > Ng. *sh* [š] /_i)	
260.	*t'âyp'- "strand"	A. *ṭibat*, pl. *ṭibab* "long strip"	*spr* "rib" (stem + *l n. suff.; C. *spīr*)	*t'âyp'- "vein, hair, sinew" (Awngi *cicifí* "hair"; corrects Ehret 1987: #115)		NOm *ts'ayp'- "root" (Bench *ts'apm* 3,3: stem + *m n. suff.)
261.	*-t'eʔ- "to lack"	A. *ṭaʔṭaʔ* "to squander rapidly one's own" (redup. stem for intens.)	*s3r, s3ir* "need" (stem + *y inchoat., i.e., become lacking, needy, + *l n. suff.); *s3ry* "needy man" (n. + *y n. suff.)	PEC *t'eʔ- or *t'eʕ- "to lack"		

THE VELAR AND LABIOVELAR OBSTRUENTS IN *PAA*

Two further points of articulation showed the full range of obstruent manners of articulation in PAA. These two series, the velars and the labiovelars, apparently fell together as simple velars in Egyptian, Semitic, and Berber, but at least in Semitic and Egyptian by separate sound shifts, as required by Eg. shift #16 (which see below). The Ethiopic branch of South Semitic does have labiovelars, which, however, are commonly attributed to Cushitic interference. This solution has been disputed, but the evidence of Semitic vowel reconstruction (see Chapter 4 above) supports the conclusion that distinct labiovelars did not exist in PS. The velars and labiovelars also merged in Omotic — although only after certain other shifts that affected the adjacent vowels (for which see Chapter 4) — but they are clearly reconstructible as separate consonant sets in PC and PCh. Five manners of articulation are indicated by both the PS and PC evidence: voiced stop, voiceless stop, voiced fricative, voiceless fricative, and ejective, requiring postulation of PAA *g and *g^w, *k and *k^w, *ɣ and *$ɣ^w$, *x and *x^w, and *k' and *k^w'. The correspondence patterns among the branches are straightforward and provide solid support for these reconstructions.

A number of interesting sound shifts operated among the velars in Egyptian. For one thing, the supposed palatal versus non-palatal distinction between Eg. *ẖ* and *ḫ* may rather have been — and in origin certainly was — a voiceless-voiced distinction, since Eg. *ẖ* normally corresponds to PC *x and *x^w and to PS *x, and Eg. *ḫ* matches with PC *ɣ and *$ɣ^w$ and PS *ɣ (recall the earlier discussion of Eg. shift #8). Exceptions to these correspondences occur in Egyptian in the environments of proximate *n* and *r*, where PAA *x^w became Eg. *ḫ*. By a different rule, PAA *x > Eg. *ḫ* and *k > Eg. *g* /#w_ (#965 and 982). The absence of the sequences *ẖw and *kw as the first two consonants of Egyptian words (at least in Faulkner 1964), in contrast to the common occurrence of *ḫw and *gw, suggests that this latter sound shift may have been more general and occurred in the environment of any proximate *w. Assimilatory voicing would make sense in these environments, whereas "depalatalization" does not. A co-occurrence constraint, by prohibiting sequences of a velar stop followed in the same root by PAA *ʕ, yielded additional Eg. *ḫ* from the PAA velar stops: the PAA sequences *gVʕ, *kVʕ, and *k^wVʕ > Eg. *ḫ3*, whereas the voiced labial velar *g^w > Eg. *ḫ* without concurrently shifting PAA *ʕ to *3* ([ʔ]), i.e., PAA *g^wVʕ > Eg. *ḫ*ᶜ (see roots #290-292, 307, 308, 337, 338, and 349). These shifts can be summarized as follows (for Eg. shifts #9-11, see discussion of labial consonants above):

Eg. #12. PAA *x^w > pre-Eg. *$ɣ^w$ /n, r,

voicing velar fricatives in the vicinity of a proximate (alveolar?) sonorant in the same word;

Eg. #13. PAA *x(w) > *ɣ(w) > Eg. *ḫ* , *k > Eg. *g* /w, y.

voicing non-ejective voiceless velar obstruents in the environment of a following or preceding PAA *w or *y; and

#14. PAA *CVʕ > Eg. *ḫ3* (C = velar stop other than PAA *gʷ);
PAA *gʷVʕ > Eg. *ḫ*ᶜ.

Contrary to what might have been expected on the basis of previous work, as late as Middle Egyptian there is little evidence of the palatalization of velars in front-vowel environments. The only clear locus of such a shift is in certain suffixal elements of the shape *-Ci (roots #310 and 323); the conditioning environment for palatalization in the few cases where it appears may thus have been that of a front vowel in an unstressed, word-final syllable. The Egyptian entry under root #295 might seem to be an isolated case of front-vowel-induced palatalization in a root-initial velar, but the general failure of palatalization in a variety of parallel environments in other roots (e.g., #280, 301, 333, 360, 362, 396, 401, and 405) makes this explanation highly doubtful. PAA *g does become Eg. *ḏ* in a number of cases. But here the conditioning environment is a following voiced dental stop, with no front vowel required to trigger the shift (roots #265, 267, and 268); the *gʷ > *ḏ* shift of #295 evinces this pattern as well. One example (#331) has been found of PAA *k > Eg. *ṯ* /#_Vt; here V probably *was* PAA *i, but the change can better be interpreted as the direct counterpart for voiceless *k of the shift of voiced *g to *ḏ*. Generalizing, PAA velar stops would seem to become palatals when preceding a proximate dental stop of equivalent voicing in the same word:

#15. PAA *g(w) > Eg. *ḏ* /#_Vd;
PAA *k(w) > Eg. *ṯ* /#_Vt.

One notable Egyptian rule, merging the velars and labiovelars, operated after #12-14 and probably after #16 (which see below):

#17. PAA *Cʷ > Eg. C (C = [+velar]).

Egyptian apparently also developed an early constraint against most pairings of velar and lateral obstruents in the C_1 and C_2 positions in a root, a situation reflected in the almost complete lack of such sequences in the available data. For lateral-initial roots the general outcome in Egyptian appears to have been for the lateral to fall together with a dental of equivalent voicing: thus PAA *dl > Eg. *d* and PAA *tl' and *ɬ > Eg. *s* when preceding a velar obstruent (#843, 850, 875, 896, 897, and 903). The fact that the ejective lateral *tl' produced *s* in this particular context instead of *t*, the voiceless counterpart of *d*, argues that the delateralization shift took place before the ejective series of

PAA had been lost in pre-Egyptian. The shift, then, was:

Eg. #3. PAA *dl > Eg. *d*, *tl' > pre-Eg. *t', *ɬ > Eg. *s* /#_VC (C = velar obstruent).

Subsequently, Eg. rules #4-7 (discussed above in the section on dentals) collapsed the PAA ejectives with *s* in the language, in consequence also converting those PAA t' that had, by rule #3, come from PAA *tl': *tl' > *t' (by shift #3) > s (by shifts #4-7).

A constraint of more general applicability in Egyptian evidently removed all sequences of non-identical velar obstruents in C_1 and C_2 positions in a root. A variety of such pairings have been noted elsewhere in Afroasiatic — *gVk', *gVɣ, *kVg, and *kʷ'Vk' in Cushitic (Ehret 1980, 1987); *gVk, *gʷVk, *kVg, and *kʷVk in Chadic (Jungraithmayr and Shimizu 1981); *gVk, *gVk', *kVk', and *k'Vk in Omotic (cf. examples in Leslau 1959); and such forms as *gk' and *gx in pPS (e.g, Arabic *jaqq* "drop excrement" for *gk' and roots #371 and 381 for the sequence *gx). But no instances appear in the available Egyptian data. What became of such sequences during the evolution of that language remains an open question.

Far fewer co-occurrence constraints affected the Semitic velars. Apart from the more general disallowance in Semitic of any consecutive identical consonants in C_1 and C_2 position in a stem, only three co-occurrence-related shifts are identified here as specifically Semitic:

PS #3. PAA *ɣ > PS *g, *x > PS *k /#_VC$_{[+laryngeal]}$

(see roots #357, 358, 372, 373, 386, and 398); a velar fricative dissimilation in roots of the shape *-ɣ$^{(w)}$Vx-:

#4. PAA *ɣ$^{(w)}$ > PS *g /#_Vx

(see #371 and 381); and a possible third shift positively attested in just one instance so far (#850), but proposed nevertheless, because it would account for the almost complete lack of the sequence *dlVk'- in Semitic (PS *ḍḳ) — just one onomatopoetic verb, *ḍaqq*, "to resound," shows that sequence in Arabic:

#5. PAA *k$^{(w)}$' > PS *k /#dlV_.

Egyptian evinces a shift

Eg. #16. PAA *xVh > Eg. *kh* (see root #386),

which partially replicates PS #3 but is limited to *xVh (and presumably also PAA *xʷVh ?). It thus appears to be a separate sound change, parallel to that seen in Semitic but of more limited scope. A similar shift also arose independently in the Rift branch of Southern Cushitic (Ehret 1980: 73-75).

The retention of labiovelars into the initial stages of the evolution of the Egyptian language, as required by the specifically Eg. shifts #11-13, shows that the merging of labiovelars with velars took place separately in the prehistories of Egyptian and PS. The placement of the pPS version of this shift within the sequence of PS sound change rules remains to be worked out; for now it can be given the same representation as the equivalent Eg. rule:

PS #6. PAA *C^{w} > C (C = [+velar]).

Proto-Chadic can be shown to have continued PAA *g as PCh *g, *k as PCh *k, and *k' as PCh *k' (and in some subgroups of Chadic, as *ɗ^{y}; Newman's rendering of PCh *k' as *'j has been changed to *k' in the present work.) In Ngizim, the Chadic velar ejective *k' became /g/ word-initially, but apparently produced a variety of outcomes in non-initial position depending upon adjacent vowel and consonant environments: g /CV_(V)C, where both C = [+voice] (e.g., roots #134 and 554); Ø /CV_, where C = [+voice] (e.g., root #108); and k /CV_, where C = [-voice] (e.g., #511).

PAA *x and *x^{w} probably lasted as fricatives into PCh, if Newman's rare instances of reconstructed *x and *x^{w} are valid. Jungraithmayr and Shimizu (1981) give only *k and *k^{w} in their comparable items, but this may reflect their usual non-recognition of PCh fricative reconstructibility, seen also for PCh *f. In Ngizim, at least, PAA *x comes out as /k/. Further, all instances so far of the Chadic correspondents to PAA roots in *ɣ show stops, not fricatives: in Ngizim word-initial /g/ but /k/ verb-stem-final (e.g., roots #163 and 164 among others), and *g or *g/*k in the PCh cases drawn from Jungraithmayr and Shimizu. Given the discrepancy between Jungraithmayr-Shimizu and Newman as to the existence of velar fricatives, the need for PCh *x, *x^{w}, *ɣ, and *ɣ^{w} remains to be solidly determined. Newman's one case of *x^{w} in a PAA root with *ɣ^{w} (#377) and his additional instance of PCh *x corresponding to PAA *x^{w} (#504) favors the conclusion, however, that velar fricatives will be required in future PCh reconstructions.

Labiovelars certainly existed in PCh, as the instances of *x^{w} and *ɣ^{w} above indicate, but their correspondence patterns with PAA labiovelars are not entirely straightforward. More often than not the connection of PAA labiovelar to PCh labiovelar is overt (e.g., roots #296, 339, 377, and 399, among numerous examples); at other times, however, vowel shifts in PCh, probably of the form *C^{w}ə > *Cə, have elided the labial feature (e.g., roots #346, 347, and 404, among others).

One notable devoicing shift, or pair of shifts, affected velars in Cushitic, namely the conversion of PAA *g to PC *k when the preceding stem consonant was PAA *d or *w:

PC #2. PAA *g > PC *k /#dV_ and /#wV_.

Potential additional, parallel environments involving preceding *#bV_ and *#yV_ for this shift will be worth looking for in future studies. A second apparent, but as yet weakly attested, PC velar sound shift dissimilated the first of two non-identical consecutive velar fricatives in a root, converting it to the equivalent stop (see roots #371 and 381):

#3. PAA *ɣ > PC *g /#_Vx-.

In Omotic the labiovelar series merged with the simple velars, according the developments depicted as Omotic sound shifts #3, 4, and 9 in Chapter 4. The fricative members of these two series produced reflexes of uncertain articulation in PO, but apparently distinct from those of PAA *k and *k^w (which both became PO *k). PAA *ɣ, *$ɣ^w$, and *x^w yielded, it appears, a consonant represented as PO *x_1, while PAA *x produced proposed PO *x_2 (see Table 1 in Chapter 2 and Table 9 at end of this chapter). The collapsing of *ɣ, *$ɣ^w$, and *x^w as one consonant in PO would require an additional PO sound shift rule preceding #3, 4, and 9; the features of such a rule remain to be defined, however, and it has not been included among the other Omotic shifts (see Appendix 4).

PAA *g	SEMITIC	EGYPTIAN	CUSHITIC	CHADIC	OMOTIC
262. *gâb- "great (especially in size but also in number)"	pPS *gb "great" (Append.1; A. *jabl* "numerous"; etc.; *jabbar* "great, mighty")		PSC *gâb- "stout, strong, thick"		*gab- "great (in size, amount)" (NOm: Mocha *gábino* "large" [stem + *n adj. suff.]; SOm: Banna *gäbri* "many" [stem + *r adj. suff.])
263. *gâb- "top"	*gbl "mountain" (stem + *l n. suff.; A. *jabal*)		PSC *gâb- "above, up, on"		
264. *gub-/*gab- "trunk"	A. *jibāl* "body" (stem + *l n. suff.)	LE *gbw* "stick"	SC: PR *gubayi "trunk" (stem + *y n. suff.)	Ng. *gùvu* "stem of a plant"	Ometo *gab- "belly"; SOm: Ari *gubi* "navel"

		SEMITIC	EGYPTIAN	CUSHITIC	CHADIC	OMOTIC
265.	*-gâd-/*-gûd- "to be big"	A. *jadd* "to be great"	*ḏd3* "fat" (stem + *r or *ʔ adj. suff.; C. *jatɛ* "to become old, mature"	*gâd-/*gûd- "big"; PSC *ăgad- "man, adult male" (*a- attrib. pref. + stem, i.e., one who is big)	*g-d- "many" (N)	SOm. *guddum- "long" (stem + *m adj. suff.); SOm: Dime *gä:d* "big" (adj. < v. by V > V:)
266.	*-găd- "to lower, put down"	A. *jadl* "to throw down" (stem + *l fin.)		*găd-/*gĭd- "to put down"	*gad "to fall" (J)	NOm *gad- "to put down" (Koyra *gad-*; Mocha *gàd-*)
267.	*-gaad- "to stay"		*ḏd* "stable, enduring" (LE "to be stable, endure, abide"; C. *jto*)	*gaad- "to stay"	WCh, CCh *gd- "house" (J; semantics: "stay" > dwell" > "dwelling")	

		SEMITIC	EGYPTIAN	CUSHITIC	CHADIC	OMOTIC
268.	*-gii d-/*-guud- "to go around; put around"	A. *jadr* "wall, enclos- ure; to wall in" (stem + *r n. suff.; v. < n.)	*ḏdḥ* "to shut up, imprison" (stem + *ḥ iter. > dur.; C. *jtah*)			Mocha *gṳ:d-* "to go around"
269.	*-gădz- "to stretch out, extend (intr.)"	A. *jaðb* "to stretch, ex- tend" (stem + *b extend.); *jaðw* "to be fat" (stem + *y inchoat.)			Ng. *gâzbər* "tall; long; deep" (stem + *b ex- tend., as in A., + *r adj. suff.)	SOm: Ari *gažmi* "long" (stem + *m adj. suff.);
270.	*-gaf- "to oppose, give trouble"	A. *jafiṣ* "refractory, obstinate" (stem + *tl' foc.); *jafw* "to oppress; molest " (stem + *w inchoat.)	*gfn* "to rebuff" (stem + *n non-fin.)	EC: Soomaali *gaf* "to offend, do a wrong to someone"		

	SEMITIC	EGYPTIAN	CUSHITIC	CHADIC	OMOTIC
271. *-gâf- "to hold, take hold of"	A. *jaff* "to collect and take away"; *jafjaf* "to hold firm, gather an keep together" (redup. as freq.)			Ng. *gáfa*- "to grasp, hold stationary object; hold out, extend" (stem + *-a incep.)	NOm: Bench *gopt* [4] "trap, net" (stem + *dl m.v.; n. < v. by V > V: ?; *V: > V in Bench)
272. *-gûf-/*-gâf- "to go down"	A. *jafjaf* "low ground; plain" (redup.); *jafy* "to throw down" (stem + *y inchoat. > tr.: become low > put low)		*gâf-/*gûf- "to descend, fall"		
273. *-gûf- "to bend, turn (intr.)"	MSA *gfw "to turn over" (stem + *w inchoat. > dur.)		EC: Oromo *guguf*- "to stoop, bend over" (redup. stem)	*gəfu "knee" (N) (Ng. ***kùfú***; stem + *w denom.)	Mocha *gu̜:p*- "to turn over"

		SEMITIC	EGYPTIAN	CUSHITIC	CHADIC	OMOTIC
274.	*-geh- "to speak"	A. *jahjah* "to cry out" (redup. stem as intens.); *jahr* "to divulge" (stem + *r dif-fus.)	*g3g3* "to chant" (re-dup. stem as freq.) (LE *g3*)	SC: PR *geh- "to speak"	CCh *g- "mouth" (J)	*geh- "to say" (Bench *gah* 4)
275.	*-guḫ-/*-giḫ- "to swell, rise, grow"	A. *jaḫḫ* "to spread" *jaḫr* "to rise on high" (stem + *r dif-fus.)	*g3b* "leaf" (stem + *b anim. de-verb.; seman-tics: see #742; C. *čōbɛ, čōōbɛ*)	*guḫ- "to swell, grow"		NW Ometo *git- "big" (stem + *y inchoat. + *t adj. suff.)
276.	*-gāl- "to show"	A. *jalw* "to reveal, dis-close" (stem + *w ext. > tr.)		PSC *gal- or *gaal- (*ˉ or *ˇ) "to look at, look over"	*gl "to show" (J); WCh, ECh *gal "to see" (J)	Mocha *'gal-* "to reveal"
277.	*-gaal- "to be alight, be afire"	MSA *gl(l) "to be alight"	*gnḫw* "star" (stem + *x^w extend.fort. + *w deverb.)			Mocha *gạ:l-* "to be melted (of butter)"

	SEMITIC	EGYPTIAN	CUSHITIC	CHADIC	OMOTIC
278. *gam- "side of the head"		*gm3* "temple (of head)" (stem + *r n. suff.)	*gamm- "mane" (reason for gemination is unclear here)	WCh, CCh *gm "head" (J)	
279. *-gâm-/*-gûm- "to break off, tear off"	pPS *gm "to cut off" (Ehret 1989)	*gmgm* "to smash, tear up, break" (redup. as intens.; C. *čomčm*)	*gâm-/*gûm- "to break to pieces"	CCh *gm "to carve wood" (J)	
280. *-gim- "to come upon, meet up with"	pPS *gm "to come together" (Append. 1)	*gmi* "to find" (stem + *y denom. > tr., > dur.?; C. *jīmī*)	EC: Soomaali *jimee* "to compare; measure" (stem + *y inchoat. > dur.; i.e, bring together in order to compare)	*g-mə "to meet" (N)	

	SEMITIC	EGYPTIAN	CUSHITIC	CHADIC	OMOTIC
281. *-găŋ-/*-gĭŋ- "to grow, grow up, mature" (Ch., Eg., Sem. **innovation**: specialization of meaning to plant growth)	A. *jans* "to ripen fully" (stem + *s' fort.)	*gnw* "branches (?)" (of trees)	*găŋ- "to become large"	some WCh *gn- "leaf" (J; semantics: see #742 below)	Mocha *gè:n-* "to be old"; *ge:no* "old man" (v. < n. after n. < PO v. *gen- by V > V: ; velar dissim.: PAA *ŋ > PO *n /#gV_ before *ŋ > *g /_-#)
282. *-guup'- "to soak; to drench, of rain" (Berber, e.g., Shilh *agafay* "cloud," implies a 2nd root shape *-gaap'-)	A. *jubb* "deep well; cistern; water-bag"; *jiban* "water in a cistern" (stem + *n n. suff.)	*igp* "cloud" (*i- attrib. pref. + stem; C. *čēpε*)	EC: Soomaali *guube* "part of camel placenta" (PC *p' > Som. *b*)	Ng. *gùɓ-* "to soak (herbs, etc., to make medicine)"	NOm *gu:p'- "cloud" (Mocha *gu:ppo* "cloud, fog"; Maji: Sheko *gɨbu* "cloud")
283. *gâr- "forest, bush"			PSC *gâr- or *gâd- "forest"	*g-r- "bush" (N)	

	SEMITIC	EGYPTIAN	CUSHITIC	CHADIC	OMOTIC
284. *-gêrʕ- "to become old"			PEC *gerʕ- "to become old"	*garə "to grow old" (N) (Ng.*gár*-)	
285. *-gĭr- "to sit"	pPS *gr "to go down" (Append.1; A. *jarr* "foot of mountain")	*gr* "to be still, be silent, be quiet; cease, desist" (C. *čō*)	*gĭr- "to sit, lie, be low"	CCh *gr "to stand" (J; semantics: sit > stay, hence stand (still))	
286. *-gŭs- "to drive away"		*gsi* "to run" (stem + *y inchoat.); *gst* "speed; run; course"	*gŭs- "to take out, drive out"		
287. *-gāš- "to chew"	A. *jasʕ* "to chew the cud" (stem + *ʕ part.; semantics: break *apart* food by chewing)		EC: Soomaali *gaso* "good grass area in mountains" (semantics: area for aninmals *to graze* in)	WCh, ECh *gs- "chin" (J; semantics: < movements of chin in chewing, as in derivation of Fr. *machoire*)	Gonga-Bench $*gaš_1$- "tooth" (Mocha *gášo* ; Bench *gaš* 2-3)

		SEMITIC	EGYPTIAN	CUSHITIC	CHADIC	OMOTIC
288.	*-guš- "to feel, run fingers over"	A. *jass* "to feel, touch"	*gs* "to anoint (someone); smear on (unguent)"; *gsw* "ointment"			SOm *guš$_1$- "claw, nail"
289.	*-gêz- "to get, gain"	pPS *gz "to get, gain" (Append.1); A. *gadan* "gift, bounty" (stem + *n n. suff.; PAA *z > BA *d n.-stem-final)		*gêz- "to get"	gɗ "granary" (J; semantics: "get" > "keep")	
290.	*-gaʕ- or *-gaaʕ- "to be sick"	MSA *gʕr "to fail" (S. "to fall ill with fever") (stem + *r diffus.)	*ḫ3yt* "disease" (stem + *y deverb. + *t n. suff.)	SC: PR *gaʕ- "to be sick"		

	SEMITIC	EGYPTIAN	CUSHITIC	CHADIC	OMOTIC
291. *-guʕ- "to become wet"	*gʕs "to expel fluid" (stem + *s' fort. or *s caus.)	*ḫ3t* "marsh" (stem + *t n. suff.)	SC: Alagwa *guʕ-* "to sink"	CCh *gʔ "to wash" (J)	Ometo: Male *goʔ-* "to flow"
292. *-guʕ- or *-guuʕ- "to kill" (#290 with *-u- tr. infix?)	A. *jaʕjaʕ* "to slaughter" (redup. stem as intens.)	*ḫ3t* "corpse" (stem + *t n. suff.); *ḫ3yt* "slaughter, massacre" (stem + *y de-verb. + *t n. suff.)	SC: Alagwa *guʕuma* "corpse" (stem + *m n. suff.)		

PAA *g^w

	SEMITIC	EGYPTIAN	CUSHITIC	CHADIC	OMOTIC
293. *g^{w}âa "cut" (n.)	A. *jaub* "to split, tear, cut through" (stem + *w de-verb. + *p' fin. fort.);		*g^{w}âa "cut" (n.)		

	SEMITIC	EGYPTIAN	CUSHITIC	CHADIC	OMOTIC
	jaib "to split, cut" (stem + *y de-verb. + *p' fin. fort.)				
294. *-g^wăb- "to not do"	A. *jabʔ* "to desist; detest, abhor" (stem + *ʔ conc., i.e., stop doing *particular* thing); *jabh* "to see water without being able to reach it" (stem + *h ampl.)	*gb* "deficiency, deprivation" LE *gbi* "to be weak, lame, deprived, deficient, parted from" (stem + *y inchoat.; C. *čbbɛ*, *jōb* "weak")	*g^wab- "to stop (intr.)"		NOm: Yem *gāw-* "to be satisfied" (i.e., not need to do)
295. *-g^wad-/*-g^wid- "to cut"	pPS *gd "to cut" (Append.1)	*ḏdb* "to sting" (stem + *b extend.)	EC: Soomaali *gud* "to circumcise"	*g^wad-/*g^wdm "spear" (J; stem + *m n. suff.)	

	SEMITIC	EGYPTIAN	CUSHITIC	CHADIC	OMOTIC
296. *g^{w}ĭd-/*g^{w}ăd- "land"			PSC *gŭd- "land, country"	*g^{w}id/*g^{w}ud "place" (J)	NOm *gad- "earth" (Ometo *gad-; Mocha *gadó* "clod of earth")
297. *-g^{w}âh- "to ooze, run out (bodily fluid)"	A. *jahiḍ* "miscarriage" (stem + *dl m.v.)	*g3p* "to lance (?) (an infection)" (stem + *p intens. of manner; i.e., make pus ooze out); LE *g3š* "to spill" (stem + *ɬ ven.; C. *čōš*)	PSC *g^{w}âhu "ulcer, sore"		
298. *-g^{w}aḫ- "to stay"	pPS *gḫ "to stay" (Append.1)	*g3ḫ* "to be weary" (stem + *ḫ iter.; i.e., stay still because of being tired)	*g^{w}aḫ- "to stay"		Ometo *geḫ- "to sleep"

	SEMITIC	EGYPTIAN	CUSHITIC	CHADIC	OMOTIC
299. *-g^weḥ- "to scrape"	pPS *gḥ "to scrape off" (Ehret 1989)		PSC *g^weḥ- "to scratch"	Ng. *gùut-* "to scrape ground" (stem + *t dur.; PC *h > Ng. Ø)	
300. *-g^waj- "to impel, make move (by pushing, pulling)	*gðb "to draw out" (MSA "to pull (out)," A."attract, draw off": stem + *b extend.)		PEC *goc- or *g'oc- "to pull toward one" (PC *dz > PEC *c; PC Cwa > Co /_c)		NOm *gač- "to impel" (Mocha *'gačč-* "to push forward"; Ari, Ometo *goč-* "pull," etc., are probable EC loans)
301. *-g^wĭl- "to bend, turn (intr.)"	pPS *gl "to turn" (Ehret 1989)	*grt* "loins" (stem + *t n. suff.; semantics: place at which the body bends; C. *člōt*)	*g^wĭlb- "knee" (stem + *b anim. deverb.)		NOm *gulbat- "knee" (probable loan < Cush.? See Cush. entry for structure; Cush. root + *t n. suff.)

	SEMITIC	EGYPTIAN	CUSHITIC	CHADIC	OMOTIC
302. *-g^{w}ar- "to turn (intr.)"			*g^{w}ar- "to turn (intr.)"	*g^{w}rp/*grf "knee; to kneel" (J; stem + *f iter.; semantics: original reference to recurrent bending of the knee?)	NOm: Bench *gart* ^{2} "to roll (intr.)" (stem + *t dur.); *gars* ^{4} "to roll (tr.)" (stem + *s caus.)
303. *-g^{w}ar-/*-g^{w}ir- "to tear off"	pPS *gr "to remove, strip" (Ehret 1989)	LE *grb* "to trim, shape" (stem + *b extend.)	*g^{w}arp-/*g^{w}irp- "to cut off" (stem + *p intens. of manner)		
304. *-g^{w}ăats- "to strip (from the ground)"	A. *jaθθ* "to cut off or down, uproot"		PSC *g^{w}ăadeets'i "eagle" (stem + *s' fort.; PSC *d /V_VC < PC *ts; semantics: < eagle's manner of seizing prey)		NOm *gots- "to plow, till" (Mocha *gós*-)

	SEMITIC	EGYPTIAN	CUSHITIC	CHADIC	OMOTIC
305. $*\text{-}g^w\hat{\imath}ts\text{-}$ "to be small"			SC: Dahalo *g*^{w}*ɨ́tstsa* "small"		NOm *gu:tsts-/ *gi:tsts- "small" (Mocha *gi:šo*; adj. < v. by V > V:); Mocha *gɨ̱:šš*- "to be little" (back-formation < adj.)
306. $*\text{-}g^w\hat{\imath}ʔ\text{-}/*\text{-}g^waʔ\text{-}$ "to sip"	pPS *gʔ "to take a sip or swallow" (Ehret 1989)		SC: Dahallo *g*^{w}*ɨ̀ʔi* "thirst"		SOm *gaʔ- "to bite"
307. $*\text{-}g^w$iiʕ-/$*\text{-}g^w$aaʕ- "to swallow"	A. *jaʕʕ* "to eat earth, clay"; *jaʕam* "to have an appetite" (stem + *m extend.)	*ḫ* ^{c}*mw* "throat" (stem + *m n. suff. or *m extend. + *w n. suff.)	$*g^w$aaʕ-/$*g^w$iiʕ- "to swallow" (Ehret 1987: $*g^w$-ʕ-)		

Velar and Labiovelar Obstruents of PAA: *k

	SEMITIC	EGYPTIAN	CUSHITIC	CHADIC	OMOTIC
308. *gʷaʕb- "throat" (root #307 + *b anim. deverb.)		LE *ḫ ᶜb* "throat"	*gʷaʕb- "throat"		
PAA *k					
309. *kaa "this" (demons.)		*ky* "other, another" (stem + *y adj. suff.; C. *kɛ*)	PSC *kaa "this" (masc. bound demons.)		SOm: Ari-Banna *ka: "this"; NOm: Mao *-ka "that"
310. *ki "you" (fem. sing. bound pron.)	A. *-ki* 2nd person fem. sing. suff. suff. (PS *-ki)	*ṯ* 2nd person fem. sing. suff. (< *ki by palatalization; see also Diakonov 1988); *ntṯ* "you (fem., sing.)" (indep. pron. base *nt-* + root)	PSC *ki "your (fem. sing.)"	*ki "you (fem. sing.)" (Ng. *kə̀m*)	

	SEMITIC	EGYPTIAN	CUSHITIC	CHADIC	OMOTIC
311. *ku, *ka "you" (masc. sing. bound pron.) (*ka as Eg., Sem., Ch. **innovation** ?)	A. *-ka* 2nd person masc. sing. suff. (PS *-ka)	*k* 2nd person masc. sing. suff. (C.-*k*); *ntk* "you (masc. sing.)" (indep. pron. base *nt-* + root)	PSC *ku "your (masc. sing.)"	*kV (*ka, *ku) "you (masc. sing.)" (Ng. *ka* , *cì*)	
312. *-kuc- or *-koc- or *-kooc- "to flow"	pPS *kθ "to flow" (Append.1)			WCh, CCh *ks "to pour" (J)	NOm: Bench *koș(k)* 4 "to flow"
313. *-kăac'- "to catch hold of"	A. *kaẓm* "to suppress one's anger; shut the door; dam off water-course" (stem + *m extend.)		*ka(a)c'- "to catch, hold fast"		Mocha *kà:č'-* "to draw the sword"

	SEMITIC	EGYPTIAN	CUSHITIC	CHADIC	OMOTIC
314. *-kŭuf-/*-kăaf- "to wrap up, cover by wrapping"	A. *kaff* "to wrap up in bandages"; *kafr* "to cover, conceal" (stem + *r diffus.)	*kf3* "to be discreet" (stem + probably *ʔ adj. suff., with v. < earlier adj.; semantics: covered > concealed > discreet)	PSC *kuuf- "to close, shut"	WCh *kp "bark (of tree)" (J)	Mocha *kà:p-* "to envelop, wrap up"
315. *-kăḫ- "to not be"	A. *kaḫt* "to clean; drive away" (stem + *t dur.; semantics: cause not to be there by cleaning off or driving away); *kaḫṣ* "to efface; be wiped away" (stem + *tl' foc.)		*kăḫ- "to not be"; *kuḫ- "to not allow, deny" (stem with *-u- tr. infix)		

	SEMITIC	EGYPTIAN	CUSHITIC	CHADIC	OMOTIC
316. *-kal- "to turn round"	MSA *kly "to bring/come home (of animals)" (stem + *y inchoat.; i.e., *return* from grazing)	*knm* "to wrap" (stem + *m extend.; C. *čl̥omlm*, with partial redup. as freq.)	*kal-/*kil- "to go round"	Ng. *kàlàkt*- "to go back, return" (stem + *k dur. + *t dur.)	Mocha *ka:llo* "turn" (n.) (n. < v. by V > V:)
317. *-kal-/*-kul- "all"	*kl(l) "all" (A. *kull*)		PSC *ʔâkale "all" (*a- attrib. pref. + stem)		SOm *kull- "all"
318. *kol- "inner shoulder"	A. *kalkal* "upper part of chest" (redup. stem)		*kolm- "nape" (stem + *m n. suff.)		
319. *-kul- "to meet"	A. *kalt*, *kalz* "to gather, assemble" (stem + *t dur.; + *z intens. of manner)	C. *čīnε* "to find" (stem + *y v. ext.; Vycichl attributes this to #297, but has to assume special conditions)	PSC *kul- "to meet"		

	SEMITIC	EGYPTIAN	CUSHITIC	CHADIC	OMOTIC
320. *-kǒɬ- "to take"	pPS *kɬ "to take away" (Ehret 1989; see also #337)		*kǒɬ- "to take hold of" (Ehret 1980: 331)		
321. *-kam- "to hold"	pPS *km "to hold" (Ap-pend.1)		PSC *kam- "to hold"	*km "to carry (load)" (J)	SOm: Ari *kam*- "to pick up"
322. *-kǔm- "to add together"	A. *kamm* "to assemble"	*km* "to total up, amount to"; *km* (y)*t* "herd of cattle" (stem + *y de-verb. + *t coll.)	*kǔm- "multitude, large number" (Agaw "cattle")		NOm *kum- "to increase (in volume, height)" (Ometo: Koyra *kum*- "to fill"; Yesma *kùmā̀* "hill")
323. *kuuna "you (pl. bound)" (root #311 + old Afro-asiatic pl. in *n, as also in #210)	MSA *-kn "you; your (fem. pl. suff.)" (PS *kəna)	*ṯn* "you" (pl. suff.; C. *-tēnɛ*); *ntṯn* "you (pl.)" (in-dep. pron. base *nt*- + root)	PSC *kuna "your (pl.)" (V-shortening is as yet unex-plained, but may well be to old morpho-logical rules)	*kun "you (pl.)" (Ng. *kùn*)	

		SEMITIC	EGYPTIAN	CUSHITIC	CHADIC	OMOTIC
324.	*kanf-/*kinf- "wing"	A. *kanaf* "wing of a bird"		*kanf-/*kinf- "wing"		*ki:p-/*ka:p- "wing" (Ometo *kep-; SOm: Ari *ka:fi* ; NOm *i: > *e by Omotic shifts #11, 12 in Chap. 4)
325.	*kâns- "loins"		*kns* "pubic region (?)" (LE "vulva")	PSC *kânsi "umbilical cord"		
326.	*-kep- "to cease, no longer function"	pPS *kp "to stop, cease" (Ap-pend.1)		PSC *kep- "to be useless, to have ceased to work well"	*kpn "old" (J; stem + *n adj. suff.)	
327.	*kop- "sole (of foot)"	MSA *kf(f) "flat of hand; claw, paw" (*kaf)	LE *kp* "sole; palm"	PEC *kob- "sandal" (PC *p > PEC *b)	*k-p- "hoof" (N) (J: *kb(n) "shoe")	

	SEMITIC	EGYPTIAN	CUSHITIC	CHADIC	OMOTIC
328. *-kâr- "to turn round, go round"	A. *karr* "to unroll itself"; *kary*, *karw* "to make in the form of balls" (stem + *y, *w inchoat.)	LE *krs* "to skip, caper, dance, jump" (stem + probably *ts diffus.)	PSC *kar- "to turn around"; *karf-/*kirf- "to turn about" (stem + *f iter.)	ECh *kr "to dance" (J)	NOm: Bench *kar* 3 "to be round"; SOm: Ari *kɛrmi* "fence" (stem + + *m n. suff.; semantics: to surround a place)
329. *-kûr- "to dig out"	pPS *kr "to dig out, scrape out" (Ehret 1989)	*krp* "to scrape out" (stem + *p intens. of manner; C. *čōrf*)	PSC *kûr- or *kûur- "to cultivate"	*kr "fields" (J); some CCh, ECh *krl "hoe" (J; stem + *l n. suff.)	
330. *-kur-/*-kar- "to cut up"	A. *kard* "to cut off, shear" (stem + *d dur.; semantics: shearing is an extended action)	LE *krt* "carnage, massacre" (stem + *t n. suff.); C. *čort* "knife" (stem + *t n. suff.)	PSC *kur- "to mince"	Ng. *kárm*- "to chop, cut down, cut off" (stem + *m extend.)	

	SEMITIC	EGYPTIAN	CUSHITIC	CHADIC	OMOTIC
331. *-kît- "to produce water"	A. *katt* "to pour out, spill"	*ṯtf* "to flow down; overflow" (stem + *f iter.)		WCh, CCh *kt "cold" (J; semantics: see #458)	Mocha *'kit-* "to draw water"
332. *-kitḫ- "to drink up, eat up" (root #331 + *ḫ iter.)	A. *katḫ* "to eat to satiety"		SC: WR *kitaḫ- "to drink"		
333. *-keetl'- "to threaten"	A. *kaṣy* "to fall into contempt" (stem + *y inchoat.)	*kṯmw* "threats" (stem + *m n. suff. + *w pl.)	EC: Afar *keexo* "violating the peace and thus creating a state of uneasiness" (*x* = [d'] < PC *tl)	some WCh *kɨr "to fear" (J; stem + *r diffus.; semantics: to feel threatened)	
334. *-kîts- "to expand (intr.)"	pPS *kθ "to increase (in size, volume, amount)" (Append.1)			some WCh *ks "long" (J)	NOm: Bench *kits* 3 "to swell"

	SEMITIC	EGYPTIAN	CUSHITIC	CHADIC	OMOTIC
335. *-kaw- "to step along"	A. *kaus* "to walk on three feet (of animal); walk slowly" (stem + *s' fort. or *ts diffus.); *kauʕ* "to walk on side of foot" (stem + *ʕ part., i.e., bending foot *away from* direction of one's progress)		*kaw- "to advance"	Ng. *kə̀má* "in front of, ahead; keep doing" (stem + *m adj. suff.)	Mocha *'kot-* "to stamp the mud" (stem + *t dur.)
336. *-kaʔ- "to cover up, enclose"		*k3p* "to cover" (stem + *p' fin. fort.; C. *kōp* "to hide"); *k3p* "hide (of fowler)" (n.< v.);	SC: PR *kaʔa "shell, sheath"; SC: PR *kaʔafu "doorway" (stem + *f iter.; semantics: item that is closed up each night)		

	SEMITIC	EGYPTIAN	CUSHITIC	CHADIC	OMOTIC
		k3pt "linen cover" (stem + *t n. suff.); *k3pw* "roof" (stem + *w deverb.)			
337. *-kâʕ- "to rise"	pPS *kʕ "to swell" (Ap-pend.1)	*ḫ3d* "dough" (stem + *d dur.); *ḫ3st* "hill-country; foreign land; desert" (stem + *s deverb. comp., i.e., raised area of land, + *t coll. suff.)	*kâʕ- "to get up"	*ka "head" (N; n.< v. by V > VV?)	Ometo: Malo *kaʔ-* "to ripen" (rise > grow > mature hence, ripen)

	SEMITIC	EGYPTIAN	CUSHITIC	CHADIC	OMOTIC
338. *-kĭʕ- "to turn (intr.), bend"	A. *kaʕz* "to make a somersault" (stem + *z intense. of manner)	*ḫ3b* "to be bent (of arm)" (stem + *b extend.); *ḫ3s* "curl on front of Red Crown" (stem + *s deverb. comp. suff.); *ḫ3m* "to bow down; bend (arm in attitude of respect)" (stem + *m extend.)	PSC *kiʕ- "to turn aside, veer off course"		NOm: Yem *kēʔā̄* "knee"

PAA *k^{w}	SEMITIC	EGYPTIAN	CUSHITIC	CHADIC	OMOTIC
339. *-k^{w}ăac- or *-k^{w}ăats- "to scratch (with an implement)"	A. *kaθʔ* "to skim" (stem + *ʔ conc.; semantics: to scrape off just the thin top layer of something)		PSC *k^{w}ăadaak^{w}- "to scrape off" (stem + *k^{w} fin.; PSC *d /V_VC < PC *ts)	WCh *k^{w}s "hoe" (J)	Mocha *'kos-* "to make fire fire by rubbing pieces of wood" (for NOm *V < PO *V: here, see #324 above)
340. *-k^{w}âd- or *-k^{w}âad- "to make a loud noise"	A. *kadkad* "to laugh immoderately" (redup. as intens.); *kadaf* "clatter of the hoofs" (stem + *f iter.)		PSC *k^{w}âad- "thunder" (possible n. < v. by V > VV?)		

	SEMITIC	EGYPTIAN	CUSHITIC	CHADIC	OMOTIC
341. *-k^wâḫ- or *-k^wâaḫ- "to become worn out"	A. *kaḫl* "infertile year; to be infertile and harm the people" (stem *l n. suff.; v. < n.)	*kḫkḫ* "to become old" (redup. stem as intens.?) tens.?)	PSC *k^waaḫ- "tiredness" (n. < v. by V > VV?)	Ng. *kwáaɓ-* "to not go well, come out badly" (stem + *p' fin. fort.)	
342. *-k^wal- "to pound"	A. *kalʔ* "to beat, whip" (stem + *ʔ conc.; semantics: whip has extremely narrow striking surface)		*k^wal- "to pound"		
343. *ink^wal- "kidney"	*kl(l) "kidney"		*ink^wal-/ *ank^wal- "kidney" (corrects Ehret 1987: #95; probable regular shifts, PAA *VN > NE *N		[Ometo: Koyra *kaláttе* ; SOm: Ari *kɛla* "kidney": separate loans < Eastern Cushitic]

	SEMITIC	EGYPTIAN	CUSHITIC	CHADIC	OMOTIC
			/#_CV, > BA *Ø, for which see Append. 4)		
344. *-k^{w}âał- "to go away"	pPS *kł "to go away" (Ehret 1989; homonymous with pPS root in #320)		PSC *k^{w}âał- "to go, travel"		
345. *k^{w}eer- "bush, brush, uncleared land"	MSA *kr m "mountain" (stem + *m n. suff.)	*k3k3* "bush (?), brush (?)" (re-dup. stem)	*k^{w}eer- "uncleared land, bush area"		
346. *k^{w}ĭr- "to twist (intr.)"	A. *karb* "to twist a rope" (stem + *b ex-tend.)		PSC *k^{w}ĭrih- or *k^{w}ĭriih- "to turn (intr.)" (stem + *h ampl.)	some WCh *krl/*krd "snake" (J; stem + probab-ly *l n. suff.; alternate shape: stem + *d dur.)	

	SEMITIC	EGYPTIAN	CUSHITIC	CHADIC	OMOTIC
347. *-k^wĭš- "to grasp"	pPS *kc "to grasp" (Ehret 1989)			WCh, CCh *ks "to take"	NOm *$kuš_2$-/*$kiš_2$- "hand" (Mocha *kišó*; Bench *kuč* [1]; Yem *kúšū*)
348. *-k^watl'- or *-k^waatl'- "to turn (intr.)	A. *kuṣūm* "to retreat, return without having obtained one's objective" (stem + *m extend.)	*kṯr* "charioteer" (stem + *l n. suff.; semantics: < turning of chariot wheels)	SC: Alagwa *kwatl-* "to stir" (expected *kwaɬ-?)	some CCh *kɬ "to kneel" (J)	
349. *-k^wâʕ- "to run away"	pPS *kʕ "to run away" (Append.1)	*ḫ3r* "to bolt (?) (of horses)" (stem + *l fin.); *ḫ3ḫ* "to be speedy; hurry" (stem + *$ɣ^w$ comp.);	PSC *k^wâʕ- "to run away"		

	SEMITIC	EGYPTIAN	CUSHITIC	CHADIC	OMOTIC
		ḫ3s "to scramble (?)" (stem + *ts diffus.)			
PAA *ɣ					
350. *ɣă "tree" (Sem., Eg. **innovation**: addition of *t n. suff.)	A. *ɣatal* "to be densely overgrown with trees" (stem + *t n. suff. + *l adj. suff.)	*ḫt* "wood; woodland; stick; pole; rod" (stem + *t n. suff., as in Sem.; see #887 for proposed etymon of C. "wood")	*ɣă "tree"		
351. *-ɣab- "to stop, stay"	A. *ɣabb* "to pass the night"; *ɣubūr* "to tarry; remain, be left" stem + *r diffus.)	*ḫbḫb* "to hobble" (redup. stem as freq.)	*ɣab- "to stay, stop, remain"		

	SEMITIC	EGYPTIAN	CUSHITIC	CHADIC	OMOTIC
352. *-ɣŭb-/*-ɣăb- "to cut"		*ḫbt* "place of execution" (stem + *t n. suff.); *ḫbḫb* "to pierce; kill" (redup. as intens.; C. *šobšεb*) *ḫbs* "to hack up (earth)" (stem + *s' fort. oř *s non-fin.)	*ɣăb-/*ɣŭb- "to cut"	some CCh, ECh *gub "hole" (J; n. < v. by V > VV [PCh *u < PAA *uu])	
353. *-ɣâf- "to fit on top of, go above or in front of"	A. *ɣafr* "to cover, veil" (stem + *r n. n. suff. < n. root seen in *ɣifār* "helmet")	*ḫft* "in front of, in accordance with, corresponding to" (stem + *t adj. suff.)	SC: Iraqw *xafi* "makeshift hut" (PC *ɣ > PSC *x)		

	SEMITIC	EGYPTIAN	CUSHITIC	CHADIC	OMOTIC
354. *ɣŏɣ- "crust"		LE *ḫḫ* "dermatitis (?)"	*ɣoɣ- "husk, rind, crust" (EC "skin, hide")	Ng. *gàgái* "earth, soil, the ground" (stem + *y n. suff.)	[Yem *gò:gó* "skin": loan < EC]
355. *ɣooɣ- "gullet"		*ḫḫ* "neck, throat" (C. *xax*)	[HEC *kokk- "throat": loan < unidentified Omotic source]		Mocha *ko:kko* "oral cavity"
356. *ɣah- "skin"		*ḫ3wt* "hide (of animal)"	*ɣah- "skin, flesh, body"		
357. *-ɣaaḫ- "to examine"	pPS *gḫ "to examine" (Append.1)	*ḫ3i* "to measure; examine (patient)" (stem + *y inchoat. > dur.; C. *šī*); *ḫ3yw* "measurements" (stem + Eg. *w* pl.);	*ɣaaḫn- "to know, understand" (stem + *n non-fin.)		

	SEMITIC	EGYPTIAN	CUSHITIC	CHADIC	OMOTIC
		ḫ3y "plumb-line" (stem + *y de-verb.)			
358. *-ɣuḫ-/*-ɣaḫ- "to flow"	A. *jaḫl* "large water-bag" (stem + *l n. suff.: *gḫl)	*ḫ3 c* "urination" (pl. *ḫ3 cw* "dis-charges (medi-cal)" (stem + *ʕ part., i.e., that which flows *out*); *ḫ3s* "creek (?); runnel (?)" (stem + *s de-verb. comp.)	PEC *g'uḥ-/ *g'aḥ- "to flow" (PEC *g' < PC *ɣ)		
359. *-ɣâl-/*-ɣûl- "to be dry"	A. *ɣalal* "to be thirsty"		PSC *xâl- or *xâal- "to be dry" (PC *ɣ > PSC *x)		NOm *kol- "dry" (PO $*x_1$ > NOm *k; Bench *kol* [2]; PO $*x_1$ > NOm *k)

	SEMITIC	EGYPTIAN	CUSHITIC	CHADIC	OMOTIC
360. *-ɣelf- "to be strong, powerful"		*ḫnf3* "arrogance (?)" (stem + *r n. suff.)	*ɣelf- or *xelf- "strength"		
361. *-ɣaɬ- "to break up, break apart (tr.)"	A. *ɣašq* "to pound, beat" (stem + *k' intens. of effect); *ɣašn* "to beat, hit" (stem + *n non-fin.)	LE *ḫšḫš* "rubble" (redup. stem as freq.); LE *ḫšb* "to mutilate" (stem + *b extend.; C. *hōš*)	Agaw *käl-/*kär- "to break, break or tear to pieces" (PC *ɣ > Agaw *k /#_, *ɬ > *l; old *l ~ *r ablaut operated here)		NOm: Yem *kálás-* "to split" (stem + *s caus.)
362. *-ɣim- "to slice, cut into"	A. *ɣumūḍ* "to penetrate" (stem + *dl m.v.)	*ḫmᶜ* "to penetrate (water, of staff)" (stem + *ʕ part.)	PEC *g'im- "to slice, cut into" (PEC *g' < PC *ɣ)	some CCh *gm "to carve (wood)" (J)	

	SEMITIC	EGYPTIAN	CUSHITIC	CHADIC	OMOTIC
363. *-ɣan-/*-ɣun- or *-ɣaŋ-/*-ɣuŋ- "to hit" (Eg., Sem. **innovation**: narrowing of meaning to beating time to music)	MSA *ɣny "to sing" (semantics: via intermediate meaning shift seen also in Eg.; stem + *y inchoat. > dur. as in 2nd Eg. entry)	*ḫn* "to clap (of hands)" (in beating time to music); *ḫni* "to play music"; (stem + *y ext. as dur.); *ḫnw* "musicians" (stem + *w* pl.)	PEC *g'an-/ *g'un- "to hit, strike" (PEC *g' < PC *ɣ; PC *ŋ > PEC *n /_-#)	some ECh *gn "mortar" (for pounding grain)	
364. *-ɣin- or *-ɣiŋ- "to twist (tr.)"	A. *ɣunj* "wry faces, grimaces" (stem + *gʷ dur.; n. < presumed earlier v. "to twist face")	*ḫnd* "to bend (wood); twist together (flower stems)" (stem + *d dur.)	PEC *g'in- "to twist (rope, string, etc.)" (PEC *g' < PC *ɣ; PC *ŋ > PEC *n /_-#)	WCh, CCh *gnɗ "to tie (rope)" (J; stem + *z intens. of manner)	

	SEMITIC	EGYPTIAN	CUSHITIC	CHADIC	OMOTIC
365. *ɣŭnts-, *ɣŭntsay- "nap, fuzz, crusty layer" (2nd root shape: adds *y n. suff.)	A. *ɣanθar* "to have thick hair" (stem + *r adj. suff., v. < earlier adj.)	*ḫnsyt* "scurf (?)" (2nd PAA root shape + *t n. suff.)	SC: Iraqw *xunsay* "crust" (2nd PAA root shape; *ɣ > PSC *x)	Ng. *gùzái* "pubic hair" (2nd PAA root shape; *nC > $C_{[+voice]}$ if *C = [-voice]); #449 also attests this rule) (J: $*^{n}gz$ "hair"; some WCh *gz(m) "beard")	NOm *ku:ts- "hair" (Bench *kust* [5]; Chara *kus-na:*) (PO $*x_1$ > NOm *k)
366. *ɣunt- "projecting surface, protrusion"	A. *ɣundar* "big and fat (young man)" (stem + *r adj. suff.); *ɣunduba-t* "swollen glands of throat" (stem + *b anim.; presumed voicing assim. in both entries, by shift *nt > nd	*ḫnt* "face; in front of, among, from, out of" (C. *šant*)	PEC *g'unt- "protrusion" (PEC *g' < PC *ɣ)		

	SEMITIC	EGYPTIAN	CUSHITIC	CHADIC	OMOTIC
	/CV_VC, where both C voiced)				
367. *-ɣâp̣- "to rise, arise"	A. *ɣafw* "to float on the water" (stem + *w inchoat.)	*ḫpr* "to come into being; become; grow up; occur, happen" (stem + *l fin., i.e., to arise; C. *šōpε*); *ḫpn* "fat (adj.)" (stem + *n adj. suff.); LE *ḫpwt* "small birds, fowl" (semanics: rise > fly; stem + *w deverb + *t coll.)	*ɣaap-/*ɣuup- "fruit" (semantics: rise > grow > ripen, mature, hence bear fruit; n. < v. by V > VV)		NOm *kap- "bird" (PO *x_1 > NOm *k; semantics: rise > fly; cf. also LE entry, which with this NOm root may conceivably reflect a PAA etymon for "bird"; Bench *kap*³)

		SEMITIC	EGYPTIAN	CUSHITIC	CHADIC	OMOTIC
368.	*-ɣar- "to become dark"	A. *ɣarb* "to pass away, depart, disappear; sunset; west" (stem + *p' fin. fort.)	*ḫ3wy* "night" (stem + *w inchoat. + *y deverb.)			NOm: *kar- "black" (Ometo *kar-ts-; Yem *kàrā̄*) (PO $*x_1$ > NOm *k)
369.	*-ɣuur-/*-ɣiir- "to join (tr.), connect"	A. *ɣarw* "glue, paste; to smear with glue" (stem + *w deverb.); *ɣarw* "to adhere" (stem + *w inchoat.)	*ḫrš* "bundle" (stem + *ɬ ven.; semantics: join by *bringing* tightly together; C. *šraš*)	*ɣuur-/*ɣiir- "to attach, fit together, join"	Ng. *gùrvà-* "to accompany, escort" (stem + *b extend. + *-a incep.)	
370.	*-ɣaat'- "to fold (tr.)" (Eg., Sem. **innovation**: "fold over, bend")	Ji. *ɣaṭḳet* "back of knee" (stem + $*k^{w}$' and. + *t n. suff.)	*ḫsf* "to spin (yarn)" (stem + *f iter.; semantics: fold over > bend > turn, + iter. > spin)	*ɣaat'- "to fold"		

	SEMITIC	EGYPTIAN	CUSHITIC	CHADIC	OMOTIC
371. *-ɣôx^w- "to bend round, form a curve"	A. *jaxw* "to hold upside down" (stem + *w inchoat.; -> *tajxiya-t* "be bent; be turned upside down")		*gox^w- "to bend, form a curve" (Append.2)		Mocha *'kukko* "hunchbacked"
372. *-ɣaaʕ- "to raise, lift, pick up"	pPS *gʕ "to pick up" (Append.1)	*ḫ c* "hill"; *ḫ ci* "to rise (of sun)" (stem + *y inchoat. > intr. as in Ng.; C. *ša*)	*ɣaaʕ- "to convey"	Ng. *gáay-* "to climb, mount" (stem + *y inchoat. > intr.)	
373. *-ɣâaʕ- "to cry loudly"	A. *jaʕr* "to low, bellow" (*gʕr, stem + *r diffus.)	*ḫ cr* "to rage" (stem + *l n. suff., v. < presumed earlier n. "rage"; C. *šaarɛ* "to beat")	*ɣaaʕ-/*ɣuuʕ- "to make a loud noise" (Append.2)	Ng. *gáad-* "to bark" (stem + *d dur.)	NOm: Bench *keʔ* 3 "to be loud"

	SEMITIC	EGYPTIAN	CUSHITIC	CHADIC	OMOTIC
PAA *ɣ^{w}					
374. *ɣ^{w}a "heat" (Eg., Sem. **innovation**: addition of *t n. suff.; short vowel required by derived verb #399)	A. *ɣatm* "oppressive heat" (stem + *t n. suff. + *m n. suff.)	*ḫt* "fire" (stem + *t n. suff.; C. (Bohairic) *xēı* ; for *ē* see #399); *ḫtt* "fiery" (n. + *t adj. suff.)	*ɣ^{w}aar- "heat" (stem + *r n. suff.)		
375. *ɣ^{w}îb-/*ɣ^{w}âb- "calabash (used as container, utensil, etc.)"		*ḫbbt* "jar" (stem with unexplained redup. + *t n. suff.)	*ɣ^{w}îb- "calabash"	Ng. *gwàbò* "large round beer gourd" (tone remains to be explained)	Mocha *'kibbo* "spatula" (< earlier sense, scoop made of section of gourd shell)

	SEMITIC	EGYPTIAN	CUSHITIC	CHADIC	OMOTIC
376. *-ɣʷal- "to grasp and take away"	A. *ɣall* "to take part of the booty, embezzle"; *ɣalb* "to snatch from" (stem + *p' fin. fort.)	*ḫnp* "to snatch, catch; steal" (stem + *p' fin. fort.; shared innovation with that seen in 2nd Sem. entry; C. *kōlp* is most probably a loan)	*ɣʷalaaf- "to catch, seize" (stem + *f iter.; original sense "to seize *many*"?)	some CCh *glɓ "to hang" (J; stem + *p' fin. fort.; semantics: fin. shifts meaning from picking up *and* taking away to just picking up)	
377. *-ɣʷîn- "to lie (down)"	A. *ɣanan* "to stay, remain; be at a place"	*ḫni* "to alight; stop, halt" (LE "to rest, tarry") (stem + *y inchoat. > dur.); *ḫnw* "resting-place, abode" (stem + *w deverb.)	PEC *g'iin-/ *g'aan- "to stay in place" (PEC *g' < PC *ɣ, *ɣʷ)	*xʷən- "to lie down" (N)	*$x_1$un-/*-$x_1$in- "to lie down" (Yem *kún-*; Ari *ginʔ-* "to fall asleep": stem + *ʔ conc.); NOm *kund-/ *kind- "to go down" (stem + *d dur.; Mocha *ki̱:nd-*; PO *x_1 > NOm *k)

	SEMITIC	EGYPTIAN	CUSHITIC	CHADIC	OMOTIC
378. *-ɣʷăp- or *-ɣʷâap- "to split (tr.)"		*ḫpš* "scimitar; battle-axe" (stem + *ɬ ven.; sematics unclear)	EC: Soomaali *goob* "pile of things that come broken up" (n. < v. by V > VV?; PC *ɣʷ > Som. *g*)	*ɣʷp "large blade" (J; WCh, CCh *gʷp "spear," some WCh, CCh *kp "knife"; other WCh *kʷ < *ɣʷ: #381)	Mocha *kà p'p'-* "to split (intr.)" (*kap't'-, stem + *dl m.v.; *a* < either PO *a or *aa, because of sound shifts seen in #324 above)
379. *-ɣʷâap- "to bend (part body)"	A. *ɣafw* "to be on the point of falling asleep, fall aslumber" (stem + *w inchoat.; semantics: < nodding of head as one drops off to sleep); Ji. *ɣɔfɔẓ́* "to wrap" (*ɣpḍ, stem + *dl m.v.)	*ḫpš* "arm; foreleg" (stem + *ɬ ven.; semantics unclear; C. *šōpš*); *ḫpdw* "buttock" (stem + *d dur.; semantics: from extended bending of buttocks in sitting or squatting)	*ɣʷaap- "to bend"		Mocha *'kap-* "to nod" (for *V: > V in this environment, see #324 above)

	SEMITIC	EGYPTIAN	CUSHITIC	CHADIC	OMOTIC
380. $*\text{-}\gamma^w ax\text{-}$ or $*\text{-}\gamma^w aax\text{-}$ "to walk about; $*\text{-}\gamma^w aax\text{-}$ "path"	A. *jaxx* "to wander from place to place" (*gx)	*ḫ3* "path, road" (C. *xo*)	$*g\text{-}\gamma\text{-}$ "to go away" (irregular voicing assim. of *x, or $*x > \gamma$ /$g^w a$_ but not with front V as in #381?)	*gk- "path(way)" (J); some WCh $*k^w ak$ "leg" (J; see #381 for proposed environment of J $*k^{(w)}$ < PAA $*\gamma^w$)	$*x_1o{:}x_2\text{-}$ "road, path" (NOm: Sheko *ko:kn*, stem + *n n. suff.; SOm: Ari *go:gi*)
381. $*\text{-}\gamma^w eex\text{-}$ "to cry out"	A. *jaxjax* "to call, cry out to; applaud" (redup. as freq.)		POT *gooh- "to cry out loudly, make a vocal din" (PC *x > POT *h /V_, PAA $*\gamma^w$ > PC $*g^w$ /#_Vx, by PC shift #3)	some WCh, rare CCh, ECh *kuk "to cry, weep" (J; for other J $*k^{(w)}$ < PAA $*\gamma^w$ /#_VC, where C is [-voice], see #378 and 380 above)	

	SEMITIC	EGYPTIAN	CUSHITIC	CHADIC	OMOTIC
382. *-ɣ^{w}ây-/ *-ɣ^{w}îy- "to be hot" (root #374 + *y inchoat.)	A. *ɣaiθ* "to shine" (stem + *ts diffus., i.e., the effect of burning hotly)	C. *hēm* "hot" (stem + *m adj. suff., added since BA *a/*ə > C. *ē* /#h_(y): see Chapter 4)	*ɣ^{w}ay-/*ɣ^{w}iy- "to be hot"		Mocha *ki̯:*- "to boil water, cook"

PAA *x

	SEMITIC	EGYPTIAN	CUSHITIC	CHADIC	OMOTIC
383. *xâb- "piece of earth, area of ground"	A. *xabt* "wide plain, sandy lowland" (stem + *t n. suff.)		*xâb- "clod, lump of earth"		
384. *-xadl- "to spill, pour"	pPS *xḏ "to wet down" (Append.1)		SC: PR *xatl- "to give birth" (PC *dl > PSC *tl)	some ECh *kl "to pour" (J; PCh *ɮ > ECh *l)	

	SEMITIC	EGYPTIAN	CUSHITIC	CHADIC	OMOTIC
385. *-xaf- "to hit"	A. *xafš* "to pelt with" (stem + *ɬ ven.); *xafq* "to give a light tap" (stem + *k^{w}' and.)		PEC *xaf- "to hit"		
386. *-xăh- "to utter"	A. *kahkah* "to roar; cry out with fear" (redup. stem as intens.)	*kh3* "to raise the voice; utter (a bellow); rage furiously" (stem + *r diffus.)	PSC *xah- "to speak"		*x_2a- or *$x_2$ah- "to utter" (NOm: Mocha *kàw-* "to scout," stem + *w inchoat.; SOm: Ari *gay-* "to say," stem + *y inchoat.)
387. *-xâj- "to rub"	A. *xaðraf* "to sharpen" (stem + *r diffus. + *f iter., i.e., to whet)		PEC *xac- "to rub off, scrape away" (PC *dz > PEC *c)		NOm *kačč- "to rub" (Mocha *'kačč-*; Yem *káaʔy-* "to tan hides, scratch"; PO *x_2 > Yem, Mocha *k*)

	SEMITIC	EGYPTIAN	CUSHITIC	CHADIC	OMOTIC
388. *xăl- "thin stalks, grass stalks"	A. *xalan*, *xala* "greens, herbs"		PEC *xal- "grazing grounds"		NOm *kall- or $*x_2$all- "stem, stalk" (Zayse *kalló* "stick": loan [expected *hall-]?; Mocha *kalló* "barley": semantics: see Sem. entry in #887)
389. *-xîɬ- "to scratch off"	A. *xašb* "to smooth, polish" (stem + *b extend.)		PSC *xîɬ-/ *hîɬ- "to scrape off" (corrects Ehret 1987: #390; occasional PSC alternance *x ~ *h occurs with proximate lateral)		
390. *-xoɬ- "to make a rough sound"	pPS *xɬ "to make a rough or creaky sound"		PSC *xoɬ- "to rasp, make a rasping sound"		

	SEMITIC	EGYPTIAN	CUSHITIC	CHADIC	OMOTIC
391. *-xan- or *-xaŋ- "to move (intr.)"	A. *xandaf* "to walk fast; step along proudly" (stem + *d dur. + *p intens. of manner)	*ẖn* "to approach, come nearer" (C. *hōn*)	EC: Yaaku -*xan*- "to go"		
392. *-xap- "to join, assemble"	Ji. *xfɔr* "to make knot in cloth" (stem + probably *r n. suff., with v. < earlier n. "knot")	LE *ẖpt* "flock (of animals)" (stem + *t n. suff.)	*xap- "to be joined, connected"	*kp "to sew" (J)	
393. *xoor- "ground"		*ẖr* "under" (C. *ha*-); *ẖrw* "base, lower part" (stem + *w n. suff.)	SC: WR *xoro "land, district, country" (PSC *VV>WR *V)		

	SEMITIC	EGYPTIAN	CUSHITIC	CHADIC	OMOTIC
394. *-xas- "to float, glide, drift" (Sem., Ch. **innovation**: "float" > "flow")	A. *xasf* "place where water appears" (stem + *f iter., i.e., recurrently flowing source of water)		*xas- "to float"	WCh, CCh *ks "to pour" (J)	NOm: Yem *kàsà* "bird" (semantics: < gliding of bird through the air)
395. *-xĭs'- "to extend, stretch out (intr.); to reach out"	H. *xāš* "to stretch out (the hands)" (MSA *š < PS *s)		EC: Soomaali *shishe* "far, distant" (< *kiš-; PC ts' > PSom *š, PC *x > *k > *sh* [š] /_i in Som.)	some WCh *ks'- "fat (n.)" (J; stem + probably *ʔ nom. suff. [represented by hyphen], used as n. rather than adj. marker)	Gonga *kič'- "to gather" (Mocha *kìč'*-; semantics: take by reaching out for)

	SEMITIC	EGYPTIAN	CUSHITIC	CHADIC	OMOTIC
396. *xiš- "little, low, small"	*xcc "meanness, low-mindedness" (Ji. *xsis* "mean"); A. *xasf* "to diminish" (stem + *f iter. > extend.)	*ẖz (y)* "weak, feeble; humble; mean" (stem + *y deverb.; *z* for expected *s remains to be explained; C. *hīsɛ*)	[EC: Soomaali *kis* "a little" (loan < other Cush. language: expected *šiy; cf. #395; PEC *š > Som. *y* /i_#)]	WCh, CCh *ks "small"	
397. *xaynz- "three"		[*ẖmt* (C. *šomnt*) "three": apparent chance resemblance; even assuming original PAA *m, with PCh, PO *m > *n assim., would yield ME *ẖmd and C. *hmt or *hɛmt]		*knɗ "three" (J)	NOm *$x_2$ayz- "three" (Mocha *kä:jjo*, Bench *kaz*[4], Yem *kèez*, Zayse *hayts*, etc.)

	SEMITIC	EGYPTIAN	CUSHITIC	CHADIC	OMOTIC
398. *-xâʕ- "to rub, scrape"	A. *kaʕz* "to scrape together with the fingers" (stem + *z intens. of manner)	*ḫ ᶜḳ* "to shave" (stem + *k' intens. of effect, i.e., to scrape off the hair; C. *hōōk*)	PSC *xâʕ- or *xâʔ- "to rub, scrape"	Ng. *káas-* "to sweep" (stem + *š non fin. or *ts diffus.)	

PAA *x^w

	SEMITIC	EGYPTIAN	CUSHITIC	CHADIC	OMOTIC
399. *x^w- "female"; *x^wat- "womb" (1st stem shape + *t n. suff.)	A. *xatūn* "relationship on the wife's side" (2nd PAA stem shape + *n n. suff.)	*ḫt* "womb, belly; body" (2nd PAA stem shape; C. *hē* ; for NAA *a, *ə > C. *ē* /#h_(y)#, see also #374, 382, and 757)	*x^w- "female"	*k^wt "belly" (J)	NOm: Yem *kàtà* "belly" (2nd PAA stem shape)

Velar and Labiovelar Obstruents of PAA: $*x^w$

	SEMITIC	EGYPTIAN	CUSHITIC	CHADIC	OMOTIC
400. $*$-x^wal- or $*$-x^waal- "to extract, take or draw out"	pPS *xl "to take off or out" (Append. 1)	LE *ḫnr* "to scatter, disperse" (stem + *r diffus.)	SC: PR $*x^w$al- "to dig up"		
401. $*$-x^win-/$*$-x^wan- or $*$-x^wiŋ-/-x^waŋ- "to inhale, take a breath" (only C. reflexes imply 2nd form with reconstructed *a)	*xnn "to speak through the nose" (A., MSA)	*ḫnm* "to breathe; smell (odors); make sweet-smelling" (stem + *m extend.; C. *šōlm*); *ḫnmw* "smell" (n.); LE *ḫnp* "to breathe" (stem + *p intens. of manner; < earlier "breathe deeply"?); LE *ḫnr* "to be hoarse" (stem + *l adj. suff., v. < earlier adj.; C. *hōl* :	$*x^w$înb- "snout" (stem + *b anim. deverb.)	Ng. *kùnkùɗ-* "to rinse (mouth)" (stem + *k dur. + *z intens. of manner); CCh, ECh $*k^w$ind "neck" (J; stem + *d dur., i.e., earlier "windpipe" < v. in sense "to breathe")	SE Ometo *kunk- "nose" (stem + *k dur., i.e., < earlier v. sense "to breathe"; PO $*x_1$ > Ometo *k; Zayse *kunké*)

	SEMITIC	EGYPTIAN	CUSHITIC	CHADIC	OMOTIC
		contraction of earlier *holol explains long V)			
402. *-x^wâr- "to split, make a hole in"	pPS *xr "to split, make a hole in" (Ap-pend.1)		*x^wâr- "to split, make a hole in" (Ap-pend.2)	Ng. *kwár̃ɓ-* "to dig up, hoe" (stem + *p' fin. fort.)	
403. *-x^war-/*-x^wir- "to attack, plunder"	A. *xarr* "to attack from ambush"; *xarb* "to devastate, destroy; be-come a robber" (stem + *p' fin. fort.)	*ḫrw, ḫrwy* "enemy" (stem + *w, *y de-verb.); *ḫrwyw, ḫrwyt* "war" (1st n. + *w, *t n. suff.)	*x^war- or *ɣ^war- "to attack" (Beja "to rob")	*xərə "to steal" (N) (Ng. *kə̀r-*)	
404. *-x^wâar- "to turn (intr.)"	pPS *xr "to turn" (Ap-pend.1)		*x^wâar- "to turn about"	Ng.*kwàr̃kwàr̃t-* "to turn around and around" (stem redup. as freq. + *t dur.)	

	SEMITIC	EGYPTIAN	CUSHITIC	CHADIC	OMOTIC
405. *-xʷir- "to rumble"	A. *xarir* "to roar; buzz; snore"; *xarxar* "to produce a rattling noise" (redup. stem as freq.)	*ḫrw* "voice; noise" (stem + *w de-verb.; C. *hr*- in *hrui* "grande voix")	SC: PR *xɨrɨ "rumble, roar" (PC *Cʷi > PSC *Cɨ)		
406. *-xʷaat- "to remove (from surface), pull, tear, or scrape off"	MSA *xtn "to circumcise" (stem + *n non-fin.; semantics: once one has been circum-cised, one stays that way)	*ẖtt* "to pluck plants" (stem + *t dur. or with redup. as freq.)	*xʷaat- "to rub, scrape (with hands, paws, etc.)"		Mocha *ka̤:t*- "to tear"
407. *-xʷayl- "to bear child" (root #399 + *y denom. + *l fin.?)	MSA *xlḳ "to be born" (stem + *kʷ' and.; seman-tics: emerging of child *into* world)	*ḫnw* "child" (stem + *w deverb.)	*xʷayl- "child; to bear child"		

PAA *k'	SEMITIC	EGYPTIAN	CUSHITIC	CHADIC	OMOTIC
408. *k'âb- "cold"		*ḳb* "cold" (n.; C. *kba*, *kbo*); *ḳbw* "cool breeze" (stem + *w n. suff.)	PEC *k'ab- "cold"		Mocha *'qäwo* "cold" (PO *b > Mocha *w* /V_)
409. *-k'ab- "to take hold of"	pPS *ḳb "to pick up" (Ehret 1989)		PEC *k'ab- "to catch, have"		
410. *-k'ĭb- "to be quiet"		*ḳbb* "calm, quiet" (redup. as dur.)	*k'ab-/*k'ib- "to be quiet"		Gonga *k'èb- "to sleep"
411. *-k'āc- or *-k'āts- "to cut off"	A. *qaθθ* "to cut down, pull out"		PSC *k'ats- "to circumcize"		Mocha *qáččo* "half"

		SEMITIC	EGYPTIAN	CUSHITIC	CHADIC	OMOTIC
412.	*-k'ad- "to stay, stop"	A. *qadʕ* "to restrain, prevent, hinder" (stem + *ʕ part.; semantics: to keep *away from*); *qadf* "to keep off, prevent" (stem + *f iter. as dur.)	*ḳd* "to sleep" (C. *kītε*); *ḳdd* "sleep" (n.; redup. as freq. > dur.?; n. < v.?)	SC: WR *qad- "to stand" (PC *k' > WR *q)		
413.	*-k'ădl- "to cut"	pPS *ḳḍ "to cut" (Ehret 1989)	LE *ḳḏw* "brambles, thorns"	*k'ădl- "to split apart"		
414.	*-k'ŭudl- "to go out; send out, drive out"	A. *qaḍḍ* "to send horsemen"		*k'uudl- "to go away"	Ng. *gùdlàdl-* "to wake up (tr.)" (redup. stem as intens.?)	Mocha *kut'í-* "to chase" (PO *k' > k /t' in Mocha; for *V: > V in this environment, see #324 above)

		SEMITIC	EGYPTIAN	CUSHITIC	CHADIC	OMOTIC
415.	*-k'âf- or *-k'âaf- "to harden, form a crust"	A. *qufūf* "to wither, dry up, dry"; *qafl* "dry, withered; to dry up, wither" (stem + *l adj. suff.; v. < adj.)	*ḳfn* "to clot (of blood)" (stem + *n non-fin.)	*k'âaf- "hull, rind" (PSC "crust") (n. < v. by V > VV?)		
416.	*-k'ăh- "to come away"	A. *qahd* "to walk with short steps" (stem + *d dur.)		*k'ăh- "to come away, part company"		
417.	*-k'êḥ- "to bite off"	*ḳḥ "to consume" (A. *qaḥḥ* "to drink in large gulps"; MSA *ḳḥm "to gnaw last shreds off bone": stem + *m extend.)		PSC *k'eḥ- "to bite"	Ng. *gáad-* "to bite" (stem + *d dur.; PCh *h > Ng. Ø)	

	SEMITIC	EGYPTIAN	CUSHITIC	CHADIC	OMOTIC
418. *-k'aj- "to seep out"	pPS *ḳð "to seep out" (Append.1)		EC: Soomaali *qaash* "pustules that form during fever" (n. < v. by V > VV; PC *dz > Som. *sh* [š])		*k'až- "to become wet, damp, moist" (NOm: Maji *k'εžiž* "wet": stem + Maji *-iz* adj. suff.; SOm *k'a(a)ž- "cold (to touch)")
419. *-k'al- "to burn (tr.)"	A. *qalw*, *qaly* "to fry in a pan; roast" (stem + *w, *y inchoat.)	*ḳrr* "to fire (pottery); broil (?)" (stem with redup. for intens.; C. *črīr* "burnt offering")	SC: PR *k'al- "to make shine"	*k^{y}'-n/*k^{y}'-l "smoke" (J) (N: *k'an-)	NOm: N. Mao *k'än-* "to burn (tr.)"; SOm: Ari *k'alal* "bright" (stem partially redup.)
420. *-k'um- or *-k'uum- "to grumble, sigh, make sounds of complaint"	MSA *ḳmḥ "to be in despair" (stem + *ḥ iter. > dur. > stat.)	*ḳm3* "to mourn" (stem + *r diffus.); *ḳmd* "to mourn" (stem + *d dur.)	PSC *k'um- or *k'uum- "to grumble"		

	SEMITIC	EGYPTIAN	CUSHITIC	CHADIC	OMOTIC
421. *-k'ăn-/*-k'ĭŋ- or *-k'ăŋ-/*-k'ĭŋ- "to grasp"	A. *qanfaš* "to snatch, gather quickly" (stem + *p intens. of manner + *ɬ ven.); *qanw* "to acquaire, procure, possess" (stem + *w inchoat.)	*ḳni* "to embrace" (stem + *y inchoat. > extend.)	*k'anc'- "to catch, hold fast" (stem + *c' extend.; corrects Ehret 1987: #141)	Ng. *gə̀n-* "to take, receive, accept"	Mocha *qàc'-* "to transport things" (stem + *c' extend. or *t' dur. intens.)
422. *k'ōoŋ- "skin"	A. *qunb* "sheath of a horse's penis" (stem + *b anim. suff.)		PEC *k'ooŋ- or *k'ooɲ- "crust"		Mocha *qóngo* "meat" (semantics: skin > meat)
423. *-k'ar- "to last, endure"	A. *qarr* "to stay permanently in a place; persist"		*k'ar- "period of time"	WCh, CCh *ɗʸar "to stand" (J)	

	SEMITIC	EGYPTIAN	CUSHITIC	CHADIC	OMOTIC
424. *k'ār- "tip, peak, point"	*ḳrn "horn; point, peak" (stem + *n n. suff.; A. *qarn*)	LE *ḳrnt* "phalli; foreskin" (stem + *n, *t n. suff.)	*k'ar- "peak, top"		Gonga *k'ar- "horn" (Mocha *qáro*) SOm: Ari *k'ari* "tusk"; *k'armi* "sharp" (stem + *m adj. suff.)
425. *-k'ĕer-/*-k'ŏor- "to cut into"	pPS *ḳr "to cut" (Ehret 1989)	*ḳrt* "depression, hollow place" (stem + *t n. suff.)	PSC *k'eer- "to cut (meat)"	Ng. *gə̀rìɗ* "cave, hollow in tree" (stem + *z intens. of manner; semantics: < underlying v. "hollow out")	Mocha *qo'rip'-* "to make a hole" (stem + *b extend. or *p' fin. fort.; PO *b, *p' > Mocha *p'* /C')

	SEMITIC	EGYPTIAN	CUSHITIC	CHADIC	OMOTIC
426. *-k'ûur-/ *-k'âar- "to become covered, go under cover"	MSA *ḳrw/y "to hide" (stem + *w/*y inchoat. > tr.)	*ḳrs* "to bury" (stem + *s caus.; C. *kaīsɛ*); *ḳrsw* "coffin" (v. stem + *w deverb.); *ḳrst* "burial" (stem + *t n. suff.)	PSC *k'uur- "to go hide"		NOm: Mocha *qärìs-* "to curtain" (stem + *s caus.); Oyda *k'u:ro* "bark"; Male *k'urubi* "skin" (stem + *b anim. deverb.)
427. *-k'âas- "to divide"	A. *qasṭ* "to separate, disperse" (stem + *t' dur. intens.); *qasm* "division, distribution; to divide, distribute" (stem + *m n. suff.; v. < n.)		PSC *k'aas- "to divide"		NOm: Mocha *'qäs-* "to open" (for *V: > V in this environment in NOm, see #324 above); SOm *k'astän- "two" (stem + *t, *n n./adj. suff., i.e., divided in two)

		SEMITIC	EGYPTIAN	CUSHITIC	CHADIC	OMOTIC
428.	*k'os- "bone"	A. *qass*, *qasqas* "to pick bone clean and suck it out"	*ḳs* "bone" (C. *kas*)		*k'aṣu "bone" (N) (J: *k's_3)	*k'os- "bone"
429.	*-k'ĕes'- "to give off heat or light"	A. *qasām* "heat of mid-day" (stem + *m n. suff.)			Ng. *gə́shăw* , *gə́zhăw* "star" (stem + *w deverb.; *sh* < pre-Ng *s /ə_, as also in #499)	NOm *k'ees'- "to burn (intr.)" (Mocha *qè:c'-* , Bench *k'ets'*[1], Yem *kíʼič-*)
430.	*-k'ăt-/*-k'ĭt- "to go down, decline"	A. *qatt* "to diminish"		*k'at- "to lie down"		Yem-Gonga *k'it- "to die" (Mocha *qìt-*)
431.	*-k'ât'- "to cut"	pPS *ḳṭ "to cut" (Append.1)		PEC *k'at'- "to cut"		Mocha *'qäč'-* "to harvest" (PO *ts' > Mocha *č'*)

		SEMITIC	EGYPTIAN	CUSHITIC	CHADIC	OMOTIC
432.	*-k'ûtl'- "to cut up"	pPS *ḳṣ "to clip" (Ehret 1989)		SC: PR *k'utl- "to cut up" (PC *tl > PSC *tl /V_-#)		Gonga *k'ut'- "to cut in two" (Mocha *'kut'*-)
433.	*-k'ey- "to excrete" (Eg., Sem. **innovation**: addition of *ʔ concisive to denote short, concentrated outflow, hence vomiting)	*ḳyʔ "to vomit" (stem + *ʔ conc.)	*ḳ3 ᶜ*, *ḳ ᶜ* "to vomit" (stem + *ʔ conc. + *ʕ part.; C. *ka*-); *ḳ3 si*, *ḳis* "to vomit" (stem + *ʔ conc. + *s' fort.; C. *kos* "vomit (n.)")		*ɗʸiis "faeces" (J; stem + *s deverb. comp.)	
434.	*-k'uʔ- "to rise"		*ḳ3i* "to be raised on high, uplifted; tall, high; exalted" (stem + *y inchoat.); *ḳ3t* , *ḳ3w* "height" (stem + *w, *t n.	PSC *k'uʔ- "to rise (out of)"		

	SEMITIC	EGYPTIAN	CUSHITIC	CHADIC	OMOTIC
		suff.); *ḳ33* "hill, high ground" (stem + *r n. suff.; C. *koyε*)			
435. *-k'oʕ- "to bend (tr.)" (joint of body)	A. *qaʕš* "to bend, bend toward one's self" (stem + *ɬ ven.)	*ḳ ᶜḥ* "to bend (arm, hand; elbow, arm, shoulder; corner; bend (of stream)" (stem + *ḥ iter.; seman- unclear; C. *kooh*)	EC: Dullay: Dopache *qoʕ-akko* "finger": stem + Dullay fem. suff.; seman- tics: fingers are the joints of the hand; PEC *k' > Dullay *q)		

	SEMITIC	EGYPTIAN	CUSHITIC	CHADIC	OMOTIC
PAA *k^w'					
436. *-k^w'-̌ "to eat"	pPS *ḳm "to eat up" (stem + *m ex-tend.; Append. 1)	ḳw "loaf or cake" (stem + *w de-verb.)	*k^w'- "to swallow"	Ng. *gágɗ-* "to chew off" (redup. stem + *z intens. of manner)	Mocha *qättó* "throat" (stem + *t n. suff.)
437. *-k^w'- "to be wet"			*k^w'- "to be wet"; PEC *k'oy- "wet" (stem + *y adj. suff.)		NOm: She *k'ai* "wet" (stem + *y adj. suff.); Mao *k'awa "wet" (stem + *w deverb. suff.)
438. *ak^w'- "water" (*a- attrib. n. pref. + root #437)			Agaw *aq^w "water" (PC *k^w' > Agaw *q^w)		NOm *ak'- "wet; water"

		SEMITIC	EGYPTIAN	CUSHITIC	CHADIC	OMOTIC
439.	*-k^{w}'- "to be thin"; *k^{w}'an- "thin" (stem + *n adj. suff.)	MSA *ḳnn "small"		*k^{w}'- "thin"; EC: S'aamakko *qonn-e* "thin" (PC *k^{w}' > Saamakko *q*)	WCh *k'n "small" (J)	
440.	*-k^{w}'ădl- "to bite"	A. *qaḍm* "to nibble at" (stem + *m ex-tend.); *qaḍʔ* "to eat up" (stem + *ʔ conc.); MSA *ḳḫʕ "to bite through" (stem + *ʕ part.)		PSC *k^{w}'ătl aaʕ- "biting insect" (stem + *ʕ part.; original v. sense "bite through," as in MSA reflex, > "to sting, bite" as of insect)		
441.	*-k^{w}'aḥ- "to pound"	A. *qaḥṭ* "to beat violent-ly" (stem + *t' dur. intens.)	*ḳḥḳḥw* "metal-workers" (redup. stem as freq. + *w pl.)	*k^{w}'aḥ(at)- "to pound" (stem + *t dur.)		

	SEMITIC	EGYPTIAN	CUSHITIC	CHADIC	OMOTIC
442. *-k^{w}'ăl- "to call" (Sem., Eg. **innovation**: narrowing of application of v. to angry calling out)	A. *qalzam* "to blame, rebuke" (stem + *z intens. of manner + *m extend.)	*ḳnd* "to be angry, furious" (stem + *d dur. > stat.; semantics: call > shout > shout in anger; C. *čōnt*)	*k^{w}'ălʔ- "to call out" (stem + *ʔ conc.)	*k'l "to count" (J)	Gonga *k'ol- "to beg" (Mocha *qòl-*)
443. *-k^{w}'al- "to make repetitive movements"	pPS *ḳl "to do, happen or move repetitively" (Append.1)		*k^{w}'al- "to move in regular short movements"		
444. *-k^{w}'îl-/*-k^{w}'âl- "to strip, tear off in strips"	pPS *ḳl "to pluck, pick" (Ehret 1989)		PSC *kɨ̂lɨ or *k'ûlu "striped, banded" (PSC *k'ɨ < PC *k^{w}'i); [some EC *k'ool- "skin": probable Omotic loan (see Omotic entry)]		NOm: Ometo *k'o:l- "skin" (n. < v. by V > V:; semantics: to strip > to skin)

	SEMITIC	EGYPTIAN	CUSHITIC	CHADIC	OMOTIC
445. $*k^{w}$'ĭlf-/$*k^{w}$'ălf- "to cover" (Sem., Cush. **innovation**: > n. "covering" > "rind, bark")	*ḳlp "bark, rind" (A. *qilf* "rind, crust"; *qalf* "to bark, rind, take off bast")		PEC *k'olf- "bark" (PC $*k^{w}$'a > PEC *k'o /_lC)		NOm: Yem *kùlf*- "to close" (PO *k' > Yem *k*)
446. *-k^{w}'aɬ- "to look for selectively"	A. *qašm* "to eat best and leave rest; sel-ect; sift" (stem + *m extend.)		$*k^{w}$'aɬ- "to look for, find" (EC: Dullay "to select")		
447. *-k^{w}'am- "to curve"	MSA *ḳmṣ "to curl up" (stem + *tl' foc.); A. *qamar* "moon; to shine with a yellowish hue" (stem + *r n. suff.; seman-tics: original ref-		$*k^{w}$'am- "to curve, bend"	some ECh $*k^{w}$ml "snake" (J; stem + *l n. suff.)	SOm *k'a:m- "ear" (seman-tics: < ear's shape; n. < v. by *V > V: operation); SOm *k'a:ms- "to hear" (SOm n. + *s caus. as denom.)

	PAA	SEMITIC	EGYPTIAN	CUSHITIC	CHADIC	OMOTIC
		erence to round shape of moon)				
448.	*-k^{w}'an- "to hit repeatedly"	A. *qann* "to flog, cudgel"	*ḳnḳn* "to beat (people); pound up (medicaments); beat out (metal" (redup. as freq.; C. *čnčn* "to play music"; semantics: see #363)	PSC *k^{w}'anaʔ- "to jab, poke, prick" (stem + *ʔ conc.)		
449.	*k^{w}'ânḩ- "egg" (root #447 + *ḩ iter.; semantics: egg curves at every point?)			*k^{w}'anḩ- "egg"	WCh *(a)k^{w}'ay "egg" (J: *k'wy) (Ng. *àgwáy* ; < pre-PCh k^{w}'anḩay, stem (+ *a- attrib. n. pref.) + *y n. suff.; PCh *N > Ø /V_C$_{[-voice]}$V, which see also	

	SEMITIC	EGYPTIAN	CUSHITIC	CHADIC	OMOTIC
				in #365 above, and PCh *h > Ø /V_VC	
450. *-k^{w}'îr-/*-k^{w}'âr- "to take a bite or swallow"	pPS *ḳr "to take a bite or swallow of" (Ehret 1989)	LE *ḳ3ḳ3* "to eat" (redup. as freq.)	PSC *k^{w}'âr- "hunger"; EC: HEC *k'urt'- "to nibble" (stem + *t' dur. intens.; < 1st PAA stem shape *k^{w}îr-)		
451. *-k^{w}'aat'- "to wet down" (root #437 + *t' dur. intens.)	A. *qaṭqaṭ* "to rain" (redup. stem as freq.); *qaṭr* "to fall or flow in drops, trickle" (stem + *r diffus.)		*k^{w}'aat'- "to wash"		

		SEMITIC	EGYPTIAN	CUSHITIC	CHADIC	OMOTIC
452.	*-kʷ'ăatl'- "to swallow" (root #437 + *tl' foc.)	A. *qaṣʕ* "to swallow water; chew; quench thirst" (stem + *ʕ part.; semantics: swallow up?); *qaṣf* "indulgence in eating, drinking" (stem + *f iter.)				NOm *k'o:d'- "to swallow" (NW Ometo *k'o:d'- "neck"; Mocha *qò:t'*- "to swallow")
453.	*-kʷ'ăayt'- "to look at"	H. *ḳeṭōr* "to look round, look everywhere" (ḳṭr, stem + *r diffus.)		PSC *kʷ'ʌ̆ʌt'- "to look at" (PC *aay > PSC *ʌʌ)		

	SEMITIC	EGYPTIAN	CUSHITIC	CHADIC	OMOTIC
454. *-kʷ'ăz- "to avoid, avoid doing" (Eg., Sem. **innovation**: meaning shift, from *avoiding* per se to *feeling a need or reason to avoid*)	A. *qazz* "to feel aversion"	LE *ḳsn* "irksome, difficult" (stem + *n adj. suff.)	PSC *kʷ'aḍ- "to leave off, let go" (PC *z > PSC *ḍ /_-#)		Mocha *qàjj-* "to refuse, abandon, disobey"

THE *PAA* ALVEOLAR AND PALATAL OBSTRUENTS

Seven other obstruent consonants hold a somewhat ambiguous position in the PAA system as set out thus far. Their correspondences across the Afroasiatic (Afrasian) family are the following:

1. PAA *dz = PS *ð (or *dʸ) = Eg. *z* = PC *dz = PCh *z = PO *ž;
2. PAA *j = PS *ð (or *dʸ) = Eg. *z* = PC *dz = PCh *z = PO *š /#_, PO *č /V_;
3. PAA *ts = PS *θ (or *tʸ) = Eg. *s* = PC *ts = PCh *s = PO *ts;
4. PAA *c = PS *θ (or *tʸ) = Eg. *s* = PC *ts = PCh *s = PO *š$_3$;
5. PAA *s' = PS *s = Eg. *s* = PC *ts' = PCh *s' (Ng *s*) = PO *s';
6. PAA *c' = PS *θ̣ (or *tʸ') = Eg. *s* = PC *c' = PCh *š' (J: *s') = PO *č'; and
7. PAA *š = PS *c = Eg. *s* = PC *š = PCh *s = PO *š.

Depending on the reconstruction chosen for the first consonant of this set of seven, two different systemic interpretations can be offered. If the PAA consonant in #1 above was *[ž], then five of the members of the set — *j, *c, *ž, *š, and *c' — could be construed as forming a palatal series, positionally equivalent to the respective voiced stop, voiceless stop, voiced fricative, voiceless fricative, and ejective found in each of the four series, labial, dental, velar, and labiovelar, already described. The two consonants, *ts and *s', would remain unaccounted for, however. Also, one notable non-parallel feature would be present — the realization of *j and *c, unlike the equivalent minus-continuant members of the four series previously considered, as affricates rather than stops.

If, on the other hand, the first consonant is reconstructed, as it is here, as *dz, then a different, more balanced system emerges, comprised of two series of affricates, one alveolar (*dz, *ts, and *s' [ts']) and the other palatal (*j, *c, and *c') with only the palatal fricative *š standing outside the pattern. Moreover, a recurrent long-term drift toward fricatization of all the certainly affricate members of this set of seven consonants is strongly apparent in the Omotic languages. It was already present in the PO word-initial reflex *š of PAA *j, in the general PO reflex *š$_3$ of PAA *c, and in the probable falling together also of PAA *ts with PO *s in word-initial environments (see Table 1 in Chapter 2). In non-initial position only did any non-glottal affricates survive in PO (*ts < PAA *ts; *č < PAA *j), and only the two ejective affricates *c' and *s' ([ts']) were fully retained. It seems thus strongly probably that PO *ž derived, too, from a PAA non-ejective affricate — hence the choice of PAA *dz as the origin of correspondence set #1 above, despite its its fricative outcome in PO.

The ejective palatal consonant of this set, PAA *c', shows up in the Chadic reconstructions of Jungraithmayr and Shimizu (1981) as *s', merging with the reflexes, also represented as *s', of PAA *t' and *s'. But the testimony of Ngizim, a West Chadic language, requires revision of that representation: PAA *c' consistently produces /j/ in Ngizim (roots #554, 561, 565, and 566), whereas PAA *t' and *s' both yield /s/ in that language, requiring that PAA *c' remained distinct in the PCh ancestry of Ngizim, even though PAA *t' and *s', as posited by Jungraithmayr and Shimizu, probably did fall together as PCh *s'. The ejective fricative representation *ŝ' has been chosen here for the PCh reflex of PAA *c', because this articulation allows its recurrent merger with PCh *s' to be seen as the direct ejective counterpart of the widespread collapsing of PAA *ŝ (PCh $*s_1$ discussed below) with *s (PCh $*s_3$) in the Chadic languages.

The correspondence pattern of the sole fricative member of the alveolar-palatal set,

PAA *ŝ = PS *c ([ts]) = Eg. *s* = PC *ŝ = PCh $*s_1$ = PO $*ŝ_1$/$*ŝ_2$

shows specifically palatal outcomes in Cushitic and Omotic, and the PS affricate representation *c (for traditional PS *s, per Faber 1985) can be explained as deriving from *ŝ by two steps, *ŝ > *č > *c [ts]. The PO reflex of PAA *ŝ is symbolized by $*ŝ_1$ in word-initial position and usually by $*ŝ_1$ non-initially as well. PO $*ŝ_2$ evidently originated as a split from $*ŝ_1$ in a restricted post-vocalic environment (see roots #347 and 735). The rule creating $*ŝ_2$,

PO #5. PAA *ŝ > PO $*ŝ_2$ /i,y_-,

is discussed in Chapter 4. The articulatory difference between $*ŝ_1$ and $*ŝ_2$ remains unclear. In keeping with the discussion of the proposed PCh reflex *ŝ' of PAA *c', the PCh counterpart of PAA *ŝ, symbolized in Jungraithmayr and Shimizu (1981) as $*s_1$, is probably also best attributed a palatal or prepalatal articulation, *[ŝ].

The distribution of the alveolar-palatal set of consonants in Semitic and Egyptian is greatly restricted by the sibilant co-occurrence constraints already described in the section dealing with the dentals. Further, Semitic seems to have eliminated sequences of ejective palatal as C_1 followed by any velar as C_2, although what such PAA sequences may have changed into in Semitic is not known. The single apparent example of such a sequence in Arabic turns out to derive from a triliteral PAA root originally containing an additional intervening consonant (*y) as the C_2 (root #565). The Cushitic evidence, in contrast, shows a number of different sequences of PAA *c' followed by a velar in the same root (Ehret 1980, 1987). Two PAA roots containing this pattern of consonants are reconstructed here, along with their Egyptian and Chadic reflexes (roots #553 and 554). What the onset of the constraint did in PS to PAA sequences of *c' plus a velar is not yet known.

Note that the Egyptian palatals, *ḏ*, *ṯ*, and *š*, do not figure at all among the reflexes of the PAA palatals (*contra* Bomhard 1988: 126 most recently, among others). The Egyptian palatals instead clearly derive primarily, albeit not entirely, from the PAA laterals (see section on laterals below).

Table 7: Afroasiatic (Afrasian) Alveolar-Palatal Correspondences

PAA	PS	Eg.	PC	PCh	PO
*dz	*ð (*d^y ?)	z	*dz	*z	*ž
*j	*ð (*d^y ?)	z	*dz	*z	*š$_1$ /#_; *č /V_
*ts	*θ (*t^y ?)	s	*ts	*s	*ts
*c	*θ (*t^y ?)	s	*ts	*s	*š$_3$ ([ʂ̌]?)
*š	*c ([ts])	s	*š	*s (*s$_1$)	*š$_1$ (*š$_2$ /i,y_)
*s'	*s	s	*ts'	*s'	*s'
*c'	*θ̣ (*t$^{y'}$?)	s	*c'	*š' (*s'~*j)	*č'

The clear implication of these data is that two pairs of these consonants fell together as single consonants in the the ancestry of Cushitic, Chadic, Semitic, and Egyptian (and, by implication, that of Berber as well). Specifically, each of these groups shows a single outcome for the voiced set of PAA affricates, *dz and *j, and also for the voiceless set, *ts and *c, explainable by one sound shift rule,

Eryth. #1. PAA *dz, *j > *dz,
PAA *ts, *c > *ts.

The reflexes of these consonants in all but Semitic favor an alveolar rather palatal result from the merger — thus the formulation of the rule given here. (The notation "Eryth." refers to a proposed primary branch of Afroasiatic, Erythraean, composed of Semitic, Egyptian, Berber, Chadic, and Cushitic, coordinate with a second branch comprising Omotic alone, for which see Chapter 6.)

These arguments require a distinctly different phonological prehistory for the PAA affricates in Omotic, possibly accounted for by a sequence of three sound shifts:

i. PAA *dz > pre-PO *ž;
ii. PAA *j > pre-PO *č,
*c > PO *š$_3$ ([ʂ̌]?).
iii. pre-PO *č > PO *š, *ts > PO *s /#_.

(Small Roman numerals are used here to distinguish these suggested shifts, which probably operated before many of the the rest of the PO and North Omotic sound change rules, discussed in Chapter 4, took effect.)

The determination of whether PAA *dz or *j or PAA *ts or *c is to be reconstructed depends entirely on attestations from Omotic, the least well known of the divisions of Afroasiatic used in this study. Lacking Omotic attestations or, in some instances, having only non-diagnostic Omotic reflexes available as yet for comparison, a significant portion of the roots containing these consonants have had to be given two alternative reconstructed forms, with both PAA *dz and *j, or both PAA *ts and *c, as the possible protophonemes. For this reason, a few additional reconstructed PAA roots, often known at present from just one division of Afroasiatic other than Omotic, but unambiguously attesting either PAA *j or PAA *dz, have been provided in Appendix 3.

	SEMITIC	EGYPTIAN	CUSHITIC	CHADIC	OMOTIC
PAA *dz					
455. *-dzac- "to fear"	cf. A. *jaθθ* "to fear"? (< PS *gθ; conjectured history: pPS *ð > PS *g /#_Vθ, as consequence of general PBA constraint disallowing consecutive sibilants in the same root)		PEC *cac- "to show fear" (Afar *sas-* "to hide"; Sidamo *shash-* "to be afraid"; *sh* = [š]; PC *dz, *ts both > PEC *c)	Ng. *zhàà* "(running) in all directions (e.g., from a hyena attack)" (presumed contraction of earlier *CVCV)	$*žaš_3š_3$- "to fear" (NOm: Zayse *žašš*-; Koyra *žášš*-; Ometo *š /$C_{[palatal]}V$_ < PO *s or $*š_3$)
456. *-dzaadl- or *-dzaatl'- "to make empty, clear"			EC: Afar *saax* "extinction, loss" (PC *dz > Afar *s*, PC *dl, *tl both > Afar *x* [d'])		NOm: Zayse *žaad'*- "to clarify"

	SEMITIC	EGYPTIAN	CUSHITIC	CHADIC	OMOTIC
457. *-dzâ aɣ- "to pierce"	A. *ðaɣɣ* "to lie with" (semantics: presumed original reference to penetration by the penis)		*dzaaɣ- "to shoot, stab, spear"	Ng. *záɡəm-* "to hurl spear, hit with thrown spear" (stem + *m extend. as fort.); some CCh *zg "to sew" (J; semantics: to pierce with a needle)	SOm: Ari *žąąg-* "to sew" (semantics: to pierce with needle, as in CCh reflex)
458. *-dzik'-/*-dzak'- "to throw down"			EC: Afar *sakuy-* "to throw" (stem + *y inchoat. > extend.; PC *dz > Afar *s*, PEC *k' > *k* /V_V)	Ng. *zəɡər əp* "falling down a slope" (stem + *r diffus. + *p intens. of manner)	SOm: Ari *žą́q-* "to throw (down)"
459. *-dzăm- "to get wet"	A. *ðamm* "to flow with mucus"		PEC *cam- "to get wet" (PC *dz > PEC *c)	*zm "cold" (J; linking of wet and cold is of wide occurrence in	NOm: Bench *ẓam* [1] "swamp"

	SEMITIC	EGYPTIAN	CUSHITIC	CHADIC	OMOTIC
				African languages; see also #204, 244, 418, 579, 604, 804, and 906)	
460. *dzar- "pole"		*z3w* "beam, baulk" (stem + *w n. suff.; C. *soī*)	PEC *carb-/ *cirb-/*curb- "thin stick" (stem + *b anim. suff.; PC *dz > PEC *c)		NOm *žar- "pole" (Dache *šara* "tree"; Nao (Maji) *tsara* "roof beam")
461. *dzix^{w}- "salt"			*dzix^{w}-/*dzax^{w}- "salt"		NOm: Bench *žeg*^{4} "salt"
462. *-dzaʔ- "to walk"	pPS *ðʔ "to walk"	*z3* "to betake one-self"			*žaʔ- "to travel" (NOm: Mocha *šà'-*; SOm: Ari *žaʔ-* "to arrive")

	SEMITIC	EGYPTIAN	CUSHITIC	CHADIC	OMOTIC
PAA *j					
463. *-jâb- "to put apart, separate (tr.)"	A. *ðabb* "to keep off, repel, forbid"	*zbn* "to steer off course, diverge" (stem + *n non-fin.)	EC: Soomaali *shabi* "to drive away" (PC *dz > Som. *sh* [š]; stem + Som. caus. *-i*, < *s caus. [by regular sound shifts *-is > *-iš *-iy > *-i*])	Ng. *zábìy-* "to clear grass, weeds from farm" (stem + *y inchoat. > dur.)	NOm: Bench *šob-k'* 2-3 "to split (tr.)" (for a proposed source of *k'*, see root #50)
464. *-jaf- "to trickle, drip, seep"	A. *ðifāf, ðufāf* "small quantity of water"; *ðifl* "thin pitch; any thin dripping fluid" (stem + *l n. suff.)		EC: Sidamo *shafo* "amniotic fluid; menses" (PC *dz > Sidamo *sh* [š])		NOm: Zayse *šapé* "waterhole, watercourse"

	SEMITIC	EGYPTIAN	CUSHITIC	CHADIC	OMOTIC
465. *-jek- "to scratch itch"	A. *ðakðak* "to tickle" (redup. stem as freq.)			Ng. *zázg-* "to rub to relieve itch" (stem with redup. as freq.; PCh *k > Ng. *g* /z(V)_-# is regular sound shift)	Maji *šiškin "nail, claw" (stem with redup. + *n n. suff.)
466. *jok'- "point, tip (of anything)"	A. *ðaqan* "chin; beard on the chin" (stem + *n n. suff.)		SC: PR *dzok'- "large blade"		*šok'- "point, tip" (NOm: Nao *šokn* "tail," stem + *n n. suff.; SOm: Ari *šóqa* "horn")
467. *-jool- "to pull off"	A. *ðaly* "to cull; pluck" stem + *y inchoat. > dur.; i.e., pluck out for discard the poor items of a set)		PEC *colool- "to remove, loosen (skin, bark, etc.)" (redup. stem; PC *dz > PEC *c)	WCh, ECh *zl "to pull" (J)	Ometo *šo:l- "to peel" (Zayse *šóol-*)

	SEMITIC	EGYPTIAN	CUSHITIC	CHADIC	OMOTIC
468. *jûl- "little, small"	A. *ðull* "to be low, vile, of obscure descent, poor; humble one-self; be meek"		*dzûl-/*dzâl- or *tsûl-/*tsâl- "little" (Append. 2)		SOm: Karo *šoli* "small" (ex-pected *šul- ?)
469. *-jôyʔ- "to pass over, go over"	A. *ðaʔal* "to walk with a light step and proudly" (stem + *l n. suff.); *ðaʔðaʔ* "to totter in walking" (re-dup. as freq.)	*s3b* "to cross water" (stem + *b extend.; *s* < presumed Old Eg. *z*)	SC: PR *dzʌʔ- "to jump over, fly across" (PC *ay > PR *ʌ)	Ng *záab-* "to wade through heavy grass" (stem + *b extend.)	Bench *šoyt* 2-3 "bird" (stem + *t n. suff.; PO *ʔ > Bench Ø /CV_(V)C)

PAA *j or *dz

	SEMITIC	EGYPTIAN	CUSHITIC	CHADIC	OMOTIC
470. *ji or *dzi "one, someone, somebody" (in-def. pron.)	*ð- "this, this one" (A. *ðā*; etc.)	*z* "man; some-one, anyone" (C. *sa*); *izwt* "crew, gang"		*zi "body" (N); *zəm "skin" (N; stem + *m n. suff.)	

	SEMITIC	EGYPTIAN	CUSHITIC	CHADIC	OMOTIC
		(*i- attrib. n. pref. + stem + *w* pl., *t* coll.)			
471. *-jiɣ- or *-dziɣ- "to be strong"			PEC *cig'g'-/ *cag'g'- "to be strong" (PC *dz > PEC *c, PC *ɣ > PEC *g')	CCh *zg(n) "man, husband" (J; stem + *n n. suff.); Ng. *zhìgóm* "brave man, great warrior" (stem + *m n. suff.; PO *z > Ng.*zh* [ž] /_i)	
472. *-jăḫ- or *-dzaḫ- "to hit repeatedly"	A. *ðaḫḫ* "to beat with the palm of the hand; pound, reduce to powder"; *ðaḫy* "to beat wool" (stem + *y inchoat. > dur.)		EC: Yaaku *-sɛhsɛh-* "to punish (by hitting with a stick)" (redup. stem as freq.; PEC *aḫ > Yaaku *ɛh*; PC *dz >PEC *c > Yaaku *s*)	Ng. *zàat-* "to pound in a mortar" (stem + *t dur.)	

	SEMITIC	EGYPTIAN	CUSHITIC	CHADIC	OMOTIC
473. *j-ḥ- or *dz-ḥ- "hut"		*zḥ* "booth, hall"		some CCh, ECh *z- "house" (J)	
474. *-jaal- or *-dzaal- "to overflow"	pPS *ðl "to flow out" (Append.1)	*znbt* "jar" (stem + *b extend. + *t n. suff.; semantics: jar is for holding, pouring water; also see #798)	EC: Soomaali *shaal* "superare qs. frontalmente (og. onda)"	WCh, some CCh *zl "to pour" (J)	
475. *-jǎam- or *-dzǎam- "to step"	A. *ðamil* "slow walk" (stem + *l n. suff.; *ðaml* "to walk slow; walk fast")	*zm3* "to arrive" (stem + *ʔ conc.)			Gonga: Mocha *šà:m-* "to take a step"

	SEMITIC	EGYPTIAN	CUSHITIC	CHADIC	OMOTIC
476. *-jêr-/*-jôr- or *-dzer-/*-dzor- "to convey, make move"	A. *ðarr* "to raise the dead"; *ðary* "to carry off" (stem + *y inchoat. > dur.)		PEC *cerr-/ *corr- "to take away, send away" (PC *dz >PEC *c)	Ng. *zár-* "to pull along"; *zə̀r̃nàk-* "to start off" (stem + *n non-fin. as incep. + *x precip.?)	
477. *-jâw- or *-dzâw- "to wear out, be used up, cease to function"	A. *ðauʕ* "to require and use up" (stem + *ʕ part.; i.e., use up implies to take out all)	*zwn* "to perish" (stem + *n non-fin.)		Ng. *zə̀nàɗ-* "to wither" (stem + *n non fin. + *z intens. of manner)	Mocha *šọ:to* "worn out" (stem + *t dur.)
478. *-jăaw- or *-dzâaw- "to sip"	A. *ðauj*, *ðaij* "to drink" (stem + *g fin. fort.); *ðauq* "to taste" (stem + *k^{w}' and.; semantics: to sip or nibble *at* something)	*zwr* "to drink" (stem + *l fin.; semantics: originally "to drink up"? C. *so*)	Agaw: Awngi *cewent* "taste" (Agaw *caw-, stem + *n non-fin. or *n n. suff. + *t n. suff.; PC *aa > Awngi *e*, PC *dz > Awngi *c*) *zh* : see #471)	BM *zəmə* "to eat" (N; stem + *m extend.); Ng. *zhìyám* "molar tooth" (2nd PAA stem shape + *m n. suff.; PO *z >	Gonga *ša:w- "to taste good" (Mocha *šà:w-*)

	SEMITIC	EGYPTIAN	CUSHITIC	CHADIC	OMOTIC
479. *jiʔ- or *dziʔ- "child, off-spring"		*z3* "son"; *z3t* "daughter" (C. *sī*-)	SC: PR *dziʔa "chick, young bird"		
480. *-jaʕ- or *-dzaʕ- "to kill (animal)"	A. *ðaʕt* "to throttle" (stem + *t dur.); *ðaʕṭ* "to slaughter" (stem + *t' dur. intens.)		HEC *ca- "to kill" (North HEC *ša-; Burji *s*-; PC *dz > PEC, HEC *c)	Ng. *zíid*- (*zàyát*) "slaughter animal by cutting throat" (stem + *y inchoat. > tr. + *d dur.)	
481. *-jiʕ- or *-dziʕ- "to spill out (intr.)"	Ji. *ðaʕar* "to spill, pour" (stem + *r diffus.)	*z3ṯ* "to make libation; pour our (water)" (stem + *tl' foc.)	SC: Kw'adza *dziʔamuko* "semen" (stem + *m n. suff. + ER *k masc. suff.; PSC *ʕ > ER *ʔ)	Ng. *záut*- "to have diarrhea" (stem + *w inchoat. + *t dur.); *zhàagә́m* "need to defecate" (< *ziag-, stem + *ɣ intens. of effect + *m n. suff.;	

	SEMITIC	EGYPTIAN	CUSHITIC	CHADIC	OMOTIC
				for PO *z > Ng. *zh* /_i, see also #471)	
PAA *ts					
482. *-ts- (*ts-, *âts-) "here/there"	*θm "there" (stem + *m n. suff.) *ʔθr "place" (2nd PAA root form + *r n. suff.)	*st* "place; grounds (of house); seat, throne; position, rank of official" (stem + *t n. suff.)	*ts-, *ʔats- "here/there" (Ehret 1980: 178 has incorrect *sa, *ʔas-)	Ng. *sə́nú* "this one, that one" (stem + *n n suff.); *sáu* "this one" (demons. pron.)	NOm *ats- "this" (Y.*āas*)
483. *îts- "brother" (Eg., Cush., Ch. **innovation**: stem + *n n. suff. > *itsan-; Omotic **innovation**: stem + *m n. suff.: *itsim-)		*sn* "brother" (stem + *n n. suff.; implies PAA V-initial etymon because *ʔi-initial stem > Eg. **isn*; C. *son*)	*itsan- or *isan- "brother" (Beja *san*; Agaw *əzan-)	*sin "brother" (J; stem + *n n. suff.)	*itsim- "brother" (NOm: Mocha *ší́mo*; Bench *ič*³; SOm: Dime *išme*; Fleming 1976b; stem + *m n. suff.)

	SEMITIC	EGYPTIAN	CUSHITIC	CHADIC	OMOTIC
484. *-tsul-/*-tsal- "to disapprove" (2nd root shape: possible old tr. derivation by addition of *-u- tr. infix)	A. *θalb* "to rebuke, scold, inveigh against" (stem + *b extend.) *θalm* "to disparage" (stem + *m ex- extend.)	*snḏ* "to fear; res- pect" (+ prep. + obj.) (stem + *dl m.v.; C. *snat* < 2nd PAA root shape)	PEC *cal- "to disapprove of" (PC *ts > PEC *c)	Ng. *sált-* "to be con- cerned, worry" (stem + *t dur. > intr.)	Yem *sòlsù* "evil, bad" (stem + NOm *ts adj. suff., i.e., bringing about disap- proval; PO *ts > Yem *s*)
485. *tsim-/*tsam- "fruit, seeds, foliage, plant growth in general"	A. *θamar* "fruit; produce, gain, profit; riches" (stem + *r n. suff.)	*sm* "grass" (C. *sīm* ; ME *smw* "pasture, herb- age, vegeta- bles": stem + *w* pl.)		WCh, CCh *sm(-n) "field, farm" (J; stem + *n n suff.); some CCh *sm "seed" (J)	NOm: Bench *sam* 4 "cabbage" (PO *ts > Bench *s* /#_)

	SEMITIC	EGYPTIAN	CUSHITIC	CHADIC	OMOTIC
486. *-tsar- "to burn low"	A. *θarw* "to be lit by the the Pleiades and the moon" (stem + *w inchoat.); *θarmad*, *θarmat* "to undercook" (stem + *m extend. + *d, *t dur.; semantics: slow cooking over low heat?)	*srf* "warm; warmth" (stem + *f iter.; semantics: earlier "give off heat over extended period"?)	*tsar-/*tsir- "to burn low" (Append.2)		NOm: Sheko *särab* "warm" (stem + *b extend > stat.; PO *ts > Shinasha *s*)
487. *-tsur- "to chatter"	A. *θarr* "to make many words"; *θarθar* "garrulous" (redup. stem as freq.)			few WCh, ECh *sr "to sing" (J)	NOm: Yem *sùr-* "to sing" (PO *ts > Yem *s*)

	SEMITIC	EGYPTIAN	CUSHITIC	CHADIC	OMOTIC
PAA *c					
488. *-cab- "to join (tr.), bring together" (Ch., Sem. **innovation**: narrowing of meaning to particular kind of joining, by sewing)	A. *θabn* "to stitch together, sew seam" (stem + *n non-fin.)		*ţsab- or *šab- "to join, put together" (corrects Ehret 1987: #243)	some CCh *sb "to sew" (J)	NOm *š₃ob- "to reconcile" (Bench *ʂob* 2-3; "reconciliation"; Mocha *šo:ṭ-* "to reconcile," < *šowṭ-, stem + *t n. suff.); [NOm *si(:)p- "to plait, sew" is a chance resemblance, for which see #211]
489. *cĕec- "to excrete"				some WCh *sis "faeces" (J; *i < PCh *ə)	NOm *š₃e:š₃- "to urinate" (Mocha *šè:ss-*; Bench *ʂeʂ* 1, Yem *šēešà* "urine")

	SEMITIC	EGYPTIAN	CUSHITIC	CHADIC	OMOTIC
490. *-cag- "to separate, set apart"	A. *θagm* "to detach easily" (stem + *m extend. > fort.)		*tsag- or *sag- "far" (i.e., in separate place; corrects Ehret 1987: #227)		NOm: Zayse *šag-* "to separate" (PO *š$_3$ > Zayse š)
491. *-câak- "to stay still, stay in place"	A. *θakm* "to dwell, abide, stay" (stem + *m extend.)	*ski* "to pass time" (stem + *y inchoat. > dur.; C. *sōk*)		Ng. *sáka* "nest"	NOm: Yem *šáakk-* "to be silent" (PO *š$_3$ > Yem š)
492. *cîl- "stomach (?)"				some ECh,WCh *sl "liver" (J)	NOm: Bench *ş̌il* ^{5} "belly" (Bench ş̌ < PO *š$_3$)
493. *-cār- "to abound in water, be very wet"	pPS *θr "to abound in water" (Append. 1)		EC: Afar *saruri* "afterbirth" (stem + *r n. suff.)		NOm *š$_3$a:r- "cloud" (Yem *šā:rù* ; Bench *ş̌art* ^{2} "to be foggy": stem + *t dur.; n. < v. by V > V:)

PAA *ts or *c	SEMITIC	EGYPTIAN	CUSHITIC	CHADIC	OMOTIC
494. *-tsâab- or *-câab- "to spoil, be ruined"	*θbr "to ruin, destroy" (A., ESA; stem + *r diffus.)	*sbi* "to be faint, perish" (stem + *y inchoat.)	*tsâab- or *sâab- or *tsâap'- or *sâap'- "to spoil"		
495. *-tsob- or *-cob- "to do wrong"		*sbt* "wrong; evil" (stem + *t n. suff.)	SC: Dahalo *tsoβ-* "to make mistake" (PSC *b > Dahalo *β* /V_; corrects Ehret 1987: #609)		
496. *-tsŭb- or *-cŭb- "to spill (tr.)"	A. *θabq* "to shed tears; pour out" (stem + *k^{w}' and.)	*sbt* "libation-jar" (stem + *t n. suff.)	PEC *cub- or *cub'- "to spill" (PC *ts > PEC *c; PC *p' > PEC *b')	some ECh *sbɗ "to pour" (J; stem + *z intens. of manner)	Mocha *šùw-* "to engender" (i.e., to beget < spill semen; PO *ts, *$š_3$ both > Mocha *š* /#_V)

		SEMITIC	EGYPTIAN	CUSHITIC	CHADIC	OMOTIC
497.	*-tsâg- or *-câg- "to rise"	A. *θajr* "broad and thick" (stem + *r adj. suff.; semantics: rise > swell in size); *θajal* "to be fat and flabby" (stem + *l adj. suff.)		*tsag- "crown of head"	ECh *sgr "long" (J gives $*s_2gr$ because of an untenable linking of this to a different root; there is **no** $*s_2$ in ECh; stem + *r adj. suff., i.e., rise > tall > long)	Gonga *šag- "to appear" (Mocha *'šäg*-); Mocha *'šug*- "to mount (male on female)" (PO *ts > Gonga *š /#_; *-u- tr. infix)
498.	*-tsag- or *-cag- or *-tsaag- or *-caag- "to not move, be at rest"	A. *θajw* "to be silent" (stem + *w inchoat.)	LE *sg3* "to be torpid, lethargic" (stem + *r adj. suff.; v. < presumed earlier adj.; C. *sōč* "to be paralyzed")	SC: PR *sag- "to rest" (PC *ts > PR *s, PR *a < either PC *a or *aa)	some WCh *sg "house" (J; semantics: stay still > stay, dwell > dwelling)	

	SEMITIC	EGYPTIAN	CUSHITIC	CHADIC	OMOTIC
499. *-tsîk'-/*-tsâk'- or *-cîk'- or *-câk'- "to pluck out, pluck off"	A. *θaqaf* "to seize, take hold of; find, obtain" (stem + *p intens. of manner)	LE *sḳr* "to pluck" (stem + *l fin.; semantics: single action of picking off/out?)	PSC *tsîk'- or *sîk'- "to remove husks, skins, etc."	WCh, CCh *sak' "to hollow out" (J; Ng. ***sháshk-***, ***shə́shk-***, stem redup. as freq.; pre-Ng. *s > *sh* /ə_ as in #429, generalized to both *s in both words)	
500. *-tsoon- or *-coon- "to smell"	A. *θanat* "to smell bad, stink" (stem + *t dur.)	*sn* "to smell (perfume); breathe (air)" (possible alternative attribution: root #224; C. *snsn*)	SLEC *coon- or *soon- "nose" (WOT, Konsoid root; conflated in Sasse 1979 with PEC *san-, < root #223, **and** PEC *siŋ-/*suŋ- < PC *ĭsŋʷ- "nose," which see under #224; PC *ts > PEC *c)	*sunə "to smell" (N) (J: *sn "to stink")	

	SEMITIC	EGYPTIAN	CUSHITIC	CHADIC	OMOTIC
501. *tsuun- or *cuun- "hair, especially pubic hair"	A. *θunna-t*, *θunan* "hair on a horse's hoof; pudenda"; MSA *θn(n) "groin"	LE *snty* "testicles" (stem + *t n. suff.; *y as LE reduction of *wy dual?)	EC: PSom *cuun "pubic hair" (PC *ts > PSom *c)	WCh, CCh *sn "hair" (J)	
502. *-tsăŋ- or *-căŋ- "to split in two, split one from the other"	A. *θanṭ* "cleft, rent" (stem + *t' dur. intens.; semantics: cleft is a *deep* split)	*sni* "to cut off (head), sever (neck)" (stem + *y inchoat.; semantics unclear)	*tsăŋ- or *săŋ- "to split, come apart"	WCh, CCh *sn "to skin" (J)	
503. *tsan- or *can- "two" (proposed source: #502, with regular PAA *ŋ > PBA *n; Eg., Berber, Sem. **innovation**: as synonym for #505)	*θny (*θany) "two"	*snw* "two" (C. *snaw* < alternate root with alternate stem V *i)		[*sər(-) "two" (N), for which see #505 below, does **not** correspond in V **nor** in 2nd C to Sem., Eg., Berber *tsan-]	

	SEMITIC	EGYPTIAN	CUSHITIC	CHADIC	OMOTIC
504. *-tsar- or *-car- "to grasp"	A. *θarabā-t* "fingers" (stem + *b anim. de-verb. suff.)		PEC *car- "to grasp" (PC *ts > PEC *c)	*sr(-n) "hand/arm" (J; stem + *n n. suff.; WCh *sar "ten," i.e., hands)	
505. *tsîr(n)- or *cîr(n)- "two" (vowel reconstruction uncertain: PAA *u, *ee, or *oo are also possible here; contrary to earlier views, this is surely a distinct root from #503)	*θər(n) "two" (MSA *θr-; Aramaic *tren*; this root, agreeing **only** in its C_1 with PS *θny "two" [503], **cannot** be considered an alternant of *θny, contra previous views)			*sər(n) "two" (N) (Ng. *shíŕí́n*; PCh *s > Ng. *sh* /_i; environment for PCh *ə > Ng. *i* remains to be fully defined; for other cases of this shift, see #471, 481, and #561)	

PAA *š	SEMITIC	EGYPTIAN	CUSHITIC	CHADIC	OMOTIC
506. *-šab- "to strike (with an implement)	MSA *sbṭ "to beat (with stick)" (stem + *t' dur. intens.; MSA *s < PS *c)		*šab- "to strike (with tool or weap-on)"	some WCh, ECh *sabr, *sibr "knife" (J; stem + *r n. suff.)	
507. *-šob- "to immerse, apply water to"	pPS *cb "to immerse" (Append.1); *cbʔ "to drink" (stem + *ʔ conc.)	*sbi* "to drink" (stem + *y inchoat.)	*šob- "to be immersed"		
508. *-šad- "to extend (lengthwise)"	pPS *cd "to extend (lengthwise)" (Append.1)				NOm: Maji *šadniz* "long" (stem + *n adj. suff. + Maji *-iz* adj. suff.)

	SEMITIC	EGYPTIAN	CUSHITIC	CHADIC	OMOTIC
509. *-šoof- "to scratch, scrape"	*cpr "to write, count" (stem + *r dif-fus.); A. *safn* "to scrape off the rind, peel" (stem + *n non-fin.)		*šoof- "to scrape"		
510. *-šaḫ- "to burn (tr.)"	A. *saḫf* "to burn" (stem + *f iter.); *saḫḫa* "hot wind"		EC: Yaaku *-šɛhɛr-* "to scorch" (stem + *r dif-fus., i.e., burn surface of; PEC *aḫ >Yaaku *ɛh*)		
511. *-šooḫ- "to wet down"	Ji. *sḫɔb* "rainclouds" (stem + *b ex-tend.; Ji. *s* < PS *c)		*šooḫ- "to secrete"	WCh *s- "to wash" (J)	Ometo: Koyra *šoh-* "to wash"

		SEMITIC	EGYPTIAN	CUSHITIC	CHADIC	OMOTIC
512.	*-šok- "to cover"	*ckk "to shut"; *ckr "to block" (stem + *r diffus.)		SC: Burunge *cok-* "to thatch"; *cokono* "thatch" (stem + *n n. suff.; PSC *š > Burunge *c*)	*skr "to close" (J; stem + *r diffus.; shared innovation with Sem. *ckr ?)	
513.	*-šîk^w- "to cut repeatedly"	*ckn "knife" (A. *sikkîn* ; MSA *skn; stem + *n n. suff.; MSA *s < PS *c); Ji. *skaʕ* "wounds on the legs" (stem + *ʕ part.; semantics: to slice *open* the skin)	*sk* "to fell (?) (trees)"	*šak^w-/*šik^w- "to cut repeatedly"	Ng. *səkwái* "small sickle" (stem + *y deverb.)	Mocha *'šikko* "knife" (wider Omotic diffusion of this word, as seen in Mao *sik-, Yem *sìkō* , etc.)

	SEMITIC	EGYPTIAN	CUSHITIC	CHADIC	OMOTIC
514. *-šuk'- or *-šuk^{w}'- "to be beaten"	A. *saqʕ* "to hit, beat" (stem + *ʕ part.; semantics: earlier "to knock *apart* ?)	cf. *sḳr* "to strike (head)," etc. (for which see #267; these roots would have become homonymous in pre-Eg.)	PEC *šuk'- "to be knocked apart, pounded up"		
515. *šuuk'- or *šuuk^{w}'- "narrow, slim"	A. *suql* "sides of abdomen just below ribs" (stem + *l n. suff.; *saqil* "slim of waist")		PEC *šuuk'- "narrow (of thing)"		
516. *-šaal- "to lap"; *-šaalk^{w}- "to lick up" (stem + *k^{w} fin.)	A. *salj* "to swallow a morsel" (stem + *g fin. fort.); *salɣaf* "to swallow, devour" (stem	*snk* "tongue" (stem + *k dur.); *snk* "to be greedy; greed" (2nd PAA root shape)	*šăalak^{w}- "to lap, lick" (2nd PAA root shape)		

	SEMITIC	EGYPTIAN	CUSHITIC	CHADIC	OMOTIC
	+ *ɣʷ comp. + *p intens. of manner)				
517. *-šul- or *-šuul- "to scratch"	A. *salt* "to wipe, wipe away; shave" (stem + *t dur.)	*srt* "thorn, spine"? (stem + *t n. suff.; cf. C. *surɛ* ; but V correspondence is not satisfactorily explained as yet)	PEC *šuull- "nail, claw" (corrects Ehret 1987: #611; n. < v. by V > VV?)		
518. *-šun- "to come close, come near"	H. *senōk* (?) "to reach" (PS *cnk: stem + *kʷ fin.; PS *c > MSA *s; Johnstone 1979 includes notation "(?)")	*sni* "to be like, resemble; imitate; conform" (stem + *y inchoat.)	EC: Afar *sune* "neighborhood" (PEC *š > Afar *s* ; semantics: nearby area)	some WCh, CCh *sn "to come" (J)	

	SEMITIC	EGYPTIAN	CUSHITIC	CHADIC	OMOTIC
519. *-šeŋ- "to be good"		*snb* "to be healthy, well; become well, recover; healthy" (stem *b extend.)	PEC *šen- "to be good" (PC *ŋ > PEC *n /_-#); Agaw: [Awngi *cənkút* "good": loan < Omotic]		NOm: Shinasha *še:ŋga* "good" (n. < v. by V > V:)
520. *šâp- "earth, ground"	A. *safan* "dust, earth" (stem + *n n. suff.)	*sp3t* "district, nome" (stem + *r, *t n. suff.)	[EC: Sidamo *shāfa* "sand": loan < Omotic (expected *saw-)]	some WCh *spm "stone" (J; stem + *m n. suff.)	*šap- "sand" (Mocha *'šawo* "earth"; SOm: Banna *ša:mmi* < *šapm-, stem + *m n. suff.)
521. *-šaap- "to cry out"	*cpd "to mourn, wail" (stem + *d dur.)	*spr* "to appeal to; petition" (stem + *l n. suff.; v. < n.; C. *sopsp*)			Ometo: Koyra *ša:p-* "to insult, argue with"

	SEMITIC	EGYPTIAN	CUSHITIC	CHADIC	OMOTIC
522. *-šup'- "to abuse, revile"	*cbb "to abuse, revile, inveigh against"		EC: Yaaku *-šub-* "to curse" (Yaaku *b* < PC *p')		
523. *-šĕr- "to shift (position)"	pPS *cr "to move" (Ehret 1989; MSA evidence requires *c)		*šĕrh- "to slip, shift position" (stem + *h ampl.)		
524. *-šoor- "to feed"	*crṭ "to swallow, gulp down" (A., MSA; stem + *t' dur. intens.); A. *sarf* "to eat a tree bare" (stem + *p intens. of manner)		PEC *šoor- "to feed"		

	SEMITIC	EGYPTIAN	CUSHITIC	CHADIC	OMOTIC
525. *-šǎawd- "to wrap around"	*cwd "black"? (proposed semantics: wrap > cover up > make dark; A. *aswad*)	*swswd* "to bandage" (redup. stem as freq.)	PSC *šǎawad- "to do by wrapping the hands around" (WR "to strangle"; Ma'a "to mold pots")		
526. *-šǎy- "to sparkle"	H. *sēḳ* "flame, spark" (*syḳ, stem + *k' intens. of effect; MSA *s < PS *c)				NOm: Bench *šayt* 4 "star" (stem + *t n. suff.)
527. *-šěeʕ- "to be scraped"	A. *saʕaf* "to be chapped around the nails" (stem + *f iter.; semantics: chapping involves many small peelings of skin)	*s ᶜs ᶜ* "to deface (?)" (redup. stem as intens.)	*šěeʕ- "to be scraped bare" (Append.2)	Ng. *sáauɗ-* "to wipe around inside of food bowl, etc., with forefinger" (stem + *w inchoat. [> dur.] + *z intens. of manner)	

	SEMITIC	EGYPTIAN	CUSHITIC	CHADIC	OMOTIC
528. *-šūʕ-/*-šāʕ- "to smell (intr.)"	A. *saʕṭ* "to make snuff medicine" (*suʕāṭ* "sharp (sense of) smell"; stem + *t' dur. intens.)		PEC *šuʕs- "to smell (tr.)" (stem + *s caus.); PEC *šuʕn- "smell, odor" (stem + *n n. suff.)		Mocha *šá'o* "odor"
PAA *s'					
529. *-s'êd- "to be (dark-) colored"	A. *sadaf* "first twilight" (stem + *f iter. or *p intens. of manner?)		PSC *ts'êd- "red"		NOm: Bench *ts'id*[1] "black" (expected *ts'id[3] ?)
530. *-s'ig- "to stay"	A. *sajm* "to delay, deter" (stem + *m extend.); *sujuww* "to be quiet, settle" (stem + *w inchoat.)		EC: Afar *sig-* "to stay, dwell" (PC *ts' > Afar *s*)	WCh *s'g "to sit" (J)	

	SEMITIC	EGYPTIAN	CUSHITIC	CHADIC	OMOTIC
531. *-s'uuɣ- or *-s'uuɣʷ- "to rub"	A. *saɣsaɣ* "to tread or roll in the dust; grease a dish abundantly" (redup. as intens.); *saɣbal* "to grease or butter; anoint the head" (stem + *b extend. + *l fin.)		PEC *cuug'- "to rub, scrub" (PC *ts' > PEC *c, PC *ɣ and *ɣʷ > PEC *g')		
532. *-s'ah- "to pound (to loosen)"	A. *sahj* "to pound, grind" (stem + *gʷ dur.); *sahk* "to grind" (stem + *k dur.)	*sh3t* "drummer" (stem + *ʔ conc. + *t n. suff.; semantics: drumming is a focused action)	SC: PR *c'aham- "chaff" (stem + *m n. suff.; semantics: chaff is loosened by threshing; PR *c' < PC *ts')		

		SEMITIC	EGYPTIAN	CUSHITIC	CHADIC	OMOTIC
533.	*-s'ik'- or *-s'ik^{w}'- "to come near"	A. *saqab* "to be or stand near" (stem + *b extend. > stat.)		PEC *cik'- "to move short distance, pass nearby" (PC *ts' > PEC *c; PC *C^{w} > PEC *C)		Ometo: Malo *s'ik'k'a* "narrow" (i.e., close together, as sides of passage)
534.	*-s'uk'- or *-s'uk^{w}'- "to strike (with tool, weapon)"	A. *saqʕ* "to hit, beat" (stem + *ʕ part., i.e., earlier "knock apart"?)	*sḳr* "to strike (head); strike down (foes)" (stem + *l fin.)	PEC *cuk'- "to strike with a tool" (PC *ts' PEC *c)		
535.	*-s'ăm- "to sour"	A. *sumūṭ* "to begin to turn sour" (stem + *ṭ' dur. intens.)	*smi* "curds" (LE "curd; cream") (stem + *y deverb.)	PEC *cam- "to rot" (PC *ts' > PEC *c)	*s'am "sour" (J)	NOm *s'a(:)m- "to be bitter" (Mocha *č'à:m-*)

		SEMITIC	EGYPTIAN	CUSHITIC	CHADIC	OMOTIC
536.	*-s'iink'- or *-s'iinkʷ'- "to become weak"	A. *isnāq* "effeminateness"		PEC *ciink'- "to become thin, weak, slight" (PC *ts' > PEC *c)		
537.	*-s'ēer- "to lower, put low"	pPS *sr "to lay down, put low" (Append.1)	*srf* "to take one's ease; rest, relief" (stem + *f iter. > dur.; C. *srfɛ*)	*ts'ēer- "to lower, lessen"	Ng. *sə́rm*- "to sit with legs out in front of one" (stem + *m ex-end.)	Gonga *č'i:r- "to perish" (Mocha *č'ì:r*- "to be finished")
538.	*-s'at-/*-s'it- "to cut into"		*sti* "to shoot (arrow); thrust (into); spear (fish)" (stem + *y inchoat. > tr.; C. *sītɛ*); *stp* "to cut up (animal); cut off (limbs)" (stem + *p intens. of	*ts'at- "to cut up"	Ng. *sə̀t*- "to sharpen to a point (pencil, etc.)"	

		SEMITIC	EGYPTIAN	CUSHITIC	CHADIC	OMOTIC
			manner); *stw* "arrow, dart" (stem + *w de-verb.; C. *sotε*)			
539.	*-s'at- "to exude" (Eg., (Sem. **innovation**: shift to outflow of water, *not* from body; root *-s'a- seen in #540 + *t dur.)	*stp "to give water" (stem + *f iter.); *sty "to drink" (stem + *y inchoat. > dur.)	*stf* "to water" (stem + *f iter. as in Sem. *stp; C. *sōtf*)	SC: Iraqw *tsat-* "to fart" (PC *ts' > Iraqw *ts*)		
540.	*-s'aw- "to flow" (root *-s'a-, seen also in #539 preceding, + *w inchoative)	pPS *sw/*sy "to flow" (Append.1)	*swnnw* "pond" (stem + *n non-fin., redup., + *w denom.)	SC: Dahalo *ts'waaḫ-* "to wash wound with hot water" (stem + *ḫ iter.)	WCh *s'awr "water" (J; stem + *r n. suff.)	NOm *s'aw- "to exude fluid" (Zaysse *č'áwa* "sweat"; Mocha *'č'ot-* "to leak" [stem + *t dur.]; She *č'om* "cloud" [stem + *m n. suff.])

		SEMITIC	EGYPTIAN	CUSHITIC	CHADIC	OMOTIC
541.	*s'iw- "daylight, sunlight"	Ji. *šum* (*šwm) "heat of the sun" (MSA *š < PS *s; stem + *m n. suff.)	*sww* "dates" (days) (stem + *w pl.); LE *sw* "day; date" (C. *sēw*, *su-*)		some WCh *s'w- "morning" (J)	
542.	*-s'aʔ- "to drink up, slurp up (liquid)"	A. *saʔb* "to quench thirst" (stem + *p' fin. fort.); *saʔad* "to drink" (stem + *d dur.)		SC: PR *č'aʔ- "to snuff, suck up" (Kw'adza "to drink"; PR *č' < PC *ts')		
543.	*-s'âʕ-/*-s'îʕ- "to burn (intr.)"	A. *saʕr* "to light or stir the fire" (stem + *r diffus.); MSA *šʕl "to spark" (stem + *l fin.; MSA *š < PS *s)		*ts'aʕ-/*ts'iʕ- "to burn (intr.)" (Append.2)		Bench, Maji *ts'iakn "ashes" (stem + *k dur., i.e., "to glow," + *n n. suff.; Bench *ts'yakn* 3,3; Maji *ts'ia:ts'o* "sun" (redup. as intens.)

	SEMITIC	EGYPTIAN	CUSHITIC	CHADIC	OMOTIC
544. *-s'iʕ- "to draw out, pull out"		*s ᶜb* "to circumcise; to take to pieces (boat)" (LE "castrated, sawed off"; stem + *b extend.)	PSC *ts'iʕ- "to be drawn out, be extracted"	some WCh *s'ᵐb "to pull" (stem + *m extend. + *b extend.)	Mocha *č'í'o* "bow, arrow, sling" (semantics: "to draw the bow")
545. *s'iʕ- "hurry, haste"	*sʕy "to hurry, run" (stem + *y denom.); A. *saʕm* "to walk very fast" (stem + *m extend. as fort.)		PEC *ciʕ- or *ciʔ- "hurry" (PC *ts' > PEC *c)		

	SEMITIC	EGYPTIAN	CUSHITIC	CHADIC	OMOTIC
PAA *c'					
546. *-c'ŭb- "to glow, burn low" (2nd root shape *-c'aab- seen in PEC v. and Banna (SOm) "white," is not as yet satisfactorily accounted for)	A. *ẓaby* "mark by branding" (stem + *y deverb.); *ẓubẓib* "to have a fever" (redup. stem)	*sb3* "star" (stem + *r n. suff.; C. *sīu*)	PEC *c'aab- "to be afire"		*č'ub- "smoke" (Yem *čūwā* ; Mocha *č'upó* , Bench *ç̌'ub* 1) SOm: Banna *č'a:wli* "white" (stem + *l adj. suff.); SOm: Ari *č'ub-* "to emit smoke"
547. *-c'of- "to flow slowly"		*sft* "oil" (stem + *t n. suff.)	*c'of- "to leak, seep"; *-c'fak'- "to soak" (stem + *k' intens. of effect)		SOm: Ari *č'afi* "wet" (for *o > Ari *a* /C[palatal]_, see also #483)

		SEMITIC	EGYPTIAN	CUSHITIC	CHADIC	OMOTIC
548.	*-c'uf-/*-c'if- "to tie together"	A. *ẓaff* "to tie together the forefeet of camel"		*c'uf-/*c'if- "to close"		
549.	*c'ohr- "trash, residue, discarded materials"	A. *ẓahr* "to throw behind, forget, neglect" (back-formation < n.; influenced by *ẓaḥr* "back," #550, i.e., "throw *behind* ")		PLEC *c'ohr- "rubbish, trash, residue"		NOm: Bench *č'or* 2-3 "leftover (of drink), residue"; SOm: Ari *č'ooré* "cow dung"
550.	*c'ohr- "lower back"	*θ̣hr "back" (A. *ẓahr*)		EC: Jiiddu *j'ooro* "kidney" (Jiiddu *j'* < PEC *c')		
551.	*-c'aḥ- "to dig"	MSA *ð̣ḥy "garden" (stem + *y deverb.)		EC: Yaaku *-c'ɛh-* "to dig" (PEC *aḥ > Yaaku *ɛh*)		

	SEMITIC	EGYPTIAN	CUSHITIC	CHADIC	OMOTIC
552. *-c'aḥ- "to beat"		*sḥm* "to crush, pound" (stem + *m extend. as fort.; C. *sōhm*); LE *sḥr* "to strike" (stem + *l fin.; semantics: single action)	PEC *c'aḥ- "to hit"	some ECh *s'- "to kill"	
553. *-c'uuk-/*-c'iik- "to rub off"		*sk* "to wipe, wipe out, wipe away" (C. *sīkε* "to mill")	PEC *c'uukk- "to rub"		
554. *c'îk'l- "jaw"			EC: Soomaali *jaqal, jiqil* "angle of the jaw" (PEC *c' > *j*, *k' > *q* in Soomaali)	Ng. *jə́gənà* "cheek" (PCh *l > Ng. *n; Kanuri borrowing *zə̀gáṭì* requires PCh *l)	

		SEMITIC	EGYPTIAN	CUSHITIC	CHADIC	OMOTIC
555.	*-c'il- "to darken, become dark colored"	*θ̣ll "to give shade" (A. *ẓill* "shadow, shade; darkness")	*snkt* , *snkkw* "darkness" (stem + *k dur. + *t n. suff.; also redup. + *w deverb.; semantics: to grow dark > darkness)	HEC, Oromo *c'il- "ember, charcoal" (not to be confused with PLEC reflex of root #251, which see; semantics: charcoal is black)		
556.	*c'ilm-/*c'alm- "black" (root #555 + *m adj. suff.)	*θ̣lm "black; darkness"			*s'ələm "black" (WCh: Buduma *tsillim* ; ECh: Sokoro *silim* : writer's reconstruction; also Greenberg 1963)	SOm: Ari *č'ɛlmi* "black"

	SEMITIC	EGYPTIAN	CUSHITIC	CHADIC	OMOTIC
557. *-c'aam- "to rest"		*smt* "hammock" (stem + *t n. suff.; semantics: resting place)	PEC *c'aamb- "to be quiet" (stem + *b extend. > stat.)	some WCh *sm "to sleep" (J)	Mocha *č'ạ:m-* "to be safe and sound"
558. *-c'em- "to become dark"	A. *aẓma* "brown; blackish"; *ẓaman* "reddish-brown" (stem + *n adj. suff.)			*s'mz "night" (J; stem + *dz extend. fort.; semantics: be *quite* dark?)	NOm: Ometo *č'e:m- "night" (Zayse *č'eemó*; n. < v. by V > V:)
559. *-c'iin- "to observe"	*θ̣n(n) "to think, suppose" (semantic influence < *znn in #200?)	*sin* "to wait" (semantics: watch > wait for)		(cf. CCh *s'n "to hear," cited under #250 above?)	Gonga *č'i:n- "to observe" (Mocha *č'ị:n-*)

	SEMITIC	EGYPTIAN	CUSHITIC	CHADIC	OMOTIC
560. *-c'ep- "to wait"	A. *ẓafr* "to sit" (stem + + *r diffus.)	*spi* "to remain over; be left out, excluded" (stem + *y inchoat., i.e., *be left* waiting)	*c'ep- or *c'eb- "to watch" (semantics: wait > watch)		
561. *-c'ap'-/*-c'ip'- "to drip"	A. *ẓabẓāb* "pustules in the face" (redup. stem as freq.)		PEC *c'ab'- "to drip" (PEC *b' < PC *p')	Ng. *jìcɓ-* "to sprinkle" (redup. stem as freq.; other PCh *Cə >Ng. $C_{[palatal]}$ i: see #471, 481, 521)	
562. *-c'âr- "to be clever"	A. *ẓarf* "to be witty, sharp of intellect, skillful, graceful, elegant" (stem + *f iter., i.e., to consistently act cleverly)	*s3i* "to be wise, prudent"; *s3w* "wisdom, prudence"; *s33* "wise man; wisdom (?)"	PSC *t^y'âr- "to be crafty, cunning" (PSC *t^y' = PC *c')		

	SEMITIC	EGYPTIAN	CUSHITIC	CHADIC	OMOTIC
563. *-c'ar-/*-c'ir- "to rise up"	A. *ẓirr* "stone with a sharp, knifelike edge"; *ẓarib* "sharp projection of a rock; (stem + *p' fin. fort.; semantics: rise to top or form very top of)		PSC *ṭʸ'aaraʕ- "to fly, jump" (stem + *ʕ part.; part.; PSC *ṭʸ' = PC *c'; PC *a > PSC *aa /#C_Caʕ,ʔ: see also #167)	*s'ar/*s'ir "to stand" (J)	Ometo: Kachama *č'era* "bird"; SOm: Ari *č'arma* "pointed" (stem + *m adj. suff.; semantics: see Arabic entries); NOm: Bench *č'ar* 2-3 "rock" (semantics: see Arabic entries)
564. *c'irf- or *c'ifr- "nail, claw"	*θ̣pr "nail, claw" (A. *ẓufr*)		SC: WR *ts'araf- "nail, claw" (PC *c' > WR *ts'; WR *a /C_CaC < PC *i or *a)		

	SEMITIC	EGYPTIAN	CUSHITIC	CHADIC	OMOTIC
565. *-c'êyg- "to shout"	A. *ẓajj* "to call for assistance in battle"	*sg* "to command"; LE *sgb* "to shriek, cry; shout; clamor; lament" (stem + *b extend.; C. *ščap*)	PSC *ʈʸ'ʌg- or *ʈʸ'eg- "to curse, bewitch" (PSC *ʈʸ' = PC *c'; PSC *ʌ < PC *ay)	WCh, CCh *š'gɮ "lion" (J. *s'gɮ; Ng. *jágádláu* : stem + *dl m.v. + *w deverb.; semantics: lion as the roarer)	*č'ayg- "to shout" (Yem *čáag-* "to shout"; Mocha *č'ẹ:g-* "to call, yell")
566. *-c'î?- or *-c'îi?- "to convey"	pPS *θ̣? "to take (away)" (Append.1)		PSC *ʈʸî?it- *ʈʸ'îi?it- "to carry" (stem + *t dur.; PSC *ʈʸ' = PC *c')	Ng. *jí* "go; take" (imperative)	
567. *-c'eʕ- "to rise"	MSA *ð̣ʕr "on, over" (stem + *r adj. suff.); A. *ẓaʕan* "to travel; set forth" (stem + *n non-fin.)		PEC *c'eʕ- "to rise"	WCh, CCh *s'(n)t "bird" (J; stem + *n non-fin. + *t n. suff.)	

THE *PAA* NASAL CONSONANTS

For at least three of the five points of articulation so far sketched out, a nasal stop can also certainly be reconstructed for PAA. PAA *m and *n must have been particularly frequent consonants. The third nasal, *ŋ, was considerably less common.

The first two represent uncomplicated reconstructions, recurring as /m/ and /n/ throughout the family in almost all environments. One unusual PCh reflex of PAA *m does appear in Jungraithmayr and Shimizu (1981), specifically in their representation of the PAA monoconsonantal roots in *m (#569 and 570). They show $*^{m}b$ in those cases, whereas Newman's (1972) work gives just the expected *m. Apparently some unusual sound shifts affected PAA *m in that particular environment in some of the Chadic languages, and Jungraithmayr and Shimizu felt it necessary to account for the shifts by reconstructing $*^{m}b$ instead of simple *m.

The PAA velar *ŋ, in contrast, has been preserved as a velar only in Eastern Cushitic, in certain languages of the Agaw and Southern branches of Cushitic, and apparently in some Chadic languages (see roots #641 and 643). In Semitic and Egyptian and also word-initially in Omotic — languages which have only *n and *m — PAA *ŋ has everywhere fallen together with PAA *n. Intervocalically in Omotic, however, *ŋ gave *ng, and in verb-stem-final position its PO reflex can be tentatively proposed to have been *g except when preceded by another PAA velar consonant in the same word, in which case its outcome was apparently *n (see root #281).

A fourth nasal, *ŋʷ, would make good systemic sense, in view of the otherwise full array of labiovelars reconstructible to PAA; but the evidence for it is as yet very meager. Three possible cases of *ŋʷ are proposed here (roots #48/49 and 224 above and #643 below), and a few other examples appear in Cushitic (cf. Ehret 1980: 272).

A fifth nasal, palatal *ɲ is represented by fifteen proposed cognate sets (roots #644-658). Its status as a valid PAA reconstruction is suspect because it appears with certainty as a distinct consonant only in Southern and Eastern Cushitic and in one Omotic language, although it may possibly have been preserved in limited contexts in one subbranch of Chadic (see root #658). Its correspondents in Semitic and Egyptian are everywhere simply /n/, as is also usually the case in Chadic in initial position. On the other hand, no consistent environment for a hypothetical conditioned splitting of the cited *ɲ from earlier *n or *ŋ seems evident. In addition, and more tellingly, a Cushitic cognate containing *ɲ can be found for each of the only two Arabic verbs which contain the extremely rare sequence of stem consonants *nr*. This sequence appears to violate a co-occurrence constraint that forbids all other pairings of alveolar sonorants (except *rn) in Semitic C_1 and C_2 position. If the PS *n in these two cognate sets (roots #646 and 651) were to derive from a nasal that was in fact not alveolar at the time the constraint took effect, as the Cushitic reflexes imply, then these occurrences of PS *nr would (at least diachronically) no longer represent a violation of the rule. (Some cases of PS *rn might be similarly explainable; others may derive from roots of the shape *rV- plus a nominal suffix or extension in *n.)

A provisional and tentative reconstruction of PAA *ɲ would therefore seem warranted despite the limited occurrence of /ɲ/ in modern-day Afroasiatic languages.

In Omotic and Chadic nasal consonants often dropped out medially in certain fricative environments; the rules involved may in both cases date to the proto-language. In Omotic this shift may have been fully general:

PO #15. PAA *N > Ø /V_C (C = [+sibilant] or PO *p ([f] /V_).

Examples involving PO $*x_1$ and $*x_2$ having not yet been identified, it remains unknown whether or not shift #15 might have had a more general environment /V_C[-contin./-voice]. The Chadic shift may have operated before just voiceless fricatives (see roots #365 and 449, in contrast to #397):

PCh #5. PAA *N > Ø /V_C (cases of C = *ts, *ẖ are known).

Finally, it should be noted that PAA *n, $*ŋ^{(w)}$, and *ɲ apparently all fell together with PAA *n in the Boreafrasian languages:

PBA #5. PAA $*ŋ^{(w)}$, *ɲ > PBA *n.

PAA *m	SEMITIC	EGYPTIAN	CUSHITIC	CHADIC	OMOTIC
568. *m- indefinite pronoun stem ("one, someone, somebody")	A. *man* "he/she/those who" (stem + *n nom. suff.)	*im* "form, shape" (*i- attrib. n. pref. + stem); *mn* "someone, so-and-so" (stem + *n nom. suff.; C. *man*)	*m- 3rd-person indefinite pronoun; PSC *mɨ "people"	*m- "person, man"; *mu(n) 1st-person pl. inclusive pron. BM *ma 1st-person dual pron.	
569. *-m- (*-mă- ?) "to be wet"; *âm- "water" (*a- attrib. n. pref. + stem)	pPS *mw/*my "to become wet" (Ehret 1989; stem + *w, *y inchoative)	*mw* "water" (stem + *w deverb.; C. *mōu*) *mwy* "to be watery" ("water" + *y denom.)		*am "water" (N) (Ng. *âm*) (J: *m$_b$-)	Gonga *am- "rain" (Mocha *'amiyo*, stem + *y n. suff.); NOm *mas- "to wash" (stem + *s caus.; Bench *mas(k)*[3], Mocha *màss*-, Yem *màs*-)

	SEMITIC	EGYPTIAN	CUSHITIC	CHADIC	OMOTIC
570. *-im- "to come"		*my* "come!"	*-ʔim (t)- "to come" (stem + *t dur.)	$*m_b$- "to come" (J)	
571. *ma, *mi "what?"	A. *mā* "what?"	*m* "what?; who?"	*ma, *mi interrogative root	*mi, *ma "what?"	NOm *ma- "what?"
572. *-ma- "to not have"	A. *mā* "not"	*m* negative imperative ("do not"); *imi* negative verb	*ma- "to avoid" (Ehret 1980: 323)	*may-(a) "hunger" (J; stem + *y deverb. suff., i.e., lacking food)	
573. *-mâc- "to walk swaying, move about disjointedly"	A. *maθʕ* "to walk in a vulgar fashion (women)" (stem + *ʕ part.; semantics unclear)	*mss* "to totter" (stem with redup. as freq.)	EC: Soomaali *mashaqo* "turbamento" (stem + *k' intens. of effect; PC *ts > Som. *sh* [š]); [PEC *macc- "to be drunk":		Gonga *maš- "to be drunk" (Mocha *'maš*-; PO *š and $*š_3$ > Gonga *š)

	SEMITIC	EGYPTIAN	CUSHITIC	CHADIC	OMOTIC
			probable Omotic loanword]		
574. *-mǎac- "to immerse, flow over"	pPS *mθ "to leak, run out" (Append. 1)	*msyt* "waterfowl"? (stem + *y n. suff. + *t coll.)	EC: Soomaali *maash* "to spread over (of rain, flood, prosperity); to drown (tr.)" (PC *ts > Som. *sh* [š])		NOm: Bench *maş̌*[1] "sedimented" (i.e., covered with sediment from stream flow)
575. *-mîc- "to chew up"	A. *maθj* "to give one to eat" (stem + *g^w dur., i.e., feed)		PEC *muc-/*mic- "to chew slowly" (PC *ts > PEC *c)		NOm *miš$_3$- "to be satiated" (Mocha *'mis-*)

	SEMITIC	EGYPTIAN	CUSHITIC	CHADIC	OMOTIC
576. *-môoc- or *-môots- "to turn (tr.)"	A. *maθmaθ* "to confuse" (redup. stem as intens. or freq.)	*msn* "to spin (?); plait (?)" (stem + *n non-fin.); *msnḫ* "to rotate; turn backwards" (stem + *n non-fin. + *ḫ iter., i.e., rotate)	PSC *môodok'- "to bend (joint of body)" (stem + *k' intens. of manner; semantics: joints bend *sharply*, at right angles; PSC *d /V_VC > PC *ts)	Ng. *mə̀st-* "to turn, tilt, change into" (stem + *t dur.)	
577. *-mac'- "to start"	A. *maẓh* "to set out on a journey" (stem + *h ampl.; semantics: journey is an extended trip)	LE *ms* "to launch"	*mac'- "to get up"		
578. *-mâd- or *-mâad- "to flow"	A. *madd* "to flow"		PSC *mâd- or *mâad- "rain"		

	SEMITIC	EGYPTIAN	CUSHITIC	CHADIC	OMOTIC
579. *-moodz- "to become wet"	pPS *mð "to wet" (Ap-pend.1)	LE *sms* "to splash" (*s caus. + stem); *mzḫ* "crocodile" ? (stem + *ḫ iter.; semantics: crocodile as animal habitually associated with water)	EC: Afar *mooyat* "waves" (stem + *t pl.; PEC *c (here < PC *dz) > Afar *y* /oo_; see also #599 below for same shift)	some WCh *mz(t) "soil" (J: stem + *t n. suff.; proposed semantics: < earlier "mud")	NOm *moodz- "to become wet" (Bench *mošt* 4 "to swim," stem + *t dur.; Zayse *mòož-* "to feel cold")
580. *-muɣʷ- "to hit"	A. *maɣθ* "to beat lightly" (stem + *ts diffus.)	LE *mḫt* "whip" (stem + *t n. suff.)	PSC *mux- "to fight" (PC *ɣʷ > PSC *x /u_-)		NOm: Yem *mùk-* "to thresh"
581. *-măh- or *-măah- "to not be able (to do)" (root #572 + *h ampl.)	A. *mahk* "to enervate (by sexual intercourse)" (stem + *k dur.)	*mhy* "to be forgetful" (stem + *y inchoat.); *mht* "forgetfulness" (stem + *t n. suff.)	PSC *măh- or *măah- "to be sterile" [borrowed into Ethiopic Sem. < unidentified Cush. source]		

	SEMITIC	EGYPTIAN	CUSHITIC	CHADIC	OMOTIC
582. *-mĭḫ- "to attack"	A. *maḫz* "to strike the chest with the fist" (stem + *z intens. of manner); *maḫn* "to beat" (stem + *n non-fin.)	*mḫ* "to hold, seize, capture" (C. *amahtɛ*, probable *i- attrib. n. pref., i.e., "capture (n.)," + *ty (*t dur. + *y denom.), rederiving v. application)	*mǎḫ-/*mĭḫ- "to attack, assail"		
583. *-maaḫ- "to get wet" (root #569 + *ḫ iter.)		*mḫi* "to drown" (stem + *y inchoat., i.e., become immersed)	*maaḫ- "to get wet"		
584. *-muj-/-maj- "to come forth, emerge, stick out"	A. *maðl* "to make known a secret" (stem + *l fin.)	*mz3* "to bring, present; extend (hand)" (stem + *ʔ conc.)	PEC *mic-/ *muc-/*mac- "to stick out, come forth" (PC *dz > PEC *c)		Gonga *mo:ččo "young grain" (n. < v. by V > V:, from *moč-)

	SEMITIC	EGYPTIAN	CUSHITIC	CHADIC	OMOTIC
585. *-mak- "to eat up"	A. *makk* "to suck out"	*mkw, mkyw* "food" (stem + *y deverb., + *w* pl.?)	*m-k- "gullet"		Yem *màkt-* "to be hungry" (stem + *t dur. > intr.)
586. *-maak'- or *-maak^{w}'- "to come back, return"		LE *mḳ3* "to come" (stem + *r diffus., removing sense of completed action)			*maak'- "to return"
587. *-mal- "to flow"; *-mălḫ- "to ooze, be viscous" (stem + *ḫ iter.; semantics: flow out bit-by-bit)	A. *malẓ* "to drop excrement" (stem + *c' extend.; semantics: < manner the stools leave the anus)	*mnḫ* "wax" (LE "wax, beeswax") (2nd PAA root shape; C. *mulh*)	*măłḫ- "to ooze out; pus" (2nd PAA root shape); [EC: PSom-III *mallay "fish": loan < Ometo]	some WCh *ml "water" (J)	NOm: Ometo *mol- "fish" (stem with *-u- tr. infix added before *u > NOm *o; semantics: to move the water in swimming > fish)

	SEMITIC	EGYPTIAN	CUSHITIC	CHADIC	OMOTIC
588. *miil- "thigh"		*mnt* "thigh; haunch" (stem + *t n. suff.)	EC: Oromo *miila* "leg"		Ometo: Koyra *minle* "thigh" (< *miln-, stem + *n n. suff.)
589. *-mǎn- "to lose, lack, be without" (root #572 + + n non-fin.)	A. *manʕ* "to refuse, hinder, prevent, repel" (stem + *ʕ part., i.e., to keep *from* having, doing)	*mn* "loss; there is not" (C. *mmon* "not"); *mni* "to die; death" (stem + *y deverb.; v. < n.)		*m-n(t)- "to forget" (N; stem + *t dur.)	NOm *ma(:)nn- "person of outcaste status, casted worker, tanner," etc. (Mocha *ma:nnó*; n. < v. by V > V:)
590. *-man-/*-mun- or *-maŋ-/ *-muŋ- or *-maɲ-/*-muɲ- "to tie up"	MSA *mnʕ "to take, catch, hold" (stem + *ʕ part.; semantics: probable underlying "to capture using a rope")	*mni* "to moor (ship)" (stem + *y inchoat. > dur.; C. *mōōnɛ*, *manɛ*); *mnḫ* "to string (beads)" (stem + *ɣʷ comp.);	*mantl-/*muntl- "to twist (e.g. in making rope)" (stem + *tl' foc.)		

	SEMITIC	EGYPTIAN	CUSHITIC	CHADIC	OMOTIC
		LE *mnṯ3* "to fasten" (stem + *tl' foc. + *ʔ conc.)			
591. *-mâr- "to bind"		*mr* "to bind" (C. *mur*, *mor*); *mrw* "weavers" (stem + *w* pl. or *w deverb.)	*mar- "to bind"		NOm: Bench *mar* 3 "to plait hair"
592. *-măar- "to be happy, fortunate, healthy"	A. *maraḥ* "to be merry and boisterous" (stem + *ḥ iter.); *marx* "to jest, sport" (stem + *x^w extend. fort.)	LE *mrd* "without defects, happy, successful, fortunate" (stem + *d dur. > stat.)	*martl- "to be without care, be merry" (stem + *tl' foc.)		NOm *ma:r- "to get well" (Mocha *mà:r-* "to get over having roundworms; Yem *màràm-* "to be healed" (stem + *m extend.)

	SEMITIC	EGYPTIAN	CUSHITIC	CHADIC	OMOTIC
593. *-mĭr-/*-măr- "to pass, pass by"	A. *marr* "to pass, pass by"	*mrt*, *mrrt* "street" (stem partially redup. + *t n. suff.)	*măr-/*mĭr- "to pass along"		
594. *-mir-/*-mar- "to take in the fingers"	pPS *mr "to brush with the fingers" (Ehret 1989)		*mar- "to wring"; EC: Yaaku *-mirmir-* "to wring" (redup. stem as intens.)	Ng. *mə̀rmə̀s-* "to rub lightly" (stem + *m extend. + *š non-fin.); *mə̀ř̃gə̀ɗ-* "to wring out" (stem + *g fin. fort. + *z intens. of manner); *mə̀ř̃tə̀k-* "to twist" (stem + *t dur. + *x precip.?)	

	SEMITIC	EGYPTIAN	CUSHITIC	CHADIC	OMOTIC
595. *-mur- "to flow"	*mrc "to marinate" (stem + *š non-fin.)	*mr* "canal; artificial lake"; *mrw* "bank" (stem + *w n. suff.; C. *mēr* implies *muur, with n. < v. by V > VV)	PSC *mur- "to flow"	*mrs "to vomit" (J; stem + *ts diffus.)	SOm: Ari *mɨri* "river, stream" (*mur-)
596. *-mas- "to become evening"	*msy "evening" (stem + *y deverb.); *ʔms (*ʔams) "yesterday" (*a- attrib. n. pref. + stem; semantics: cf. English *eve* denoting "the day before," as in "on the eve of")	*msyt* "supper" (i.e., evening meal) (stem + *y deverb. + *t n. suff.)	SC: PR *amas- "night" (*a- attrib. n. pref. + stem; corrects Ehret 1980: 297)		NOm: Yem *màskō* "morning star, Venus" (stem + *k dur.?, i.e., shine at dusk, with shift from evening to morning reference)

	SEMITIC	EGYPTIAN	CUSHITIC	CHADIC	OMOTIC
597. *-mâat'- "to trade, barter, sell, buy"			EC: Yaaku *-maat'-* "to sell"	*masə "to buy" (N) (J: *ms' "to sell"; Ng. *más-* "to buy")	
598. *-matl'-/*-mitl'- "to empy, empty out"	pPS *mṣ "to draw out" (Ehret 1989)	*mṯwn* "arena" (stem + *w inchoat. + *n n. suff.; semantics: area of open ground; *m- agent n. pref. + Eg. v. *ṯwn* "to gore with horn" seems a bit far-fetched)	*matl-/*mitl- "to be empty"		

	SEMITIC	EGYPTIAN	CUSHITIC	CHADIC	OMOTIC
599. *moots- "baby"	A. *maθāna-t* "womb; bladder" (stem + *n n. suff.)	*ms* "child; calf" (C. *mas*); *msi* "to give birth; produce; create" (stem + *y deverb.; C. *mīsɛ*)	EC: Afar *mooy*, *moota* "baby goat" (PEC *c (here < PC *ts) > Afar *y* /oo_; 2nd shape: stem + *t n. suff.)		NOm: Mocha *mo:sso* "baby"
600. *-maaw- "to die" (root #572 + *w inchoat.; PS, Eg., Ch **innovation**: integration of *t dur. into stem)	*mwt "to die" (A. *mawt*)	*mwt*, *mt* "to die" (C. *mu*)	EC: PSom-II *-umaaw-/ *-am-w(t)- "to die"	*mətə "to die" (N) (Ng. *mə̀t-*) (J: *mwt)	
601. *-max^w- "to move water about" (root #570 + *x^w extend. fort.?)	pPS *mx "to produce water, fluid" (Ehret 1989)	*mḫ3* "a boat" (stem + *r n. suff.)	PSC *max^w- "hippopotamus"		

	SEMITIC	EGYPTIAN	CUSHITIC	CHADIC	OMOTIC
602. *-môx^w- "to bend"		*mḫ3* "to incline (one's heart)" (stem + *ʔ conc.)	*môx^w- "to bend"		
603. *-maʔ-/*-miʔ- "to bend, fold (tr.)"		*m3s* "to kneel" (stem + *š non-fin. or *s' fort.; semantics: see Cush. entry in #576); *m3st* "knee; hock" (above v.+ *t n. suff.)	PSC *maʔ- or *maʕ- "to bend, fold"	*ma "to return" (N; semantics: bend >turn > turn back, return)	Mocha *'mi 'o* "bundle"
604. *-māʔ-/*-mīʔ- "to be wet"	pPS *mʔ "to be wet" (Append.1)	*m3ᶜ* "bank (of river)" (stem + *ʕ part., i.e., bank is off to the side of the water)	*maʔ-/*miʔ- "to be wet"	Ng. *màmà* "coldness" (redup. stem, as intens. (?); semantics: see #458)	NOm: Yem *mèʔ-* "to wash"

	SEMITIC	EGYPTIAN	CUSHITIC	CHADIC	OMOTIC
605. *-m-ʔ- "to go toward"		*m3ᶜ* "to lead, guide, direct; send, dispatch; set out (on journey)" (stem + *ʕ part., i.e., send, set *out*)	*-mʔ- "to start toward"		
606. *-măaʕ- "to eat"	A. *maʕq* "to drink greedily" (stem + *k' intens. of effect)		PEC *maaʕ- "to eat, feed" (Afar *maaqo* "food"; *maaqiyo* "canine tooth": stem + *y deverb.; Afar *q* = [ʕ]; Yaaku *mεε'* "mouth")	some WCh *m- "mouth" (J) (Ng. *mìyó*, stem + *y deverb)	NOm *meʔ- "to eat" (Bench *mʔ¹*)
607. *-mĭʕ-/*-mŭʕ- "to handle"	pPS *mʕ "to rub" (Ehret 1989)		PSC *muʕ(ut)- "to handle lightly" (stem + *t dur.)		Mocha *mì'o* "handle" (n.)

PAA *n

	SEMITIC	EGYPTIAN	CUSHITIC	CHADIC	OMOTIC
608. *nê(e) "with"			PSC *nêe "with"	Ng. *naa* "with"	*-ne, *-nä "and"
609. *ni "of" (genitive)		*n* "of" (C. *n*-)	SC: Dahalo -*ni* genitive suff. of possessor n.	*n- "of" (genitive)	NOm: Yem -*n*, -*ni* genitive connector
610. *-năb- "to call"	*nb "to call, cry" (Ehret 1989)		EC: Arbore *náab* "meeting place of village" (n. < v. by V > VV; i.e., place of public speaking and debate)	WCh, CCh *nb "to count" (J)	*nab- "to call" (SOm *na:b- "name": n. < v. by V > V:; NOm: Mocha *nàb*- "to speak loudly")

	SEMITIC	EGYPTIAN	CUSHITIC	CHADIC	OMOTIC
611. *-nǎf-/*-nǐf- "to exhale"	pPS *np "to inhale, exhale" (Ehret 1989); *ʔnp (*ʔanp) "nose" (*a- attrib. n. pref. + stem)	*nft* "breath; wind" (stem + *t n. suff.); *nf3* "to blow (out of nose)" (stem + *r diffus.); *nfyt* "fan" (stem + *y inchoat. as dur. + *t n. suff.); C. *nīfε* "to breathe" (stem + *y inchoat. > dur.)	EC: Soomaali *naf* "vita; anima"; PEC *nafs-/nefs- "to breathe" (n. "breath," seen in Som. "vita," + *s caus. as deverb.)		Mocha *nàp-* "to blow"

	SEMITIC	EGYPTIAN	CUSHITIC	CHADIC	OMOTIC
612. *-neg- or *-nag- "to watch"	A. *najθ*, *najš* "to examine, test, investigate" (stem + *θ diffus., + *ɬ ven.); *najnaj* "to consider a thing indolently" (stem redup. as freq. > dur.)		EC: Soomaali *neg* "to be still, unmoving; be calm" (semantics: watch > wait > not move; PEC *a and *e > Som. *e* /n_g)	WCh, CCh *nag "to see" (J)	
613. *-nugʷ- "to seep"	pPS *ng "to seep, ooze" (Append.1)	cf. *ngsgs* "to overflow" (but see #833 for alternative suggested source and for proposed morphology)	*ʔangʷ-/*ʔungʷ- "breast" (< *anugʷ-: *a- attrib. deverb. + stem; semantics: from secreting of milk by the breast)		

	SEMITIC	EGYPTIAN	CUSHITIC	CHADIC	OMOTIC
614. *-neh- "to be slight"	A. *nahš* "to be thin, lean" (stem + *ɬ ven.; semantics unclear)	*nhy* "some, a little, few" (stem + *y deverb.)	*neh- "to be thin"		
615. *-noh- "to bite into hungrily"	pPS *nh "to bite into hungrily" (Append.1)		EC: Soomaali *nohnoh* "violent hunger" (redup. stem as intens.)	some WCh *neen "hunger" (J; stem + *n n. suff., probable earlier *nahin)	
616. *-nĭḫ- or *-nĕeḫ- or *-nĭiḫ- "to last, endure, abide"	A. *naḫāḫa-t* "patience"	*nḫḫ* "eternity" (stem with redup. as intens.; C. *ɛnɛh*, probable *a- attrib. pref. + stem)	PSC *nĭḫ- or *nĕeḫ- or *nĭiḫ- "to live, be alive"		

	SEMITIC	EGYPTIAN	CUSHITIC	CHADIC	OMOTIC
617. *-naj- "to become low"	*nðl "bad, worthless, despised" (stem + *l adj. suff.; A. *naðl*); Ji. *nðɔḱ* "to sink like a stone; sink into the ground" stem + *k' intens. of effect)		EC: Soomaali *nash* "fontanelle" (semantics: fontanelle forms slight depression in baby's skull; PC *dz > Som. *sh* [š]); Agaw: [Awngi *ɨncu* "thin": loan < Omotic + *in- concom.?]	WCh, CCh *nz "to sit (down)" (J)	Maji: Nao *nač̌u* "thin" (semantics: low > flat > thin)
618. *-nik^{w}- "to be deficient, little, or few"	A. *nakd* "little, a trifle" (stem + *d dur. > stat., i.e., < earlier "to be little"); *niks* "weak, powerless" (stem + *s deverb. comp.)	*nkt* "some, a little" (stem + *t n. suff.)	*nik^{w}-/*nuk^{w}- "to fall short"		

	SEMITIC	EGYPTIAN	CUSHITIC	CHADIC	OMOTIC
619. *-nok'- "to run out (of water)"	A. *naqṭ* "to fall in drops" (stem + *t' dur. intens.; only dur. connotation persists here); *naqf* "to strain (wine); water" (stem + *f iter.)	*nḳwt* "moisture" (stem + *w inchoat., i.e., to become moist, + *t n. suff.; C. *lōk* "to be fresh, cool")	*-nok'- "to flow"		SOm *no(:)q- "water" (n. < v. by V > V: ? Ari *noqá*)
620. *-nuuk'- "to suck"	pPS *nḳ "to suck" (Append. i)	*snḳ* "to suckle, nurse" (Eg. *s- caus. + stem; C. *sōnk*)	*nuuk'- "to suck in"		
621. *nim-/*nam- "person"	A. *nummā* "somebody, anybody"	*inm* "skin" (*i- attrib. n. pref. + stem; semantics: person > body > skin; C. *anom* < earlier *inam)	PEC *nam-/ *nim-/*num- "person"	*nəm "person" (Ng. *nə̀n* "someone"; *m > *n assim.; J: ECh *lm "person": nasal dissim.)	NOm: Kafa *ana:mo* "man, male" (*a- attrib. n. pref. + stem; V > V: shift is not yet explained)

	SEMITIC	EGYPTIAN	CUSHITIC	CHADIC	OMOTIC
622. *-naatl'- "to call to"	A. *naṣṣ* "to announce, state explicitly"; *naṣḥ* "to advise and admonish sincerely" (stem + *ḥ iter.)	*nḏ* "to consult, enquire about, call upon, utter" (PAA *tl' > *dl > Eg. *ḏ* /n_)	*naatl- "to shout, yell"		
623. *-nuz- "to join (tr.)"			EC: Soomaali *nud* "to join (tr.)" (PEC *z > Soomaali *d*)	WCh, ECh *nɗ "to tie (rope)"	
624. *-naʔ- or *-naaʔ- "to scratch"			PSC *naʔ- or *naaʔ- "to scratch, mark by scratching"	Ng. *náay-* "to grind on a grindstone" (stem + *y inchoat. > dur.)	

	SEMITIC	EGYPTIAN	CUSHITIC	CHADIC	OMOTIC
625. *-nûʔ- "to suck in, snuff (up)"	pPS *nʔ "to suck in" (Append.1)	*n3w* "breeze" (stem + *w denom.; semantics: snuff > blow > blow, of wind)	PSC *nûʔ-, *nûnuʔ- "to suck"		
626. *-naʕ- "to be soft"	A. *naʕʕ* "weak, without strength"; *naʕnaʕ* "to become flaccid again (after an erection)" (redup. as intens.?); MSA *nʕm "soft, smooth; to soften" (stem + *m adj. suff.; v. < adj.)	*n ᶜi* "to be mild, merciful, lenient" (stem + *y inchoat.; C. *na*, *naa*)	*naʕ- "to be tender, soft"		

	SEMITIC	EGYPTIAN	CUSHITIC	CHADIC	OMOTIC
627. *-naaʕ-/*-niiʕ- "to go/come"	A. *naʕj* "to pace vigorously along" (stem + *gʷ dur.)	$n^{c}i$ "to travel" (stem + *y inchoat. > dur.; C. *na*, *nu*, *nuɛ*); $n^{c}t$ "expedition" (stem + *t n. suff.)	*naaʕ- "to go"	Ng. *nì* "to come, go"; *nài* "to come"	SOm: Banna *ni?*- "to come"
628. *-noʕ- "to scrape off"		n^{cc} "smooth" (stem with redup. as iter.?)	PSC *noʕ- "to scrape, scratch"	Ng. *nà*- "to flay, skin"	

PAA *ŋ

	SEMITIC	EGYPTIAN	CUSHITIC	CHADIC	OMOTIC
629. *-ŋoc'- "to be damaged, not function right"	A. *naẓar* "to have a fault or vice, be pale and haggard, be frail" (stem + probably *r adj. suff.)	*nss* "to do damage (to)" (stem + *s caus.? C. *lōōs*, *lōs* "to smash, break to pieces")	PEC *ŋoc'c'- "non-bearing male animal (neutered, too young, or too old and decrepit)"		

	SEMITIC	EGYPTIAN	CUSHITIC	CHADIC	OMOTIC
630. *-ŋĕd- "to take (bit of food or drink) into the mouth"	A. *nadf* "to drink by draughts; eat" (stem + *f iter.)	*ndb*, *ndbdb* "to sip" (stem + *b extend., with redup. as freq.)	*ŋĕd- "to bite"	CCh *nd "to eat" (J; PO *ŋ > *n in most CCh)	
631. *-ŋodl- "to grip tightly"	A. *naḍw* "to pull out, unsheathe, strip, put off" stem + *w inchoat. > dur.); *naḍy* "to draw the sword" (stem + *y inchoat. > dur.)	*nḏrw* "to grasp, hold fast, catch; take possession" (stem + *r or *l n. suff. + *w denom.; C. *nuj* "to put, place")	EC: Arbore *ŋoḍ-* "to pinch" (PC *dl > Arbore *ḍ*)		
632. *-ŋek'-/*-ŋok'- "to look at intently"	pPS *nḳ "to look at closely" (Append.1)		PEC *ŋek'-/ *ŋok'- "to look at intently"		

	SEMITIC	EGYPTIAN	CUSHITIC	CHADIC	OMOTIC
633. *-ŋal-/*-ŋ-l- "to cry out"		LE *nrḫ* "to abuse, revile" (stem + *ḫ iter.)	PEC *ŋal- "to express strong feelings"	ECh: Somrai *nul "to weep, cry" (J; PCh *ŋ > Somrai *n; presumed PCh *ŋəl < pre-PCh *ŋil- or *ŋul-)	
634. *-ŋaɬ- "to fasten"	A. *našb* "to adhere firmly, be fastened to" (stem + *b extend.); *našṭ* "to make knot in rope" (stem + *t' dur. intens. > intens.)	LE *nšp* "gate" (stem + *p intens. of manner or *p' fin. fort.; semantics: fasten securely?)	*ŋaɬ- or *ŋal- "to tie, knot" (Append.2)	Ng.*ǹtl*- "to tighten down" (PCh $*ɬ_2$ > Ng. *tl*, *ŋ > Ng. *n*)	

	SEMITIC	EGYPTIAN	CUSHITIC	CHADIC	OMOTIC
635. *-ŋiɬ- "to cut"	pPS *nɬ "to cut" (Ehret 1989)	*nšnš* "to tear up (documents)" (redup. stem as freq.); LE *nšd* "to tear up" (stem + *d dur.)	PEC *ŋalʕ-/ *ŋilʕ- "to stab" (stem + *ʕ part. > and., i.e., cut *into*; PC *ɬ > PEC *l)		
636. *-ŋôm- "to use the mouth (other than in eating)"	A. *namm* "breath, breeze"	*nmi* "to shout, low" (stem + *y in-choat.)	PSC *ŋûm- "to pucker the the lips (as in blowing)" (PC *o > PSC *u /_$C_{[+labial]}$)		NOm *no:n- "mouth" (Yem *nòonā*, Bench *non* [4]; presumed assim., *no:m- > *no:n; n. < v. by V > V:)

	SEMITIC	EGYPTIAN	CUSHITIC	CHADIC	OMOTIC
637. *ŋaan- "boy"		*nn* "child" (C. *lɛlu* "child, boy"; *u < ME *a /N_, N = nasal)	SC: Burunge *naw* "small boy" (< pre-PR *ŋaanaw, stem *w n. suff.; PSC $*C_1VC_1 > C_1$ /#_VC); PSC *ʔiŋǎan- "brother" (*i- attrib. pref. + stem; corrects Ehret 1980: 292)	some WCh *nan "brother" (J)	NOm *na:m- "son" (Mocha *nà:mo* ; Bench *nam* 3 "daughter," *nans* 2 "son"; stem with nasal dissim., *nVn > *nVm; tonal correspondence unclear)
638. *-ŋaat'- "to spread (intr.)"	A. *naṭṭ* "to extend, stretch"; *naṭw* "to stretch; be distant" (stem + *w inchoat.)		*ŋaat'- "to spread apart, become separated" (Append.2)		

	SEMITIC	EGYPTIAN	CUSHITIC	CHADIC	OMOTIC
639. *-ŋiit'- "to darken"	A. *naṭf* "to snuff a candle" (stem + *p intens. of manner)		NAgaw *ŋicir "black(ness)" (stem + *r adj. suff.; Agaw *i < PC *ii; PC *t' > NAgaw *c)		
640. *-ŋaaw- "to blaze" (*ŋ is required by derived noun, root #641 following)	A. *nauḍ* "to shine, flash" (stem + *dl m.v.)	*nwḫ* "to heat; be scorched" (stem + $*\gamma^{w}$ comp.)		Ng. *nàwà* "day, period of daylight"; *nàwà-* "to spend the day" (v. < n.; PCh *ŋ > Ng. *n*)	SOm *now- "fire"; NOm: Kafa *na:to* "ashes" (stem + *t n. suff.)
641. *-ŋîiwr- "flames, firelight" (root #640 + *r n. suff.)	*nwr "light; to shine"		PSC *ŋûur- "flare, blaze"	*ŋurŋ "embers" (J: WCh *ŋrŋ ashes"; some WCh, ECh *nurn "charcoal"; stem + *ŋ n. suff.)	

	SEMITIC	EGYPTIAN	CUSHITIC	CHADIC	OMOTIC
642. *ŋaʕw- "python" (?)		$n^{c}w$ "serpent"	PEC *ŋaʕw- "crocodile"		

Proposed PAA *ŋʷ

	SEMITIC	EGYPTIAN	CUSHITIC	CHADIC	OMOTIC
643. *-ŋʷâɬ- or *-ŋʷâaɬ- "to run or seep out"	pPS *nɬ "to overflow, run out" (Ehret 1989)	*nšw* "pemphigus; issue (from wound)" (stem + *w deverb.); *nšwt* "mucus" (previous word + *t n. suff.)	PSC *ŋʷâaɬ- "gums" (semantics: gums are coated with saliva, the outflow of oral membranes of which gums a part; n. < v. by V > VV?)	CCh: Masa *ŋɬ/*ɲɬ "sand" (J; semantics: sand forms the streambed, over which water flows)	

Proposed PAA *ɲ	SEMITIC	EGYPTIAN	CUSHITIC	CHADIC	OMOTIC
644. *-ɲiḫ- "to shape to a point"	A. *naḫt* "to shave, plane, smooth; scratch; saw off; carve wood or stone" (stem + *t dur.); *naḫḏ* "to make thin and sharp" (stem + *dl m.v., i.e., form point > tr.)	*nḫḏt* "tooth; tusk" (stem + *dl m. v., i.e., form a point, + *t n. suff.)	PEC *ɲiḫ-/*ɲuḫ- "to shape to a point"	some WCh *ɲaw "horn" (J; stem + *w deverb.; *ɲ may be 2ndary palatalization here of *nihaw, because other posited word-initial *ɲ appear as *n in J: see #645, 646, and 653)	
645. *-ɲuuk'- "to rub" (Eg., Sem. **innovation**: "to rub" > "to scrape")	pPS *nḳ "to scrape" (Append.1)	*nḳm* "to be bald" (stem + *m ex-tend. > stat.); LE *nḳ ᶜ* "to scrape, in-cise; polish (?)" (stem + *ʕ part.; semantics:	PSC *nʸuuk'- "to rub" (PSC *nʸ = *ɲ)	WCh *nk' "to grind" (J)	

	SEMITIC	EGYPTIAN	CUSHITIC	CHADIC	OMOTIC
		scrape *off* roughness)			
646. *-ɲer- "to fear"	A. *narz* "to hide oneself for fear" (stem + *z intens. of manner)	*nri* "to fear; overawe" (stem + *y inchoat. > dur.); *nrw* "fear, dread; terrible one" (stem + *w deverb.)	SC: Kw'adza *nyelesiko* "thing of supernatural danger" (stem + PR *s agent n. suff. + ER *k masc. gender suff.)	some CCh, ECh *naar "to fear" (J; reconstruction error? Expected *nar)	
647. *-ɲîr- "to be frail"			PEC *ɲar-/*ɲir- "to be frail"; PEC *ɲurk'- "weak" (stem + *k' intens. of effect; i.e., < earlier v. "to be greatly weakened"?); SC: WR *nark^{w}- "to be poor"		Gonga *nir- "to be soft, loose, flexible" (Mocha *'niro* "soft, flexible, mellow")

	SEMITIC	EGYPTIAN	CUSHITIC	CHADIC	OMOTIC
			(stem + *k^w fin.; semantics unclear; PSC *ɲ > WR *n)		
648. *-ɲiit'-/*-ɲāat'- "to hurt, ache, be in pain"	A. *naṭf* "to suffer from indigestion" (stem + *f iter.; semantics: indigestion is accompanied by lingering or recurrent pain)	*nspw* "wounds" (stem + *p intens. of manner + Eg. pl. in *w*)	EC: Sidamo *niit'-* "to have labor pains" (PEC *ɲ > Sidamo *n*)		NOm: Bench *ɲats'*[2] "headache" (PO *V: > Bench V)
649. *-ɲaw- "to come to, arrive at" (*ŋ and *a are reconstructed because they are required in derived root #651 below)	A. *naub* "to come upon; be near" (stem + *p' fin.fort.); *nauš* "to advance" (stem + *ɬ ven.)	*nwy* "to return (to); come (to); bring back" (stem + *y inchoat. > dur.)	Beja *nuw* "to offer, present to" (stem + *-u- tr. infix as caus.; PC *ɲ > Beja *n*)		

	SEMITIC	EGYPTIAN	CUSHITIC	CHADIC	OMOTIC
650. *-ɲaw- "to be moist, damp"		*nwy* "water" (stem + *y deverb.)	PEC *ɲawr- "damp, moist" (stem + *r adj. suff.)	Ng. *nàwə́k* , pl. *nàwàwín* "saliva" (PAA *ɲ > Ng. *n*)	
651. *-ɲawr- "to move toward, come toward" (#649 + *r diffus.; semantics: from closed- to open-ended action)	A. *narš* "to reach for, take in one's hand" (stem + *ɬ ven.)	*nr* "to charge (after enemy)"	PEC *ɲawr- "to arrive, come up to"		
652. *-ɲoxʷ- "to hold in the mouth"	A. *naxr* "to gnaw" (stem + *r diffus.); *naxb* "to bite" (stem + *p' fin. fort.)		*ɲox- "to suck" (Append.2)		

	SEMITIC	EGYPTIAN	CUSHITIC	CHADIC	OMOTIC
653. *-ɲay- "to speak loudly"	A. *nairab* "to slander, utter lies" (stem + *r diffus. + *b extend.; cognates outside Sem. indicate this is *not* a case of CayCaC modification of an original triliteral)	*nis* "to make summons, invocation; summon; evoke; invoke; recite" (stem + *c' extend.)	PEC *ɲayln- or *ɲaylm- "quarrel" (stem + *l n. suff. + *n or *m n. suff.); EC: Soomaali *geyr* "anger; resentment" (stem + *r n. suff.; PEC *ɲ > Som. *g*)	Ng. *náang-* "to abuse, berate, insult" (stem + *n non-fin. + *g fin. fort.; PAA *ɲ > Ng. *n*)	
654. *-ɲay-/*-ɲaw- "to rise, swell, expand"	pPS *ny/*nw "to rise, expand" (Append.1); MSA *nwb "big" (stem + *b extend. > stat., adj. < earlier v.)		EC: Soomaali *gawar* "altura brulla"; (stem + *r n. suff.; PEC *ɲ > Som.*g*); PEC *ɲayln- "very long hair" (stem + *l adj. suff. + *n n. suff.)	*nə "to ripen" (N) (J: *nay, *niy) (Ng. *náwà-*, stem + *-a incep., i.e., become ripe); some ECh *nyl "grass" (J; stem + *l n. suff.; semantics: see #742)	

	SEMITIC	EGYPTIAN	CUSHITIC	CHADIC	OMOTIC
655. *ɲâʔ- "light, slight"	A. *naʔnaʔ* "weak" (re-dup. stem as intens.)		PEC *ɲaʔayl- "narrow, thin" (stem + EC *-ayl adj. suff. < *y + *l adj. suffixes)		NOm *ɲaʔ- "child" (Mocha *'na 'o*; Bench *ɲaʔ* 3; Yem *nàa*)
656. *-ɲîʕ- "to rise (in elevation), swell (in size)"	A. *naʕš* "to elevate, raise the fallen" (stem + *ɬ ven.); *naʕẓ* "to have an erection" (stem + *c' extend.)	LE $n^{c}r$ "ship's mast" (stem + *l n. suff.)	PSC $*n^{y}$îʕ- "to thicken" (PSC $*n^{y}$ = PC *ɲ; corrects Ehret 1980: 186)		
657. *k'âɲ- "yellow"		*ḳni* "to be yellow (?), of eyes"; *ḳnit* "yellow pig-ment, yellow-ness" (v. + *t n. suff.)	PSC *k'ân^{y}- "yellow, tan, yellow-gray" (PSC $*n^{y}$ = PC *ɲ)		

	SEMITIC	EGYPTIAN	CUSHITIC	CHADIC	OMOTIC
658. *-z-ɲ- "to open"		*zn* "to open"		some ECh *ɗɲ "to open" (J)	
PAA *n or *ŋ or *ɲ					
659. *-nah- or *-ŋah- or *-ɲah- "to avoid"	A. *nahnah* "to refrain from" (redup. stem as freq. > dur.)	*nh* "to escape (death); dread" (C. *1εh* "fear, anxiety")	SC: Iraqw *nahat-* "to hide" (stem + *t dur.; PC *ŋ, *ɲ > Iraqw *n* /#_)		
660. *-noh- or *-ŋoh- or *-ɲoh- "to cry out"	*nhḳ "to bray" (stem + *k' intens. of effect); MSA *nhs "to sigh" (stem + *š non-fin.; MSA *s < *š); A. *nahm* "to shout to camels; cry out" (stem + *m extend.)	*nhm* "to shout" (stem + *m extend. as fort.); *nhmhm* "to roar" (redup. 1st v. as intens.; C. (Bohairic) *1hεm*); *nhp* "to mourn" (stem + *p in-			Yem *nòon-* "to murmur" (prePO *nohn-, stem + *n non-fin. > *no:n-)

	SEMITIC	EGYPTIAN	CUSHITIC	CHADIC	OMOTIC
		tens. of manner; C. *nεhpε*)			
661. *-naxʷ- or *-ŋaxʷ- or *-ɲaxʷ- "to surprise"	A. *naxṭ* "to fall upon suddenly" (stem + *t' dur. intens., here just intens.)	LE *nḫnḫ* "to attack" (redup. stem as intens.)	SC: WR *naxʷ- "to startle" (PSC *ŋ, ɲ > WR *n /#_)		

PAA *ŋ or *ɲ

	SEMITIC	EGYPTIAN	CUSHITIC	CHADIC	OMOTIC
662. *-ŋêep'- or *-ɲêep'- "to stick one thing into another"	pPS *nb "to prick" (Ehret 1989)	*npḏ* "to slaughter" (stem + *dl m.v.); *npḏt* "sharp knife" (stem + *t n. suff.)	EC: Soomaali *jeeb* "to make a precise cut in" (PC *ŋ, *ɲ > PSom *g > Som. *j* /#_e; PC *p' > Som. *b*)	Ng. *nəɓk-* "to join, consolidate" (stem + *k dur.; semantics: cf. English *stick*, i.e., be thrust in and remain stuck)	Yem *nèeb-* "to hunt" (semantics: to pierce with arrow, spear)

THE LARYNGEAL CONSONANTS OF *PAA*

A sixth point of articulation in proto-Afroasiatic covers the PAA pharyngeals and glottals, *ʕ, *ʔ, *ḥ, and *h.

In Omotic and Chadic the pharyngeal feature dropped out in the proto-language, although in Omotic the two pharyngeals left behind the evidence of their former presence in pre-PO in the form of a fronting shift, PAA *a > PO *e before a following PAA *ʕ or *ḥ (see Chapter 4, Omotic rule #1). The loss of pharyngeality in both PO and PCh took the specific form,

PAA *ʕ > *ʔ, *ḥ > *h [PO #2 and PCh #2].

This pattern is also universally attested in the numerous separate instances of deletion of the pharyngeal feature in Cushitic prehistory — in the Ma'a language of Southern Cushitic and also in the East Rift subgroup of Southern Cushitic; in Beja; and, from the Eastern branch of Cushitic, separately in Yaaku, proto-Highland Eastern Cushitic, and several languages of the Soomaali subgroup (Sasse 1979; Ehret 1980, 1987; Ehret and Ali 1985). Clearly, in some profound fashion, *ʕ and *ʔ, and *ḥ and *h, form natural phonological pairings. In the case of the former pair, it may be that PAA *ʕ is better reconstructed as originally a stop, an articulation observed in a number of modern-day Cushitic languages (J. Pia, pers. com., for Soomaali, and the writer's own fieldwork for Southern Cushitic languages). Proto-Chadic at first regularly maintained the resulting *h and *ʔ, although both sounds were then recurrently deleted in the subsequent evolution of the various Chadic languages (e.g., the loss of medial *h in proto-West Chadic seen in root #449, and the complete loss of all PCh *ʔ and *h in the Ngizim language).

In the PS and PC reconstructions and in early Egyptian, however, the full four-way distinction was maintained among the laryngeals, with usually one-to-one correspondences of *ʕ to *ʕ, *ʔ to *ʔ, *ḥ to *ḥ, and *h to *h in each.

The most notable exceptions to this pattern appear in Egyptian. PAA *ʕ often produces Eg. *i* in the environment #_VC, while PAA *ʔ less commonly yielded *i* in the same context. A combination of shifts appear to explain these outcomes. The sequence PAA *ʕi probably generally became a sequence rendered as *i* in Egyptian, while other *ʕV also went to *i* if the following consonant was *s* or *z*. A third shift, it appears, changed PAA *ʔV to Eg. *i* when it preceded a sonorant. A shift of more limited scope can be proposed to have converted both PAA *ʔu(u) and *ʕu(u) to Eg. written *w* in the environment of a following voiceless fricative (examples with following */#_f and /#_s have been noted: #665, 673, and 713). In addition, PAA *ʔ was voiced to ᶜ ([ʕ]) in Egyptian before a following PAA *n or *r and apparently *g, at least in cases where the intervening vowel was *a(a); while, as noted above in the discussion of velars, PAA *ʕ devoiced to Eg. *3* ([ʔ]) following PAA *g, *k, or *kʷ in the same stem. PAA *ʕ also devoiced to Eg. *3* after a preceding PAA *d or *z (roots #157 and 206). In summary,

Eg. #18. PAA *ʕi > Eg. *i* ;

#19. PAA *ʕ > Eg. *i* /#_V[+cont./+dental];

#20. PAA *ʔ > Eg. *i* /#_VS, S = sonorant;

#21. some PAA *ʕu > Eg. *w* (/#_{s,f};

#22. PAA *ʔ > Eg. *ᶜ* /_VC, C = n, r, or g (V = a, aa ?); and

#23. PAA *ʕ > Eg. *3* /[+voice/+dental]V_.

Dissimilation in continuancy rather than in voicing marked PAA *h and *ḫ following *ɣ in an Egyptian stem, with both becoming a glottal stop (Eg.*3*) in such instances (roots #356 and 357). PAA *h and *ḫ also changed to *3* in conjunction with a preceding *g in all the instances so far identified (roots #274, 275, 297, and 298). Lastly, the complete absence of *h ᶜ* and *ᶜh* sequences in the C_1 and C_2 positions in Egyptian requires some kind of dissimilatory or assimilatory shifts to have taken place. One example, with PAA *h initial, shows *hʕ becaming Eg. *h3* (#802). An opposite assimilation, of *ʕh to Eg.*ᶜḥ*, would seem to provide a plausible accounting for the lack of *ᶜh* and the surfeit of *ᶜḥ* in Egyptian; but the direct attestations for such a change remain to be identified. To sum up,

#24. PAA *H > Eg. *3* /C[+voice/+velar]V_ (H = *h or *ḫ), and

#25. PAA *hʕ > Eg. *h3*; and

#26. PAA *ʕh > Eg. *ᶜḥ* (?).

Sequences pairing Eg. *ḥ* , *h* , *ẖ*, or *ḫ* with each other are also absent in the data. A possible Egyptian outcome for one such a sequence has been suggested in the evidence presented here (#745); if valid, it would imply a rule,

#27. PAA *ḫɣ > Eg. *ḥ3*.

For Semitic, a different kind of exception to the usual patterns can be proposed. A shift,

PS #7. PAA *ʔ > PS *ʕ /#ɬ_r#,

is attested in the only two known examples of this particular environment (roots #887 and 889).

Semitic also developed a sweeping constraint against the co-occurrence of PAA *ʕ, *ʔ, *ħ, and *h in the C_1 and C_2 positions in a stem; the only exceptions seem to be *ʕh and a single instance of *ʔh*, the overtly onomatopoetic formation seen in root #716. In general, it appears that PAA *ʕ and *ʔ became PS *w in C_2 position in such sequences (roots #765 and 800-802); what became of *ħ and *h in the same circumstances remains to be investigated.

It should be noted that Mocha words have been recorded by Leslau (1959) both with initial vowel and with initial glottal stop (represented as /'/). The difference is probably an artifact of recording because no regularity of correspondence between Leslau's glottal stop or its absence and the PAA pharyngeal-glottal consonants has so far been discovered. Marking of the glottal stop has therefore been disregarded in the citations of Mocha data below.

PAA *ʕ	SEMITIC	EGYPTIAN	CUSHITIC	CHADIC	OMOTIC
663. *-ʕâb- "to shine"	A. *ʕab*, *ʕabb* "sunlight"; *ʕabw* "to shine, be bright" (stem + *w denom.)	*ᶜb3* "to glitter" (stem + *r diffus.)	*ʕab- "to burn, shine"		NOm *a:b- "sun" (Yem *àwà* ; Bench *ab* 3 "day"; n. < v. by V > V:); Ometo: Koyra *ʔaw-* "to shine (of sun)" (PO *b > Koyra *w* /V_)
664. *-ʕob- "to take a swallow"	A. *ʕabb* "to drink keeping mouth close to the water or without breathing"	*ᶜb* "meal"	PEC *ʕob- "to take a bite or swallow" (Afar, NSom "to drink"; Bayso "to bite")		

	SEMITIC	EGYPTIAN	CUSHITIC	CHADIC	OMOTIC
665. *-ʕŭc- "to swallow liquid or soft food"	pPS *ʕθ "to swallow (liquid, soft food?)" (Append.1)	*wsḫ* "cup" (stem + *ɣʷ comp.; semantics: to drink > thing drunk out of)	EC: Afar *quus* "breakfast" (n. < v. by V > VV; *q* = [ʕ])		NOm *uš₃- "to drink" (Bench (Bench *uʂ(k)* [1]
666. *-ʕac'- "to repeat, do again"	A. *ʕaẓb* "to persevere patiently" (stem + *b extend.); *ʕaẓl* "to stick fast together (copulating dogs)" (stem + *l fin.)		EC: Yaaku *-εc'-* "to repeat; to return (intr.)" (PEC *a > Yaaku ε /*ʕ, *ʕ > Yaaku Ø v.-stem-initial)		
667. *ʕî d- "to raise, lift"	A. *ʕadn* "to take out of the ground; grow high" (stem + *n non-fin., i.e., grow high);	*idn* "to lay out (?) (enclosure)" (stem + *n non-fin.; semantics: to raise > build)	*ʕâdh-/*ʕîdh- "to put up high" (stem + *h ampl.)		SOm: Dime *e:do* "mountain" (n. < v. by V > V:; for *i > *e /#_d in SOm, see also #668 following)

	SEMITIC	EGYPTIAN	CUSHITIC	CHADIC	OMOTIC
	ʕadq "to gather" (stem + *k' intens. of effect, i.e., repeated picking up)				
668. *ʕid- "person"			*ʕad-/*ʕid- "body of a person"		*id- "person" (SOm *ed-)
669. *-ʕŭdl- "to grip"	A. *ʕuḍw*, *ʕiḍw* "limb, member" (stem + *w deverb.); *ʕuḍm* "handle of the plow, plowtail" (stem + *m n. suff.)		*ʕadl-/*ʕudl- "to grip"		NOm: Bench *ut* '1 "to catch"

	SEMITIC	EGYPTIAN	CUSHITIC	CHADIC	OMOTIC
670. *-ʕudl- or *-ʕuudl- "to cut off"	A. *ʕaḍḍ* "to cut, lop, prune"	*ᶜḏ* "to hack up, destroy"; *ᶜḏt* "slaughter, massacre" (stem + *t n. suff.)	SC: Iraqw *alʕutl-* "to circumcise" (WR *al- v. pref. of conseq. action + stem; PC *dl > Iraqw *tl*)		
671. *-ʕadz- "to be wrong, bad, ill; do or function wrong-ly"	A. *ʕaðw* "to hurt, in-jure; slander; turn from what is good" (stem + *w inchoat.)	*izft* "wrong, wrongdoing, falsehood" (stem + *f iter. > dur., "to do wrong," + *t n. suff.)	EC: Afar *qaas* "lawless per-son" (n. < v. by V > VV); EC: Soomaali *cashi* "to be struck by an illness" stem + Som. *-i* caus.; *c* = [ʕ]; PC *dz > Som. *sh* [š])		SOm: Ari *ą̈ž-* "to become ill"

	SEMITIC	EGYPTIAN	CUSHITIC	CHADIC	OMOTIC
672. *-ʕaaf- "to see"	Ugaritic *ʕpʕp-m* "eyes" (redup. stem + *m pl.)		EC: Sidamo *aaf-* "to know"		*a:p- "eye" (Mocha *a:pó*; Bench *ap*[1]; Yem *āāfā*) SOm *a:f- "to see" (Ari *áa̧f-* "to find")
673. *-ʕĭf-/*-ʕŭf-/ *-ʕăf- "to utter"	A. *ʕafr* "to scold" (stem + *r diffus.); *ʕafk* "to speak confusedly" (stem + *k dur.)	*wf3* "to talk about, discuss" (stem + *r diffus. or *r n. suff., with v. < earlier n.)	PSC *ʕif- "to utter"		*ap-/*ip- "to weep, cry" (NOm: Mocha *àp-*; SOm: Dime *if-*; etc.); NOm: Kafa *ufo* "curse"
674. *-ʕăg- "to take a mouthful"	A. *ʕajm* "to bite, chew" (stem + *m extend., i.e., to chew)		*ʕăg- "to take a swallow" (Ehret (1987: "to drink")		

	SEMITIC	EGYPTIAN	CUSHITIC	CHADIC	OMOTIC
675. *ʕâag- "grain" (Eg., Ch. **innovation**: *ʕâagaw- "cooked grain," stem + *w n. suff.)		ᶜ*gwt* "a preparation of grain" (stem + *w n. suff. + *t n. suff.)	*ʕaag- "grain species"	Ng. *áagǎw* "pounded, cooked grain" (stem + *w n. suff.)	
676. *-ʕaj-/*-ʕij- "to bite"	pPS *ʕð "to bite" (Ehret 1989)	LE *ispw* "to ache with hunger, lack food" (stem + *p intens. of manner + *w inchoat., i.e., be ready to bite into food ravenously)			*ač-/*ič- "to bite; tooth" (NOm *ač- "tooth" [Yem *àʔyà*]; SOm: Ari *átsi* "teeth"; SOm *ats-/*its- "to eat")
677. *-ʕǎak- or *-ʕǎakʷ- "to attack"	A. *ʕakk* "to attack; beat, whip, flog"		PSC *ʕǎak- or *ʕǎakʷ- "to attack"		

	SEMITIC	EGYPTIAN	CUSHITIC	CHADIC	OMOTIC
678. *-ʕik'-/*-ʕak'- "to rise up"	A. *ʕaql* "to ascend mountain" (stem + *l fin., i.e., reach peak); *ʕaqw* "to be hoisted, raised high" (stem + *w inchoat.); MSA **ʕḳr* "to grow big" (stem + *r adj suff., v. < presumed earlier adj.)		SC: Iraqw *ʕaqmit-* "to fly" (stem + SC *m intr. + *t dur.)		NOm *ik'- "to rise up" (Ometo *ek'- "to stand"; Maji: She *ik'* "big") NOm: Yem *àkàmā* "big" (stem + *m adj. suff.)
679. *-ʕal- "to ascend, go up"	*ʕl (*ʕal) "on, above"	^{c}r "to mount up, ascend" (C. *ōl*, *ol*)	PEC *ʕal- "mountain"		NOm: Maji *al-* "to sit" (stand > stay > sit)
680. *ʕal- "jaw"		^{c}r ^{c}r "chin" (redup. stem)	*ʕal- "cheek"		

	SEMITIC	EGYPTIAN	CUSHITIC	CHADIC	OMOTIC
681. *-ʕil- "to move to and fro"	pPS *ʕl "to move to to and fro" (Append.1)	*inry* "to shudder" (stem + *r dif-fus. + *y in-choat. > dur.)	Soomaali *cillaal* "to impede, make deviate, turn aside" (partially re-dup. stem; Som. *c* = [ʕ])	some ECh *ʔl "snake" (J)	
682. *-ʕâam- "to raise; tip of anything"	*ʕmc "to bear; carry (load)" (stem + *š non-fin.) A. *ʕamʕam* "to enlarge" (redup. stem as freq. > dur.); *ʕamd* "to support, prop up" (stem + *d dur.)	*ᶜmm* "brain" (stem with redup.? Or stem + *m n. suff.? Sem-antics: top of head > what is contained in upper part of head)	*ʕâam- "to rise, swell; point, tip; thorn" (last meaning: possible bor-rowing from Omotic?)	some CCh, ECh *ʔam "to take" (J; semantics: raise > lift, carry > take)	NOm *am- "thorn" (Bench *amu* [2,3] "thorny"); NOm: Yem *àamà* "mountain"

	SEMITIC	EGYPTIAN	CUSHITIC	CHADIC	OMOTIC
683. *-ʕīm- "to apply, put into effect"	pPS *ʕm "to apply, put into effect" (Append.1)	*imi* "to give; place; cause" (imper.) (C. *ma*)	SC: Iraqw *ʕimamis-* "to continue (doing)" (stem + SC *m intr. + *s caus.)		*im- "to give" (Mocha *'im-*; Yem *í́m-*)
684. *-ʕôom- "to stop (intr.)"	A. *ʕamn* "to stay, abide" (stem + *n non-fin.)		PSC *ʕôom- "to stop (intr.)"		
685. *-ʕăn- or *-ʕăŋ- "to bend, turn"	pPS *ʕn "to curve away from" (Ehret 1989)	^{c}*nn* "to turn back; come back; bring back" (stem with re-dup. as intens.; C. *on* "again")	PSC *ʕănk^{w}a "flexible, soft" (stem + *k^{w} fin.; semantics: > finished condition, i.e., be bendable?)		
686. *-ʕan- or *-ʕaan- "to come into view, appear"	A. *ʕann* "to present itself to view, appear, happen"	^{c}*nḏw* "dawn" (stem + *dl m.v. + *w deverb.)	PSC *ʕaan- or *ʕeen- "sight, view" (n. < v. by V > VV?)		

	SEMITIC	EGYPTIAN	CUSHITIC	CHADIC	OMOTIC
687. *-ʕâan- "to seep (of bodily fluid)"	A. *ʕunūd* "to bleed so as not to be staunched" (stem + *d dur.)	*ᶜnd* "an unguent" (stem + *d dur., < presumed earlier "drip (of body) with oil"); LE *ᶜnṯ* "oil man (?)" (stem + *tl' foc., < earlier "to anoint"?)	*ʕaanf- "snot, mucus" (stem + *f iter., i.e., < presumed earlier "to drip (of nose)"); PLEC *ʕaan- "milk"; PEC *ʕand'uuf- "saliva" (stem + *dl m.v. + *f iter..; PEC *d' < PC *dl; semantics: earlier "produce saliva," both a m.v. and a repeated action) PC *ʕâanrab- "tongue" (stem + *r diffus. or *r n. suff. + *b anim. suff.)	Ng. *ányí* "milk; breast; teat (animal)" (probable separate derivation from that seen in PLEC "milk")	NOm: Yem *ánnā* "blood"

	SEMITIC	EGYPTIAN	CUSHITIC	CHADIC	OMOTIC
688. *-ʕôn- "to swallow"	A. *ʕanjar* "to smack the lips" (stem + *g fin. fort. + *r diffus.)	*ᶜn ᶜn* "chin" (redup. stem; see "chin" in #680 for parallel formation)	*ʕûn-/*ʕôn- "to swallow"	ECh: Mokilko *ʔòn ɗá* "to suck" (J; stem + *z intens. of manner + *-a incep. [< *ḫ iter.?])	
689. *ʕăŋ-/*ʕĭŋ- "tip, peak, top"	Ji. *ʕinn* "(bull) try to mount (cow)" (semantics: n. "top" > v. "to get on top")	*ᶜnt* "nail, claw; pick" (stem + *t n. suff.; C. *ynɛ*)	PSC *ʕăŋ- "head; above"		Gonga *eŋgo "brain" (Mocha *e:ŋgó*; < pre-PO *ìŋg- (n. < v. by V > V: ; semantics: see #682 above); Ometo: Malo *angutsa* "thorn" (stem + Ometo *ts n. suff.)

	SEMITIC	EGYPTIAN	CUSHITIC	CHADIC	OMOTIC
690. *-ʕanɣʷ- "to rise, grow" (root #689 + ɣʷ comp.)		ᶜ*nḫ* "to live; life; person" (C. *ōnh*)	*ʕanɣʷ- "top"		NOm *aŋg- "to grow, increase" (Maji: Sheko *anga* "many"; Gonga *àːŋg- "to be fat"; single example so far of PAA *ɣʷ > NOm *g /N_)
691. *-ʕĕŋ- "to move in a confused manner"		LE ᶜ*n*ᶜ*n* "to confound; flounder" (redup. stem as intens.)	*ʕĕŋ- "to be drunk"		
692. *-ʕūp-/*-ʕīp- "to convey, make move"	A. *ʕafš* "to gather, collect, especially worthless things" (stem + *ɬ ven.)	ᶜ*pi* "to traverse (a waterway); pass (by)" (stem + *y inchoat.)	SC: Burunge *ilaʕup-* "to push" (WR *al(a)- v. pref. of concomitant action + stem; PC *u and *o > PSC *u /_p)		Ometo: Koyra *ep-* "to take"; Bench *opt* ² "to walk" (stem + *t dur. as intr.; this form implies 3rd root shape *ʕap-)

	SEMITIC	EGYPTIAN	CUSHITIC	CHADIC	OMOTIC
693. *-ʕar- "to become still"	A. *ʕarš* "to stay, abide" (stem + *ɬ ven.; semantics unclear); *ʕarḍ* "to die without an illness" (stem + *dl m.v.)		PSC *ʕar- "to fall asleep"		
694. *ʕarf- "cloud" (root #695 + *f iter.? If so, semantics are unclear)	Ugaritic *ʕrp-t* "cloud"		Beja *afra* "cloud" (metathesis of stem; PC *ʕ > Beja Ø)		
695. *-ʕir- "to be raised; sky"	pPS *ʕr "to be raised" (Append.1)	*ꜥꜣ* "pillar, column"	*ʕir- "rain" or "sky" (loan < Omotic?; semantics: rain > sky and sky > rain are recurrent Afri- meaning shifts)	WCh, CCh *-rm "mountain" (J; stem + *m n. suff.)	NOm *ir- "rain" (Yem *ìrò*; semantics: see Cushitic entry); NOm: Ometo *irts'- "wet" (stem + *t' dur. intens.)

	SEMITIC	EGYPTIAN	CUSHITIC	CHADIC	OMOTIC
696. *-ʕŏr-/*-ʕĕr- "to burn brightly (intr.)"	pPS *ʕr "to burn (intr.), shine" (Append.1)		*ʕŏr-/*ʕĕr- "to burn (intr.)"; [Agaw *arb-/ *arf- "moon": probable old loan < Omotic]		*erp- "moon" (stem + *f iter., i.e., < earlier v. "to shine, glimer, glow"; Bench *ʔyarp* 2)
697. *ʕûur- "strength"	pPS *ʕr "hard, firm, strong" (Append.1)	*c3* "greatness" (C. *o*); *c3* , *c3i* "great; rich" (stem + *y adj. suff.)	PSC *ʕûr- or *ʕûur- "strength" (corrects Ehret 1980: 279)		
698. *-ʕis- "to be(come) heavy"	A. *ʕasn*, *ʕusn*, *ʕisn* "fat" (stem + *n adj. suff.)	*is* "old, ancient" (semantics: be heavy > mature > become old; C. *aas*)	PEC *ʕusl-/ *ʕisl-/*ʕasl- "heavy" (stem + *l adj. suff.)		

	SEMITIC	EGYPTIAN	CUSHITIC	CHADIC	OMOTIC
699. *-ʕăs'- "to burn (intr.?)"	cf. *ʔst (*ʔəst) "fire"? (but this item fails regular sound correspondence in its initial C and has variant stem V)		*ʕats'- "to burn, shine" (PEC *ʕac-/*ʕic- "to shine, glow")	CCh *-s' "sun" (J)	*as'- "to burn (tr.)"; NOm: Yem *ássā* "moon" (semantics: burn > shine, glow)
700. *-ʕiš-/*-ʕuš- "to stick up"	MSA *ʕsm "to heap up" (stem + *m extend.; MSA *s < PS *c)		EC: Soomaali *cisal* "penis of bull, ram, or billy-goat" (stem + *l n. suff.; PEC *š > PSom *s; Som. *c* = [ʕ])		*uš₁(um)- "horn" (stem + *m n. suff.)
701. *-ʕat-/*-ʕit-/ *-ʕut- "to stop (tr.?)"	A. *ʕatm* "to desist from; tarry, be too late" (stem + *m extend.)	LE *itḫ* "to tie up" (stem + *ḫ iter., i.e., an extended action that restricts further movement; C. *ōth*)	*ʕat-/*ʕit- "to stop, restrain from"		NOm *ut- "to sit" (semantics: stop (intr.) > stay > sit)

	SEMITIC	EGYPTIAN	CUSHITIC	CHADIC	OMOTIC
702. *-ʕat'- "to present"	A. *ʕaṭan* "gift, present" (stem + *n n. suff.); *ʕaṭw* "to give, grant" (stem + *w de-nom.)	*isw* "reward" (stem + *w deverb.)			NOm: Maji *ats'- "to give"
703. *-ʕatl'- "to become fat, thick"	A. *ʕaṣṣ* "to be hard, firm, strong"	*ᶜḏ* "to fatten (?)"; *ᶜḏ* "fat, grease" (C. *ōt*)	*ʕatl- "to swell, be-come fat"		SW Ometo *ad'- "big"
704. *-ʕâts- "to ask for, beg"	A. *ʕaθθ* "to importune"		EC: Yaaku *-ɛs-* "to beg" (PEC *a > Yaaku *ɛ* /*ʕ, *ʕ >Yaaku Ø stem-initial-ly, PC *ts > Yaaku *s*)	Ng. *ásásá* "let's hear it" (listeners' res-ponse when storyteller an-nounces tale or riddle; redup. stem as intens.)	Mocha *'äčč-* "to ask

	SEMITIC	EGYPTIAN	CUSHITIC	CHADIC	OMOTIC
705. *-ʕīts- "to stop (tr.)"	A. *ʕaθʕaθ* "to stay, abide" (redup. stem as freq. > dur.)	*isḳ* "to hinder; linger; wait" (stem + *k' intens. of effect, i.e., extended stopping; C. *ōsk*)	EC: Yaaku *-es-* "to hinder, prevent; stop (tr.)" (PC *ts > Yaaku *s*, *i > Yaaku *e*, *ʕ > Yaaku Ø v.-stem-initial)		NOm: Bench *yits* 2 "to stop (tr.)"
706. *-ʕâyg- "to go down"	A. *ʕajb* "tail-bone; hind part" (stem + *b anim. suff.; semantics: that which is sat down on)	LE *ᶜg3* "to drown" (stem + *ʔ conc.; semantics: go down > sink (into the water) > drown)	*ʕâyg- "to go down"		
707. *-ʕuz- "young"	A. *ʕuzl* "weak" (stem + *l adj. suff.)	*id* "boy" (*idyt* "girl")	*ʕazz- "new, young"		Ometo: Zayse *uzze* "heifer"

	SEMITIC	EGYPTIAN	CUSHITIC	CHADIC	OMOTIC
708. *-ʕâʕ- "to cry"	A. *ʕaʔiha-t* "clamour" (stem + *h ampl.; dis-sim. of consecu-tive identical C: *ʕ > *ʔ /ʕ_)	*ʿʿi* "to jabber" (stem + *y in-choat. > dur.)	PSC *ʕâʕ- or *ʕâʔ- "to cry, low, bleat, etc."		

PAA *ʔ

	SEMITIC	EGYPTIAN	CUSHITIC	CHADIC	OMOTIC
709. *-ʔaab-/*-ʔiib- "to burn, give off heat, glow"	A. *ʔabt* "hot; to be hot" (stem + *t adj. suff.)	*3bw* "to brand, scorch the skin"; *3bt* "brand" (n.); *3bd* "month" (stem + *d dur., < presumed earli-er v. "to shine (moon)"; C. *ɛbot*)	EC: HEC *iib- "to be warm"; EC: Afar *abaab-* "to reflect"; *abaabo* "reflection of light on sur-face" (redup. stem as freq.)	Ng. *àván* "embers" (stem + *n n. suff.; possible alternative attri-bution #663; but semantic fit is better here; also tonal correspondence probably coun-ter-indicates #663)	

	SEMITIC	EGYPTIAN	CUSHITIC	CHADIC	OMOTIC
710. *-ʔabz-/*-ʔibz- "to blaze" (root #709 + *z intens. of manner)		*3zb* "fierce, glowing (of radiance)" (metathesis of *3bz)	PEC *ʔabz-/*ʔibz- "fire"		
711. *-ʔĭb- "to sit, stay"	A. *ʔubūd* "to stop, halt" (stem + *d dur.)	*3b* "to tarry, stay; cease"	PSC *ʔĭb- "to recline"	WCh *-b- "to get tired" (J)	
712. *-ʔadl- "to act in anger"	A. *ʔaḍḍ* "to vex, torment; grieve"; *ʔaḍam* "anger, envy" (stem + *m n. suff.)	*3d* "to be savage; be aggessive; be angry; attack; anger"? (requires positing Eg. *ḏ* > *d* /#3_, as yet known only in this word, but not yet counterindicated either)	EC: Arbore *aḍ-* "to fight" (PC *dl > Arbore *ḍ*); SC: PR *ʔatlag- or *ʔatlag^w- "to swear oath" (stem + probably *g fin. fort., implying correctness of 1st form; PC *dl > PR *tl)		

	SEMITIC	EGYPTIAN	CUSHITIC	CHADIC	OMOTIC
713. *-ʔûuf- "to blow"		*wf 3* "lungs" (stem + *r n. suff.; C. *wof*)	*ʔûff-/*ʔûuf- "to blow"		
714. *-ʔăg- or *-ʔăg^w- "to arrange"		LE *ᶜg3* "to position (?)" (stem + *ʔ conc.)	PSC *ʔăgan- "even, straight" (stem + *n adj. suff.; *C^w, *C > *C /_- + -aC- suff. in PSC)		
715. *-ʔaɣ- or *-ʔaaɣ- "to be satis-factory"		*3ḫ* "useful, bene-ficial" (LE "to please")	*ʔaɣ- or *ʔaaɣ- "to be enough"		
716. *-ʔah- or *-ʔaah- "to moan"	A. *ʔahh* "to be grieved and sigh"	*3hw* "misery, pain" (stem + *w de-verb.)	SC: Iraqw *ah-* "to low (of cattle)"		

	SEMITIC	EGYPTIAN	CUSHITIC	CHADIC	OMOTIC
717. *-ʔâak^w- "to burn (of fire); fire (n.)"	A. *ʔakk* "to be very hot"		*ʔaak^w-/*ʔiik^w- "fire" (corrects Ehret 1987; EC: Arbore *ʔeeg*, loan < SC); *ʔâak^w- "to burn (intr.)" (Append.2)	*ak^{w}a/*aku "fire" (N) (Ng. *ákâ*) (J: *-kw)	
718. *ʔâl- "base of neck"	A. *ʔalal* "shoulders"		*ʔâl- "neck"		
719. *ʔîl- "oath"	A. *ʔalw* "to swear, take an oath" (stem + *w denom.)	LE *iri* "to swear (an oath" (stem + *y denom.)	PSC *ʔîlo "oath"		
720. *-ʔil-/*-ʔal- "to see"; *ʔĭl- "eye"		*irt* "eye" (stem + *t n. suff.; C. *ya*)	*ʔĭl- "eye"; PSC *ʔiley- "to know" (stem + *y in-choat. > dur.)	*ʔal "to see" (J)	NOm: Mao *al- "to know"

		SEMITIC	EGYPTIAN	CUSHITIC	CHADIC	OMOTIC
721.	*-ʔoɬ- "to speak loudly"	pPS *ʔɬ "to speak out" (Append.1)		PSC *ʔoɬ- "to insult, abuse"		
722.	*-ʔâm- "to heat"	A. *ʔamaj* "to be very hot" (stem + *g fin. fort., here as just fort.)	*3m* "to burn up (tr.); burn (of brazier)"	PSC *ʔânt- "to cook" (stem + *t dur.; *m > *n /_t)		NOm: Mao *a:ms- "moon" (stem + Omotic *ts n. suff.?; semantics: to give off heat > glow, shine)
723.	*-ʔam- "to intend"	pPS *ʔm "to intend" (Ehret 1989)		SC: PR *ʔamaɬ- "to choose" (stem + *ɬ ven., i.e., intend for oneself)		
724.	*ʔân-/*ʔîn- or *ân-/*în- "I"	*ʔn "I"		*ʔâni "I"	*nV (*na ?) "I" (after Kraft 1974, Shryock 1990)	NOm: Maji *in- "I"

	SEMITIC	EGYPTIAN	CUSHITIC	CHADIC	OMOTIC
725. *ʔănn-/*ʔĭnn- or *ănn-/*ĭnn- "we" (pl. of #724 by adding *-(a)C- where C = preceding stem-final C, is implied in Eg. reflex)	*ʔnn "we"; *-na suffixed 1st-person pl. pron.	*inn* "we" (C. *anon*, < earlier shape *inan-, stem of #724 + PAA pl. by redup. of stem-final C according to pattern *-aC-)	*ʔănn-/*ʔĭnn- "we"; PSC *ʔan- "our"		NOm *nona/ *nuna/*nina "we" (< prePO *inun- ?; Yem *ìnnò*; Bench *nuna* 1,3, *nin* 1)
726. *ʔîns- "one, someone, person" (indef. pron.)	*ʔns "person, man" (A. *ʔins*)		PEC *ʔis- "self" (PC *ns > PEC *s /#ʔV_-#)		NOm *is- "one" (Yem *ìsà*; *N > PO Ø /_s)
727. *ʔânt-/*ʔînt- or *ânt-/*înt- "you (sing.)"	*ʔnt "you (sing.)"		*ʔânt- "you (sing.)"		*int- "you (sing.)" ? (according to Fleming 1974; Bench *yint* 2 "you (polite)")

	SEMITIC	EGYPTIAN	CUSHITIC	CHADIC	OMOTIC
728. *-ʔânxʷ- "to listen; ear" (root #723 + *xʷ extend. fort.; *m > /n/ ([ŋ]) /_ *xʷ)		ᶜ*nḫwy* "ears" (stem + *wy* dual)	*ʔânxʷ-/*ʔînxʷ- "to listen, pay attention to" (Agaw "ear"; Append.2)		
729. *-ʔâr- "to know"	A. *ʔarub* "to be wise, prudent" (stem + *b extend. > stat.)		*ʔâr- "to know" (PSC "to see")		*ar- "to know" (Bench *er* ³)
730. *-ʔark'- "to notice, become aware of" (root #729 + *k' intens. of effect)	A. *ʔaraq* "to wake, be awake, sleepless"	ᶜ*rḳ* "to perceive"	*ʔark'- "to see"		
731. *-ʔaš- "to walk; leg"			EC: Dullay *ašš-* "to go"	*asə "foot/leg" (N) (ECh *ʔsn [J]); *(a)sə "to come" (N)	NOm: Maji *aš₁- "foot"

	SEMITIC	EGYPTIAN	CUSHITIC	CHADIC	OMOTIC
732. *-ʔāat- "to set out for"	A. *ʔaty* "to arrive; visit; meet" (stem + *y inchoat.)		EC: Soomaali *aad* "to go into, set out for"		NOm: Bench *at* 2 "to arrive"
733. *ʔâts- "body"			*ʔâts-/*ʔîts- *ʔûts- "torso"		NOm *ats- "person" (Mocha *'ašo* ; Bench *ats* 3)
734. *ʔăw- "tall, high, long, big"	A. *ʔauq* "to be higher than" (stem + *k' intens. of effect)	*3w* "long; length"; *3wy* "to extend (the arm)" (stem + *y denom.); C. *wu* "to be long" (stem + *y denom.)	EC: Afar *awaq* "climbing, exiting" (stem + *ʕ part., i.e., be so high as to rise out of; Afar *q* = [ʕ])		Mocha *awwó* "fat"; Yem *àw* "great, big"

	SEMITIC	EGYPTIAN	CUSHITIC	CHADIC	OMOTIC
735. *ʔâayš- "flesh, meat"		*3is* "viscera"	Agaw: Awngi *əšši* "meat" (PC *š > Awngi š /_i)		*a:yš$_2$- "flesh, meat" (Wolayta *ašo*, Basketo *a:yš* Yem *àšà*, Bench *aç̌* 4 "meat"; Mocha *'aččo* "body"; Ari *a:yzi* "skin")
736. *-ʔaz- "to hold"	A. *ʔazm* "to adhere, be firmly attached" (stem + *m extend.)		*ʔaz- or *ʕaz- "to hold"		
737. *-ʔaz- "to bite"	A. *ʔazm* "to bite with all the teeth; bite into pieces" (stem + *m extend.)		*ʔazx^w- "to gnaw" (stem + *x^w extend. fort.; Ehret 1987 has "to chew")		

PAA *ḩ	SEMITIC	EGYPTIAN	CUSHITIC	CHADIC	OMOTIC
738. *-ḩâb-/*-ḩûb- "to hold"	*ḩbs "to hold tight" (stem + *s' fort.)	*ḩb* "to catch (of fish and fowl)"	*ḩâb-/*ḩûb- "bicep, upper arm"		
739. *-ḩaab- "to speak out, proclaim"		*ḩb* "to mourn; to celebrate a triumph; festival"; *ḩby* "to be festal, make festival" (stem + *y denom.)	PSC *ḩaab- "to speak"		
740. *-ḩăc-/*-ḩîc- "to rub against"	A. *ḩaθm* "to rub, rub off" (stem + *m extend.)		EC: Afar *cisiyo* "grinding" (stem + *y deverb.); Afar *cisik* "shuffling along on one's buttocks"(stem+*k dur.; *c* = [ḩ])		NOm: Bench *(h)ašt* 1 "ointment" (stem + *t n. suff., i.e., that which is rubbed on one)

	SEMITIC	EGYPTIAN	CUSHITIC	CHADIC	OMOTIC
741. *-ḫâc'- "to curve, bend round"	A. *ḫaẓr* "to surround with a wall; enclose cattle in a fold" (stem + *r n. suff.; v. < presumed earlier n. "enclosure, fold")	*ḫsi* "to spin yarn" (stem + *y inchoat. > dur.; C. *hōs*, *hōōs*, *hus* "thread")	PSC *ḫâty'- "snake" (PSC *ty' = PC *c')	some WCh *-sk "snake" (J; stem + *k dur.; semantics: < manner of movement of snake)	
742. *-ḫêd- "to become fat, grow"	A. *ḫadb* "to bulge, be convex, be hunchbacked" (stem + *b extend. > stat.) *ḫadr* "to swell and get hard" (stem + *r adj. suff.: *ḫudurr* "thick, swollen")		*ḫêd- "to grow, grow up, mature" (PSC "to be fat")	some ECh *hd "leaf" (J; semantics: cf. etymology of English, German *grass*; for other parallel derivations, see #275, 282, 653, 831, 864, 865, 963, 984, and 1003)	

	SEMITIC	EGYPTIAN	CUSHITIC	CHADIC	OMOTIC
743. *-ḥudl- or *-ḥuudl- "to twist (tr.)"	A. *ḥaḍrab* "to twist tightly" (stem + *r diffus. + *p' fin. fort.)		SC: PR *ḥutl- "to twist fiber (into string or rope)" (PC *dl > PSC *tl)		
744. *-ḥaf- "to lay"	pPS *ḥp "to put down" (Append.1)	*ḥfd* "to sit" (stem + + *d dur. as stative > intr.); *ḥf3t* "crawling posture" (stem + *r diffus. + *t n. suff.)	*ḥaf- "to flatten, lay flat"		
745. *-ḥaɣ- "to feint, make as if to do"	A. *ḥaɣḥaɣ* "to be on point of speaking, but abstain" (redup. stem); *ḥaɣw* "to suppose, be of opinion, assert without	*ḥ3rw* "decoy-duck; bait in general" (stem + *l fin. + *w deverb.; see discussion of laryngeals for possible sound shifts)?	PEC *ḥag'- "to make as if to do something" (PEC *g' < PC *ɣ)		

	SEMITIC	EGYPTIAN	CUSHITIC	CHADIC	OMOTIC
	sufficient foundation" (stem + *w inchoat.)				
746. *-ḫeek- or *-ḫeek^{w}- "to go down"	A. *ḫakš* "to shrink" (stem + *ɬ ven.)		*ḫeek- or *ḫeek^{w}- "to go down"		
747. *-ḫâm-/*-ḫîm- "to strip away (hair, skin, etc.)"	pPS *ḫm "to remove (hair, skin, etc.)" (Append. 1)	*ḫmm* "surgeon's knife (?)" (redup. to derive n.?; C. *hom*); LE *ḫms* "to castrate; slay, slaughter" (stem + *s' fort. or *t' dur. intens.)	*ḫam- "hair"; PSC *ḫîm- "strip" (n.)	some WCh *hm "to carve (wood)" (J)	

	SEMITIC	EGYPTIAN	CUSHITIC	CHADIC	OMOTIC
748. *-ḥam- "to spoil (intr.)" (Sem., Eg. **innovation**: to spoil > to sour)	A. *ḥamḍ* "to be sour, acid" (stem + *dl m.v.); *ḥamat* "to be rank, spoiled" (stem + *t dur. or *t adj. suff. with v. < earlier adj.)	*ḥm3t* "salt" (stem + *r adj. suff. + *t n. suff.; semantics: sour > bitter > salty; C. *hmu*)	*ḥam- "to go bad, spoil"		
749. *-ḥam- or "to warm up"	A. *ḥamm* "to make hot, heat"; *aḥmar* "red" (stem with *a- attrib. pref. + *r adj. suff.)	C. *hmom* "to be(come) hot" (partially redup. stem as intens.)	PSC *ḥam- "to be warm"		
750. *-ḥin-/*-ḥan- "to set out, lay out, put into use"		*ḥn* "to provide, equip" (C. *sahnε* "to procure": *s- caus. + stem);		CCh *hn "to build" (J); WCh *hinɗ "to stand up" (J; stem + *z intens. of manner)	NOm: Maji *han-* "to put, place"

	SEMITIC	EGYPTIAN	CUSHITIC	CHADIC	OMOTIC
		ḫnw "cattle, possessions" (stem + *w deverb.); *ḫnb* "to convey" (stem + *b extend.)			
751. *-ḫînk-/*-ḫânk- "to carry (to or from)" (root #750 + *k dur.)		*ḫnk* "to present, offer; be burdened" (C. *hōnk*, *hank*)	*ḫînk- "to remove, take away"		
752. *-ḫōn- "to stick up, project, protrude"		*ḫnn* "phallus" (n. < v. by redup. of C /_#?); *ḫnwt* "horn" (stem + *w denom. + *t n. suff.); *ḫnḫnt* "swelling" (re-	SC: Dahalo *ḫòntò* "crown of head" (stem + *t n. suff.)		

	SEMITIC	EGYPTIAN	CUSHITIC	CHADIC	OMOTIC
		dup. as freq. + *t n. suff.)			
753. *-ḫuun-/*-ḫiin-/ *-ḫaan- "to bite into"	pPS *ḫn "to bite into" (Append.1)	*ḫnt* "greed" (stem + *t n. suff.); *ḫnty* "to be covetous, greedy" (preceding n. + *y denom.; semantics: hungry for, in metaphorical sense)	*ḫank'- "palate" (stem + *k' intens. of effect); PSC *ḫuntl- "to chew" (stem + *dl m.v.; PC *dl > PSC *tl); PEC *ḫiinc'-/ *ḫaanc'- "to chew" (stem (stem + *c' extend.); PLEC *ḫanc'uf- "saliva" (stem + *c' extend. + *f iter., i.e., chewing produces saliva)		

	SEMITIC	EGYPTIAN	CUSHITIC	CHADIC	OMOTIC
754. *-ḥap- "to take hold of"	pPS *ḥp "to take hold of" (Append.1)	*ḥpt* "to embrace" (stem + *t n. suff., v. < n. seen in C. *hpot* "brasse," i.e., length of two *arms*)	PSC *ḥap- "to clasp"		
755. *-ḥup- or *-ḥuup- "mouthful"	A. *ḥafas* "to eat" (stem + *s caus. as de-nom.)	*ḥpd* "to open (mouth)" (stem + *d dur.)	PSC *ḥup- or *ḥuup- "breath"		
756. *-ḥap'- "to hasten"	A. *ḥabj* "to walk fast" (stem + $*g^w$ dur.)	*ḥpwty* "runner" (stem + *w inchoat. + *t, *y n. suff.); *ḥpgt* "leaping dance" (stem + $*g^w$ dur. + *t n. suff.) LE *ḥpt* "to travel, hurry" (stem + *t dur.)	EC: Yaaku *-hɛbisom-* "to go fast" (stem + Yaaku *-isom-* v. ext.; PC *p' > Yaaku *b*; PC *ḥa > Yaaku *hɛ*)		Mocha *apà:pin-* "to be fast" (re-dup. stem + *n adj. suff.; v. < earlier adj.)

	SEMITIC	EGYPTIAN	CUSHITIC	CHADIC	OMOTIC
757. *-ḫĕr- "to scrape off"	pPS *ḫr "to scratch, scrape" (Ehret 1989); *ḫrθ "to plow" (stem + *ts diffus.)	*ḫ3y* "to be naked" (stem + *y inchoat., i.e., be scraped bare; C. *hēy* ; for *ē* < PBA *a, see #399)	PSC *ḫĕr- "to shave"		
758. *-ḫâs'- "to feel bad"	pPS *ḫs "to feel bad, give vent to bad feelings" (Append.1)	LE *ḫs3* "fierce; savage; terrible" (stem + *r or *ʔ adj. suff.)	SC: Dahalo *ḫáts'ts'i* "sorrow" (< PC *ḫâts'-)		
759. *-ḫetl'-/*-ḫotl'- "to scratch"	A. *ḫaṣṣ* "to shave; rub off the hair"		*ḫetl-/*ḫotl- "to scratch"		Mocha *at'a:to* "thorn" (stem + *t n. suff.)
760. *-ḫâw- "to hack"		*ḫwi* "to beat, smite, strike; thresh" (stem + *y inchoat. > dur.; C. *hī*)	PSC *ḫâaw- or *hâaw- "ax" (n. < v. by V > VV)		

	SEMITIC	EGYPTIAN	CUSHITIC	CHADIC	OMOTIC
761. *-ḫ-y-/*-ḫ-w- "to travel"	pPS *ḫy/*ḫw "to move (intr.)" (Append.1)	*ḫwi* "to tread, roam" (stem + *y inchoat. > dur.)	SC: PR *ḫuyu(ma) "journey" (stem + *m n. suff.)		
762. *-ḫâaz- "to cut into"	A. *ḫazz* "to cut, make incisions, carve"	*ḫsḳ* "to cut off (head); cut out (heart)" (stem + *kʷ' and.); *ḫsḳt* "chopper" (previous v. + *t n. suff.)	PSC *ḫâaḍ- "to cut into, gash" (PSC *ḍ < PC *z verb-stem-finally); EC: Arbore *hezzú* "sign, mark" (PC *ḫa > Arbore *he*)		

	SEMITIC	EGYPTIAN	CUSHITIC	CHADIC	OMOTIC
763. *-ḫîz- "to increase in size or amount (intr.)"	A. *ḫazfar* "to fill" (stem + *f iter. + *r adj. suff., with v. < presumed earlier adj. "full"); *ḫazn* "rough, elevated ground" (stem + *n n. suff.)		*ḫîz- "to be stout"		NOm: Bench *ez* [2-3] "big"
764. *-ḫôz- "to dig"		*ḫzp* "garden" (stem + *p intens. of manner, i.e., < earlier "to till")	PSC *ḫôḍ- "to dig hole" (PSC *ḍ < PC *z verb-stem-finally)		

	SEMITIC	EGYPTIAN	CUSHITIC	CHADIC	OMOTIC
765. *-ḫôʔ- "to spill (intr.)"	A. *ḫauḍ* "to collect water; make a reservoir" (stem + *dl m.v.)	*ḫ3i* "to drip, drop" (stem + *y inchoat. > dur.); *ḫ3yt* "flood-water" (previous v. + *t n. suff.)	PSC *ḫôʔ-, *ḫôʕ-, *hôʔ-, or *hôʕ- "to spill" (Ehret 1980: 310 left out alternative forms in *ḫ)		
766. *-ḫĕʕ- or *-ḫĕeʕ- "to be weak"		*ḫᶜ3w* "children" (stem + *r n. suff. + *w* pl.)	PSC *ḫĕeʕ-, *ḫĕeʔ-, *hĕeʕ-, or *hĕeʔ- "weak, feeble" (adj. < v. by V > VV?)		

PAA *h

	SEMITIC	EGYPTIAN	CUSHITIC	CHADIC	OMOTIC
767. *h- "this/that" (demons. base); *ha "this/that one"	*hā- demons. stem (in A. in near demons.; in Syriac in far and near demons.)		*ha "this one" (PSC *ha; EC: Afar *ah*); PSC *hû or *hûu "that"		*ha- "this" (base in near demons.; Yem *hān* , Male *hay*, Oyda *ha*-, etc.)

		SEMITIC	EGYPTIAN	CUSHITIC	CHADIC	OMOTIC
768.	*hâa "open ground, area outside residence"		*h* "courtyard"	*hâ(a) "outside"	CCh *hy, *hn, *ht "earth, soil" (J; stem + *y, *n, *t n. suff.)	
769.	*-hu- or *-huu- "to fall"	A. *huwiyy* "to fall; die" (stem + *y in-choat.)		SC: PR *hu- "to fall"		
770.	*-hab- "to beat, strike with weapon"	*hb "to hit" (Ap-pend.1)	*hbķ* "to beat up" (stem + *k' in-tens. of effect)	EC: Soomaali *habbi* "to beat some-one with a stick" (stem + *s caus. > Som. -*i*)		Mocha *àwur-* "to throw a spear" (stem + *r diffus.; PO *b > Mocha *w* /V_V)
771.	*-hăad- "to move along, proceed" (Sem., Eg. **innova-tion**: move > move toward)	A. *hadf* "to appear, en-ter; approach" (stem + *f iter. > dur.)	LE *hd* "to encroach"	*hăad- "to go along"		

	SEMITIC	EGYPTIAN	CUSHITIC	CHADIC	OMOTIC
772. *-hĭd- or *-hĭid- "to drive"	A. *hady* "to lead on the right path; follow, imitate" (stem + *y inchoat.; semantics: drive > send, direct (on right path), + *y inchoat. > follow)	*hd* "to attack; assault (n.)" (LE "to drive off"); *hdhd* "charge (of army)" (redup. stem as intens.)	PSC *hĭd- or *hĭid- "to drive (animals)"		
773. *-h-d- "to rest"	A. *hadʔ* "to rest, calm down, subside; keep quiet; halt; stop, abide" (stem + *ʕ conc.); *hudūn* "to calm down" (stem + *n non-fin.)	*hdmw* "footstool" (stem + *m extend. + *w deverb.; semantics: thing to rest on)	*-h-dr- "to stay the night" (stem + *r diffus.)		

	SEMITIC	EGYPTIAN	CUSHITIC	CHADIC	OMOTIC
774. *-hŏj- "to wet down"	A. *haðb* "to flow" (stem + *b extend.)		EC: Sidamo *hoshōsh-* "to erode soil" (redup. as intens.; PC *dz > Sidamo *sh* [š])		NOm: Yem *hōʔyā* "soil, mud" (PO *č > Yem *ʔy*)
775. *-hâl-/*-hîl- "to cry, call out"	pPS *hl "to shout" (Append. 1)	*hnw* "praise" (stem + *w deverb.)	*hâl-/*hîl- "to cry"		
776. *hāl-/*hīl- "other" (probably demon. root #767 + *l n./adj. suff.)		*hnw* "associates, family" (stem + *w* pl.)	*hāl-/*hīl- "other"		
777. *-hal- "to become thoroughly wet, pour heavily (intr.)"	A. *hall* "to pour down violently"; *halb* "to moisten by lasting rain or snow" (stem + *b extend.)	*hnw* "waves" (stem + *w deverb.); LE *hr* "canal"	*hal- "spring (of water)"		NOm: Sezo *hult-* "wet" (stem with *-u- tr. infix, + *t adj. suff.)

	SEMITIC	EGYPTIAN	CUSHITIC	CHADIC	OMOTIC
778. *-heel- "to grip, take hold of"	pPS *hl "to grasp and take out" (Append.1)		*heel- "to seize, catch hold of"		Ometo: Malo *yel-* "to bear (child)" (semantics: cf. English "bear"; PO *h > Malo *y* /#_eC)
779. *-hâm- "to go away"	pPS *hm "to go away; send away" (Ehret 1989)	*hmt* "fare (for conveyance)" (stem + *t n. suff.); LE *hmw* "fare" (stem + *w deverb.)			NOm $*h_1am$- "to go" (Mocha *hàmm-*; Bench *ham(nk)*-3; Yem *àm*-)
780. *-ham- or *-haam-	A. *hamm* "to be concerned at, solicitous about, purpose, intend, strive after"	*hmhmt* "war shout" (redup. stem as intens. + *t n. suff.); LE *hm* "cry of satisfaction, shout"	SC: Alagwa *hamhami* "eagerness, zeal, concern" redup. stem as intens.?)		

		SEMITIC	EGYPTIAN	CUSHITIC	CHADIC	OMOTIC
781.	*-hom- "to take into the mouth"	pPS *hm "to take into the mouth (food or drink)" (Ehret 1989)		*-ohm-/*-ehm- "to eat" (corrects Ehret 1987: #543)	CCh *ham "to eat hard things; to chew" (J)	Mocha *hùma:n-* "to be thirsty" (stem + *n adj. suff.; v. < adj.)
782.	*-hûum- "to lower"	pPS *hm "to lower, put down" (Ehret 1989)		PSC *hûmb- "to crouch" (stem + *b extend.)	ECh *-unt "to sit down" (J; stem + *t dur.)	
783.	*-hăp- "to put up, put above"	A. *haft* "to fly to and fro, flit, hover" (stem + *t dur. as intr.)		PSC *hăp- "to put up, put above, put on top of"		
784.	*-hip'- "to rub"	A. *habj* "to scratch so that blood flows" (stem + *g fin. fort. or $*g^w$ dur.)		PSC *hip'- "to rub"		

		SEMITIC	EGYPTIAN	CUSHITIC	CHADIC	OMOTIC
785.	*-hup'- "point, tip"	A. *habbār* "sharp" (stem + *r adj. suff.)		EC: Soomaali *hub* "weapon" (PC *p' > Som.*b*)		NOm $*h_1up'$- "tip, point" (NE Ometo *hup'- "head"; Mocha *huba:tto* "awl": stem + *t n. suff.)
786.	*har- "flow (n.)"	A. *hurr* "to bring on diarrhea; leak; pour out"	*hrp* "to be immersed" (stem + *p intens. of manner; C. *hōrp*) LE *hrnw* "waters" (stem + *n n. suff. + *w* pl.)	PEC *har- "pond, stream"		
787.	*-har- or *-haar- "to cut into"	pPS *hr "to cut into, cut away" (Ehret 1989)		PSC *haar- "spear" (n.< v. by V > VV?)		

	SEMITIC	EGYPTIAN	CUSHITIC	CHADIC	OMOTIC
788. *-hăr- "to become lit"		*hr w*, *h3w* "day, daytime" (stem + *w deverb.; C. *hou*)	*hur- "to light" (tr. by *-u- infix)		Mocha *hàr*- "to dawn"
789. *-her-/*-hor- "to go rapidly on foot"	A. *harab* "to flee, run away" (stem + *b extend.)		*horr-/*herr- "to go on foot" (PEC "to run away")		
790. *-hur- "to feel good"		*hr w* "pleasing; to be pleased; be at peace" (stem + *w deverb.)	PEC *hur- "to recover from illness"		
791. *-haas- "voice" (Sem., Eg. **innovation**: addition of *b extend., imputing meaning "to count")	A. *ḥass*, *ḥiss* "voice"; *ḥsb "to count" (stem + *b extend.)	*ḥsb* "to count, reckon, reckon with" (stem + *b extend.)	PEC *haassaw- "to converse, chat" (stem + *w denom.)		

	SEMITIC	EGYPTIAN	CUSHITIC	CHADIC	OMOTIC
792. *haas'- "sand"	*ḥs "sand" (Ji. *ḥaši* "soil"; MSA *š < PS *s)		*haats'- "sand"		
793. *-hes'- "to sing"		*ḥsi* "to sing" (stem + *y inchoat. > dur.; C. *hōs*)	[EC: PSom *hees "to sing": loan from Omotic (expected Som. *heš < PEC *hec-)		Ometo: Malo *yes's'*- "to sing" (for PO *h > Malo *y* /#_eC, see also #778)
794. *-hat'- "to overflow"	A. *haṭf* "to milk; rain" (stem + *f iter.); *haṭl*, *huṭl* "continuous rain" (stem + *l n. suff.)		SC: PR *hats'- "to be full"		NOm: Dorze, Dache *hats'e* "water" (distinct root from that seen in #1014); SOm: Ari *hats'*- "to wash"

	SEMITIC	EGYPTIAN	CUSHITIC	CHADIC	OMOTIC
795. *-hăat'- "to come toward"	A. *haṭʕ* "to run away, frightened, with one's eyes fixed on the object of fear" (stem + *ʕ part.)	LE *hsmḳ* "to storm, assault" (stem + *m extend. + *k' intens. of effect)	PSC *hăat'- "to come near"		
796. *-hatl'- "to stop (intr.)"	MSA *hṣḳ "hobble, rope" (stem + *k' intens. of effect)		PEC *haj'- "to be still, unmoving" (PC *tl > PEC *j')		
797. *-hâys'- "to lap"	A. *ḥasw* "to drink, sip, lap" (stem + *w inchoat. > dur.)				Gonga, Bench *hays'- "tongue" (Bench *eyts'*$^{2\text{-}3}$; Mocha *'hač'awo*)

	SEMITIC	EGYPTIAN	CUSHITIC	CHADIC	OMOTIC
798. *hǎz- "flow (n.)"	A. *hazhāz* "flowing abundantly" (redup. stem as intens.)	*ḥz3* "milk; mucus; dough" (stem + *r n. suff.); *ḥzt* "water-jar" (stem + *t n. suff.)	*hǎz- "flow of water"	CCh, ECh *-ɗk "saliva" (J; stem + probably *k sing. suff. of liquids, seen in Ng. entry in #124, etc.)	
799. *-hôoz- "to speak"	pPS *hz "to speak out" (Append.1)	*ḥzi* "to praise; favor (someone)" (stem + *y inchoat. > dur.; C. *hasīɛ*)	*hôoz- "to tell"		Ometo: Gidicho *ho:d-* "to say" (PO *z > Gidicho *d* /V_)
800. *-heeʔ- "to convey"	Ji. *hɔ́ɬ* (*hwɬ) "to take by force" (stem + *ɬ ven.)	*h3b* "to send" (stem + *b extend.; C. *hōb*)	*heeʔ- "to bring"		
801. *-hooʔ- "to burn, become hot"	A. *haub* "heat of fire" (stem + *b extend. > stat.)	*h3wt* "flame" (stem + *w inchoat. + *t n. suff.)	*hooʔ- or *ʔooh- "to burn"		NW Ometo *hoʔ- "warm"

	SEMITIC	EGYPTIAN	CUSHITIC	CHADIC	OMOTIC
802. *-hăʕ- "to arrive"	A. *hauʔ* "to come to, reach, come with, bring" (stem + *ʔ conc.); *haus* "to step vigorously; walk around" (stem + *s' fort. or *š non-fin.)	*h3yt* "portal" (stem + *y inchoat. + *t n. suff.)	PSC *hăʕ- "to arrive"		

THE LATERALS AND *r IN *PAA*

Four laterals, *l, *dl, *ɬ, and *tl', along with a flap *r, must be postulated for PAA.

The most straightforward reconstruction is that of *r. In PS, PC, and PCh it produced *r in all environments. In Omotic it persisted as *r in non-initial contexts, but became PO *d word-initially. In pre-Egyptian its reflexes were probably /r/ in all positions; but by Middle Egyptian *r was widely weakening to *3* ([ʔ]) when occurring as the final consonant in a word. In some environments the consonant seems to have resisted such weakening, however; in particular, it remained *r* in biconsonantal words when the preceding consonant was Eg. *g*, *m*, *n*, or *w*, or one of the two voiceless fricatives *š* or *x* (see roots #285, 393, 591, 595, 646, 651, 884, and 974), and also following another *r* (/#(C)r_, as in #175).

Less often, there are cases in Egyptian of medial weakening of *r, one oft-noted example being *irṯt* "milk." which came sometimes to be rendered *i3tt* (*irṯt > *irtt [*ṯ > t assimilation] > *i3tt*). But on the whole the examples of medial weakening involve only those penultimate *r where the ultimate consonant is a suffix of high productivity in Middle Egyptian, normally the suffixes *i* ~ *y*, *w*, or *t*. These cases are thus suspect as instances involving affixation subsequent to the operation of the shift *r > *3* /_#. In other cases the affix may still have been felt by speakers to be only optionally present and therefore still indirectly indicating a potentially word-final affixless environment; in such an environment the *r > *3* shift would have applied, with generalization to the case where the affix did appear. Even the word for "milk" might be considered a special case of this process — its particular history giving it the appearance of involving a double suffixation of *t*.

The reflexes of PAA *l were only somewhat more varied than those of *r. In PS, PC, PCh, and PO it remained *l. Newman fails to account for it in his reconstruction of PCh, but Jungraithmayr and Shimizu (1981) provide a clear demonstration of its presence in proto-Chadic. In the Gonga subgroup of Omotic, *l became proto-Gonga *n word-initially when the following consonant was labial, and proto-Gonga *d in other word-initial environments (see Mocha examples of *l below, and Table 1, Chapter 2). But in the rest of Omotic, and non-initially in Gonga, its reflexes are generally /l/, except for assimilation to /n/ in the restricted environment of a proximate nasal in several North Omotic tongues (again see Table 1).

In ancient Egyptian, a distinct /l/ was not marked in the script. In the early written records, PAA *l produced Eg. *r* in word-final position and occasionally in what would have been final position, but for addition of one of the highly productive Egyptian suffixes mentioned above. All cases of word-final *r* in ME and LE data — except those of *gr*, *mr*, *nr*, *rr*, and *wr* and of *šr* and *xr* noted above — can thus be taken normally to represent PAA *l, since *r would regularly have yielded Eg. *3*. Word-initially PAA *l also yielded Eg. *i* (*y) in instances where the following vowel was *i. In all other environments PAA *l appears normally as Eg. *n*. In at least one word-initial context, preceding a PAA *b (#_Vb), PAA *r would have fallen together with *l in Egyptian, because it produces the same outcome, *n*, as does PAA *l in such an environment (roots #927-930).

The Egyptological literature on the consonant *l often holds that Egyptian had a spoken [l] but no grapheme to represent it, and so relied on *n*, *r*, and *i* to fill the gap. This seems extraordinarily puzzling, given that the scribes did not adapt their script from that of some other language of considerably differing phonology, but evolved it on their own; that they seem fully to have represented in their script all the other early consonant distinctions; and that they seem eventually, if belatedly, to have taken account of most other changes in the consonant system of Egyptian. Moreover, the regularity of the orthographical correspondences revealed in the comparative data presented here — coupled with the fact that [r], [y] (*i*), and [n] are such natural, common, and unremarkable phonetic outcomes of original *l in the described environments — would make far better sense if the graphic correspondences were phonetically rather than scribally motivated.

And in fact, a reexamination of the Coptic outcomes of PAA *l, *n, and *r, viewed in the light of the correspondences established here, compels exactly that conclusion — that ancient Egyptian orthography reflects the actual phonemic history not of just a scribal dialect (Vycichl 1983), but of the language as a whole, both spoken and written. In words that were not borrowed and that are certainly traceable back to Middle Egyptian, Coptic (and Demotic) *l* is as likely to derive from PAA *n, *ŋ, or *ɲ (which fell together as Eg. *n*) as from PAA *l. Moreover, Coptic *l* appears as a reflex of these several PAA nasals and of PAA *l only if one of a restricted set of consonants co-occurs with it in the same word; otherwise both PAA *l and the PAA non-labial nasals yield Coptic *n*. These data thus impel one to the conclusion that most PAA *n and *l merged as actual *n* ([n]) in Old Egyptian, with new *l* arising subsequently in Demotic times by split from such Eg. *n* . Other *l* entered the language in word borrowings, principally from Semitic and Greek, completing the rephonemicization of /l/ in Demotic and Coptic.

Two periods of sound change lie behind this phonological history. The first period started off with six sound shift rules dating no later than the beginning of Old Egyptian. First,

> Eg. #30. PAA *r > pre-Eg. *l /#_V(V)C[+obstruent,+labial] (#927-933, and 941).

A shift of more sweeping affect then removed most word-final *r from the language:

> #31. PAA *r > Eg. *3* /C_(t, w, y)# (C ≠ *g*, *m*, *n* , *r*, *w*, *š*, or *x*).

It was followed by

Eg. #32. PAA *l > Eg. *r* /_(t, w, y)#,

remedying the defective distribution of Eg. *r* created by sound shift #31, but conversely beginning the elimination of the phoneme /l/ from the language. More PAA *l were removed by two other shifts,

#33. PAA *l > Eg. *i* ([y]) /#_iC (instances of /#_ib and /#_iʕC have been observed so far: #808, 809, 834, and 835), and

#34. PAA *l > Eg. *r* /#nV_C (#633).

Finally, a sixth rule,

#35. PAA *l > Eg. *n*,

eliminated from early Egyptian all the remaining *l. These six rules together account naturally and succinctly for Old and Middle Egyptian orthography — for the shift of most PAA *r to *3* word- or stem-finally; for the realization of PAA *l as *r* in the same environments; and for the representation of all other PAA *l, and some word-initial *r, as *n*.

A second set of sound shifts, dating to the period between Middle Egyptian and Coptic, then completed the process initiated by shifts #30-35. First, new *l* were created from ME *n* in a variety of restricted environments, most of them involving a proximate voiced labial or another nasal in the same word:

#36. ME *n* > *l* /#_Vb_Vb (single instance, #810, but no counter-examples known);

#37. ME *n* > *l* /#{š, h}V_{m, l}, /#_(V){s, š, h}V{m,b}#, and /#_V{m,b}{s, š, h}, where *s*, *š*, and *h* are the attested Coptic consonants (hence in #401, 629, 659, 661 (first entry), 810 (third entry), and 827, but not in #661 (second entry) and 817);

#38. ME *n* > *l* /#_Vḳ (#619, 822, and also C. *lkō* "sycamore fig" < ME *nḳ* ᶜ*wt*);

#39. ME *n* > *l* /#C_1V_C_2 (either C_1 or C_2 = *m*; 316, 587); and

#40. ME *nn* > *l (V) l V* (#637; single example, but no counter-examples have been identified).

Outside of these instances, however, all ME *n* — whether deriving ultimately from PAA *l, *n, *ɲ, *ŋ, or *r — normally produced *n* in Coptic (for Coptic *n* < PAA *l, see roots #442, 484, 803, 804, 814, 817, 819, 831, and

969; for Coptic *n* < PAA *n, *ŋ, or *ɲ, see 48, 198, 323, 366, 391, 448, 568, 589, 590, 609, 611, 616, 620, 621, 626, 627, 631, 685, 689, 690, 725, 952, 970, and 983; and for Coptic *n* from PAA *r, see #927-930, 933, and 941).

This history of PAA *l, *n, and *r in Egyptian has the added virtue of providing a plausible and simple explanation of one seemingly irregular source for word-initial *l* in certain Coptic words. These particular *l* replaced the grapheme for *r*, which had been used in the Demotic or Late Egyptian forms of the same words. With one exception, none of these words can be traced back earlier in Egyptian than some point in the Late Egyptian period, and most are generally argued to be Semitic borrowings in which the orginal consonant was PS *l (Cerny 1976; Vycichl 1983). Given this latter information and the phonological history sketched out above, the explanation seems relatively straightforward. Initially, in Late Egyptian, *r* would have been adapted to mark the rare borrowed [l], lacking as a native sound in the Egyptian of that period; and then, in later centuries, such [l] would have become part of the new post-Late-Egyptian /l/ created by rules #36-40, and so would no longer have been represented by *r*, but by a new symbol encompassing all of the newly phonemic /l/.

The one case of Coptic word-initial *l* which truly derives from PAA *r (root #926) is one of three examples (another notable case being #679) attesting a separate pre-Coptic sound shift rule in a very restricted but sharply defined environment:

Eg. #41. ME *r* > Coptic *l* /#(C)_o(C)# and /#o_#.

Of the remaining three PAA laterals, *ɬ was surely a voiceless lateral fricative; the correspondences point clearly and consistently in this direction. PAA *dl and *tl', on the other hand, were most probably articulated as affricates. A minus-continuant articulation is indicated by their reflexes in all four branches of Cushitic: by the Beja retroflex stops /ḍ/ for PAA *dl and /ṭ/ for PAA *tl'; by the Agaw voiced stop *d for *dl and the ejective stop *t' for *tl'; by the PEC stop *d' (either retroflex or implosive) for *dl, and PEC *j (['j]) for *tl' (Ehret 1987); and by their maintenance in PSC as the lateral affricates reconstructed respectively as *tl and dl. The same feature is attested in Omotic, in which *dl and *tl' fell together as the PO implosive stop *d' ([ɗ]) whereas PAA *ɬ and *l collapsed into PO *l. And it is paralleled in Egyptian, which changed *dl and *tl' to the respective palatal saffricate or stops *ḏ* and *ṯ*, but PAA *ɬ to the equivalent fricative palatal *š*. Only in Chadic, where the two consonants widely yield lateral fricatives, and in Semitic, where PAA *tl' shifted to pre-PS *s' (*ṣ) — filling the slot in the consonant system vacated by the Boreafrican collapsing of PAA *s' with *s (NAA shift #1) — are continuant reflexes notably present; and even then the PS *ṣ may actually have been realized as an ejective affricate [ts'] (as a variety of scholars have argued).

Newman's published reconstructions (1977) posit only *ɬ for PCh, but

Jungraithmayr and Shimizu propose four laterals, which fit very well with the four laterals of PC. Their PC *l corresponds to PAA *l, their *ɬ (or *$ɬ_1$) to PAA *tl', their *$ɬ_2$ to PAA *ɬ, and their *ɮ to PAA *dl. As with their reconstruction of the alveolar sibilants, one of their reconstructed laterals, *ɬ (*$ɬ_1$), acts as a catch-all category into which a lateral fricative or affricate is placed whenever the data are insufficient to establish which specific lateral is involved. Thus PAA *ɬ is normally reflected in Jungraithmayr and Shimizu's *$ɬ_2$, but occasionally in their *ɬ. The evidence cited from Ngizim, finally, is quite clear: PAA *dl yields Ngizim /dl/, both *ɬ and *tl' become Ngizim /tl/, and PAA *l commonly gives Ngizim /n/, but sometimes /l/ (e.g., root #804; the factors conditioning these particular reflexes remain to be worked out).

Table 8: Afroasiatic (Afrasian) Lateral Correspondences

PAA	PS	Eg.	PC	PCh	PO
*l	*l	*n, r, i*	*l	*l (Ng. /n/)	*l
*dl	*ḏ	*ḏ*	*dl	*ɮ (Ng. /dl/	*d'
*ɬ	*ɬ	*š*	*ɬ	*ɬ (*$ɬ_2$) (Ng. /tl/)	*l
*tl'	*ṣ	*ṯ*	*tl ([tl'])	*tl (*$ɬ_1$) (Ng. /tl/)	*d'

(Note that the notation *tl in Cushitic symbolizes the *ejective* lateral affricate [tl'].)

A fairly extensive co-occurrence constraint in Egyptian limits the variety of possible consonant sequences in Egyptian involving the PAA laterals. In particular, it disallows lateral obstruents (or, as they became in Egyptian, palatal obstruents) before following velar obstruents in the same word, with the result that PAA *ɬ and *tl' became Eg. *s* (rather than *š* and *ṯ* respectively) and *dl became Eg. *d* (rather than expected *ḏ*) in such environments. The constraint apparently affected some but not all sequences of the opposite order, with a velar as C_1 and a lateral obstruent as C_2. For further discussion of this shift or set of shifts, see the materials on Eg. rule #3 in the section above on Afroasiatic velars and labiovelars. Another Egyptian sound shift of consequence for the laterals,

Eg. #28. PAA *tl' > pre-Eg. *dl > Eg. *ḏ* /#_Vʕ,

accounts for the absence of the sequence *ṯ* *ᶜ* in the language (roots #922 and 923).

The distribution of PAA laterals may also have been subject to a very ancient and widespread constraint against the co-occurrence of any two non-identical lateral *obstruents* as C_1 and C_2 of a root. Whether this restriction existed in Omotic is not as yet known; perhaps like the constraint barring the co-occurrence of non-identical labials (discussed earlier), it did not operate in that branch. But it seems on present evidence to have been a general feature of the Semitic, Egyptian, Chadic, and probably Cushitic divisions of the family.

	SEMITIC	EGYPTIAN	CUSHITIC	CHADIC	OMOTIC
PAA *l					
803. *la "at, to"	*l- "to, at" (A. *li* ; Ji. *l*- ; etc.)	*n* "to, for" (C. *n*-)	*la "at"		
804. *-lâ-/*-lî- "to be moist, damp"	*lyn "to become soft" (stem + *n non-fin.)	*nt* "water" (stem + *t n. suff.; C. *nut*)	*lâ-/*-lî- "to be moist, damp"	*ly "cold" (J; stem + *y adj. suff.; Ng. *láyí* ; semantics: see #458); WCh, CCh *lw "rain, sky" (J; stem + *w deverb.)	Ometo: Dache *lim*- "to swim" (stem + *m extend.)
805. *-lâa- "to strike down"	pPS *lt "to hit repeatedly" (stem + *t dur. > iter.; Ehret 1989)	*ni* "to drive away, rebuff; throw down (enemy); parry (missile)" (stem + *y inchoat. > dur.)	PSC *lâa- "to kill (by beating)"		

	SEMITIC	EGYPTIAN	CUSHITIC	CHADIC	OMOTIC
806. *lð "true"	A. *la*- "truly, indeed, certainly"		*lð "true"		NOm *loʔ- "good" (stem + *ʔ adj. suff.; Mocha *dóʔa*) Mocha *dọ:*- "to be good" (stem + *w de-nom.; PO *l > Mocha *d* /#_V)
807. *-lîb- or *-lîib- "to sit"	pPS *lb "to stay" (Ehret 1989)		PSC *lîib- "buttocks" (n. < v. by V > VV?)		
808. *-lib- "to lap"	pPS *lb "to lap up" (Ehret 1989)	*ib* "thirsty man" (possibly n. < v. by VV?); *ibt* "thirst" (stem + *t n. suff.); *ibi* "to be thirsty" (1st n. + *y de-			NOm *alib- "tongue" (*a- attrib. deverb. pref. + stem)

	SEMITIC	EGYPTIAN	CUSHITIC	CHADIC	OMOTIC
		nom.; C. *ybε*); *ibḫ* "tooth" (stem + *ḫ iter., i.e., < v. "to chew")			
809. *1īb- "heart"	*lbb "heart" (A. *lubb* "middle"); A. *labān* "chest" (stem + *n n. suff.)	*ib* "heart"	*l-b- "chest, breast"	CCh *lb "belly" (J)	NOm *lib- "heart" (Yem *nībā*; Gonga: S. Mao *yibba*, Mocha *nı́bbo*, etc.)
810. *-lib-/*-lab- "to burn (intr.)"	MSA *lbḳ "to light" (stem + *ḳʷ and.)	*nbi* "flame; to burn (intr.)" (stem + *y denom.; stem + *y in-choat. > dur.; *nbibi* "to be hot" (re-dup. > intens.); C. *loblεb* "ardor of love" (redup. stem as		some WCh *libn "charcoal" (J; stem + *n n. suff.)	

	SEMITIC	EGYPTIAN	CUSHITIC	CHADIC	OMOTIC
		intens.); C. *1ōbš* "to burn; be hot" (stem + *ɣʷ comp.? ME *ḫ* often > C. š /_#)			
811. *-1âf- "to rise"	A. *1aff* "to be densely grown" (semantics: rise > grow > grow densely)	*nfnft* "to leap" (stem redup. as intens. + *t dur., < earlier "hop, bound"?)	SC: Alagwa *1af-* "to swell"	*1p(-t) "to jump" (J; stem + *t dur.; shared innovation with Eg.?)	Mocha *'daparo* "hump" (stem + *r n. suff.)
812. *-1ef- "to wrap, fold"	pPS *1p "to wrap, fold up" (Ehret 1989)		*1ef- "to wrap"		
813. *1eg?- "bull (?)"		*ng3* "long-horned bull"	*1e?g- or *1eg?- "calf" or "bull-calf"		

	SEMITIC	EGYPTIAN	CUSHITIC	CHADIC	OMOTIC
814. *-lâg^{w}- or *-lâag^{w}- "to speak"	A. *lajab* "to cry out, clamor" (stem + *b extend.); *lajlaj* "to repeat words frequently in speech" (redup. as freq.)	*ngg* "to cackle" (redup. stem as freq.; C. *nočnč* "to banter": fully redup. stem)	PSC *lâag^{w}- "news" (n. < v. by V > VV?)		
815. *-laaɣ- "to turn, turn back, change direction"	A. *lagz* "to alter, change shape of a thing, distort" (stem + *z intens. of manner, i.e., distort)	*nḫ3ḫ3* "to ruffle (?) (hair)" stem + *r diffus., redup. as freq.)	PEC *laag'- "to return" (PEC *g' < PC *ɣ)	some CCh *lg "back" (J has *g for PAA *ɣ)	
816. *-lîɣ-/*-lûɣ- "to be raised"	A. *laɣd* "to prick the ears" (stem + *d dur.)	*nḫ3* "pendulous" (stem + *r or *ʔ adj. suff.)	PEC *lig'- "to rise up" (PEC *g' < PC *ɣ)	some CCh *lg "to hang" (J has *g for PAA *ɣ)	Mocha *'dokko* "upper part of door"

	SEMITIC	EGYPTIAN	CUSHITIC	CHADIC	OMOTIC
817. *-loh- "to rise, go up"		*nhp* "to rise early in the morning" (stem + *p' fin. fort.); *nhpw* "early morning" (previous v. + *w deverb.); *nhzi* "to wake" (stem + *z intens. of manner or *dz extend. fort. + *y inchoat.; C. *nεhsε*)	PSC *lohiʕ- "to put out new growth" (stem + *ʕ part., i.e., put *out* new shoots, etc.)		

	SEMITIC	EGYPTIAN	CUSHITIC	CHADIC	OMOTIC
818. *-lĕḫ- "to notice, pay attention"	A. *laḫaẓ* "to regard, notice, comprehend" (stem + *c' extend.); *laḫn* "to understand, comprehend" (stem + *n non-fin.)	*nḫr* "to resemble" (stem + *l fin.; semantics: cf. English "to *look* like")	PSC *lĕḫ- "to listen for, be on the look-out for"		
819. *-lĕeḫ- "to come out"	pPS *lḫ "to come toward" (Append.1)	*nḫm* "to take away, carry off; withdraw (oneself?)" (stem + *m extend.; C. *nuhm* "to save," i.e., withdraw from danger, keep)	*lĕeḫ- "to come out" (Ehret 1987 has incorrect *leḫ-)		

	SEMITIC	EGYPTIAN	CUSHITIC	CHADIC	OMOTIC
820. *laj- or *ladz- "light (of fire, day)"	A. *laðʕ* "to burn; brand, cauterize" (stem + *ʕ part.; i.e., burn *off* bit of skin)	*ns* "flame" (presumed Old Eg. *nz)	PEC *lac- "day" (PC *dz > PEC *c)		
821. *-lak- "to hold with the tongue"	pPS *lk "to put the tongue to" (Append.1)		SC: Dahalo *lakkaʕ-* "to swallow" (stem + *ʕ part.)	*lk(ɗ) "to lick" (J; stem + *z intens. of manner); some WCh *lk "tongue" (J)	
822. *-lak'- "to lap up"	pPS *lḳ "to lap" (Ehret 1989)	C. *lōks* "to bite, sting" (stem + *s' fort.?)	*lak'- or *ɬak'- "to lap up" (Ehret 1987 notes only *ɬak'- as a possible etymon)		

		SEMITIC	EGYPTIAN	CUSHITIC	CHADIC	OMOTIC
823.	*-lâk'- *-lâak'- "to show, bring to (one's) notice or attention"	A. *laqf* "to comprehend quickly" (stem + *p intens. of manner); *liqy*, *luqy* "to meet, encounter; perceive, find" (stem + *y inchoat.; semantics: de-caus. but not de-tr., i.e., "perceive, find" < "show")		PSC *lâk'- or *lâak'- "to show"		
824.	*-lăm-/*-lĭm- "to move"	A. *lamṭ* "to be moved, restless, agitated; totter" (stem + *t' dur. intens.)	*nmi* "to travel, traverse" (stem + *y inchoat. > dur.)	PSC *lănk- "to dash about, flit about, move about quickly" (stem + *k dur. with assim. of *m to /n/ before suff. *k)		Gonga: S.Mao *nɨm-* "to go" (PO *l > Gonga *n)

	SEMITIC	EGYPTIAN	CUSHITIC	CHADIC	OMOTIC
825. *-lep'- "to move along"	A. *labṭ* "to pass" (stem + *t' dur. intens., i.e., go completely by); MSA *lbd "to become; start, keep on" (stem + *d dur.)		PEC *leb'- "to move along" (PEC *b' < PC *p')		
826. *-laas- "to become weak, be in a weakened state"	A. *lasam* "to grow silent (from weariness)" (stem + *m extend.)		*laas- "to be soft, weak, limp"		

	SEMITIC	EGYPTIAN	CUSHITIC	CHADIC	OMOTIC
827. *-lis'- "to lick" (Ch., Berber, and Eg. shared **innovation**: *aləs-/*iləs- "tongue": *a-/*i- attrib. n. pref. + stem; PS *lisn "tongue" is a separate and distinct derivation from the same verb root)	pPS *ls "to lick, lap" (Ehret 1989); *lsn "tongue" (*lisn ~ *lasn, rather than just *lisn as in Diakonov 1975; stem + *n n. suff.)	*ns* "tongue" (presumed pre-Eg. *aləs with regular *a- > Ø some /#_CVC; C. *las*); *nsb* "to lap up" tend.; C. *lapsī* "mouthful; to bite": metathesis of ME n. + *y deverb., with v. < n.)	EC: [Arbore leč'- "to lick": loan < unidentified Omotic language (expected Arbore *lis-)]	*aləsi "tongue" (N; *a- attrib. n. pref. + stem) J: *-ls3)	SOm: Dime *lits'*- "to lick"
828. *-laš- "to hold onto"	MSA *lsx "to get hold of" (stem + *x precip.; MSA *s < PS *c)		SC: Dahalo *las*- "to pull" (Dahalo *s* < PC *š /V-#)		

	SEMITIC	EGYPTIAN	CUSHITIC	CHADIC	OMOTIC
829. *-l-t'- "to splatter"	A. *laṭx* "to soil, bespatter" (stem + *x extend. fort.)			some WCh *ls's' "to vomit" (J; stem with redup. as intens.)	
830. *-laaw- "to pick up"	H. *lōf* "to receive, get" (*lwf, stem + *f iter. > dur.)	*nw, nwy* "to gather, collect" (stem + *y inchoat. as dur.)	*laaw- "to take hold of"	CCh *lw "sky" (J; semantics: pick up > raise, put above > above)	
831. *-lăax- "to increase (intr.)" (Sem., Eg., Ch. **innovaion**: "increase" > "grow in size")	A. *laxaṣ* "to be swollen (all around the the eye)" (stem + *tl' foc.); *laxt* "big, corpulent" (stem + *t adj. suff.)	*nḫ* "to be old" (semantics: to grow > to mature, hence become old); *nḫt* "strong; stiff; hard" (stem + *t adj. suff.; C. *nšot* "to become hard")		some WCh *lks "grass" (J; stem + *s deverb. comp. suff.; semantics: see #742 above)	Gonga *da:k- "to add" (Mocha *dà:k-*)

	SEMITIC	EGYPTIAN	CUSHITIC	CHADIC	OMOTIC
832. *-lôx^w- "to move toward"	A. *laxy* "to present, bestow upon" (stem + *y inchoat. > tr.)		*lôx^w- "to move toward"		Ometo: Basketo *luk-* "to go"
833. *-lâyg^w- "to trickle" (root #804 + *y inchoat. + *g^w dur.)	A. *lajaḥ* "running eyes" (stem + * ḥ iter.); *lujj* "high sea; the deep; immense mass of water"	*ngsgs* "to overflow" (stem + *s' fort., *š non-fin., or *ts diffus., redup. as intens.; but see #613 for alternative possible attribution)	*lâyg^w- "to trickle"		
834. *-liʕ- "to shine"	A. *laʕʕ* "to shine"	*iᶜḥ* "moon" (stem + *ḥ iter.; semantics: earlier "to glimmer, glow"; C. *ooh*)	*laʕ-/*liʕ- or *ɬaʕ-/*ɬiʕ- "to shine, give off heat" (corrects Ehret 1987: #335)		Ometo: Male *leʔe* "ashes"

	SEMITIC	EGYPTIAN	CUSHITIC	CHADIC	OMOTIC
835. *-liʕɓ- "to move (tr.), convey"		*i ᶜb* "to present (to)"	*liʕɓ- or *ɬiʕɓ- "to convey, make move"	some CCh *lb "to carry" (J)	

PAA *dl

	SEMITIC	EGYPTIAN	CUSHITIC	CHADIC	OMOTIC
836. *dlâ/dlî "call, cry (n.)"	A. *ḍuwwa-t* "noise, tumult" (stem + probably *w n. suff. as in Eg.)	*ḏwi* "to call upon (god)" (stem + *w n. suff. + *y denom.)	*dlâ/dlî or *tlâ/*tlî "utterance"	Ng. *dládlìy-* "to beseech" (redup. stem as intens. + *y denom.)	
837. *-dlâ- "to grow, swell"	A. *ḍawāt* "tumor, swelling" (stem + *w inchoat. or *w deverb. + *t n. suff.)	*ḏt* "body (of person)" (stem + *t n. suff.); *ḏw* "mountain" (stem + *w deverb.; C. *tou*)	*dlâw-/*dlûw- "to live, be, become, grow" (stem + *w inchoat.)	Ng. *dláyâ* "ulcer" (stem + *y deverb.)	

	SEMITIC	EGYPTIAN	CUSHITIC	CHADIC	OMOTIC
838. *-dlab-/*-dlib- "to put the hand to"	pPS *ḍb "to take in the hand" (Ehret 1989)		EC: Afar *xabba-hee* "to grab, grasp, seize" (*hee* "to put"; *x* = [d'] < PC *dl); PSC *tlibiʕ- "to push" (stem + *ʕ part. > and.; PC *dl > PSC *tl)		
839. *-dlabʕ-/*-dlibʕ- "to stretch out (intr.)" (root #838 + *ʕ part.; Sem., Eg. **in-novation**: narrowing of meaning to tr. stretching out of arms)	A. *ḍabʕ* "to stretch out arm against; arm; armpit"	*ḏb^c* "to point the finger (at); finger, thumb" (C. *tēēbɛ*; probable case of Eg. /i/ > C. *ē* in open syllable, but if so, then not in one of the usual consonant environments of that shift)	EC: Soomaali *dhabbac* "to lie in prone position" (*dh* = [d'] < PC *dl; *c* = [ʕ]); EC: [Afar *xabqe* "armpit" (*x* = [d'], *q* = [ʕ]): loan < Sem.?]		

	SEMITIC	EGYPTIAN	CUSHITIC	CHADIC	OMOTIC
840. *-dlib- "to suffer loss, be damaged"	A. *ḍabas* "to be malignant" (stem + *s' fort.?); *ḍaban* "loss, defect" (stem + *n n. suff.)	LE *ḏb ḏb* "to destroy" (redup. stem as intens.)	EC: Soomaali *dhib* "to cause difficulty, bother, hinder" (*dh* = [d'] < PC *dl)	Ng. *dlə́bgən-* "to become spoiled, ruined; become physically or morally deteriorated" (stem + *g fin. fort. + *n non-fin.)	
841. *-dlaf-/*-dluf- "to rise above"	pPS *ḍp "to raise, increase; rise" (Append.1)	*ḏf 3* "to be provided; abound (in supplies)" (stem + *r diffus., i.e., to rise in quantity, hence, to abound)	PSC *tlaf- "to drift, glide, rise (through the air)" (revises Ehret 1989: #377; PC *dl > PSC *tl)	some WCh *lpn "sky" (J; stem + *n n. suff.; PCh *ɮ often > WCh *l; but cf. #811 above as possible alternative attribution for this root)	Mocha *t'ṵ:p'-* "to jump up" (PO *p > Mocha *p'* /C'V_); SOm: Ari *d'ap-* "to get up"

	SEMITIC	EGYPTIAN	CUSHITIC	CHADIC	OMOTIC
842. *-dlêf-/*-dlôf- "to flow out"	pPS *ḍp "to excrete" (Append.1)	*ḏfḏf* "to drip" (re-dup. stem as freq.)	EC: Yaaku *-dɛpaʔam-* "to leak" (stem + *ʔ conc., i.e. leaks have a narrow focus of action, + *m extend.; PC *dl > Yaaku *d*, PC *f > Yaaku *p*)		Gonga *t'u:p- "to gush; spring of water" (Mocha *t'ụ:p'-* "to gush out," *t'ú:p'p'o* "spring"; PO *p > p' /C'V_ in Mocha)
843. *-dleg- "to pay atten-tion to"		*dgi* "to look, see, behold" (stem + *y inchoat. > dur.)	*dleg- "to listen to"		
844. *-dlog- "to be bent, curved"	A. *ḍajʕ* "to lie on the side; deviate" (stem + *ʕ part., i.e., de-viate); *ḍajam* "crookedness;		EC: Afar *xogga* "thigh" (x = [d'] < PC *dl; semantics: < bending of leg in moving, sit-ting, etc.)	Ng. *dlágd-* "to move off the road; pass off to the side of road, de-tour" (stem + *d dur.)	

	SEMITIC	EGYPTIAN	CUSHITIC	CHADIC	OMOTIC
	to be crooked" (stem + *m n. suff.; v. < n.)				
845. *-dlōog^{w}-/ *-dlēeg^{w}- "to call out"	A. *ḍajj* "to cry out"; *ḍajar* "to roar" (stem + *r diffus.)			Ng. *dlùgùn*, pl. *dlùgwàgwín* "name" (stem + *n n. suff.; proposed PCh shift *oo > *uu /_C^{w})	NOm: Yem *tèeg-* "to call" (PO *t' > Yem *t*)
846. *-dlah- "to heat"	A. *ḍahb* "to bring on a change by fire" (stem + *b ex- tend.)		SC: PR *tlah- "to warm" (PC *dl > PR *tl)		
847. *-dlaḫ- "to swell"	A. *ḍaḫḍaḫ* "to undulate" (redup. stem as freq.)		*dlaḫ- "to get bigger"		

	SEMITIC	EGYPTIAN	CUSHITIC	CHADIC	OMOTIC
848. *-dl-kʷ- "to go bad"	A. *ḍakz* "to slander" (stem + *z intens. of manner; semantics: to call someone bad)		PSC *tlakʷ- "to be bad" (PC *dl > PSC *tl)	Ng. *dləgwàɗ-* "to rot" (stem + *z intens. of manner)	
849. *-dleek'- "to squeeze"			*dleek'- "to squeeze"	Ng. *dləgùɗ* "wrestling" (stem + *z intens. of manner)	
850. *-dlôkʷ'- "to push"	A. *ḍakk*, *ḍakḍak* "to press"; *ḍakz* "to press violently" (stem + *z intens. of manner; for proposed shift of *k' > *k, see PS rule #5)	*dḳr* "to press (?) (against)" (stem + *l fin. > fin. > fort.?; C. *tōkr* "to touch")	EC: Soomaali *dhaqaaji* "to make move, push" (stem with redup. as freq. + Som. *-i* caus.; *dh* = [d'] < PC *dl; PC PC *k' > Som. *q* > *j* /_i)		NOm *t'uk'- "to push" (Yem *tūg-*; Mocha *'t'uq-*)

	SEMITIC	EGYPTIAN	CUSHITIC	CHADIC	OMOTIC
851. *-dlum- "to be finished, ended, made useless"			*dlam-/*dlim- *dlum- "to end"	Ng. *dləmàt-* "to become useless, spoil" (stem + *t dur.)	Mocha *t'u:me* "widow" (n. < v. by V > V:)
852. *-dlâp'-/*-dlîp'- "to descend, go down"	A. *ḍabb* "to adhere to the ground"; *ḍabʔ* "to adhere to the ground; throw on the ground" (stem + *ʔ conc.)		*dlib- or *dlip- or *dlip'- "to fall"	Ng. *dláɓ(a)-* "to sit, remain, stay; reside; be, become" (stem + *-a incep, i.e, "become")	Gonga: S. Mao *t'ä:p-* "to sit" (PS *p' > S. Mao *p*)
853. *-dlăp'-/*-dlĭp'- "to pay"	A. *ḍabs* "to press for payment" (stem + *s caus., i.e., make pay)	*ḏbȝ* "payments; reward; compensation; to repay" (stem + *r n. suff.; C. *tōōbɛ*, *toob*)	*dlăp'-/*dlĭp'- "to pay"		

	SEMITIC	EGYPTIAN	CUSHITIC	CHADIC	OMOTIC
854. *-dlāp'-/*-dlīp'- "to set on top of" (Sem, Eg., Ch., Cush. **innovation**: "set on top of" > "cover")	A. *ḍabw* "to take refuge" (stem + *w inchoat.); *ḍabʔ* "to seek refuge: (stem + *ʔ conc.)	*ḏb3* "to clothe; stop up, block" (stem + *ʔ conc., i.e., stop up)	*dlab-/*dlib- "to cover"? (EC shapes require *b; other Cush. allow *p')	*ɮɓ "to close" (J)	NOm: Bench *t'ep'* 2 "to load" (semantics: a load is placed on top of one's back, head, or shoulders)
855. *-dlir- "to harm"	A. *ḍarr* "to damage, injure"	*ḏrt* "harm (?)" (stem + *t n. suff.)	EC: Yaaku *-der-* "to bewitch" (Yaaku *e* < PC *i /_C-; PC *dl > Yaaku *d*)	Ng. *dlə̀rá* "internal bodily ache or pain"	
856. *-dl^r- "to cut"	A. *ḍarb* "to cut off" (stem + *p' fin. fort.)	*ḏ3i* "to pierce, transfix" (stem + *y inchoat. > dur.)		Ng. *dlár̃d-* "to cut, rip, abrade" (stem + *d dur.); *dlə́r̃d-* "to snap off several" (stem + *d dur.)	

	SEMITIC	EGYPTIAN	CUSHITIC	CHADIC	OMOTIC
857. *-dlay-/*-dlaw- "to bite"	pPS *ḍw "to bite" (Ehret 1989)	LE *ḍwt* "midge" (i.e., biting insect)	*dlay-/*dlaw- "to bite" (Append.2)		NOm: Ometo *d'ay- "to bite"
858. *-dlaʔ- "to go from"		*ḏ3i* "to ferry; go across (sky)" (stem + *y inchoat. > dur.; C. *jī*-)	PSC *tlaʔ- "to desert, run away" (PC *dl > PSC *tl)		
859. *-dlăʔ- "to decline, become low"	A. *ḍaʔal* "to make oneself small" (stem + *l adj. suff.)	*ḏ3t* "remainder; deficiency"	SC: PR *tlatlaʔ- "afternoon" (redup. stem as dur.?; PC *dl > PR *tl)	CCh *ɮ- "to fall" (J)	Mocha *t'à:'o* "place" (semantics: < presumed earlier sense "ground": ground is below one; n. < v. by V > V:)

	SEMITIC	EGYPTIAN	CUSHITIC	CHADIC	OMOTIC
860. *-dlii?- "to expand"		*ḏ3 i* "to extend (arm); reach out"	EC: Yaaku *dee?ɛu* "fat, thick" (stem + *w de-verb.; PC *ii > Yaaku *ee* ; PC *dl > Yaaku *d*)		
861. *-dleʕ-/*-dloʕ- "to feel weak, be worn out"	pPS *ḏʕ "weak" (Ap-pend.1)	LE *ḏ ͨm* "to faint" (stem + *m extend.)	PSC *tleʕ-/*tloʕ- "to be tired" (PC *dl > PSC *tl)		

PAA *ɬ

	SEMITIC	EGYPTIAN	CUSHITIC	CHADIC	OMOTIC
862. *-âaɬ- "to burn (intr.)"	A. *šayy* "to roast; hot water" (stem + + *y inchoat. > dur.; 2nd meaning: stem + *y deverb.); *?ašar* "to shine (light-ning)" (stem + *r diffus.)	*šw* "sun, sunlight" (stem + *w de-verb.); *3 šr* "to roast; roast (meat)" (stem + *l or *r n. suff.; v. < n.; C. *ōrš* "to burn, roast")	*âaɬ- "to burn"		NOm: Maji *a:lu* "fire"

	SEMITIC	EGYPTIAN	CUSHITIC	CHADIC	OMOTIC
863. *-ɬĕ- "to stand up, get up" (Sem., Eg. **innovation**: addition of *w inchoative to stem)	pPS *ɬw "to rise" (stem + *w inchoat.; Append.1); pPS *ɬm "up, above" (stem + *m adj. suff.; Ehret 1989)	*šw* "to ascend" (stem + *w inchoat.)	PSC *ɬĕm- "to rise off the ground" (stem + *m extend.)	*ɬa "to stand up" (N) (Ng.*tlà*-)	
864. *-ɬâb- "to grow, increase, add on"	*ɬb "mature man; gray hair"; H. *ɬeb* "to climb, rise"	*šbn* "to mix" (stem + *n non-fin.; semantics: mixing involves the ongoing addition of ingredients: C. *šōnb*, metathesized stem); *šbnt* "various" (previous v. + *t n. suff.)	PSC *ɬâb- "foliage, vegetation" (semantics: see #742: Chadic entry	WCh (BB) *ɬb1 "mountain" (J; stem + *l n. suff.; PCh $*ɬ_2$ > BB *ɬ)	

	SEMITIC	EGYPTIAN	CUSHITIC	CHADIC	OMOTIC
865. *-ɬâf- "to live, grow"	Ji. *ɬfɔr* "to wake up after sleeping through an illness" (*ɬpr, stem + *r diffus.)		PSC *ɬâf- "to grow"; PSC *ɬâfi "health, breath, life"	*ɬ$_2$p "leaf; grass" (J; semantics: see #742)	
866. *-ɬŭf- "to expand, increase" (root #866 with *-u- tr. infix [also tonal shift as found in Chadic cases])	A. *šafaf* "to increase, multiply"; *ɬpḳ "to be abundant" (stem + *k' intens. of effect)	*šf* "to swell" (C. *šaafε*, *šafε*)	PSC *ɬûf- or *ɬûuf- "to swell"	some CCh *ɬf "to count" (J; semantics: to increase, multiply > to add > to count; PCh *ɬ$_2$ > CCh *ɬ)	
867. *-ɬuuf- "to sip"	*ɬp(t) "lip" (stem + *t n. suff.)		PSC *ɬuuf- "to sip; lip"		
868. *ɬâg- "to be much, many"	pPS *ɬg "to be large in number, size" (Append.1)		*ɬâg- "much"		NOm: Ometo *la:g- "many" (nom. < v. by V > V:)

	SEMITIC	EGYPTIAN	CUSHITIC	CHADIC	OMOTIC
869. *-ɬăɣ- "to be excited, stirred up"	A. *šaɣz* "to behave impudently against; stir up discord, excite a tumult" (stem + *z intens. of manner); *šaɣf* "to inspire with violent love" (stem + *p intens. of manner)		PSC *ɬăx- "to be angry, quarrel" (PC *ɣ > PSC *x)		
870. *-ɬeeh- "to shine" (this root is included because #871 following derives from it)	A. *šahab* "to shine, flare" (stem + probably *p' fin. fort., i.e., to *flare*)	*šhb* "hot wind" (stem + *b extend., n. < v. seen in C. *šōhb* "to parch, burn up")			
871. *-ɬêeh- "moon"	*ɬh-, *ɬhr "moon" (2nd shape: stem + *r n. suff.)		*ɬêeh- "moon"		

	SEMITIC	EGYPTIAN	CUSHITIC	CHADIC	OMOTIC
872. *-ɬăḥ- "to burn (tr.)"	A. *šaḥḥar* "soot" (stem + *r n. suff.); *šaḥtār* "soot" (stem + *t adj. suff., i.e., burnt, + *r n. suff.)	*š3m* "to be hot; burn" (1st meaning: stem + *m adj. suff.; 2nd meaning: stem + *m extend.)	*ɬăḥ- "to burn (tr.)"		
873. *-ɬîiḥ- "to scrape off"	pPS *ɬḥ "to scrape off" (Ehret 1989)	LE *šḥḳ* "to dust (?); chaff" (stem + *k' intens. of effect; C. *šhīč*, *šhīj*)	EC: Afar *liic* "claws of a type of crab" (*c* = [ḥ]; PC *ɬ > EC *l)	Ng. *tlàat-* "to strip bark" (stem + *t dur.); *tláaɗ-* "to scratch (itch); scrape out" (stem + *z intens. of manner)	Mocha *dịː-* "to grind" (stem + *y inchoat. > dur.; PO *h > Mocha Ø /V_VC)
874. *-ɬăak^{w}- "to pierce"	*ɬkk "to pierce; thorn"		PSC *ɬăak^{w}- "to stab, pierce"	WCh, ECh *ɬk "hole" (J: attested so far from languages which merge PCh *$ɬ_1$, *$ɬ_2$)	

	SEMITIC	EGYPTIAN	CUSHITIC	CHADIC	OMOTIC
875. *-ɬikʷ- "to bite"	A. *šakm* "to bite" (stem + probably *m n. suff., with v. < earlier n. "bite")	*skn* "to be greedy" (stem + *n non-fin.)	*ĭɬikʷ- "tooth" (*i- attrib. n. pref. + stem; corrects Ehret 1987: #342)		
876. *-ɬakʷ'- "to become visible, emerge into view"	A. *šaqq* "dawn"; *ɬḳr "to redden, lighten" (stem + *r diffus., i.e., light of rising sun); *ɬrḳ "to rise (sun, moon)"? (metahesis of *ɬḳr, stem + *r n. suff., with v. < pPS n.?)		PSC *ɬakʷ'- "to present, bring into view"		

	SEMITIC	EGYPTIAN	CUSHITIC	CHADIC	OMOTIC
877. *ɬâm- "two"	*ɬmʔl "left hand, left side"? (stem + *ʔ adj. suff. + *l n. suff.; proposed semantics: *2nd hand*, i.e., not the primary hand)		*ɬâ(a)m- "two"		*lam- "two" (Bench *nam* 4)
878. *-ɬăam- "to leave"	pPS *ɬm "to depart" (Append.1)	*šm* "to go; walk; set out"; *šms* "to bring, present" (stem + *s caus.); *šmw* "traveller" (stem + *w deverb.); *šmt* "gait; walking" (stem + *t n. suff.)	PSC *ɬam- or *ɬaam- "to leave, leave off"		Gonga *dà:m- "to send away" (Mocha "to exile")

	SEMITIC	EGYPTIAN	CUSHITIC	CHADIC	OMOTIC
879. *-ɬuum- "to harm"		*šm* "drug"; *šm3w* "distress; disease" (stem + *r diffus. + *w deverb.)	PSC *ɬuum- "to wish harm on"		
880. *-ɬîŋ- "to run out (of fluid)"	A. *šann* "to pour out slowly, water the wine"	*šnyt* "storm" (stem + *y inchoat. > dur. + *t n. n. suff.); *šnᶜ* "storm-cloud" (stem + *ʕ part.; semantics: what rain pours *out of*); LE *šni* "to rain, storm" (stem + *y inchoat. > dur.)	PSC *ɬimp- "to have a runny nose" (stem + *p intens. of manner; PSC *ɨ < PC *i /_mp; assim. of *ŋ to following labial)	Ng. *tlə́n* "mucus"; *tlə̀n-* "to blow nose" (PCh *ŋ > Ng. *n*)	Gonga *deng- "mud" (Mocha 'dängo ; PO *l > Gonga *d /#_)

	SEMITIC	EGYPTIAN	CUSHITIC	CHADIC	OMOTIC
881. *-ɬap-/*-ɬip- "to go down, decline"	A. *šaff* "to lessen, diminish"; *šafw* "to be near setting" (stem + *w inchoat.); MSA *ɬfḳ "twilight" (stem + *k$^{w'}$ and.; semantics: < going *away* of sun)		*ɬap-/*ɬip- "to fall"		
882. *ɬap'-/*ɬip'- "ribcage" (distinct root from #809)			*ɬap'- "rib"		SOm: Ari dial. *lip'a*, *liɓa* "belly, heart" (Fleming 1974)
883. *-ɬup'- "to burn (intr.)"	A. *šabb* "to light fire, kindle"		EC: S'aamakko *lub'as-* "to burn (tr.)" (stem + *s caus.; PC *ɬ > PEC *l, *p' > PEC *b')		

	SEMITIC	EGYPTIAN	CUSHITIC	CHADIC	OMOTIC
884. *-ɬâr- "to cover up"	A. *šarnaq* "to change into a chrysalis" (stem + *n non-fin. + *k' intens. of effect)	*šr* "to stop up, block" (C. *šōr*)	PSC *ɬâr- or *ɬâḍ- "to cover up"	Ng. *tlář́ám* "dry outer shell of sorghum stalk" (stem + *m n. suff.)	
885. *-ɬăw- "to take" (Eg., Sem. **innovation**: take > take out)	pPS *ɬw "to draw (out)" (Ehret 1989)	*šw* , *šwy* "to be empty; be lacking" (stem + *y inchoat., i.e., taken out of; C. *šuo* "bare")	PSC *ɬăw- "to get"		
886. *-ɬow- "to cover over"		*šwyt* "shadow, shade" (stem + *y inchoat., i.e., become covered, hence be in shade" (stem + *t n. suff.)	*ɬow- "to enfold, enclose"		

	SEMITIC	EGYPTIAN	CUSHITIC	CHADIC	OMOTIC
887. *ɬaʔ- or *ɬaaʔ- "grassy area, low vegetation, scrub"	*ɬʕr (*ɬaʕr) "grass stalks" (MSA "dry grass, straw"; A. "trees, plants, vegetation; thicket"; West Semitic "barley") (stem + *r n. suff.)	*š3* "field, meadow, country" (V correspondence in C. *šɛ* "wood" favors its placement here rather than with the ME root in #350; semantics: see A. entry here)	SC: WR *ɬaʔa "bush, weeds" (PR *a < PSC *a or *aa)		
888. *ɬŏʔ- "cattle" (sing. *ɬŏw- "cow") (Eg., Sem. **innovation**: generalization of pl. to domestic animals in general, then narrowing in PS and Eg. to different specific animals	*ɬʔ (*ɬaʔ) "sheep"	*š3* "pig" (C. *šɛ*)	*ɬŏw, pl. *ɬŏʔ- "cow" (modifies Ehret 1987: #337)	*ɬa "cow" (N) (J: $*ɬ_2$-) (Ng. *tlà*)	

	SEMITIC	EGYPTIAN	CUSHITIC	CHADIC	OMOTIC
889. *ɬ-ʔr- or *ɬ-rʔ- "hair" (possible vowel reconstructions: *a, *aa, *e, or *o)	*ɬʕr "hair" (A. *šaʕr*)	*šr3* "hair"		*ɬ₂araw "root" (J; stem + *w n. suff.)	
890. *-ɬêʕ- "to cut off"	A. *šaʕb* "to split, cut" (stem + *p' fin. fort., i.e., split)	*š ᶜ* "to cut off"; *š ᶜt* "knife"; *š ᶜd* "to cut; cut off; cut down" (stem + *d dur.; C. *šōōt*, *šɛt*)	PSC *ɬêʕ- or *ɬêʔ- "to slice"	*ɬa "to cut" (N) (J: *ɬ₂-)	
891. *ɬaʕf-/*ɬiʕf- "to claw, paw"	*ɬʕp (*ɬaʕp) "foot"		*ɬaʕf-/*ɬiʕf- or *laʕf-/*liʕf- "to claw, scratch"		

PAA *tl'	SEMITIC	EGYPTIAN	CUSHITIC	CHADIC	OMOTIC
892. *-tl'ab- "to stick into"	A. *ṣibār* "stopper, cork" (stem + *r n. suff.)		*tlab-/*tlib- "to stick, stick into, stuff"	WCh *ɬɓ "to shoot" (J; cf. PCh *ɬɓ "to throw"?)	
893. *-tl'ab-/*-tl'ub- "to make quick movements"	A. *ṣabṣāb* "fast, swift; alert" (redup. stem as intens.)	*ṯbn* "to be quick" (stem + probably *n adj. suff., with v. < earlier adj.); *ṯbhn* "to prance, leap (of animals)" (stem + *h ampl. + *n non-fin.)	PEC *j'ub- or *j'ub'- "to move quickly about"; PEC *j'abbal- "to be agitated" (stem + probably *l adj. suff., with v. < earlier adj.; PEC *j' < PC *tl)		
894. *-tl'ab- "to spill, pour"	pPS *ṣɓ "to pour out" (Ehret 1989)	*ṯbt* "vase" (stem + *t n. suff.; i.e., *water* pot)	*tlab-/*tlib-/*tlub- "to rain"		SOm: Ari *d'ɛbi* "semen"

	SEMITIC	EGYPTIAN	CUSHITIC	CHADIC	OMOTIC
895. *-tl'af- "to turn (tr.)"	A. *ṣafḫ* "to turn aside" (stem + *ḫ iter.; semantics unclear: keep veering off?); *taṣaffuq* "to roll about" (stem + *k' intens. of effect)		PEC *j'af- "to stir" (PEC *j' < PC *tl)		
896. *-tl'eeɣ- "to stick out or up"	A. *ṣaɣṣaɣ* "to comb up hair so as to be neither curly nor smooth" (redup. stem as freq.)	*sḫn* "swelling (?)" (stem + *n n. suff.)	PEC *j'eeg'- "to stick up or out" (PEC *j' < PC *tl, g' < PC *ɣ or *ɣʷ)	WCh, CCh *ɬg "knife" (J)	
897. *-tl'iiɣʷ- "to descend, go down"	pPS *ṣɣ "to become low" (Append.1)	*sḫm* "to founder (?) (ship)" (stem + *m extend.)	*tliiɣʷ- or *tliixʷ- "to lie"		

	SEMITIC	EGYPTIAN	CUSHITIC	CHADIC	OMOTIC
898. *-tl'ih- "to run away, flee (from); to chase"		*ṯhm* "to harry; to hunt" (stem + *m extend.)	PEC *j'ah-/*j'ih- "to avoid, keep away from" (PC *tl > PEC *j')		
899. *-tl'âḫ- "to be loud, exuberant"	A. *ṣaḫīr* "bray" (stem + *r n. suff.)	*ṯḫḫ* "to exult" (stem with redup. as intens.); *ṯḫw* "to rejoice; joy" (stem + *w deverb.)	PSC *tlâḫ- or *dlâḫ- "tumult" (PC *tl > PSC *dl)		
900. *-tl'ôoḫ- "to join (intr.)"	A. *ṣaḫb* "companionship; friendship" (and variety of derivative meanings; stem + *b anim. deverb., i.e., "friend, panion," or + *b extend. > stat., be a friend?)	*ṯḫn* "to meet; engage" (stem + *n non-fin.)	PSC *tlôoḫ- or *dlôoḫ- "to be attached, adhere" (PC *tl > PSC *dl)		

		SEMITIC	EGYPTIAN	CUSHITIC	CHADIC	OMOTIC
901.	*-tl'ik^w-/ *-tl'ak^w- "to fool"	A. *ṣakik* "weak and stupid"		*tlak^w-/*tlik^w- "to fool"		
902.	*-tl'ok'- "to beat"	pPS *ṣḳ "to beat" (Append.1)	[cf. *sḳr* "to strike; clap; etc." (for which see #514 and 534; these three roots would probably have become identical in their consonants in ME]	*tlok'- "to beat"		
903.	*-tl'ook'- "to rub"	A. *ṣaql* "to smooth, polish" (stem + *l adj. suff.; v. < adj. seen in *ṣaqīl* "smooth")	*sḳr* "to knead" (stem + *l fin. > fort.)	*tlook'- "to grind"	few CCh *ɬg "to grind" (this CCh *ɬ < PCh *ɬ, *$ɬ_2$, or *s_3; *g presumably < PCh *k')	

		SEMITIC	EGYPTIAN	CUSHITIC	CHADIC	OMOTIC
904.	*-tl'ak^{w}'-/ *-tl'ik^{w}'- "to ooze, be thick (of fluid matter)"	A. *ṣaqr* "sour milk; to be very sour" (stem + *r adj. suff.; v. < n.)		*tl ak^{w}'- "to ooze" (Ap-pend.2)		Mocha *t'é:qqo* "dry dung of hen" (n. < v. by V > V:; *q* = [k']; < pre-PO *tl'ik^{w}'-)
905.	*-tl'âl- "to burn, make hot"	pPS *ṣl "to burn (something)" (Ehret 1989)	*ṯnr* "eager" (stem + *r or *l adj. suff.)	*tl al al- or *dl al al- "to heat" (cor-rects Ehret 1980: 328)	Ng. *tlán-* "to become light; dawn" (PCh *l > Ng. *n*)	
906.	*-tl'âl- "to wet down"	A. *ṣal* , *ṣil* "rain"; *ṣalat* "to pour out" (stem + *t dur.); MSA *ṣl(l) "ravine" (i.e, place of water when it rains)	LE *ṯnf* "drinking" (stem + *f iter.)	PEC *j'all al- "to become wet and cold" (stem with redup. as intens.; PEC *j' < PC *tl)		Gonga *t'all- "clean" (Mocha *'t'ällo* ; seman-tics: to wet down > to wash > to clean)

	SEMITIC	EGYPTIAN	CUSHITIC	CHADIC	OMOTIC
907. *-tl'il- "to clench the teeth"	A. *ṣald* "to gnash" (stem + *d dur.); *ṣalqam* "to gnash teeth" (stem + *k' intens. of effect + *m extend.)		PEC *j'ill- "to clench the teeth" (PEC *j' < PC *tl)		
908. *-tl'im-/*-tl'um- "to ooze, be viscous"	A. *ṣimx* "ear-wax" (stem + *x^w extend. extend. fort.; semantics: ear-wax as matter continually produced by ear?)	*ṯms* "to be be smeared" (stem + *s caus., i.e., be made to ooze)	PEC *j'im- "to ooze, seep"; PEC *j'umm- "viscous fluid" (PEC *j' < PC *tl)		

	SEMITIC	EGYPTIAN	CUSHITIC	CHADIC	OMOTIC
909. *-tl'in- "to rise"	MSA *ṣnʕ "to stand on hind legs (to feed)" (stem + *ʕ part.; semantics: stretch *out* in order to reach above)	*ṯni* "to lift up; promote" (stem + *y inchoat. > dur.)	*tlin- "to get well"	*ɬnk "to hang" (J; stem + *k dur.); WCh, CCh *ln(l) "mountain" (J; stem + *l n. suff.)	
910. *-tl'ip-/*-tl'up- "to hit" (Sem., Ch. **innovation**: semantic narrowing to hitting with the hand)	*ṣpḳ "to clap" (stem + *k' intens. of effect); A. *ṣafḥ* "to clap palms of hands (stem + *ḥ iter.); *ṣafʕ* "to cuff; box the ear" (stem + *ʕ part.; semantics: cuffing knocks the head *away* from the hitter)		*tlip-/*tlup- "to hit"	Ng. *tləp-* "to clap"	

		SEMITIC	EGYPTIAN	CUSHITIC	CHADIC	OMOTIC
911.	*-tl'etl'- "to fix the eyes upon"	A. *šaṣw* "to be rigidly fixed on (eyes)" (stem + *w inchoat.; dissim. where $C_1 = C_2$: *tl'Vtl' > *ɬVtl')		PEC *j'ej'j'- "to intend, expect, want" (PEC *j' < PC *tl)		
912.	*-tl'aw-/*-tl'ay- "to split (tr.)"	A. *ṣauḥ* "to split, cleave" (stem + *ḥ iter.; semantics: to split by chopping); *ṣaur* "to cut in pieces, dissect" (stem + *r diffus.)	*ṯwn* "to gore; stick (into)" (stem + *n non-fin.)	EC: Yaaku *-jee-* "to split" (Yaaku *j* < PC *tl, *ee* < *ay)		
913.	*-tl'ow- "to flow"	pPS *ṣw "to flow" (Append.1)		*tlow- "to flow"		*d'um- "cloud" (stem + *m n. suff.; pre-PO *d'owm-)

	SEMITIC	EGYPTIAN	CUSHITIC	CHADIC	OMOTIC
914. *-tl'uw- "to rise"	MSA *ṣwr "to stand, stay" (stem + *r diffus. > dur.); A. *ṣauḫ* "steep bank; mountain-side" (stem + *ḫ iter.; semantics unclear); A. *ṣaur* "riverbank" (stem + *r n. suff.)	*ṯw3*, *tw3* "to support, sustain, hold up" (stem + *ʔ conc.); *ṯit*, *ṯwt* "dais" (stem + *t n. suff.; alternate root shape *-tl'-y- seems attested in 1st form)		*ɬw "meat" (J) (Ng.*tlùwái*, stem + *y deverb.; semantics: rise > grow > live, + *y deverb. > animal (i.e., living creature) > meat)	NOm: Maji t'umu "mountain" (stem + *m n. suff.)
915. *-tl'āy- "to produce or apply fluid"	pPS *ṣy "to produce or apply fluid" (Append.1)		EC: Soomaali *dhay* "to smear (unguent)" (PC *tl > Som. *dh* [d'])		NOm *d'ian-, *d'iam- "breast" (stem + *n/*m n. suff.; semantics: breast secretes milk; Mocha *t'änó*, Bench *t'yam* 2)

	SEMITIC	EGYPTIAN	CUSHITIC	CHADIC	OMOTIC
916. *tl'ayŋ- "moisture, wetness, wet matter" (root #915 + *ŋ n. suff.)	A. *ṣunayy* "a little water in a ravine" (Sem. dimin. by the pattern CuCayC)	*ṯni* "basin" (stem + *y n. suff.; semantics: basin is a container for liquid)	*tlayŋ-/*tliŋ- "moisture, wet matter"		
917. *-tl'iy- "to set down, lower"	A. *ṣaid* "to cause one to bend the neck" (stem + *dl m.v. > tr.; earlier "bowed down"); *ṣair* "to bend, incline" (stem + *r diffus.)		PEC *j'iyab- or *j'iyab'- "to set, lower, put low" (stem + *b extend. or *p' fin. fort.); PEC *j'iyann- "to lie down" (stem + *n non-fin.; PEC *j' < PC *tl)		
918. *-tl'ĭz- "to raise"	A. *šazw* "to be high" (stem + *w inchoat.)	*ṯzi* "to raise; lift up; go up" (stem + *y inchoat., i.e, to go up; C. *jīsɛ*)	*tlăz-/*tlĭz- "cloud"	Ng. *tlə́ɗ-* "to raise (orphaned animal, child)" (tr. by *-u- tr. infix + tone shift)	

	SEMITIC	EGYPTIAN	CUSHITIC	CHADIC	OMOTIC
919. *tl'ˇ-z- "tall, high, long" (probable *tl'iiz-, adj. < v. in #918 by V > VV; occurrence of PSC *ee (or *e?) for expected *ii probably reflects phonetic influence of PC root in #254)			PSC *tled-, *tleed-, *dled-, or *dleed- "long" (also PSC *tlĕduw- or *dlĕduw- "to lengthen": stem + *w denom.) (corrects Ehret 1980: 216) (PC *tl > PSC *dl, *z > *d /V_-#)	some CCh *ɬɗ "long (of stick)" (J)	
920. *-tl'ôz- or *-tl'ûz- "to glow"	A. *ašzar* "red" (stem + + *r adj. suff.)				Gonga *t'ojj- "star" (Mocha *'t'ojjo*; PO *zz > Gonga *jj)
921. *-tl'oʔ- "to grab"		*ṯ3w* "to take up, seize, snatch; don; rob, steal" (stem + *w inchoat. > dur.);	*tloʔ- "to seize in the fingers"	CCh *ɬ- "to take" (J)	

	SEMITIC	EGYPTIAN	CUSHITIC	CHADIC	OMOTIC
		ṯ3r "to make fast; fasten; take possession of" (stem + *l fin.)			
922. *-tl'aʕ- "to strike (with implement)"		*ḏᶜ* "to spear (fish)"	*tlaʕ- "to hit"	WCh, CCh *ɬ- "to kill" (J)	
923. *-tl'iiʕ- "to blow"	A. *ṣaʕad* "to draw (breath)" (stem + *d dur.; semantics: earlier "breathe")	*ḏᶜ* "storm, storm-wind" (LE "gale, storm"; C. *jo*)	PEC *j'iiʕ-/ *j'aaʕ- "to blow, expel air" (PEC *j' < PC *tl)		

PAA *r

	SEMITIC	EGYPTIAN	CUSHITIC	CHADIC	OMOTIC
924. *ar- "at, by"		*r* "to, at, concerning" (C. *ɛ-*, *ɛro*)	*ʔar- "with, by" (epenthesis of *ʔ to fit in with usual word structures)		

	SEMITIC	EGYPTIAN	CUSHITIC	CHADIC	OMOTIC
925. *ra/*ri "wet place"	A. *rayy* "to be sufficiently watered" (stem + *y denom.)		*ra-/*ri- "patch of moisture"		
926. *-râ-, *-râw- "to continue, keep on"	pPS *rw/*ry "to move along, continue, keep on" (Append.1)	*rwi* "to go away, depart; pass away, advance" (stem + *y inchoat. > dur.; C. *1o*) *rwwt* "departure" (stem partially redup. + *t n. suff.); *rwt* "gate" (stem + *t n. suff.); LE *rwyt* "waiting place" (stem + *y inchoat. + *t n.	PSC *ra- "to stay, remain"; PSC *rât- "to continue onward" (stem + *t dur.); EC: Arbore *rot-*, *root-* "to travel on foot" (< *rawt-, stem + *t dur.)	Ng.*ráakə́n-* "to walk, travel, go" (stem + *k dur. + *n non-fin.)	SOm *dowt- "foot" (Dime *dɔ:to*, Ari *du:ti*, 2nd stem + *t n. suff.); [SOm: Ari *ra̤a̤t-* "to lie down": loanword (expected *daat-)]

	SEMITIC	EGYPTIAN	CUSHITIC	CHADIC	OMOTIC
		suff.); LE *rwḏ* "to persist; remain firm; persevere" (stem + *dl m.v.)			
927. *-rab- "to be destroyed, perish"; *-rŭb- "to destroy, kill (many?)" (tr. by *-u- infix)		*nbḏ* "destructive" (stem + *dl m.v., i.e., < earlier v. "be destructive"; C. *nobε* "sin" [Demotic *nby* "harm"])	EC: Afar *rab-* "to die"	Ng. *rə̀b-* "to kill in great numbers, massacre"; *rə̀bg-* "to destroy, raze" (stem + *g fin. fort.); *rəbn "lion" (J; WCh "leopard"; 2nd PAA stem + *n n. suff.; *not* cognate of PS *lab- "lioness": PC *r ≠ PS *l)	Gonga *dub-n- "corpse" (2nd PAA stem + *n n. suff.; Mocha *ˌduba'no*)

	SEMITIC	EGYPTIAN	CUSHITIC	CHADIC	OMOTIC
928. *-rŏb-/*-rĕb- "to put above"	pPS *rb "to raise, increase" (Ehret 1989)	*nb3* "carrying-pole" (stem + *r n. suff.)	*roob- or *roop- "above; sky" (n. < v. by V> VV); EC: Afar *rabrab-* "to put one on top of the other" (redup. stem as freq. = iter.; PC *e, *o > Afar *a*)		SOm *do:b-/ *de:b- "rain" (n. < v. by V > V:); NOm: Bench *deb* [1] "head" (n. < v. by V > V:)
929. *-roob- "to tighten by twisting"	pPS *rb "to tie" (Ehret 1989)	*nb* "to tie"; *nbd* "to plait, wrap up" (stem + *d dur.)	EC: Afar *roboq-* "to squeeze, wrench" (stem + *ʕ part.; semantics: < earlier "to wrench *loose*"? Afar *q* = [ʕ]; Afar *o* here < PEC *oo)		

		SEMITIC	EGYPTIAN	CUSHITIC	CHADIC	OMOTIC
930.	*-ruub- "to send" (Sem., Eg. **innovation**: "send" > "direct," hence "command, rule")	pPS *rb "to put in good order" (hence to exercise dominion) (Ehret 1989)	*nb* "lord, master, owner" (C. *nēb*); *nbt* "lady, mistress" (semantics: see Sem. reflex)	EC: Afar *ruub-* "to send"		
931.	*-r-d- "to walk" (Agaw *a allows PAA vowel reconstructions *a, *aa, *o, or *e)	pPS *rd "to step along" (Append.1)	LE *rdḥ* "to advance" (stem + *ḥ iter. > dur.)	*-r-d- "to go on foot"; Agaw: NAgaw *dad- "road, path" (PC *r > Agaw *d /#_)		
932.	*-r̂-dl- "to flow out"	A. *raḍb* "to stream violently" (stem + *p' fin. fort., here only as fort.)	*rḏw* "efflux (of body)" (stem + + *w denom.)		Ng. *rádl-* "to become wet; wet; melt"; *rə̀dl-* "to moisten" (tr. by *-u- infix > Ng. ə)	

	SEMITIC	EGYPTIAN	CUSHITIC	CHADIC	OMOTIC
933. *-râf-/*-rîf- "to break off, detach"	A. *raft* "to break into small pieces; smash a bone" (stem + *t dur.)	*nft* "to detach, loosen" (stem + *t dur.; C. *nuft*, *nutf*); *nf ᶜ* "to remove" (stem + *ʕ part.); *nfnfn* "to unroll" (re-dup. stem + *n non-fin.)	*rif- "to break off"	Ng. *ráfiíwà* "sorghum chaff" (stem + probab-ly *y inchoat. + *w deverb.; semantics: chaff is material brok-en off the ear of the grain)	Gonga *dap- "to cut down" (Mocha *'dap-* "to clear for-est")
934. *-reg-/*-rog- "to increase (in size or quantity) (tr.)"	A. *rujūḫ* "to sink [of scale], weigh over; surpass" (stem + *ḫ iter. > dur.)		*reg-/*rog- "to increase (tr.)"		
935. *-rig-/*-rag- "to move (intr.), walk"	*rgl "foot" (stem + *l n. suff.; A. *rijl*)		*ragad-/*rigid- "foot" (stem + *d dur.; n. < extended v.)	Ng. *rə̀g-* "to migrate, move living quarters"	

	SEMITIC	EGYPTIAN	CUSHITIC	CHADIC	OMOTIC
936. *-râɣʷ- "to pierce"	A. *raɣθ* "to pierce repeatedly" (stem + *ts diffus.)	*rḫs* "to slaughter" (stem + *s' fort. or *c' extend.)	PSC *râxʷ- "to bleed cattle (by shooting with a special kind of arrow)" (PC *ɣʷ > PSC *xʷ)		
937. *-rĭh-/*-răh- "to go down, lower oneself"	pPS *rh "to stay in a place, be still" (Ehret 1989) (semantics: sit > stay)			Ng. *ráaɓ-* "to knock down" (stem + *p' fin. fort.)	Gonga *dih- "to fall" (Mocha *dìh-*); SOm: Dime *dah-* "to sit"
938. *-ruk- "to bend (intr.)"	pPS *rk "to bend, turn" (Ehret 1989); *rkb "knee" (stem + *b anim. suff.)	*rkrk* "to creep; snake" (redup. stem as freq.)	*ruk-/*rak- "to turn" EC: NSom *ruug* "kneecap" (PC *k > Som. *g* /V_; n. < v. by V > VV)	WCh, CCh *rkn "snake" (J; stem + *n n. suff.)	

		SEMITIC	EGYPTIAN	CUSHITIC	CHADIC	OMOTIC
939.	*-rĭk'- or *-rĭkʷ'- "to bend down"	A. *raqd* "to go to sleep, sleep" (stem + *d dur.)	*rḳ* "to incline; turn aside" (C. *rīkɛ*); *rḳw* "tilting (of balance)"	PSC *rĭk'e "hindquarters" (PC *k', *kʷ' > PSC *k' /i_)		
940.	*-rep- "to strike"	pPS *rp "to knock" (Ehret 1989)		*rep- or *reb- "to strike"		
941.	*-rip- "to tie together; to sew"	pPS *rp "to tie together" (Ehret 1989)	*npnpt* "hem" (redup. stem as freq. + *t n. suff.)	EC: Afar *rib*- "to sew" (PC *p > EC *b)	*rp "to sew" (J)	

	SEMITIC	EGYPTIAN	CUSHITIC	CHADIC	OMOTIC
942. *-rǎw-/*-rǎy- "to rise"	A. *rawaḫ* "to be wide, spacious" (stem + *ḫ iter. > dur., i.e., to expand, widen)	*ris*, *rs* "to wake; be watchful, vigilant" (stem + *š non-fin.; C. *roys*); *rwdw* "stairway" (stem + *d dur. + *w deverb.; semantics: < v. to climb stairs); LE *rwḏ* , *rḏ* "to flourish" (stem + *dl m.v.)	*r-w- "to rise"; *r-w-m- "to grow" (stem + *m extend.)	Ng. *ràwà-* "to grow up" (stem + *-a incep.); *rw "sky" (J)	NOm: Ometo *du:nn- "termite mound" (< *r-wn-, stem + *n n. suff.; Zayse *dunné*); Yem *dàys-* "to add" (stem + *s caus., i.e., raise > increase in number or amount)
943. *-reyb- "to stop (doing)"	pPS *rb "to stop (intr.)" (Ehret 1989)		*reyb- "to forbid" (corrects Ehret 1987: #359)		

	SEMITIC	EGYPTIAN	CUSHITIC	CHADIC	OMOTIC
944. *rĭiz- "foot"		Eg. *rd* "foot" (C. *rat* ; alternative possible source: #931; but vowel correspondences better fit this attribution)	*rĭiz-/*răaz- "footprint, sole of foot" (Append.2; corrects Ehret 1980: 329)		
945. *-rŭz- "to become lost"	pPS *rz "to get used up, worn out, lose function" (Append.1)		*ruz- "to disappear, get lost"		Mocha *dò:jj-* "to be absent-minded" (V length not yet explained; PO *zz > Mocha *jj*)
946. *-rûʔ- "to stick up"	A. *raʔb* "to put forth grass again after being mowed" (stem + *b extend.);		PSC *rûʔ- "lump, bump, mound"		

	SEMITIC	EGYPTIAN	CUSHITIC	CHADIC	OMOTIC
	*r?s "head" (stem + *s deverb. comp.)				
947. *-raaʕ- "to move along"	pPS *rʕ "to move" (Append.1)		*raaʕ- "to accompany, follow"		
948. *-raaʕ- "to be raised"	pPS *rʕ "to rise" (Append.1)	*r ͨ* "sun; day" (C. *rī*)	SC: Dahalo *raaʕ*- "to be suspended"		

THE *PAA* GLIDES

Finally, the PAA consonant inventory contained the two glides or "semivowels" *w and *y. Both have been retained quite generally across the family and so are easily reconstructed. In one environment, medially in triconsonantal roots, *y and *w coalesced with a preceding short vowel in PS, Egyptian, PCh and presumably Berber, but remained distinct in PC and PO. This development was posited in Chapter 3 as a shared innovation, PNE sound shift #1, supporting a North Erythraean branch of the family excluding Cushitic. Medial /y/ and /w/ are of course again today common features in Semitic languages, simply because many new medial *y and *w were created later on in the Boreafrasian subgroups, via the addition of extensions and nominal suffixes to biconsonantal roots of the shapes *CVy and *CVw (e.g., see root #836, among others, for a shared Egyptian and Semitic innovation of this kind). Other *y continue to be produced by modern Semitic morphological operations.

Jungraithmayr and Shimizu (1981) reconstruct both *y and a less common glottalized glide *'y, although it is not clear from their data that the sound *'y is actually to be traced back to PCh. A number of modern Chadic languages, among them Ngizim, also maintain both /y/ and /'y/ in their consonant inventories. This distinction is a reconstructible feature of proto-Nilo-Saharan (Ehret, work in progress). As only *y seems traceable to PAA, *'y probably thus originally entered Chadic phonology via Nilo-Saharan loanwords in early Chadic. In Ngizim both /y/ and some /'y/ can derive from PAA *y; a possible conditioning environments of the split in Ngizim may be the following:

PCh *y > Ngizim *'y* /#_VC,
> Ngizim *y* /#_V-#.

But more data are needed to substantiate this suggestion.

One additional glide, $*h^w$, may possibly have existed in PAA. But thus far only four potential examples can be suggested, all with the hypothesized consonant occurring in stem-initial position (#1012-1015 in Appendix 3). If valid, $*h^w$ would account for PO $*h_2$, the Omotic outcomes of which are /h/ or /w/ in different of the Ometo languages, /h/ in the Bench and Maji subgroups, and /w/ in the Gonga and Yem subgroups (see Table 1 in Chapter 2). The possibility that such $*h^w$ might trace back to PAA is at present hardly more than a conjecture, although one certainly worthy of future scholarly consideration.

PAA *w	SEMITIC	EGYPTIAN	CUSHITIC	CHADIC	OMOTIC
949. *wa-/*wi- "what?"		*wy* "how ...!"	Agaw *wä/*wɨ "what?"	*wa "who?" (N)	*w- "what?"
950. *-wêeb- "to burn (intr.)"	A. *wabṣ* "to flash" (stem + *tl' foc.)	*wbd* "to burn; heat; be scalded" (stem + *d dur.); *wbḫ* "to be bright" (stem + $*\gamma^w$ comp.; C. *wbaš*) *wbn* "to rise, shine (of sun); glitter" (stem + *n non-fin., as incep. in "rise (of sun)"); *wbnw* "eastern; the East" (v. "to	EC: Soomaali *woob* "yellow; yolk" (semantics: words for "yellow" commonly derive from verbs for "to burn, shine," e.g., English *yellow* and *yolk* both)	ECh *wb "to roast" (J)	NOm: Bench *obar* 3,3 "sun" (stem + *r n. suff.)

	SEMITIC	EGYPTIAN	CUSHITIC	CHADIC	OMOTIC
		rise" + *w deverb.)			
951. *-wěc- "to be hard, solid" (Sem., Eg. **innovation**: added meaning "firm," hence, figuratively, "firmly established, strong")	*wθḳ "to be fixed, firm, solid, established" (stem + *k' intens. of effect)	*wsr* "strong; powerful; wealthy, influential" (stem + *r or *l adj. suff.)			*wiš₃- "to be dry" (NOm: Yem *ìšma ~ ìčma* "dry": stem + *m adj. suff.; SOm *woč-)
952. *-wăc'- "to pass"	A. *wuẓūb* "to practice without interruption; continue" (stem + *b extend.)	*wsṯn* "to travel freely; be unhindered" (stem + *tl' foc. + *n non-fin.; semantics of foc. ext. unclear; C. *wostn*)	PSC *wăt^{y}'- "to cross" (PSC *t^{y}' = PC *c')		NOm: Yem *òčō* "leg" (PO *č' > Yem /č/; semantics: pass > walk, step > foot; stem + *w n. suff.)

	SEMITIC	EGYPTIAN	CUSHITIC	CHADIC	OMOTIC
953. *-wic'- "to swallow"		*wsrt* "neck" (stem + + *r n. suff. + *t n. suff.)			SOm *wuč'- "to drink"
954. *-wad- "to move (tr.)"	pPS *wd "to move" (Append.1)	*wdi* "to place, put" (stem + *y inchoat. > dur., i.e., to become moved)	*wad- "to move" (PSC "to carry"; PEC "to pass")		NOm: Zayse *wod-* "to put down"
955. *-wadl- "to flow"	A. *waḍx* "to half-fill a bucket" (stem + *x precip., i.e., hasty and hence incomplete filling?)	*wḏb* "riverbank; riparian lands; seashore" (stem + *b extend., i.e., place where water recurrently flows); *wḏḥ* "to pour out" (stem + *ḥ iter.; C. *wōth*)			NOm: Ometo *wad'- "to swim" (semantics: flow > float > swim)

	SEMITIC	EGYPTIAN	CUSHITIC	CHADIC	OMOTIC
956. *-wadl- "to turn back, bend back (tr.)"	A. *waḍn* "to lay close one upon the other, double, fold; twist, entwine" (stem + *n non-fin.)	*wḏb* "to fold over; turn back; revert" (stem + *b extend.; C. *wōtb* "to turn, change")	PSC *watl- "to return" (PC *dl > PSC *tl)		Ometo: Malo *wad'a* "forearm" (semantics: forearm bends back toward upper arm at the elbow)
957. *-wăadl- "to leave abruptly"	A. *waḍf* "to go apace, hasten" (stem + *f iter.)	*wḏi* "to depart; stray (of cattle)" (stem + *y inchoat. > dur., i.e., to stray); *wḏ3* "to go, set out, proceed" (stem + *r diffus.)	EC: Dullay *waad'd'-* "to be fast, hurry" (stem + *dl m.v.: PC *dl > Dullay *d'*)		Mocha *wà:t'-* "to uproot" (i.e., take out abruptly, tr. application of root)

	SEMITIC	EGYPTIAN	CUSHITIC	CHADIC	OMOTIC
958. *-wăag- "lower face"	*wgn/*wgm "face" (stem + *n, *m n. suff.: *wagn, *wagm)	*wgi* "to chew" (stem + *y denom.); *wgyt* "jaw" (previous v. + *t n. suff.; C.*wooče*)	*wăak- "lower face" (Append.2)		
959. *-waag- "to despise"	pPS *wg "to fear, hate" (Ehret 1989)	*wgg* "miserable, disreputable; woe, weakness, want" (C# redup. as deverb.)	*waak- "to hate"		
960. *-wâḫ- "to cut"		*wḫ3* "to hew (stone)" (stem + *r diffus.); *wḫs* "to cut off (hair)" (stem + *c' extend.)	*wâḫr- or *wârḫ- "large blade" (stem + *r n. suff.)		

	SEMITIC	EGYPTIAN	CUSHITIC	CHADIC	OMOTIC
961. *-wâḫ- "to look"		*wḫ*ᶜ "to investigate" (stem + *ʕ part.; semantics: "look *out* for"?; C. *wεh*)	PSC *wâḫ- "to see"	WCh, CCh *w- "to see" (J)	
962. *-waaḫ- "to keep on, continue"	A. *waḫm* "to go toward a place, try to get there" (stem + *m extend.)	*wḫm* "to repeat (an action)" (stem + *m extend.; C. *wōhm*)	*waaḫ- "to spread, expand"		
963. *-wâj- "to grow in size"	A. *waðar* "to be fat and fleshy" (stem + *r adj. suff.)		EC: Dullay: Harso *wašala* "(uncircumcised) penis" (stem + *l n. suff.; PC *dz > Harso *š*)	*wzm "grass" (J) (Ng. *àzə́m*) (stem + *m n. suff.; semantics: see #742)	NOm: Yem *wàʔyā* "branch" (semantics: growth in a tree takes form of growing new branches)

	SEMITIC	EGYPTIAN	CUSHITIC	CHADIC	OMOTIC
964. *-wĭj- "to intertwine, to bind by twining together"	A. *waδam* "strap running through the handles of a bucket" (stem + *m n. suff.)		EC: Sidamo *wosshaado* "snare (trap)," *wosshaad-* "to lay traps" (stem + *d dur.)		NOm: Yem *wiʔy-* "to weave" (PO *č > Yem *ʔy*)
965. *-wak- "to cut apart"	A. *wakz* "to pierce" (stem + *z intens. of manner)	*wgs* "to cut open, gut (fish, etc.)" (stem + *ts diffus.; C. *wōčs*); *wgp* "to triturate" (stem + *p intens. of manner; C. *wōčp*)	*wak-/*wik- "to cut off"		
966. *-wăk'- or *-wĕk'- or or *-wăkʷ'- "to separate husk, rind, chaff, etc."	A. *waqs* "mange, dry scab, scurf; to take crust off a wound" (stem + *s deverb. comp.; v. < n.)	LE *wḳm* "to grind, winnow" (stem + *m extend.)			Mocha *wòq-* "to screen grain"; Mocha *óqqo* "bark" (< v. in sense "to peel, de-bark")

	SEMITIC	EGYPTIAN	CUSHITIC	CHADIC	OMOTIC
967. *-wek'- "to burn (intr.)"	A. *waqd* "to ignite and burn; kindle" (stem + *d dur.)		EC: Dullay *oqaḫy- "sun; sunbeam" (stem + *ḫ iter. > dur. + *y de-verb.; semantics: < earlier "to shine"; PC *k' > Dullay *q)	some WCh *wk'y/*yk'y "smoke" (J; stem + *y de-verb.)	
968. *-wel- or *-wal- "to go round"	A. *walm* "leather girth, tether, rope" (stem + *m n. suff.); *walh* "to be confused" (stem + *h ampl.)		*wal- or *wel- "to go round"		NOm: Yem *wòl-* "to return" (semantics: go round > turn > return)

	SEMITIC	EGYPTIAN	CUSHITIC	CHADIC	OMOTIC
969. *-wil- "to hasten, hurry"	A. *wulūb* "to hasten" (stem + *b ex-tend.); *walq* "to be nimble, agile, active; hasten" (stem + *k' intens. of effect)	*wni* "to hasten, hurry" (stem + *y inchoat. > dur.; C. *wynε*)	*wal-/*wil- "to hurry"		
970. *-wan- "to open (tr.)"		*wn* "to open; open up; rip open" C. *wōn*)	EC: Soomaali *wandhar* "to separate, spread apart; open in two lengthwise" (stem + *dl m.v. + *r dif-fus.; PC *dl > Som. *dh* [d'])	*wan "to open" (J)	

		SEMITIC	EGYPTIAN	CUSHITIC	CHADIC	OMOTIC
971.	*-wap'- "to be above, be at the top, form the tip or peak"	A. *wabʔ* "to point with the fingers to" (stem + *ʔ conc.); *wabh* "to be haughty, arrogant, proud" (stem + *h ampl.)	*wpt* "horns; top (of head); brow; top (of mountain)" (stem + *t n. suff.)	*wab- or *wap'- "to perform the role of clan-head"; *waber- or *wap'er- "hereditary clan-head" (for both roots, see Append.2)	CCh *wɓ "breast" (J; semantics: nipple as forming a tip)	
972.	*-war-/*-wir- "to call out"	A. *warwar* "to speak fast" (redup. stem as intens.)		*war- "to call out; news, report"	Ng. *wə̀rd-* "to cry out" (stem + *d dur.)	Gonga *wor- "news" (Mocha *wóro*)
973.	*war- "light"	A. *wary* "to burn, blaze" (stem + *y denom.)		SC: Iraqw *warʔes-* "to flash (of lightning)" (stem + SC *ʔ n. suff. + *s caus. as denom.; corrects Ehret 1980: 312)		NOm: S. Mao *wəro* "moon"

	SEMITIC	EGYPTIAN	CUSHITIC	CHADIC	OMOTIC
974. *-wăr-/*wĭr- "to grow (person, animal)"	pPS *wr "to grow, increase in size" (Ehret 1989)	*wr* "greatness of size"; *wr*, *wrr* "great; much, many"	SC: PR *war- "mature young person" (corrects Ehret 1980: 311-312)	CCh *wr "old" (J)	NOm: Ometo *orde "big" (stem *war- + *d dur. > stat.); Gonga *wur- "male animal" (i.e., the generally *larger* sex; Mocha *wuró* < *wer-)
975. *-waar- "to soak (intr.)"	A. *warq* "dropping blood or pus" (stem + $*k^{w}$' and.); and.); *wary* "festering pus" (stem + *y deverb.)	*wryt* "cloth for straining liquids" (stem + *y inchoat. + *t n. suff.); *wrḫ* "to anoint, smear on" (stem + *ḫ iter.)	*warb- "to hold water" (stem + *b extend.; example of *VV > *V /C_C- + C ext.)		*wa:r- "fish"; SOm: Ari-Banna *wa:r- "to swim"

	SEMITIC	EGYPTIAN	CUSHITIC	CHADIC	OMOTIC
976. *-wir- "to turn (intr.)"	A. *warab* "to be awry, aslant, oblique, diagonal" (stem + *b extend.)	*wrryt* "chariot" (redup. stem as freq. + *y, *t n. suff.; semantics: < turning of wheels)	*wark-/*wirk- "to go round" (stem + *k dur.)		NOm: Yem *wòryā* "elbow" (stem + *y deverb.; semantics: turn > bend)
977. *-wis- "to fall asleep" (Sem., Ch. **innovation**: derivation of v. "to sleep" by addition of *n non-fin.)	*wsn "to sleep" (stem + *n non-fin.)	*wsš* "to die out (of a race)" (stem + *ɬ ven.; semantics unclear)	PEC *wisl- "to dream" (stem + probably *l n. suff., with v. < earlier n.)	WCh, CCh *wsn, *sn "to sleep" (J) (N: *s-n-; stem + *n non-fin.)	
978. *-wiš- "to form dirt, rubbish"	*wcx "dirt" (stem + probably $*x^w$ extend. fort.; semantics: < earlier v. "to collect (of dirt, intr.)";		EC: Yaaku *ošobu* "foam" (stem + *p' fin. fort.; Yaaku *b* < PC *p'; PC *wi > *u > Yaaku *o* /#_C)		

	SEMITIC	EGYPTIAN	CUSHITIC	CHADIC	OMOTIC
	A. *wasab* "dirt; to be dirty" (stem + *b extend. > stat.)				
979. *-wetl'- "to destroy"	A. *waṣm* "to break; ruin, destroy, spoil" (stem + *m extend. as fort.)		EC: Soomaali *war* "massacrare, sterminare" (PC *tl' > PSom *d' > Som. *r* /V_, *e > Som. *a*)		NOm *wod'- "to kill"
980. *-wīitl'- "to stand"	A. *wuṣūd* "to last, stand firm, remain, abide" (stem + *d dur.)	*wṯz* "to raise, lift up" (stem + *dz extend. fort.)		*wɨk "to stand" (J; stem + *k dur.)	NOm: Bench *yi:t'-* 2 "to stand" (POm *w > Bench *y* /#_i:C)

	SEMITIC	EGYPTIAN	CUSHITIC	CHADIC	OMOTIC
981. *-wits- or *-wic- "to twist (tr.)"	pPS *wθ "to twist" (Append.1)		SC: Dahalo *witstsik'ir-* "to twist fiber into string" (stem + *k' intens. of effect + *r n. suff.; v. < earlier n., as argued in Ehret 1980: 312; also corrects reconstruction there)	ECh *w-s "to spin (thread)" (J)	
982. *-wax- "to look at"	A. *waxx* "intention"; *waxy* "to advance straight forward, intend" (stem + *y inchoat. > dur.)	*wḫ3* "to seek" (stem + *r diffus.; C. *wōš*)	PEC *wax- "to watch"		

	SEMITIC	EGYPTIAN	CUSHITIC	CHADIC	OMOTIC
983. *-wayn- "to grow" (root seen also in #984 + *n non-fin.; Eg., Sem. **innovation**: "grow" > "live," whence Eg. "be, exist")	A. ***wank*** "to dwell amongst" (stem + *k dur.)	*wnn* "to be, exist" (stem with redup. as dur.; C. *wn-* "there is"); *wnb* "flower" (stem *b anim. deverb., < v. in sense "grow," hence "bloom")	*wayn- "to become, grow"	*wn "full" (J)	NOm: Yem *íɲɲà* "big" (< *wayn- + -ya, stem + *y adj. suff.); SOm: Dime *wann-* , *o:n-* "to become" (possible EC loanword)
984. *-wǎys- "to expand" (root seen also in #983 + probably *s caus. as denom. with pre-PAA root *way thus having been a n. or adj.)	pPS *ws "to grow, increase (in size)" (Append.1; A. A. *wisb* "grass and herbs" (stem + *b anim. deverb.; semantics: see see #742); *wsṭ "to expand"	*wsḫ* "broad, wide; breadth" (stem + *ɣʷ comp.; C. *waššɛ* , < metath. of earlier *waššɛ)	PEC *ways-, *wayš- or *weš- "to swell; swelling"; corrects Ehret 1991: #46)	Ng. *wùs-* "to swell up due to infection, sprain, etc."	

	SEMITIC	EGYPTIAN	CUSHITIC	CHADIC	OMOTIC
	(stem + *t' dur. intens. > dur.)				
985. *wiz- "organ of chest"	A. *wudd*, *widd*, *wadd* "love; desire, wish" (i.e., < earlier heart (or liver) as seat of affections)	*wdd* "gall; gall bladder" (stem with redup., possibly for diminutive, as occurs in SC)	PEC *wizn-/ *wazn- "heart" (stem + *n n. suff.)	*wəɗi "breast; milk" (N; stem + *y n. suff.?)	NOm: [Ometo *wizn- "heart": loan < EC]
986. *-wǎʔ- or *-wǎaʔ- "to glow, burn (of fire)"	A. *waʔr* "to make the fire to flare" (stem + *r diffus.); *waʔm* "very warm, hot" (stem + *m adj. suff.)	*w3m* "to bake (?)" (stem + *m extend.); LE *w(3)w(3)w* "sheen" (redup. stem as freq., i.e., to glitter, + *w deverb.); *w3i* "to roast (?) (grain)" (stem + *y inchoat. > dur.);	SC: Ma'a *wa 'ú* "smoke" (corrects Ehret 1980: 313)	Ng. *wìiɗà* "bright light; lightning" (stem + *z intens. of manner); some WCh *wt "fire" (J; stem + *t n. suff.)	

	SEMITIC	EGYPTIAN	CUSHITIC	CHADIC	OMOTIC
		w3w3t "fiery one (?)" (redup. stem as intens. + *t n. suff.)			
987. *-wâaʔ- "to get up to leave, start out, come or go forth"	A. *waʔl* "to take refuge with, escape, try to escape; hasten to" (stem + *l fin. *waʔr* "to frighten away" (stem + *r diffus.; semantics: to put to flight?)	*w3t* "road, way" (stem + *t n. suff.); *w3r* "to flee" (stem + *l fin. > intens.) LE *w3i* "to go; march against" (stem + *y inchoat. > dur.)	*waaʔ- "to rise, go out"	*w-, *wt "to pass by, go out, come, go" (J; 2nd shape: stem + *t dur.)	NOm *w- "to come" (Mocha *wa̠:-*; Bench *w-³*); SOm: Ari *woʔ-* "to stand up"
988. *-wāʕ- "to grasp, take hold of"	A. *waʕb* "to take hold of all" (stem + *p' fin. fort.); *waʕy* "to gather and	LE *wᶜf* "to subdue; curb; bind" (stem + *f iter. > dur.)	SC: PR *waʕ- "to apply, put to"		NOm: Yem *wōʔr-* "to carry" (stem + *r diffus. > dur.)

	SEMITIC	EGYPTIAN	CUSHITIC	CHADIC	OMOTIC
	preserve in one place; grasp together and put in a vessel" (stem + *y inchoat. > dur.)				
989. *-wǎʕ- "to run, run out (fluid)"	A. *waʕy* "pus" (stem + *y deverb.)	*w ᶜb* "pure; to bathe, cleanse, purify" (stem + *b extend.; C. *wop*); *w ᶜr* "to rush forth (child at birth)" (stem + *l fin.)	PSC *waʕ- or *waaʕ- "to spill out, flow"	*wa "to give birth" (N)	NOm: Yem *wòʔr-* "to float" (stem + *r diffus.)
990. *-waaʕ- "to yell"	A. *waʕwaʕ* "to scream, bark, howl, yell"	*w ᶜ ʒ* "curse; to curse" (stem + *r n. suff.; v. < n.; C. *wa*)	*wa(a)ʕ- "to yell"	*wa "to call" (N)	

PAA *y	SEMITIC	EGYPTIAN	CUSHITIC	CHADIC	OMOTIC
991. *-yo- "to say"		*i* "to say"	*yo- "to say"		NOm: Ometo *y- "to say"
992. *-yab- "to protect"		*ibw* "refuge, shelter" (stem + *w deverb.)	PSC *yab- "to protect"		
993. *-yed- "to grasp" (Eg., Sem. **innovation**: derivation of n. for "hand")	*yd (*yad) "hand"	*yd* "hand"	EC: Soomaali *yed* "to give to" (cf. etymology of English "give")		NOm: Ari *yẹd-* "to seize"
994. *-yŭf- "to swell"	A. *yafʕ* "to ascend; grow up" (stem + *ʕ part.; semantics: grow up < swell *out*)		*yŭf- "to swell"		

	SEMITIC	EGYPTIAN	CUSHITIC	CHADIC	OMOTIC
995. *-yag^{w}- "to come out"; *-yug^{w}- "to put out" (root with *-u- tr. infix)			PSC *yug- "to pull out, pull off" (PC *g^{w} > PSC *g /Cu_-)	some CCh *yag^{w} "to come, take a walk"	Mocha *'yug-* "to throw" (i.e., cast out)
996. *-yah- "to respond, speak out in response" (Eg., Sem. **innovation**: narrowing of meaning to loud kinds of response)	A. *yahr* "importunity; quarrelsomeness" (stem + *r n. suff.)	*ihhy* "rejoicing" (stem with redup. for intens. + *y deverb.; i.e., rejoicing is vocal response to happy events)	PSC *yah- "to admit," i.e., respond to accusation or query); PSC *yahas- "to ask (question)" (stem + *s caus.)		
997. *-yak- "to rise"; *-yuk- "to raise" (root with *-u- tr. infix)		*ikn* "to draw water" (tr. stem + *n non-fin.)	*yak- "to rise"; *yuk- "to raise" (corrects Ehret 1987: #562);		NOm: Maji *yakiz* "many" (stem + Maji *-iz* adj. suff.; semantics: rise > in-

	SEMITIC	EGYPTIAN	CUSHITIC	CHADIC	OMOTIC
			SC: Alagwa *yukuhus-* "to put load on top of another" (stem + *h ampl. + *s caus.)		crease in number)
998. *-yak^w- or *-yaak^w- "to conceal"		*ikm* "shield" (stem + *m n. suff.)	SC: WR *yak^w- "to hide" (PC *VV > WR *V)		
999. *-yak'- "to be aware of, knowledgeable about"	A. *yaqaẓ* "to be awake, awake" (stem + *c' extend.); *yaqn* "to know for certain; certainly; anything certain, sure" (stem + *n n. suff.; v. < n.)	*iḳr* "trustworthy; skilful; excellent; superior (in rank)" (stem + *l adj. suff.)	*(y)ak'- "to know" (Append.2)		

	SEMITIC	EGYPTIAN	CUSHITIC	CHADIC	OMOTIC
1000. *yâl- "mane"	A. *yalab* "skin of the back of wild animals" (stem + *b anim. suff.)		SC: Dahalo *jálala* "mane" (Daha- *j* < PSC *y; stem + *l n. suff.)		
1001. *-yuɬ- "to shout"	A. *yašš* "to be joyous, rejoice, exult"	*išnn* "war-cry" (stem + *n n. suff., with redup. as intens.)	EC: Soomaali *yulqan* "hum, buzz; to emit indistinct hum, buzz" (stem + *k' in- tens. of effect + *n or *m n. suff.; PC *ɬ > PEC *l, PC *k' > Som. *q*; PC *m > Som. *n* /_#)		

	SEMITIC	EGYPTIAN	CUSHITIC	CHADIC	OMOTIC
1002. *yam- "body of water"; *-yam- "to submerge, go under water"	*ym (*yam) "sea"	*ym* "river; sea" (C. *ειom* [yom])	Beja *yam* "water"; EC: Soomaali *yumbo* "to immerge" (stem with *-u- tr. infix + *b extend. + form of *w inchoat., hence intr. sense here)	Ng. *'yàm*- "to submerge, go under water"	
1003. *-yaar- "to grow (up), grow large"		*i3w* "old man" (stem + *w deverb.); *i3yt* "old woman" (previous n. + *t fem.); *i3wi* "to be aged, attain old age" (1st n. + *y denom.);	PSC *yaar-/*ʔaar- "to grow (in size)" (PC *y > *y/ʔ alternance in several PSC roots; see also #1005)	CCh *yr "grass" (J; semantics: see #742)	

	SEMITIC	EGYPTIAN	CUSHITIC	CHADIC	OMOTIC
		i3t "old age" (stem + *t n. suff.; C. *ōɛ*)			
1004. *-yâw- "to produce young"		*iwr* "to conceive; become pregnant" (stem + *r diffus.; semantics: pregnancy is a period of time, not a single event; C. *ōō*)	*yuw-/*yaw- "child"	*yw "to give birth" (J) (Ng.*'yáw-*)	
1005. *yaw-, *yawr- "bull" (2nd shape: stem + *r n. suff.; possible n. derivation < v. in #1004)		*iw3* "ox"	*yaw-/*ʔaw- "bull" (PEC *ʔawr-)		

	SEMITIC	EGYPTIAN	CUSHITIC	CHADIC	OMOTIC
1006. *yax^w-/*yux^w- "side"		*iḫmt* "bank (of river" (stem + *m, *t n. suff.)	*yax^w-/*yux^w- "waist"		
1007. *-yâʔ- "to come"		*ii*, *iw* "to come" (stem + *y/*w inchoat. > dur.; C. *y*)	*yaʔ- "to walk"	*yá "to come" (imperative stem) (N)	NOm *yeʔ- "to come" (Yem *y-̀*; Bench *yeʔ-*3)
1008. *-yăʔ- "to drip"		*i3dt* "dew; pouring rain" (stem + *d dur. + *t n. suff.; C. *yōtε*)	*yaʔ- "to flow"	Ng. *yau* "to leak, drip" (*yà-)	Gonga *yo(y)o "rainy season" (Mocha *yò:o*) (stem + *w deverb., redup., with regular *ʔ > Ø /V_VC)
1009. *-yuʔ- "to notice"	A. *yaʔs* "to know" (stem + *š non-fin.)		*yuʔ- "to look at" (Append.2)	Ng. *yà-* "to feel something external to oneself (e.g., cold, heat)"	

	SEMITIC	EGYPTIAN	CUSHITIC	CHADIC	OMOTIC
1010. *-yaʕ- "to die"		*i* ᶜ "tomb"	*yaʕ- "to die"		
PAA vowel-only or *y-initial root					
1011. *i or *yi "me, my" (bound 1st-person sing. pronoun)	*-i "me, my" (suff.)	*i* "I, me, my" (suffixed 1st-person pron.)	*i or *yi "my" (PSC *-i, *ayi; 2nd form: *a- attrib. pref. + stem; EC: Afar *yi* ; etc.)	*i "me, my" (bound pron.)	SOm: Ari *i* "I, me, my"

SOURCES OF PRENASALIZED STOPS IN AFROASIATIC

A final issue to be considered is whether PAA had prenasalized stops (*^{N}C). Four such consonants, *^{m}b, *^{n}d, *^{n}g, and *^{n}g^{w}, can be suggested for proto-Chadic (see Jungraithmayr and Shimizu 1981), and these four turn up in particular as word-initial consonants in Ngizim, which has been cited frequently in the data above. This kind of consonant appears nowhere else in Afroasiatic as a reconstructible feature, and is not traceable on present evidence to PAA.

Three sources of the putative PCh *^{N}C can be proposed. Firstly, it is clear that loanwords from Nilo-Saharan — a family in which phonemic *^{m}b, *^{n}d, *^{n}ḍ (a prepalatal), *^{n}g, and *^{n}gw *are* reconstructible (Ehret, work in progress) — account for at least some of the Chadic attestations. The PCh roots *^{m}b^{w}n "big" and *^{n}gr "to snore" (Jungraithmayr and Shimizu 1981: 40, 245) are just such borrowings. In the Chadic language Ngizim, the majority of NC-initial words can be traced to Nilo-Saharan, many of them visibly loans from Kanuri (Schuh 1981). In Chadic languages spoken in the Plateau region of northern Nigeria, Niger-Congo loanwords may also in some cases have been the source of prenasalized stops.

A probable second source of prenasals in early Chadic was a morphological process, known from three of the four branches of Cushitic but not yet demonstrated elsewhere (and in particular not yet demonstrated to be productive in particular Chadic languages). A fossil PAA instance of this process may also be present in the old root for "kidney" (root #343 above). In this operation, a prefix of the shape *in- marks an action or condition concomitant in some way on the action of the verb to which it attaches. Examples in Cushitic include

(1) Beja *ḍib* - "to fall, go down" versus *inḍib* "sunset";

(2) Agaw *caq-/*caɣ- "to urinate" versus *ɨncaɣ- "to fill" (earlier sense of verb root probably was "to pour"); and

(3) Iraqw (SC) *hlaw*- "to get, find" versus *inhlaw*- "to remember" (reverse semantics of English *forget*, prefix *for*- plus *get*).

More rarely, in Southern Cushitic and apparently also in Chadic (see roots #18 and 365), this prefix can derive one noun from another, with the derived noun denoting a feature or aspect of the item named by the original noun, or else a resemblant or related thing.

The Southern Cushitic reflexes of this concomitive prefix reveal it to have been originally vowel-initial in structure. In the West Rift subgroup, Iraqw shows it as /in-/, but Burunge has /hin-/, with epenthetic /h/ bringing its shape into conformity with the usual consonant-initial pattern of the family. In Dahalo conformity is achieved in an opposite fashion, through deletion of the vowel, producing a shape *N- for this marker; an example is Dahalo *ngaasið-* "to explain" — *N-kaas-is-, concomitive marker *in- + stem + *s causative (> Dahalo *-VD stem-final) — from a Cushitic root seen also in proto-Soomaali *kas "to know, understand." (Ehret 1980 treats such Dahalo items as requiring reconstructed PSC *ᴺC consonants, but the explanation offered here is much to be preferred.)

If this prefixation was also operative in pre- or proto-Chadic, as there is reason to believe, then there too it could plausibly have taken the shape *N-. The question of its presence in the prehistory of the Chadic division of Afroasiatic remains to be systematically investigated, but the preliminary indications are favorable to the postulation. A number of plausible examples of a PCh prefix of the shape *N- and having a concomitive implication can be and have been proposed in the data already covered in this chapter (roots #4, 17, 33, 35, 51, 56, 124, 168, 208, and 365); one of these is an especially powerful indicator, because it comprises a reconstructed pair of Chadic roots, one of them the extended noun, and the other the clearly related, unprefixed root from which it derives (see #33, *ᵐɓɗ "to look for" versus *ɓɗ "to show"). The nine examples so far given provisional identification combine the *N- prefix with *b-, *p-, *t-, *z- (PCh *ɗ), and *ɣ-initial stems, and in each case yield the positionally equivalent voiced prenasal stop in their Chadic reflexes, i.e., *N- + either *b or *p > *ᵐb, + *t or *d > *ⁿd, + *ɗ (PAA *z) > *ⁿd, and + *ɣ > ⁿg. The possible effects of such prefixation on stems beginning in voiceless continuants or in liquids remain to be explored.

A third source of *ᴺC in Jungraithmayr and Shimizu has an extremely restricted range of effect: two cases of *ᵐb in their work (#569 and 570), as discussed above in the section on the PAA nasals, apparently represent their representation of the PCh reflex of PAA *m in single-consonant roots, a reflex written simply as *m in the reconstruction of Newman (1977).

THE *PAA* CONSONANT INVENTORY

The consonants of PAA reconstructed on the basis of the evidence presented here include forty firmly established phonemes, one provisional though probable member of the set (*ɲ), and one possible additional item (*ŋʷ). Their basic correspondences across the five major divisions of the family, Semitic, Egyptian, Chadic, Cushitic, and Omotic, are shown in the following table. The variety of subsidiary regular sound changes affecting these consonants in the different branches have been dealt with in the relevant sections of the present chapter. One further PAA consonant, *hʷ, may conceivably have existed also (see Appendix 3, roots #1012-1015), but is not dealt with here.

The consonant columns in Table 9 below have been put in a slightly different order than was used above in the extended tabulations of the cognate data. The intention there was to place next to each other the language groups that are best attested and thus could provide the fullest bodies of evidence. Hence the Semitic, Egyptian, and Cushitic reflexes were alotted the second, third, and fourth columns respectively, and the Chadic and Omotic attestations were relegated to the fifth and sixth columns. In Table 9 a different objective prevails — to order the divisions of the family according to their relative closeness of relationship, as proposed in Chapter 6, so as to bring into sharper relief any patterns of consonantal sound change that might be shared among the different divisions. Semitic and Egyptian, as members (along with Berber, which is not included in the table) of the Boreafrasian subgroup, thus appear first. Chadic, as the subgroup next closest in relationship to Semitic, Egyptian, and Berber, has the third column, while Cushitic and Omotic, posited to be successively more distantly related to the North Erythraean group, take up respectively the fifth and sixth columns.

Table 9: Consonants of Proto-Afroasiatic (Proto-Afrasian)

PAA	PS	Eg.	PCh	PC	PO
*b	*b	b	*b	*b	*b
*c	*θ (*t^{y}?)	s	*s	*ts	*š$_{3}$
*c'	*θ̣ (*t^{y}'?)	s	*š' (S: *s')	*c'	*č'
*d	*d	d	*d	*d	*d
*dl	*ḍ (*ɮ)	ḏ	*ɮ	*dl	*d'
*dz	*ð (*d^{y}?)	z	*z	*dz	*ž
*f	*p	f	*f	*f	*p
*g	*g	g	*g	*g	*g
*g^{w}	*g	g	*g^{w}	*g^{w}	*g
*ɣ	*ɣ	ḫ	*ɣ ? (Ng. *g*)	*ɣ	*x$_{1}$
*ɣ^{w}	*ɣ	ḫ	*ɣ^{w} ? (Ng. *gw*)	*ɣ^{w}	*x$_{1}$
*h	*h	h	*h	*h	*h$_{1}$
*ḥ	*ḥ	ḥ	*h	*ḥ	Ø, *h$_{1}$/#_; *h$_{1}$ /V_
*j	*ð (*d^{y}?)	z	*z	*dz	*š$_{1}$ /#_; *č /V_
*k	*k	k	*k	*k	*k
*k^{w}	*k	k	*k^{w}	*k^{w}	*k
*k'	*ḳ (*k')	ḳ	*k'	*k'	*k'
*k^{w}'	*ḳ (*k')	ḳ	*k^{w}'	*k^{w}'	*k'
*l	*l	n (*i* /#_i; r /_#)	*l	*l	*l
*ɬ	*ɬ	š	*ɬ	*ɬ	*l
*m	*m	m	*m	*m	*m
*n	*n	n	*n	*n	*n

Table 9: Consonants of Proto-Afroasiatic (Afrasian) (continued)

PAA	PS	Eg.	PCh	PC	PO
*ŋ	*n	n	*ŋ (Ng. _n_)	*ŋ	*n /#_ ; *ng /V_V; *g /V_-#
*ŋ^{w} ?	*n	n	(?)	*ŋ^{w}	(?)
*ɲ (?)	*n	n	(*ɲ?)(Ng. _n_)	*ɲ	*ɲ /#_
*p	*p	p	*p	*p	*p
*p'	*b	p	*ɓ	*p'	*p'
*r	*r	r (_3_ /_#)	*r	*r	*d /#_; *r /V_
*s	*s	s	*s$_3$ (N: *ṣ)	*s	*s
*s'	*s	s	*s'	*ts'	*s'
*š	*c	s	*s (*s$_1$)	*š	*š$_1$ (*š$_2$ /i_)
*t	*t	t	*t	*t	*t
*t'	*ṭ (*t')	s	*s'	*t'	*ts'
*tl'	*ṣ (*s')	ṯ	*tl (*ɬ$_1$)	*tl [tl']	*d'
*ts	*θ (*t^{y}?)	s	*s	*ts	*ts
*w	*w	w	*w	*w	*w
*x	*x	ẖ	*x ? (Ng. _k_)	*x	*x$_2$
*x^{w}	*x	ẖ	*x^{w} ? (Ng. _kw_)	*x^{w}	*x$_1$?
*y	*y	_i_, y	*y	*y	*y
*z	*z	z	*ɗ	*z	*z
*ʔ	*ʔ	_3_ [ʔ]	*ʔ, Ø	*ʔ	*ʔ, Ø
*ʕ	*ʕ	_c_ [ʕ]	*ʔ, Ø	*ʕ	*ʔ, Ø

6

THE SUBCLASSIFICATION OF AFROASIATIC (AFRASIAN)

The systematic phonological reconstruction of proto-Afroasiatic (proto-Afrasian) laid out in the previous chapters provides a strong and consistent demonstration of a particular subclassification of the family. Chadic, Berber, Egyptian, and Semitic together form one major genetic division of Afroasiatic, called here North Erythraean. Within that division, Egyptian, Semitic, and Berber belong to one subgroup, termed Boreafrasian, while Chadic forms the second subgroup. Cushitic and Omotic stand as separate branches of still more distant relationship to North Erythraean as a whole and to each other.

THE BOREAFRASIAN SUBGROUP

The genetic subgrouping of Afroasiatic most firmly established by the data is Boreafrasian (BA), its name reflecting the historical and modern locations of two of its three subgroups. It consists of Egyptian, Semitic, and Berber.

Two classes of phonological innovations place the case for Boreafrasian on an exceptionally strong footing. The first of these by itself puts the issue virtually beyond doubt. It is composed of two laws, of sweeping scope and consequence, with apparent point-for-point congruence in their specific effects in Semitic and Egyptian and seemingly also in Berber:

(1) a co-occurrence constraint disallowing all sequences of PAA *t followed by any dental or alveolar obstruent in C_1 and C_2 positions in a root (PBA rule #3); and

(2) a co-occurrence constraint disallowing in the same environment any sequences of sibilants (PBA rule #4).

A fuller presentation of these constraints was made in the discussion of the PAA dental set in Chapter 5 above. A survey of Berber vocabulary indicates that the same kinds of sequences are generally lacking there also. In contrast, these two co-occurrence constraints are clearly *not* present in Chadic, Cushitic, or Omotic.

A second notable phonological development diagnostic of the Boreafrasian grouping is a shared sequence of two sound shifts — neither of them inherently dependent upon, or a consequence of, the other, but the second of them necessarily arising later in time because its full environment was defined by the operation of the first rule:

PBA #1. PAA *s', *s > PBA *s, followed by

#2. PAA *h > PBA *ḫ /#_Vs.

(This set of shifts was also discussed in the dental section of Chapter 5.) The two rules are overtly lacking in Cushitic. Direct evidence for or against the second rule of the sequence is missing in Chadic and Omotic because of the loss, in both PCh and PO, of the feature [+ pharyngeal] (see section on pharyngeal consonants in Chapter 5, and also the PO sound changes discussed in Chapter 4). Indirectly, however, its presence in Chadic and Omotic prehistory is ruled out by the absence in those branches of the prior rule of the sequence, PBA #2 — an absence directly attested in both proto-Chadic and proto-Omotic by the preservation of distinct reflexes of PAA *s' and *s.

Three further phonological innovations, each of broad systemic effect, can be placed at the PBA stage. One of these, PBA shift #7 (for which see Appendix 4), dropped terminal vowels (TVs), with the consequent development, only at that point in time, of "sonants" and of the associated kinds of root structures postulated for the family as a whole by Diakonov (1988) (see Chapter 3). The second, PBA #6 (see Appendix 4 for PBA sound shifts) deleted the PAA tonal distinctions, well attested for Omotic, Cushitic, and Chadic, but lacking from Semitic, Egyptian, and Berber. Still another sound shift, PBA #5, can be proposed to have merged the PAA velar and palatal nasals with PBA *n.

One other PBA rule, #8, changing PAA *z to *d in noun-stem-final environments, deserves special recognition. With a sharply defined, restricted environment and a unique product, it seems a particularly strong indicator of the unity of the Boreafrasian subgroup. The probable precondition for this shift was the loss of TVs in PBA (shift #7), a development which would have converted most noun-stem-final *z into word-final consonants. In contrast, verb-stem-final *z in PBA, it can be argued, remained unaffected by this shift because conjugational affixations normally kept such *z from occupying a consistently word-final position.

One major morphological modification can be identified as a specifically PBA innovation, namely, the shift of the remaining productive verb extensions to a prefixal locus of application. The most notable example is that of the PAA *s causative. The positioning of the causative in PO, PC, and PCh, and isolated lexicalized occurrences in Eg. (e.g., root #878 and probably others noted in Table 3) and Semitic (Ehret 1989 and examples cited in Table 3), all show it originally to have been a suffix like the rest of the early Afroasiatic (Afrasian) verb extensions (for all of which see Chapter 3). The probable precondition for this shift in the positioning of *s causative was the general decay in PBA of the Afroasiatic suffixal extension system, leaving the causative as one of the last productive verb suffixes; as such it could very plausibly have moved to preverbal position, in syntagmatic conformity with the other major set of verb affixes, the predominantly prefixal conjugational morphemes. In Semitic at least two other extensions, *t continuative and *n extendative, can be shown as well to have moved to a prefixal position (see Chapter 3).

The comparative data of Chapter 5 also reveal a goodly number of word-specific innovations supporting the Boreafrasian subgroup. These include cases of shared semantic innovation in a morphologically unmodified root (#59, 191, 237, 363, 454, 645, 839, 885, 930, 983, and 996, among others); at least one notable lexical innovation — a word for "two" — limited to Boreafrasian, but usually treated as if it were an actual PAA root (see root #503 in conjunction with #505 and 877); and a number innovated derived roots (#11, 259, 350, 374, 539, and 863, again among others).

The breakdown of relationships among the three Boreafrasian subgroups, Semitic, Egyptian, and Berber, remains to be established. But there are at least two salient indicators of a possible closer connection between Egyptian and Berber; (a) a sound shift found merging of the reflexes of PAA *p and *p' distinct from the reflexes of *b and *f (see root #282); and (b) one root-specific semantic innovation that appears to connect Egyptian with Berber to the exclusion of Semitic (root #59). The first of these is a particularly striking common development, because it appears elsewhere in Afroasiatic only in the East Rift subgroup of Southern Cushitic. Everywhere else the pattern is for PAA *p', if it does not maintain a distinct reflex of its own, to merge with *b. If indeed a validly shared innovation, it would require us to restate Egyptian sound shift #10 as an Egypto-Berber rule:

EgB #l. PAA *p' > EgB *p.

A good deal more evidence would be needed, however, to move this proposition beyond its current status as an arresting hypothesis in need of future investigation.

THE NORTH ERYTHRAEAN SUB-BRANCH

At the next deeper level of relationship, Boreafrasian and Chadic can be seen to form a division of the family excluding Cushitic and Omotic.

The most notable set of phonological evidence for this branching consists of the sequence of three vowel sound shifts, PNE rules #1-3 (discussed in Chapter 4). These shifts together contracted the PAA system from five vowels, each occurring both long and short, to a proto-PNE set of five vowels in two tiers — a centralized set of two members, *ə and *a (or *ä), and a peripheral set of three members, *i, *u, and *a (or *aa). An additional PNE sound shift brought the PAA verb stems of the shape *-VC- into conformity with the more usual consonant-initial patterns of PAA stems, via a metathetical sound shift,

PNE #4. PAA *-VC- (v. roots) > *-CV-

(see roots #159, 570, and 862). The operation of the rule apparently was blocked where such roots had previously added a suffix; compare the Egyptian and Semitic suffixed forms of the verb root of #862, which instead took the shape *-ʔVC(V)C-, conforming to the usual root structure patterns by inserting a stem-initial epenthetic glottal stop.

One additional pair of phonological developments, supportive of both the Chado-North branch and the Boreafrasian subgroup, may well account for the failure of the concomitive prefix, provisionally reconstructed in Chapter 5 for Cushitic and Chadic, to surface in Boreafrasian. This proposed history would consist of two sound shifts, the first dating to the proto-North Erythraean period and the second to the subsequent proto-Boreafrasian era:

PNE #5. Eryth. *in- (concom. pref.) > PNE *N- /#_CV,

creating word-initial nasal-stop clusters, followed in later times by

PBA #8. PNE *N- > PBA Ø /#_CV,

which brought the Boreafrasian languages back into conformity with the more ancient Afroasiatic word-initial patterns. In contrast, such clusters can be proposed to have been sustained in proto-Chadic because the proto-Chadic language spread into regions, in the Chad Basin, where the earlier areal phonological tendencies prominently included that feature word-initially.

The Chadic languages also share with the Boreafrasian group the use of a prefixed nominalizer, the instrument-agent marker in *m (see end of Chapter 3 above for discussion of why this prefix should not be reconstructed for proto-Cushitic). A further morphological feature, the *s deverbative complement suffix, is not yet known outside of Chadic and Boreafrasian (see the several examples of it in the data of Chapter 5) and so seems also a probable North Erythraean innovation.

In addition, a considerable variety of root-specific innovations attest to the validity of North Erythraean. At least sixteen root derivational and semantic innovations, inferable for Boreafrasian and Chadic languages and specifically counter-indicated for Cushitic and/or Omotic, are noted in the data of Chapter 5 (roots #159, 194, 219, 223, 225, 281, 311, 394, 488, 600, 675, 827, 831, 910, and 977). Among these is a root often treated as if it were the PAA word for "tooth" (#223); but the wider comparative evidence requires it to have had an originally less specific meaning, "point," with the semantic narrowing to "tooth" being a feature of the Chadic and Boreafrasian attestations (although apparently separately derived in the isolated instance of the Omotic language, Bench). One notable lexical innovation, of a new word for "two" (#505) displacing from use the posited PAA root for that meaning (#877), can also be placed at the PNE stage.

THE ERYTHRAEAN BRANCH OF AFROASIATIC

At a still deeper level of relationship, Cushitic together with Chadic and Boreafrasian can be proposed to form one primary branch of the family coordinate with Omotic as the other primary branch. This idea is not original to the present work (e.g., see Fleming 1974), but it is reaffirmed by the evidence given here. The probable location of the early Afroasiatic (Afrasian) speech communities from which the Cushitic and North Erythraean languages would have derived must have been situated, by this classification, somewhere along the Red Sea regions of northeastern Africa (Ehret 1979a and 1979b); hence the name Erythraean can be applied specifically to this proposed branch (the use of this term does *not at all* imply a speech area *straddling* that sea).

The evidence for an Erythraean branch is of varying kinds. One very strong indicator is morphological and relates to the rise of grammatical gender marking. Some markers of *natural* gender probably do go back to PAA. The *t feminine found widely in Afroasiatic outside Omotic may just possibly appear in a few scattered instances in Omotic languages (Bender 1990); and the Kafa nominal TVs, *-e* feminine and *-o* masculine, may show regular phonological correspondence to PAA *i/*u (PAA *i/*u > NOm *e/*o, at least for most /C_C; see Chapter 4), an opposition which serves to distinguish feminine/masculine in the second- and third-person singular bound pronouns of Erythraean (roots #209 and 310/311), in some demonstratives found elsewhere in the family (e.g., Ehret 1980: 289, 296), and in some Southern Cushitic nouns (Ehret 1980: 50). But Hayward (1987) is surely correct in seeing PO as, in fact, originally lacking *grammatical* gender in nouns. The development of grammatical gender throughout the rest of Afroasiatic appears therefore as a particularly striking innovation supporting an Erythraean branch distinct from Omotic. It seems probable, too, that Omotic never had the full range of verb extensional markers reconstructed from the pre-proto-Semitic, Chadic, and Cushitic evidence (see Chapter 3 above).

A number of root-specific innovations also support a primary branching between Omotic and the rest of Afroasiatic. Two of these concern third-person pronominal forms found in both Cushitic and North Erythraean, that innovate directly upon a simpler base form still visible in Omotic reconstruction:

(1) Erythraean *si "she," *su "he" built from an originally non-gender-marked form *is/*si, by substituting the masculine marker *u and reinterpreting the form containing *i as feminine (root #209);

(2) Erythraean *sun- "they" constructed from older *su, *usu, present in the Omotic evidence (root #210), by addition of PAA *n plural suffix, and remodeled in some languages into *(u)sun-/*(i)sin- "they (masculine/feminine)," after the corresponding *su/*si singular pronouns.

In short, it can be argued that the original PAA third-person pronouns were *si singular and *su plural, where the base was *s-, and *-i and *-u marked singular and plural respectively (for the origins of these as old number markers, see also evidence in Ehret 1980: 49-50). In proto-Erythraean they were developed into gender distinguishing pronouns by a reanalysis of *i/*u as the respective feminine and masculine markers *i and *u, which were originally indicative of natural, rather than grammatical, gender.

A third pronominal set known from Cushitic and North Erythraean, the *ku/*ki singular masculine/feminine bound pronoun (#310/311), lacks a prototype in Omotic. But its vocalic structuring of gender marking, parallel to that of *su/*si "he"/"she" suggests that it too arose as part of the same round of pronoun formation and thus similarly constitutes an innovation diagnostic of an Erythraean branch.

Four additional root-specific indicators also unambiguously support an Erythraean branch. Three are cases showing shared semantic development in Cushitic, North Erythraean, and/or Boreafrasian, but preservation in Omotic of a logically earlier meaning (roots #101, 194, and 854). The fourth involves a contrast in the suffixes applied to the same simple root, setting off the Cushitic and North Erythraean languages from Omotic (root #483).

At least one strong sound shift rule also strikingly sets the proposed Erythraean languages apart from Omotic,

Eryth. #1. PAA *j > Eryth. *dz,
PAA *c > Eryth. *ts,

as discussed in the section on the alveolars and palatals in Chapter 5. Proto-Omotic, in contrast, changed these sounds around in different fashions (see PO rules #i-iii in Appendix 4).

The most widely found co-occurrence constraint in Afroasiatic, disallowing non-identical labial consonants (other than *w) in C_1 and C_2 positions, may be also an innovation common to the whole family except Omotic (see section on labials in Chapter 5 and also Appendix 4); but more examples need to be found before this attribution can be considered fully established.

THE CUSHITIC SUB-BRANCH OF ERYTHRAEAN

Cushitic itself is a very deep and diverse division of the Afroasiatic family, internally of possibly as great a time depth and degree of divergence as the entire North Erythraean sub-branch. Its overall coherence as a distinct sub-branch is attested so far by three known sound shifts. One of the three,

PC #1. PAA *b > PC *m /#_Vn,

is not entirely unique to Cushitic within Afroasiatic. But the other two shifts,

#2. PAA *g > PC *k /#dV_ or /#wV_, and

#3. PAA $*\gamma^{(w)}$ > PC $*g^{(w)}$ /#_Vx,

and especially the former, are arrestingly different and surely diagnostic indicators (see sections on labials and velars in Chapter 5). Each of these three shifts is attested in Beja as well as the other Cushitic branches. Additional confirmation of the coherence of Cushitic and the correctness of including Beja in it emerges from the evidence of lexical innovation (Ehret 1979a).

It has been suggested on morphological grounds in one major work (Hetzron 1980) that Beja stands apart as a group distinct from the rest of the Cushitic branches. From this perspective the Agaw, Eastern Cushitic, and Southern Cushitic divisions together would form one primary branch of Cushitic, and Beja a second. But the segregation of Beja rests largely on its lack of features found in other Cushitic. Because Beja is a single language with no close relatives that might provide additional evidence, and is moreover a language relatively poorly covered in the literature, the gaps could well be due to loss of features once present (cf. the case of English within the Germanic grouping of languages). In contrast, the phonological historical evidence indicates — relatively weakly, but on quite positive grounds — a genetic subgrouping of Southern and Eastern Cushitic into one branch, leaving Agaw and Beja as coequal second and third primary branches of Cushitic (Ehret 1987). That subgrouping, accordingly, is the one followed here.

OVERALL SUBCLASSIFICATORY SCHEME

These classificatory arguments rest on a considerable body of evidence backed up by systematic phonological reconstruction. The historically more recent branchings posited here — Boreafrasian and North Erythraean — seem amply supported by that evidence. The proposed earliest division of the family, into coordinate Erythraean and Omotic branches, stands on a less solid footing as yet. But the idea of placing Cushitic and Omotic together in a common branch of the family, as was once generally assumed by scholars and as some students of Afroasiatic wish again to assert, finds no support whatsoever. Within Boreafrasian, the relationships among Semitic, Egyptian, and Berber need to be reexamined in the light of the new materials developed here; for now, these three are treated as if they were equidistantly related members of the subgroup, although some evidence can been adduced for the proposition that Egyptian and Berber might form a North African subgroup coordinate with Semitic. (An earlier, very limited effort by the writer at Afroasiatic subclassification (Ehret 1979a) reached conclusions similar to those arrived at here, *inter alia* joining Berber with Semitic in a Semito-Berber subgroup of Boreafrasian; but the evidence used there was far inferior in quality to, and in many cases controverted as well by, the findings of the current work.)

The unified subclassification of the family proposed here has therefore the structure (as depicted in Table 10):

Table 10: Subclassification of Afroasiatic (Afrasian)

- I. Omotic
    - A. North Omotic
    - B. South Omotic
- II. Erythraean
    - A. Cushitic
        - 1. Beja
        - 2. Agaw
        - 3. East-South Cushitic
            - a. Eastern Cushitic
            - b. Southern Cushitic
    - B. North Erythraean
        - 1. Chadic
        - 2. Boreafrasian
            - a. Egyptian
            - b. Berber
            - c. Semitic

Appendices

Appendix 1
Pre-Proto-Semitic Roots
(Additional to those presented in Ehret 1989)

In this appendix, Arabic verbs are usually cited in their *maṣdar* forms; the notation "MSA" refers to proto-Modern Southern Arabian roots, as reconstructed from their representations in Johnstone 1977 and 1981.

	Related forms in Arabic	extension (or suffix)	reconstructed root
(#5)	*baht* "to surprise and seize" *bahr* "astonishment" MSA *bhẓ̌ "to start up in fright"	*t durative *r noun suffix *dl middle voice	*bh "to sneak up on and surprise"
(#14)	*balʔaz* "to flee; jump, run"	*ʔ concisive; *z intensive (manner)	*bl "to proceed, move along"
	bulūq "to reach, come to" *balḥas* "to flee from fear" *balhas* "to walk fast"	*kʷ' andative *ḥ iterative; *s' fortative *h amplificative; *s' fortative or *š non-finitive	
(#20)	*barbaṣ* "to water ground abundantly" *bard* "to be cold; cold (n. and adj.)" *baraṣ* "to water the ground before tilling" *barḍ* "to flow scantily" *barɣ* "spittle, drivel"	*b extendative; *tl' focative *d durative (> stative) *tl' focative *dl middle voice *ɣʷ complementive	*br "to be moist"

	Related forms in Arabic	extension (or suffix)	reconstructed root
	burūk "to rain continuously" *birniq* "mud"	*k durative *n non-finitive; *k' intensive (effect)	
(#52)	*fartan* "to speak indistinctly and incoherently" *farḍ* "to predict, announce; divine comandment"	*ṭ durative; *n non-finitive *dl middle voice	*pr "to speak"
(#79)	*fuqfūq* "intellect, sagacity" *faqim* "intelligent, ingenious" *fiqh* "knowledge, learning; intelligence, understanding" (*faqah* "to surpass in knowledge of law or divinity")	(reduplicated stem) *m adjective or noun suffix *h amplificative	*pḳ "to be wise, intelligent"
(#88)	*faṭfaṭ* "to drop excrement" *faṭʔ* "to break wind, drop excrement" *faṭḫ* "to give birth"	(reduplicated stem as frequentative) *ʔ concisive *ḫ iterative (semantics unclear)	*pṭ "to excrete"
(#89)	*faṭʔ* "to shatter" *faṭr* "split, rent; to split, cleave" *faṭm* "to cut off" *faṭḫ* "to widen, make broad"	*ʔ concisive *r noun suffix (v. < n.) *m extendative as fortative *ḫ iterative (> extendative sense)	*pṭ "to break apart"

	Related forms in Arabic	extension (or suffix)	reconstructed root
(#113)	*bart* "to cut"	*t durative	*br "to cut"
	barx "cut (of a sword)"	*x precipitive	
	baršaq "to cut into pieces"	*ɬ venitive; *k' intensive (effect)	
	barkaʕ "to cut, cut off"	*k^w finitive; *ʕ partive	
	barw, *bary* "to plan, shave"	*w, *y inchoative (> tr.)	
(#114)	*baṣṣ* "to exude"	(none)	*bṣ "to exude"
	baṣʕ "to flow, stream"	*ʕ partive (i.e., flow *out*)	
	baṣq "to spit"	*k' intensive (effect)	
	bazr "to blow the nose"	*r diffusive	*bz "to secrete, let leak"
	bazɣ "to bleed with a lancet; lancet"	*ɣ intensive (effect)	
	bazq "to spit"	*k' intensive (effect)	
	bazl "to tap a cask"	*l finitive	
	bazm "to milk a camel"	*m extendative	
(#117)	*baʕj* "to split, slit"	*g finitive fortative	*bʕ "to cut with a blade"
	baʕṭ "to slaughter, kill"	*t' durative intensive	
	baʕq "to slaughter"	*k' intensive (effect)	
	baʕk "to strike arm or leg with sword"	*k^w finitive	
	baʕkar "to cut off"	*k^w finitive; *r diffusive	

	Related forms in Arabic	extension (or suffix)	reconstructed root
(#123)	*daθθ* "slight rain"	(none)	*dθ "to spill down"
	daθṭ "to open and void tumor"	*t' durative intensive	
	daθq "to pour out"	*k' intensive (effect)	
(#131)	*daḩḩ* "to lie with"	(none)	*dḩ "to lie prone"
	daḩb "to lie with"	*b extendative	
	daḩbaʔ "to lie with"	*b extendative; *ʔ concisive	
	daḩj "to lie with"	*g^w durative	
	daḩz "to sleep with"	*z intensive (manner)	
	daḩs "to sprawl"	*š non-finitive or *s' fortative	
	daḩḑ "to sprawl"	*dl middle voice	
	daḩm "to lie with"	*m extendative	
	daḩmal "to stretch on the ground to be trodden on"	*m extendative; *l finitive	
	daḩw "to lie with"	*w inchoative (> durative)	
(#133)	*dakk*, *dakdak* "to fill a well with earth"	(none); (reduplicated stem as freqentative)	*dk "heap (of earth)" (PS *dək ?)
	dukk "low hill, hillock"	(none)	
	daks "to heap up a quantity of earth"	*s causative (as denominative) or *š non-finitive	

	Related forms in Arabic	extension (or suffix)	reconstructed root
(#139)	*damdam* "to fix in the ground"	(reduplicated stem as intensive)	*dm "to join two things by inserting one thing into the other"
	dumūj "to be inserted, joined; work one thing into the other (teeth of a wheel)"	*g^w durative	
	dumūq "to enter without permission; enter into one's hiding-place"	*k' intensive (effect)	
(#145)	*dafdaf* "to skim ground in flying"	(reduplicated stem as frequentative > durative)	*dp "to touch; to put the hands on"
	dafr "to push back"	*r diffusive	
	dafš "to push with the hand, push back, buffet"	*ɬ venitive	
	dafʕ "to push back, keep off, ward off; push towards"	*ʕ partive	
(#155)	*daxaj* "blackness"	*g finitive fortative	*dx "to cover over, conceal from view"
	daxs "to be concealed or buried in the ground" (MSA *dxšr "lair, hole")	*s' fortative (MSA: same verb root plus *r noun suffix)	
	daxmar "to cover, veil"	*m extendative; *r diffusive or *r noun suffix (with v. < n.)	
	daxan "darkness" (MSA "dark-colored")	*n adjective or noun suffix	
(#157)	*daʕdaʕ* "to fill the dish"	(reduplicated stem as intensive)	*dʕ "to put into, stick into"
	daʕs "to pierce; fill"	*s' fortative	
	daʕlaq "to go deep into the water"	*l finitive; *k' intensive (effect)	

	Related forms in Arabic	extension (or suffix)	reconstructed root
(#196)	*zalx* "to pierce with a lance"	*x precipitive	*zl "to cut"
	zalq "to shave the head"	*k' intensive (effect)	
	zalm "to cut off, maim"	*m as fortative	
(#221)	*samīʔ* "heaven; roof"	*ʔ adjective suffix (< "above")	*sm "above; high"
	samk "to raise to a great height"	$*k^w$ finitive	
	sumuww "to be high, elevated, sublime; rise high and be visible"	*w inchoative/denominative	
(#240)	*ṭabr* "to conceal one's self, hide"	*r diffusive	*ṭb "to cover"
	ṭabs "black"	*s deverbatove complement suffix (semantic linkage of covering with darkness or blackness appears also in #155 above)	
	ṭabq "to cover, veil; close"	$*k^{w}$' andative	
(#245)	*ṭahbal* "to travel; set out on a journey"	*b extendative (first sense); *l finitive (second sense)	*ṭh "to come"
	ṭahs "to enter a country, come to"	*s causative (> tr. sense)	
	ṭahlab "to travel into a country"	*l finitive; *b extendative	
	ṭahw "to travel into a country"	*w inchoative	

	Related forms in Arabic	extension (or suffix)	reconstructed root
(#250)	*ṭalb* "to wish, demand, ask, seek; long for"	*b extendative (i.e., long for)	*ṭl "to observe"
	ṭalsam "to fix the eyes on the ground"	*s' fortative; *m extendative	
	ṭalʕ "sight, perception"	*ʕ partive (< earlier "view, see *from* a distance"?)	
(#256)	*ṭurʔān* "bad"	*ʔ concisive or *ʔ adjective suffix; *n adjective suffix	*ṭr "to be dirty"
	ṭarḫ "mud in the water"	*ḫ iterative	
	ṭarfas "to be muddy"	*f iterative; *š non-finitive (?)	
	ṭarq "to befoul the water; befouled water"	*k' intensive (effect)	
(#262)	*jabj* "to recover and regain strength"	*g^w durative	*gb "great"
	jabbār "strong, powerful"	*r adjective suffix	
	jabl "numerous"	*l adjective suffix	
(#280)	*jamār* "crowd, people" (*jamr* "to unite for a purpose")	*r noun suffix (v. < n.)	*gm "to come together"
	jamʕ "to gather, assemble, keep together; unite, reconcile; crowd, assembly"	*ʕ partive (bring together what was previously *apart*?)	
	jaml "to gather, assemble" (*jumul* "troop; addition")	*l noun suffix (v. < n.)	
	jamhar "to assemble, heap up (*jumhur* "principal part or majority; totality, all; troop, crowd; people, public")	*h amplificative; *r noun suffix (v. < n.)	

	Related forms in Arabic	extension (or suffix)	reconstructed root
(#285)	*jarr* "foot of a mountain; valley"	(none)	*gr "to go down"
	jarbaz "to fall"	*b extendative; *z intensive (manner)	
	jurθum "root, origin; earth round the foot of a tree"	*ts diffusive; *m noun suffix	
	jarjam "to throw down"	*g finitive fortative; *m as fortative	
	jardal "to stumble, fall"	*d durative; *l finitive	
	jarfas "to throw on the ground"	*p intensive (manner); *s lexicalized PAA causative	
(#289)	*jazʔ* "to take a part of"	*ʔ concisive	*gz "to get, gain, take"
	jazʕ "to give a part of one's fortune to another"	*ʕ partive (as andative)	
	jazw "to subdue, subjugate"	*w inchoative (> tr.)	
(#295)	*jadd* "to cut, lop, prune"	(none)	*gd "to cut"
	jadʕ "to cut off the ears, nose, etc.; maim, mutilate"	*ʕ partive	
	jadf "to cut off"	*p intensive (manner)	
	jadm "to cut off"	*m as fortative	
(#298)	*jaḥjaḥ* "to desist"	(reduplicated stem as intensive)	*gḥ "to stay"
	jaḥr "to remain behind"	*r diffusive	
	ijḥām "to abstain, desist"	*m extendative	
	jaḥw "to stay, remain"	*w inchoative (> durative)	

	Related forms in Arabic	extension (or suffix)	reconstructed root
(#312)	***kaθθ*** "to drop excrement"	(none)	*kθ "to flow"
	kaθb "to pour out"	*p' finitive fortative	
	kuθūʕ "to have diarrhea"	*ʕ partive (i.e., flow *out*)	
	kuθw "a little milk"	*w deverbative	
(#321)	***kamz*** "to roll into a ball with the hands"	*z intensive (manner)	*km "to hold"
	kamš "to grasp"	*ŧ venitive	
	kamhal "to gather"	*h amplificative; *l finitive	
(#326)	***kaff*** "to avert, stay; desist, refrain"	(none)	*kp "to stop, cease"
	kafkaf "to repel repeatedly, prevent, hinder, restrain"	(reduplicated stem as frequentative)	
	kaft "to prevent, hinder"	*t durative	
(#334)	***kaθθ*** "to be thick, condensed"	(none)	*kθ "to increase (in size, number)
	kaθʔ "to grow, be high and densely grown"	*ʔ concisive	
	kaθb "to gather, heap up"	*b extendative	
	kaθj "to gather stores for one's family"	*g^{w} durative	
	kaθḫ "to gather, collect"	*ḫ iterative	
	kaθr, ***kaθîr*** "much, many"	*r adjective suffix	
	kaθf "dense crowd, throng, great quantity"	*f iterative	
	kaθl "great quantity; to gather, heap up"	*l noun suffix (v. < n.)	
	kaθm "to heap up; fill"	*m extendative	
	kuθw "heaped up earth"	*w deverbative	

	Related forms in Arabic	extension (or suffix)	reconstructed root
(#337)	*kuʕb* "breast, bosom" (*kuʕub* "to have swelling breast, swell")	*b animate deverbative suffix (v. < n.)	*kʕ "to swell"
	kaʕθab "thick"	*ts diffusive; *b extendative	
	kaʕir "big-bellied and fat" (*kaʕar* "to be big-bellied and fat")	*r adjective suffix (v. < adj.)	
(#349)	*kaʕkaʕ* "to render timorous, frighten off"	(reduplicated stem as intensive)	*kʕ "to run away"
	ikʕāt "to depart hurriedly"	*t durative	
	kaʕtar "to run fast, hasten, hurry"	*t durative; *r diffusive	
	kaʕsam "to turn the back and flee"	*s' fortative; *m extendative	
(#357)	*jaħjaħ* "to examine a thing and bring it speedily to a conclusion"	(reduplicated stem as intensive)	*għ "to examine"
	ijħāð "to look sharply at"	*dz extendative fortative	
	jaħm "to open the eyes and fix them on something"	*m extendative	
(#372)	*jaʕjaʕ* "to hold fast"	(reduplicated stem as intensive)	*gʕ "to pick up"
	jaʕb "to gather"	*b extendative	
	jaʕl "to put, place, pile; put upon; give"	*l finitive	
	jaʕw "heap, dung-hill; to gather dung in a heap"	*w deverbative (v. < n.)	

	Related forms in Arabic	extension (or suffix)	reconstructed root
(#384)	*xaḍxaḍ* "to rinse"	(reduplicated stem as frequentative)	*xḍ "to wet down"
	xaḍb "to dye (especially red)"	*p' finitive fortative	
	xaḍil "moist, wet, fresh and tender" (*xaḍal* "to be moist, wet; get moistened")	*l adjective suffix (v. < adj.)	
(#390)	*xašš* "to call forth a noise"	(none)	*xɬ "to make a rough or creaky sound"
	xašxaš "to make a noise, clatter"	(reduplicated stem as intensive)	
	xašram "to make a noise in eating"	*r diffusive; *m extendative	
	xašf "to creak"	*f iterative	
(#400)	*xalj* "to draw, attract"	$*g^w$ durative	*xl "to take off or out"
	xalj "to tear out"	*g finitive fortative	
	xals "to snatch away clandestinely"	*s' fortative	
	xalʕ "to draw out slowly, take from beneath; pull off, strip"	*ʕ partive	

	Related forms in Arabic	extension (or suffix)	reconstructed root
(#402)	*xurr* "hole in the millstone to put the corn in"	(none)	*xr "to split, make a hole in"
	xarb "to pierce; split, tear" (*xarb* "round hole")	*p' finitive fortative	
	xart "to pierce, make holes"	*t durative	
	xarʕ "to split, break"	*ʕ partive	
	xarq "to tear; rent, cleft, split"	*k' intensive (effect)	
	MSA *xrs "gap-toothed"	*s deverbative complement suffix	
(#404)	*xaraf* "to be delirious; delirium"	*f iterative	*xr "to turn"
	xarfaš "to mix, mix up, confuse"	*f iterative; *ɬ venitive	
	xarm "to deviate"	*m extendative	
(#418)	*qaðf* "to vomit, expectorate"	*p intensive (manner)	*ḳð "to seep out"
	qaðim "perennial wells in the rock"	*m noun suffix	
	qaðy "to exude a white matter (eye)"	*y inchoative	
(#431)	*qaṭṭ* "to cut"	(none)	*ḳṭ "to cut"
	qaṭb "to cut"	*b extendative	
	qaṭʕ "to cut, cut off, lop, amputate"	*ʕ partive	
	qaṭl "to cut off, amputate, behead"	*l finitive	
(#436)	*qamm* "to eat all"	(none)	*ḳm "to eat up"
	qamḫ "to take medicine in a solid form"	*ḫ iterative	
	qamʕ "to drink out greedily"	*ʕ partive (i.e., drink *out*)	
	qumʕūl "large cup"	*ʕ partive; *l noun suffix	

	Related forms in Arabic	extension (or suffix)	reconstructed root
(#443)	*qalqal* "to move, shake, agitate; resound, stammer"	(reduplicated stem as intensive/ frequentative)	*ḳl "to do, happen, or move repetitively"
	qald "to befall every day"	*d durative	
	qalaq "to be agitated, shaken; quake, quiver"	*k' intensive (effect)	
(#474)	*ðalq* "to drop excrement"	*kʷ' andative	*ðl "to flow out"
	ðullāḫ "watered milk"	*ḫ iterative	
	ðalam "shallow mouth of a river"	*m noun suffix	
(#493)	*θarr* "to abound in water, milk, etc."	(none)	*θr "to abound in water"
	θarθāra-t "overflowing, gushing"	(reduplicated stem as intensive)	
	θard "light rain"	*d durative	
	θarṭ "fluid manure"	*t' durative intensive	
	θurʕuṭ "thin and fluid"	*ʕ partive; *t' durative intensive	
	θarmaṭ "to be muddy, composed of thin mud"	*m extendative; *t' durative intensive	
(#507)	*sabsab* "to cause to flow"	(reduplicated stem as intensive)	*cb "to immerse"
	sabḫ "to swim; float"	*ḫ iterative	
	sabal "rain"	*l noun suffix	
	MSA: Jibbāli *sɔ̄ɣ* (*sbɣ) "to dye" (PS *cbɣ)	*ɣ intensive (effect) (dyeing is the highly visible effect of immersing in the dyeing liquid)	

	Related forms in Arabic	extension (or suffix)	reconstructed root
(#508)	***sadad*** "straightness"	(none)	*cd "to extend length-wise"
	sadr "to let hair hang down"	*r diffusive	
	sadʕ "to stretch out, spread"	*ʕ partive (i.e., stretch *out*)	
	sadw "to reach for"	*w inchoative (> tr.)	
(#537)	***sarʔ*** "to lay eggs"	*ʔ concisive	*sr "to lay down, put low"
	saras "to be impotent, be weak"	*š non-finitive	
	saraq "to be weak"	*k' intensive (effect)	
	sarak "to grow weak and thin"	*k durative	
	sarw "to lay eggs, spawn; undress self"	*w inchoative (> tr.)	
(#540)	***saux*** "to sink in the mud"	*x^w extendative fortative	*sw/*sy "to flow"
	sauhaq "juicy, full of sap"	*h amplificative; *k' intensive (effect)	
	saib "to flow, run"	*b extendative	
	saiḥ "to flow on surface, spread; melt"	*ḥ iterative	
	saix "to sink in anything soft"	(see ***saux***)	
	saiʕ "to flow, dissolve, move, undulate"	*ʕ partive (i.e., dissolve)	
	saiɣ "to flow or glide easily down the throat"	*ɣ intensive (effect)	
	sīf, pl. ***asyāf*** "riverbank, sea-coast, shore"	*f iterative (i.e., a place of continually moving water)	
	sail "river, stream; torrent; to flow, run"	*l noun suffix (v. < n.)	

	Related forms in Arabic	extension (or suffix)	reconstructed root
(#566)	*ẓaʔb* "to marry" (semantics: *take* a wife)	*p' finitive fortative	*θ̣ʔ "to take (away)"
	ẓaʔf "to push away, drive off, expel"	*p intensive (manner)	
	ẓaʔm "to marry another's sister"	*m extendative	
(#574)	*maθθ* "to perspire, ooze"	(none)	*mθ "to leak, run out"
	maθmaθ "to leak"	(reduplicated stem as frequentative)	
(#579)	*maðʕ* "to flow"	*ʕ partive (i.e., flow *out*)	*mð "to wet"
	maðq "to mix with water"	*k^{w}' andative	
	maðy "to lose sperm without intercourse"	*y inchoative	
(#604)	*maʔd* "to become juicy and begin to grow; be tender; juicy, tender"	*d durative	*mʔ "to be wet, produce fluid"
	maʔar "to break open again (wound)"	*r diffusive	
	maʔš "to wash the ground"	*ɬ venitive	
(#613)	*najj* "to bleed, suppurate"	(none)	*ng "to seep, ooze"
	najx "to bring wind and rain"	*x^{w} extendative fortative	
	najd "to drip with perspiration"	*d durative	
	najl "outflowing water, spring; to abound with springs of water"	*l noun suffix (v. < n.)	
	najf "to milk (a sheep) well"	*f iterative	
	najw "pouring cloud"	*w deverbative	

	Related forms in Arabic	extension (or suffix)	reconstructed root
(#615)	*nahs* "to seize flesh with the front teeth and tear it off; bite"	*s' fortative	*nh "to bite into (hungrily?)"
	nahsar "voracious; to consume, swallow"	*s' fortative; *r adjective suffix (v. < adj.) or *r diffusive	
	nahš "to sting, bite, bith with the front or molar teeth"	*ɬ venitive	
	nahšal "to bite; eat very greedily"	*ɬ venitive; *l finitive (i.e., eat up)	
	nahak "to suck out the breast; drink out"	*k durative	
	nahal "to quench one's thirst"	*l finitive	
	nahal "first draught; to take the first draught"	*l noun suffix (v. < n.)	
	naham "ravenous hunger"	*m noun suffix	
(#620)	*naqθ*, *naqḫ*, *naqt*, *naqy* "to suck the marrow out of a bone"	*ts diffusive; *ḫ iterative; *t durative; *y inchoative (> durative)	*nḳ "to suck"
	naqʕ "to quench one's thirst"	*ʕ partive (semantics unclear)	
	naqm "to eat greedily"	*m extendative as fortative	
(#625)	*naʔaj* "to eat slowly and slightly masticating"	*g^w durative	*nʔ "to suck in"
	naʔîṭ "to breathe heavily"	*t' durative intensive	
	naʔaf "to drink one's fill"	*p intensive (manner)	

	Related forms in Arabic	extension (or suffix)	reconstructed root
(#632)	*tanqīb* "to examine minutely"	*b extendative	*nḳ "to look at closely"
	naqθ "to examine"	*ts diffusive	
	naqd "to cast a stealthy glance upon"	*d durative	
	tanqîr "to examine, test"	*r diffusive	
	naqš "to investigate"	*ɬ venitive	
	MSA *nḳl "to choose"	*l finitive	
(#645)	*naqb* "to till or cultivate the ground; hollow out, excavate"	*b extendative	*nḳ "to scrape"
	naqθ "to excavate and lay bare"	*ts diffusive	
	naqḥ "to shell, peel"	*ḥ iterative	
	naqr "to whet the mill-stones"	*r diffusive	
	naqš "to paint, imprint; embroider, engrave, chisel, carve in stone"	*ɬ venitive	
(#654)	*nauʔ* "to rise with difficulty"	*ʔ concisive	*nw/*ny "to rise, expand"
	nauṭ "to tie and suspend one thing to another; don"	*t' durative intensive (> durative)	
	nauf "to tower over, hang over; be long and high"	*p intensive (manner)	
	nauh "to be high, elevated, sublime"	*h amplificative	
	nayy "fat"	(none)	
	naiṭ "to be far distant"	*t' durative intensive	
	MSA *nwb "big"	*b extendative (> stative?)	

	Related forms in Arabic	extension (or suffix)	reconstructed root
(#665)	*ʕaθθ* "to eat up wool (moth); bite"	(none)	*ʕθ "to swallow (liquid, soft food?)"
	ʕaθj "to drink in small quantities but long and much"	*g^w durative	
	ʕaθlab "to swallow the water greedily"	*l finitive; *p' finitive fortative	
(#681)	*ʕall* "to repeat, do over again"	(none)	*ʕl "to move to and fro"
	ʕalʕāl "waving to and fro"	(reduplicated stem as frequentative)	
	ʕalaz "to be restless"	*z intensive of manner	
	ʕalḑ "to shake a thing to pull it out"	*ḑ middle voice	
	ʕalah "to be intoxicated; to run to and fro in terror"	*h amplificative	
(#683)	*ʕamd* "to purpose, resolve upon; attend to, undertake"	*d durative	*ʕm "to apply, put into effect"
	ʕamal "deed, action; occupation; work; to work, perform; do; practise, profes; produce an effect"	*l noun suffix (v. < n.)	
	ʕamr "to cultivate and inhabit land"	*r diffusive	
(#695)	*ʕarb* "to swell and suppurate"	*b extendative	*ʕr "to be raised"
	ʕarj "to mount"	*g finitive fortative	
	ʕard "to shoot up, grow"	*d durative	
	ʕarš "to build"	*ɬ venitive	

	Related forms in Arabic	extension (or suffix)	reconstructed root
(#696)	*ʕart* "to lighten, flash, shine"	*t durative	*ʕr "to burn (intr.), shine"
	ʕarš "to be kindled and kept burning"	*ɬ venitive	
	ʕarṣ "to lighten continually"	*tl' focative	
(#697)	*ʕard*, *ʕardal* "hard, firm, stiff"	*d durative; *l adjective suffix	*ʕr "hard, firm, strong"
	ʕarz "to be thick and strong"	*z intensive (manner)	
	ʕart "to be hard"	*t adjective suffix (with v. < adj.)	
(#721)	*ʔašb* "to blame"	*p' finitive fortative	*ʔɬ "to speak out"
	ʔašr "boisterous merriment; to be merry"	*r noun suffix (with v. < n.)	
	ʔašy "to invent lies"	*y inchoative	
(#744)	*ḥafʔ* "to throw on the ground"	*ʔ concisive	*ḥp "to put down"
	ḥafr "to lie with"	*r diffusive	
	ḥafṣ "to drop"	*tl' focative	
	ḥafḍ "to let fall, drop"	*dl middle voice	
(#747)	*ḥamr* "to scrape off; skin"	*r diffusive	*ḥm "to remove (hair, skin, etc.)"
	ḥamṣ "to take a mote out of the eye"	*tl' focative	
	ḥamṭ "to peel, pare"	*t' durative intensive (> durative)	
(#753)	*ḥanjar* "throat, gullet"	*g^w durative; *r noun suffix	*ḥn "to bite into"
	ḥank "to chew" (*ḥanak* "palate")	*k durative (n. < v.)	
	ḥanaš "sting"	*ɬ venitive (< earlier "get stung")	

	Related forms in Arabic	extension (or suffix)	reconstructed root
(#754)	*ḫafš* "to gather, grasp; assemble"	*ɬ venitive	*ḫp "to take hold of"
	ḫafṯ "to collect, gather"	*tl' focative	
	ḫafl "crowd, large assembly; to assemble"	*l noun suffix (v. < n.)	
	ḫafn "to take a handful; give little"	*n noun suffix (v. < presumed earlier n. "handful")	
(#758)	*ḫass* "to be moved with compassion"	(none)	*ḫs "to feel bad, give vent to bad feelings"
	ḫasḫas "to complain of pain"	(reduplicated stem as intensive)	
	ḫasd "to envy"	*d durative	
	ḫasif "to bear a grudge against, treat roughly"	*p intensive (manner)	
	ḫasl "to despise; grow mean"	*l finitive	
	ḫask "to be angry with"	*k durative	
(#761)	*ḫauz* "to walk slowly"	*z intensive (manner)	*ḫy/*ḫw "to move (intr.)"
	ḫaul "to come upon, come to"	*l finitive	
	ḫayas "to approach"	*š non-finitive	
(#770)	*habt* "to beat, strike down"	*t durative	*hb "to hit"
	habj "to beat, cudgel"	*g^w durative	
	habš "to beat"	*ɬ venitive	
(#775)	*hall* "to shout for joy, exult, cry out"	(none)	*hl "to shout"
	halhal "to repeat a voice, or raise and lower it alternatively; bewail the dead"	(reduplicated stem as frequentative)	
	halb "to scold, revile"	*b extendative	

	Related forms in Arabic	extension (or suffix)	reconstructed root
	halj "to tell incredible things"	*g^{w} durative	
	hals "to laugh, jest, crack jokes"	*s' fortative or *š non-finitive	
(#778)	*halt* "to bark, peel; uproot"	*t durative	*hl "to grasp and take out"
	halḍ "to draw or pull out"	*dl middle voice	
	halmaṭ "to take, gather"	*m extendative; *t' durative intensive (> durative)	
(#799)	*hazaj* "to modulate one's voice, trill, quaver"	*g^{w} durative	*hz "to speak out"
	hazl "jest, joke, sport; obscene talk or action"	*l noun suffix	
	hazmaj "to talk without interruption"	*m extendative; *g^{w} durative	
(#819)	*laḥḥ* "to approach, be near"	(none)	*lḥ "to come toward"
	laḥb "to go straight on, quickly along"	*b extendative	
	laḥq "to reach, overtake; pursue"	*k^{w}' andative	
(#821)	*lakḥ* "to lick"	*ḥ iterative	*lk "to put the tongue to"
	lakʕ "to sting"	*ʕ partive (> andative)	
	lakan "to speak with an impediment"	*n non-finitive or *n noun suffix, with v. < earlier n.	

	Related forms in Arabic	extension (or suffix)	reconstructed root
(#841)	*ḍafr* "sand-hill"	*r noun suffix	*ḍp "to rise; to raise, increase"
	ḍafṭ "to ride continually on"	*t' durative intensive	
	ḍafn "to load"	*n non-finitive	
	ḍafw "to abound; abundance"	*w inchoative or *w deverbative	
(#842)	*ḍafʕ* "to drop excrement"	*ʕ partive	*ḍp "to excrete"
	ḍafq "to ease the bowels once"	*k' intensive (effect)	
	ḍafn "to ease the bowels"	*n non-finitive	
(#861)	*ḍaʕḍaʕ* "weak"	(reduplicated stem; semantics unclear)	*ḍʕ "weak"
	ḍaʕf "to be weak, grow weak and thin"	*f iterative (> extendative)	
	ḍaʕal "to be weak"	*l adjective suffix (with v. < presumed earlier adj.)	
(#863)	*tašwad* "to stand high"	*d durative	*ɬw "to rise"
	šauðab "tall and handsome"	*dz extendative fortative; *b extendative (> stative?)	
	šaul "to ascend; be raised, lifted up"	*l finitive	
	šauh "to rise higher"	*h amplificative	
(#868)	*šajb* "to stretch, lengthen"	*b extendative	*ɬg "to be much, many"
	šajar "to be many, be numerous"	*r adjective suffix (v. < presumed earlier adj.)	
	šajʕam "long"	*ʕ partive; *m adjective suffix	

Related forms in Arabic	extension (or suffix)	reconstructed root
(#878) *šamr* "to walk with a light step"	*r diffusive	*ɬm "to depart"
šamjar "to flee in terror"	*g finitive fortative; *r diffusive	
šamz "to run away"	*z intensive of manner	
(#897) *ṣaɣar* "to be small, paltry, insignificant"	*r adjective suffix	*ṣɣ "to become low"
ṣaɣil "small"	*l adjective suffix	
ṣaɣw "to turn towards setting (sun)"	*w inchoative	
(#902) *ṣaqb* "to beat with the fist"	*b extendative	*ṣḳ "to beat"
ṣaqr "to beat; break stones"	*r diffusive	
ṣaqʕ "to beat"	*ʕ partive (earlier "to break by beating"?)	
ṣaql "to beat"	*l noun suffix? (earlier n. "beating"?)	
(#913) *ṣaub* "to pour out; heavy shower"	*p' finitive fortative	*ṣw "to flow"
ṣaur "river-bank"	*r noun suffix	
ṣauṭ "pattering of drops"	*t' durative intensive	
ṣaum "to drop excrement"	*m extendative	
taṣayyuʕ "to overflow the banks"	*ʕ partive	
(#915) *taṣyīʔ* "to wash the head not quite clean"	*ʔ concisive	*ṣy "to produce or apply fluid"
ṣayyib "pouring out rain; heavy rain"	*b extendative	
ṣair "to go to the water, return (from it)"	*r diffusive	
taṣyīg "to soak bread, etc., in fat or sauce"	*ɣ intensive (effect)	
taṣayyuʕ "to overflow the banks"	*ʕ partive	

	Related forms in Arabic	extension (or suffix)	reconstructed root
(#926)	***rauḫ*** "to go away, depart"	*ḫ iterative	*rw/*ry "to move along, continue, keep on"
	raud "to come and go, go to and fro, roam about; move to and fro; shift"	*d durative	
	raus "to step along haughtily"	*s' fortative	
	rauṭ "to flee into the mountains and dunes"	*t' durative intensive	
	rais "to walk pompously with violent movements of the body"	*s' fortative	
	raih "to come and go"	*h amplificative	
(#931)	***radb*** "trodden road which ceases suddenly"	*p' finitive fortative	*rd "to step along"
	radaj "to move slowly and step by step"	*g^w durative	
	radf "to come behind another, follow"	*f iterative	
	rady "to go away"	*y inchoative (> durative)	
(#945)	***ruzʔ*** "to diminish; damage, befall and harm"	*ʔ concisive	*rz "to get used up, worn out, lose function"
	razāḫ "to break down from tiredness and emaciation; be jaded"	*ḫ iterative	
	razaɣ "to be in a plight"	*$ɣ^w$ complementive	
	ruzūm "to be so weak and emaciated as not to be able to rise; die"	*m extendative as fortative	
(#947)	***raʕj*** "to move, agitate"	*g finitive fortative	*rʕ "to move"
	raʕs "to walk slowly"	*š non-finitive (?)	
	raʕṣ "to move, shake, pull, draw, drag"	*tl' focative	

	Related forms in Arabic	extension (or suffix)	reconstructed root
(#948)	*raʕraʕ* "to cause to thrive; thrive and grow"	(reduplicated stem as intensive)	*rʕ "to rise"
	raʕaj "to be very numerous"	*g finitive fortative	
	raʕn "jutting part of a mountain; promontory"	*n noun suffix	
(#954)	*wadʕ* "to put down; deposit; leave behind; take leave of and wish good journey to; abandon, forsake; let along, let be done, admit, allow; leave undone"	*ʕ partive	*wd "to move"
	wads "to depart"	*s' fortative or *š non-finitive	
	wadq "to approach, be near, be within reach of"	$*k^{w}$' andative	
(#981)	*waθʔ* "to sprain one's wrist"	*ʔ concisive	*wθ "to twist"
	waθal "rope of bast"	*l noun suffix	
	waθy "to be sprained, bruised, injured (hand)"	*y inchoative	
(#984)	*wisb* "grass and herbs"	*b animate deverbative	*ws "to grow, increase"
	wisʕ, *wusʕ*, *wasʕ* "width, capacity, extent; plenteousness, wealth"	*ʕ partive (< earlier v. sense "to grow out"?)	
	wasq "to gather and heap up"	*k' intensive (effect)	

Related forms in Arabic	extension (or suffix)	reconstructed root
(Appendix 3: #1023)		
ḫaðð "to cut off entirely"	(none)	*ḫð "to cut off"
ḫaðf "to cut off part of one's hair"	*f iterative	
ḫaðlam "to shave and sharpen to a point"	*l finitive; *m extendative	
ḫaðm "to cut off"	*m extendative	

Appendix 2
Proto-Cushitic Roots

(Additional to those presented in Ehret 1987)

	CUSHITIC ROOT	ATTESTATIONS
(#24)	*bǎts'- "front"	PSC *bǎts'a or *bǎt'a "face" PEC *bac- or *b'ac- "front" (PC *ts' > PEC *c)
(#61)	*paʔr- or *baʔr- "cultivated ground"	EC: PSom *baar "to cultivate; cultivated field" (PC *VʔC > PSom *VVC; PC *p > PSom *b) Agaw: Chamir *baruw-* "to cultivate" (stem+*w inchoat.; PC *p > Chamir *b*)
(#371)	*gox^{w}- "to bend, form a curve"	SC: Iraqw *gongoxi* "elbow" (< redup. stem *go-gox-, with regular epenthetic nasal insertion; PC *x^{w} > PSC *x /o_) EC: Soomaali *guho* "hump; curve (of road, river, coast, etc.)" (PEC *x > Som. *h* /V_; PC *ox^{w} > PEC ux; see #717 below for more general rule involved here)
(#373)	*ɣaaʕ-/*-ɣuuʕ- "to make a loud noise"	PSC *xaaʕ- "to make a noise (vocal)" PEC *g'uuʕ- "to cry loudly"
(#402)	*x^{w}âr- "to split, make a hole in"	PSC *x^{w}âr- "honeycomb" (semantics: honeycomb is composed of a myriad of small holes) PEC *xaarr- "hole, gap, space" (n. < v. by stem-vowel lengthening); *xor- "to split" (regular PC *C^{w}a > PEC *Co /_r)

	CUSHITIC ROOT	ATTESTATIONS
(#467)	*dzûl-/dzâl- or *tsûl-/*tsâl- "little"	PEC *cal- "narrow" (PC *dz, *ts > PEC *c) Agaw: Awngi *cəllí* "few"
(#486)	*tsar-/*tsir- "to burn low"	PSC *sir- or *tsir- "to cook, prepare food" EC: Yaaku *-sar-* "to burn" (PC *ts > Yaaku *s*) NAgaw *sär-/*cär- "to be red"
(#527)	*šĕeʕ- "to be scraped bare"	PSC *šĕeʕ- or *šĕeʔ- "to be abraded, be raw (of skin)" PEC *šeeʕ- "to be bare, clear"
(#543)	*ts'aʕ-/*ts'iʕ- "to burn"	PSC *ts'iʕ- or *t'iʕ- "to get hot" PEC *caʕʕ- "to burn" (PC *ts' > PEC *c)
(#635)	*ŋaɬ- or *ŋal- "to tie, knot"	EC: Soomaali *galaan*, Afar *galum* "muzzle to tie mouth of camel" (stem + *m n. suff.; PEC *ŋ > Som., Afar *g* /#_; PC *ɬ > PEC *l) Beja *naal* "Knoten, Glied in Grass-, Strohhalm" (n. < v. by VV > V; PC *ŋ > Beja *n*)
(#638)	*ŋaat'- "to spread apart, become separated"	EC: Soomaali *gaadh* "special, particular" (semantics: distinct from rest, *separate* in characteristics; PEC *ŋ > Soomaali *g*, PEC *t' > Soomaali *dh* [d']) Agaw: Chamir *ŋaša* "person with wide-apart teeth" (PC *t' > Chamir *š*)
(#652)	*ɲox- "to suck"	PSC *nʸox- "to suckle" EC: Afar *nak-* "to drink" (PEC *ɲ > Afar *n*, *o > Afar *a* /#C_C)

	CUSHITIC ROOT	ATTESTATIONS
(#717)	*ʔâak^{w}- "to burn (intr.)"	PSC *ʔâk^{w}- or *ʔâak$^{w'}$- "to be bright, be brightly colored" EC: Arbore *ʔoog*- "to burn" (PEC *o < *a, *u < *o /_C^{w}; see #371 above and 904 below for other examples of this shift)
(#728)	*ʔânx^{w}-/*ʔînx^{w}- "to listen, pay attention to"	PSC *ʔâx^{w}- "to listen" (PC *NC > PSC *C /#ʔV_-#, C = [-voice]) EC: Dullay *ʔaxx-/*ʔixx- "eye" (PEC: same *NC > *C shift as in PSC) Agaw *ɨnq^{w}(äq^{w})- "ear" (Awngi "ear; to hear") Beja *angwiil* "ear" (stem + *l n. suff.; PC *x^{w} > Beja *gw* /n_VC, C = [+voice]; corrects Ehret 1987: #410)
(#857)	*dlay-/*dlaw- "to bite"	SC: WR *tlu- "to chew" (< alternate vocalization *dluw-; PC *dl > PSC *tl) EC: Arbore *ḍow*- "to taste" (< *d'aw-; PC *dl > Arbore *ḍ*) Yaaku *-deet*- "to eat" (*-d'ay-t-, stem + *t durative; PC *dl > Yaaku *d*)
(#904)	*tlak$^{w'}$- "to ooze"	PSC *dlak$^{w'}$- "to ooze, be thick or viscous" (PC *tl > PSC *dl) PEC *j'ok'- "to produce fluid" (PEC *o < *a /_C^{w}: see #717 above for moe general rule involved here; PC *tl > PEC *j')
(#944)	*rĭiz-/*răaz- "footprint, sole of foot"	SC: Ma'a *i-rirá* "track of animal" (PC *z > PSC *d > Ma'a *r* /V_V#; PSC *ˇ word-tone > Ma'a CvCv́) EC: SLEC *raaz- "footprint, sole of foot" (Soomaali *raad*; Arbore *rass*)
(#958)	*wăak- "lower face"	PSC *wăkar- or *wăakar- "area under chin" (stem + *r n. suff.) EC: PSom-III *weeji (< *waaki) "face"

CUSHITIC ROOT	ATTESTATIONS
(#971) *wab- or *wap'- "to perform office of hereditary clan-head"; *waber- or *wap'er- "hereditary clan-head"	SC: Iraqw *wawutmo* "clan-head" (stem + *t n. suff. + SC *m sing. suff.; PSC *p' > WR *b > Iraqw *w* /V_) EC: Soomaali *waber* "hereditary clan-head" (stem + *r n. suff.; PC *p' > PEC *b' > Som. *b*) Agaw: Kemant *wämbär* "hereditary tribal priest-chief" (stem + *r n. suff.; PC *p' > pre-Agaw *b > Agaw *mb /#CV_Vr)
(#999) *yak'- "to know"	EC: Soomaali *aqoo* "to know" (stem + *w inchoat. > dur.; < pre-PSom. *-yak'- with assimilation of original stem-initial *y to prefix conjugational *y- person marking Agaw *aq- "to know" (*y > Ø /#_aC usually in Agaw)
(#1009) *yuʔ- "to look at"	SC: Burunge *yuʔud-* "to look" (stem + *t durative; PSC *t > Burunge *d* /V_-#) EC: Yaaku *-yo'yo'-* "to peep at" (reduplicated stem as freq.; PEC *u > Yaaku *o* if following C ≠ geminate)

Appendix 3
Additional Proposed PAA Roots

	SEMITIC	EGYPTIAN	CUSHITIC	CHADIC	OMOTIC
Possible cases of conjectured PAA *h^w					
1012. *-h^wâk-/*-h^wîk "to increase (in volume, extent, or size)" (Ch., Cush. **innovation**: additional meaning, "to fill up")			EC: Soomaali *hig* "to fill, sate"; *higaag* "swelling" (stem partially redup. as intens.; PEC *k > Som. *g* /V_)	some CCh *wk "full"; Ng. *wákà* "plant which is growing; on top of, high; up high"	NOm *h_2a:k "far" (Bench *hak* [4], Yem *wòokà*, Zayse *haakó* ; nom. < v. by V > V:)
1013. *-h^wats- "to darken, become dim, be obscured"			EC: Sidamo *hassh*- "to become dark" (*hassho* "night"; PC *ts >Sidamo *sh* [š])	few ECh *ws "to hide" (J)	NOm: Yem *wàssī* "midnight" (PO *h_2 > Yem *w*, *ts > Yem *s*)

	SEMITIC	EGYPTIAN	CUSHITIC	CHADIC	OMOTIC
1014. *-h^wats- or *-h^waats- "to flow, run"	A. *haθhaθ* "to pour down rain or snow (of cloud)" (redup. stem as intens.)	*hsmk* "to wade (?)" (stem + *m extend. + *k dur.)		some WCh *ws "blood" (J; semantics: flow > bleed)	NOm *h_2a:tsts- "water" (n. < v. by V >V:?); Ometo: Malo *hatsad'*- "to swim" (stem + *dl m.v.)
1015. *-h^wǎy- "to listen to, pay attention to" (Eg., Sem. **innovation**: "pay attention to" > "watch over," hence "protect")	A. *haiman* "to guard, protect" (stem + *m n. suff. or *m extend. + *n non-fin.)	*hi* "husband" (C. *haī* ; semantics: husband as protector of family; may imply alternate root shape *h^wiy-)	PEC *hayy- "wisdom, wise advice" (semantics: hear > understand > be wise")		NOm *$h_2$ay- "ear" (Ometo *$h_2$ayts-; Bench *(h)ay* 4, Mocha *wà:mo* < *way- + *m n. suff.; Yem *wèes*- "to hear"; NOm n. + *s caus. as denom.)

	SEMITIC	EGYPTIAN	CUSHITIC	CHADIC	OMOTIC
Additional PAA *dz					
1016. *-dzaw- "to be moist"	*ðwb, *ðyb "to melt" (stem + *b extend.)				NOm: Maji *čou* "cold" (semantics: see #458)
1017. *-gǒodz- "to be merry"	A. *jaðil* "merry" (stem + *l adj. suff.)				*go:ž- "to be drunk" (Bench *gož̧* [1]; Zayse *góožž-*)
1018. *-widz- "to scorn, have low opinion of"	A. *wazʔ* "to accuse, scold, put to scorn, despise" (stem + *ʔ conc.)				SOm: Ari *yi̧ž-* "to hate"
Additional PAA *j					
1019. *-jak- "to burn (intr.)"	A. *ðakw* "to blaze" (stem + *w inchoat. > dur.)				SOm: Ari *šakmi* "bright" (stem + *m adj. suff.)

	SEMITIC	EGYPTIAN	CUSHITIC	CHADIC	OMOTIC
1020. *-poj- "to spread apart (tr.)"	A. *faðð* "alone; to be alone, isolated"; *infiðāḫ* "to spread legs apart to make water" (stem + *ḫ iter. > dur.)		EC: Soomaali *bashiici* "to open slightly" (stem + *ʕ part. + *s caus. (> Som. *-i*); PC *p > Som. *b*, *dz > Som. *sh* [š], *o > Som. *a*; Som. *c* = [ʕ])		SOm: Ari *fo č*- "to open"
1021. *-k'iij- "to take a sip"	A. *qaðm* "to sip" (stem + *m extend.)				NOm: Sheko *k'i:š*- "to drink"
1022. *-ʕăaj- "to take from view, put out of sight"	MSA *ʕaðl "to be dark, moonless" (stem + *l adj. suff.)	*iz* "tomb"			*a:č- "to hide" (NOm: Bench *ač* [1]; SOm: Ari *aač*-)

	SEMITIC	EGYPTIAN	CUSHITIC	CHADIC	OMOTIC
1023. *-ḫăj- "to cut off"	pPS *ḫð "to cut off" (Append.1)		EC: Soomaali *xash* "sawdust, shaving, chip" (*x* = [ḫ]; PC *dz > Som. *sh* [š])		NOm: Mocha *hàčč-* "to sharpen; cut with adze"
1024. *-ɬăaj- "to find, get" (Sem., Eg. **innovation**: addition of *p intens. ext.)	A. *šaðf* "to get, obtain" (stem + *p in-intens. of man-ner)	*šzp* "to take, accept, reserve" (stem + *p intens. of manner)			Gonga *da:č- "to find" (Mocha *dà:č*-; PO *l > Gonga *d /#_)

Appendix 4

Summary of Numbered Sound Shift Rules

1. Pre-proto-Semitic (pPS) and proto-Semitic (PS) sound shifts:

#1. PNE *i, *u, *ə > PS *ə;
PNE *a, *ä > PS *a /#C_C(C).
#2. PAA *tl' > PS *ɬ /$C_{[+sibilant]}$.
#3. PAA *ɣ > PS *g, *x > PS *k /#_$VC_{[+laryngeal]}$.
#4. PAA $*ɣ^{(w)}$ > PS *g /#_Vx.
#5. PAA $*k^{(w)'}$ > PS *k /#dlV_.
#6. PAA $*C^{w}$ > C (C = [+velar]).
#7. PAA *ʔ > PS *ʕ /#ɬ_r#.
#8. PBA $*C_1VC_1$ > PS ? (uncertain; just one proposed example so far: #911)

2. Egyptian sound shifts:

#1. PNE *ə > Old Eg. /i/,
PNE *ä > Old Eg. /a/.
#2. PAA *h > Eg. *ḫ* /_Vz.
#3. PAA *dl > Eg. *d*, *tl' > pre-Eg. *t', *ɬ > Eg. *s* /#_VC (C = velar obstruent).
#4. PAA *t' > pre-Eg. *ts'.
#5. PAA *c > pre-Eg. *ts,
PAA *c' > pre-Eg. *ts',
PAA *j > pre-Eg. *dz (presuming *c = [č], *j = [ǯ]), and
PAA *ŝ > s.
#6. pre-Eg. *ts' > pre-Eg. *ts (de-glottalization).
#7. pre-Eg. *ts > Old Eg., ME *s*,
pre-Eg. *dz > Old Eg. *z* (de-affrication).
#8. Old Eg. *z* > ME *s* .
#9. PAA *f > Eg. *p* /#_$VC_{[+continuant/-voice]}$ and /#_Vr.
#10. PAA *p' > pre-Eg. *p.
#11. Eg. *p* > Eg. *b* /#dlV_ .
#12. PAA $*x^{w}$ > pre-Eg. $*ɣ^{w}$ /n, r.
#13. PAA $*x^{(w)}$ > $*ɣ^{(w)}$ > Eg. *ḫ*, *k > Eg. *g* /w, y.

#14. PAA *CVʕ > Eg. *ḫ3* (C = velar stop other than PAA *gʷ),
PAA *gʷVʕ > Eg. *ḫ ᶜ*.
#15. PAA *g⁽ʷ⁾ > Eg. *ḏ* /#_Vd,
PAA *k⁽ʷ⁾ > Eg. *ṯ* /#_Vt.
#16. PAA *xVh > Eg. *kh* (see root #402).
#17. PAA *C[+labial,+velar] > Eg. *C* [+velar].
#18. PAA *ʕi > Eg. *i* .
#19. PAA *ʕ > Eg. *i* /#_V[+cont./+dental].
#20. PAA *ʔ > Eg. *i* /#_VS, S = sonorant.
#21. some PAA *ʕu > Eg. *w* (/#_{f,s}.
#22. PAA *ʔ > Eg. *ᶜ* /_VC, C = n, r, or g (V = a, aa ?).
#23. PAA *ʕ > Eg. *3* /[+voice/+dental]V_.
#24. PAA *H > Eg. *3* /C[+voice/+velar]V_ (H = *h or *ḫ).
#25. PAA *hʕ > Eg. *h3*,
#26. PAA *ʕh > Eg.*ᶜḫ* (?).
#27. PAA *ḫɣ > Eg. *ḫ3*.
#28. PAA *tl' > pre-Eg. *dl /#_Vʕ.
#29. PAA *C[+lateral,+obstruent] > Eg. *C* [+palatal,+obstruent].
#30. PAA *r > pre-Eg. *l /#_V(V)C[+obstruent,+labial].
#31. PAA *r > Eg. *3* /C_(t, w, y)# (C ≠ *g*, *m*, *n*, *r*, *w*, *š*, or *x*).
#32. PAA *l > Eg. *r* /_(t, w, y)#.
#33. PAA *l > Eg. *i* ([y]) /#_iC (instances of /#_ib and /#_iʕC have been observed so far).
#34. PAA *l > Eg. *r* /#nV_C.
#35. PAA *l > Eg. *n*.
#36. ME *n* > Coptic (C.) *l* /#_Vb_Vb.
#37. ME *n* > C. *l* /#_(V){s, š, h}V(m,b)# and /#_V{m,b}{s, š, h}.
#38. ME *n* > C. *l* /#_Vḳ.
#39. ME *n* > C. *l* /#C_1V_C_2 (either C_1 or C_2 = *m*).
#40. ME *nn* > C. *l (V) l V*.
#41. PAA *r (> ME *r*) > C. *l* /#(C)_o(C)# and /#o _#.

3. Proposed Egypto-Berber (EgB) sound shift:

#1. PAA *p' > EgB *p (before *p, *f > proto-Berber *f)

4. Proto-Boreafrasian (PBA) sound shifts:

#1. PAA *s', *s > PBA *s.
#2. PAA *h > PBA *ḫ /#_Vs.

#3. PAA *t > ? (unknown) /#_VC (C = dental/alveolar obstruent)
#4. PAA *z > *d, other *C[+sibilant] > ? (unknown) in the environment of a proximate sibilant in the same word.
#5. PAA *ŋ (w), *ɲ > PBA *n.
#6. Loss of phonemic tone.
#7. PAA *V > PBA Ø /_# in nominals.
#8. PAA *z > PBA *d /_-# (noun-stem-final).
#9. PNE *N- > PBA Ø /#_CV (deleting N created by PNE shift #5 in section 6 below)

5. Proto-Chadic (PCh) sound shifts:

#1. PNE *a [aa], *ä > PCh *a
#2. [+pharyngeal] > [-pharyngeal] (PAA *ʕ > PCh *ʔ, *ḩ > PCh *h.
#3. PAA *t', *s' > PCh *s', PAA *c' > PCh *ŝ'.
#4. Eryth. *dz > PCh *z, *ts > PCh *s.
#5. PAA *N > Ø /V_C (cases of C = *ts, *ḩ are known).

6. Proto-North Erythraean (PNE) sound shifts:

#1. PAA *Vy, *Vw > PNE *VV /#C__C.
#2. PAA *ee > pre-PNE *i,
PAA *oo > pre-PNE *u.
#3. pre-PNE *o, *e, *a (< PAA *o, *e, *a) > PNE *ä,
pre-PNE *u, *i (created by #2) > PNE *ə.
#4. PAA *-VC- verb roots > PNE *-CV-.
#5. Eryth. *in- (concom. pref.) > *N- /#_C.

7. Proto-Cushitic (PC) sound shifts:

#1. PAA *b > PC *m /#_Vn.
#2. PAA *g > PC *k /#dV_ and /#wV_.
#3. PAA *ɣ > PC *g /#_Vx-.

8. Proto-Erythraean (Eryth.) sound shift:

#1. PAA *j, *dz > Eryth. *dz,
PAA *c, *ts > Eryth. *ts

9. Proto-Omotic (PO) and North Omotic (NOm) sound shifts:

i. PAA *dz > pre-PO *ž;
ii. PAA *j > pre-PO *č;
PAA *c > PO *$\check{s}_3$ ([š̢]?).
iii. pre-PO *č > PO *š, *ts > PO *s /#_.
#1. PAA *a(a) > PO *e(:) /_C- (C = PAA *ʕ or *ḥ).
#2. [+pharyngeal] > [-pharyngeal] (PAA *ʕ > PO *ʔ, *ḥ > PO *h).
#3. PAA *C^wa > *Co /#_C_2 (C_2 = *l, *dl, and *c, in the examples so far noted).
#4. PAA *C^w > PO *C /#_V, V ≠ i(:).
#5. PAA *š > PO *$\check{s}_2$ /i, y_.
#6. PAA *VNC > PO *V:C (C = [-voice]).
#7. PAA *u > NOm *o, PAA *i > NO *e.
[7a. */e/ -> *[i] /#N_C (N = nasal);
*[i] /#l_$C_{[+labial/+voice]}$ (PO *l < PAA *l and *ɬ);
*[i] /#b, p_r;
*[i] /#S_K (S = PO *s, *s', or *š; K = PO *k, *k^w, or *ʔ); and
*[e] elsewhere;
[7b. */o/ -> *[u] /#C_$C_{[+labial]}$;
*[u], */e/ -> [i] /#(ʔ)_C;
*[u], */e/ -> [i] /#k, x, k'_C (C = PO *t, *t', *s');
*[u], */e/ -> [i] /#(ʔ)_C- (but not /#(ʔ)_CC-);
*[u], */e/ -> [i] /#$C_{[+labial]}$_C_2 (C_2 = ts, c'); and
*[o] elsewhere.]
#8. PAA *a > PO *o /#C_1_$C_{[+labial]}$, C_1 = PAA *z, *j.
#9. PAA *C^w > PO *C (deleting all remaining labiovelars).
#10. PAA *e(:) > NOm *i(:) /#S_C (S = sibilant; C = *d, *n, or *r);
#11. PO *V: > NOm *V /#C[+velar, -voice]_C, where PAA root had *ˆ tone.
#12. NOm *u > Ometo *o, *i > Ometo *e /#(ʔ)_$C_{[-continuant, -voice]}$
#13. PO *u > NOm *u: /#C_P (C = voiced oral stop, P = voiceless labial).
#14. PO *V: > NOm *V /#C_C- + -(V)C- suffix.
#15. PAA *N > NOm (or PO?) Ø /V_C (C = [+sibilant] or PO *p ([f] /V_).

References

Allan, E. J.

1976. "Kullo." In M. L. Bender (ed.), *The Non-Semitic Languages of Ethiopia*, pp. 324-350. East Lansing: African Studies Center, Michigan State University.

Appleyard, D. L.

1984. "The internal classification of the Agaw languages: a comparative and historical phonology." In James Bynon (ed.), *Current Progress in Afro-Asiatic Linguistics*, pp. 33-67. Amsterdam, Philadelphia: John Benjamins Publishing Co.

n.d. "Proto-Agaw Roots." Unpublished typescript.

Arvanites, Linda.

1990. *The Glottalic Phonemes of proto-Eastern Cushitic.* Ph.D. dissertation, University of California at Los Angeles.

Bender, M. L.

1971. "The languages of Ethiopia: a new lexicostatistical classification and some problems of diffusion." *Anthropological Linguistics* 13 (5): 165-288.

1975. *Omotic: A New Afroasiatic Family.* Carbondale: University Museum, Southern Illinois University.

1988. "Proto-Omotic phonology and lexicon." In M. Bechhaus-Gerst and F. Serzisko (ed.), *Cushitic-Omotic. Papers from the International Symposium on Cushitic and Omotic Languages, Cologne, January 6-9, 1986* , pp. 1221-159. Hamburg: Buske.

1989. "Gender in Omotic." *Journal of Afroasiatic Languages* 2 (2): 203-221.

1990. "A survey of Omotic grammemes." In P. Baldi (ed.), *Linguistic Change and Reconstruction Methodology.* Berlin, New York: de Gruyter.

Bomhard, A. R.

1988. "The reconstruction of the proto-Semitic consonant system." In Y. L. Arbeitman (ed.), *A Semitic/Afrasian Gathering in Re-*

membrance of Albert Ehrman. Amsterdam, Philadelphia: John Benjamins Publishing Co.

Breeze, M.
1990. "A sketch of the phonology and grammar of Gimira (Benchnon)." In R. Hayward (ed.), *Omotic Language Studies* (which see below), pp. 1-67.

Callender, J. B.
1975. *Middle Egyptian*. Malibu: Undena Publications.

Cerny, J.
1976. *Coptic Etymological Dictionary*. Cambridge: Cambridge University Press.

Cohen, D.
1968. "Langues chamito-sémitiques." In A. Martinet (ed.), *Le Langage*. Bruges: Encyclopédie de la Pleiade.

Cohen, M.
1947. *Essai comparatif sur le vocabulaire et la phonétique du chamito-sémitique*. Paris.

Diakonov, I. M. (Diakonoff)
1965. *Semito-Hamitic Languages: an Essay in Classification*. Moscow: "Nauka" Publishing House.
1970. "Problems of root structure in Proto-Semitic." *Archiv Orientální* 38: 453-480.
1975. "On root structure in Proto-Semitic." In J. and T. Bynon (ed.), (ed.), *Hamito-Semitica*, pp. 133-151. The Hague, Paris: Mouton.
1981. "Earliest Semites in Asia." *Altorientalische Forschungen* 8: 23-74.
1988. *Afrasian Languages*. Moscow: "Nauka" Publishers, Central Department of Oriental Literature.

Ehret, C.
1979a. "Omotic and the subgrouping of the Afroasiatic language family." In R. L. Hess (ed.), *Proceedings of the Fifth International Conference on Ethiopian Studies, Session B, April 13-18, 1979, Chicago, USA*, pp. 51-62. Chicago: Office of Publication Services, University of Illinois at Chicago Circle.
1979b. "On the antiquity of agriculture in Ethiopia." *Journal of African History* 20: 161-177.

1980. *The Historical Reconstruction of Southern Cushitic Phonology and Vocabulary*. Kölner Beiträge zur Afrikanistik, B.5. Berlin: Reimer.
1987. "Proto-Cushitic Reconstruction." *Sprache und Geschichte in Afrika* 8: 7-180.
1989. "The origin of third consonants in Semitic roots: an internal reconstruction (applied to Arabic)." *Journal of Afroasiatic Languages* 2 (2): 109-202.
1991. "Revising the Consonants of proto-Eastern Cushitic." *Studies in African Linguistics* 22 (3): 1-65.
MS. *The Historical Reconstruction of Nilo-Saharan..*

Ehret, C., and M. N. Ali.
1985. "The subclassification of Soomaali." In T. Labahn (ed.), *Proceedings of the Second International Congress of Somali Studies*, pp. 201-269. Hamburg: Buske.

Faber, A.
1985. *Semitic Sibilants: A Study in Comparative Lexicography.* (Manuscript)

Faulkner, R. O.
1964. *A Concise Dictionary of Middle Egyptian.* Oxford: Griffith Institute.

Fleming, H. C.
1969. "The classification of West Cushitic within Hamito-Semitic." In J. Butler (ed.), *Eastern African History*, pp. 3-27. New York: Praeger.
1974. "Omotic as an Afroasiatic family." *Studies in African Linguistics,* Supplement 5, pp. 81-94.
1976a. "Cushitic and Omotic." In M. L. Bender, et al. (ed.), *Language in Ethiopia*, pp. 34-53. London: Oxford University Press.
1976b. "Omotic Overview." In M. L. Bender (ed.), *The Non-Semitic Languages of Ethiopia*, pp. 299-323. East Lansing: African Studies Center, Michigan State University.
1977. Oral presentation, Conference on Cushitic Origins, School of Oriental and African Studies, London, June 1977.

Greenberg, J. H.
1963. *The Languages of Africa.* Bloomington: Indiana University Research Center in Anthropology, Folklore, and Linguistics. (Also reprinted in several later years)

Hayward, R. J.
1982. "Notes on the Koyra language." *Afrika und Ubersee* 65: 211-268.
1984a. *The Arbore Language: A First Investigation.* Hamburg: Buske.
1984b. "A reconstruction of some root extensions of the Eastern Cushitic verb." In J. Bynon (ed.), *Current Progress* (for which see Appleyard 1984), pp. 69-109.
1987. "Terminal vowels in Ometo nominals." In H. Jungraithmayr and W. W. Müller (ed.), *Proceedings 4th International Hamito-Semitic Congress*, pp. 215-231. Amsterdam, Philadelphia: John Benjamins Publishing Co.
1990. *Omotic Language Studies.* London: School of Oriental and African Studies, University of London.

Hetzron, R.
1978. "The nominal system of Awngi (Southern Agaw)." *Bulletin of the School of Oriental and African Studies* 41: 121-141.
1980. "The limits of Cushitic." *Sprache und Geshichte in Afrika* 2: 7-126.

Johnstone, T. M.
1977. *Harsūsi Lexicon.* London: Oxford University Press.
1981. *Jibbāli Lexicon.* Oxford, New York: Oxford University Press.

Jungraithmayr, H., and K. Shimizu.
1981. *Chadic Lexical Roots,* Vol. II. Berlin: Reimer.

Kraft, C. H.
1974. "Reconstruction of Chadic pronouns I: possessives, object and independent sets—an interim report." In E. Voeltz (ed.), *Third Annual Conference on African Linguistics*, pp. 69-94. Bloomington: Indiana University Publications, African Series, vol. 7.

Lesko, L. H.
1982-1990. *A Dictionary of Late Egyptian,* vols. 1-5. Berkeley: B.C. Scribe Publications.

Leslau, W.
1959. *A Dictionary of Moča.* Berkeley, Los Angeles: University of California Press.

Martinet, A.
1975. "Remarques sur le consonantisme sémitique." In A. Martinet, *Evolutions des langues et reconstruction.* Vendome: Presses Universitaires de France.

Moscati, S. (ed.)
1964. *An Introduction to the Comparative Grammar of the Semitic Languages.* Wiesbaden: Harrassowitz.

Newman, P.
1977. "Chadic classification and reconstructions." *Afroasiatic Linguistics* 5, 1: 1-42.

Newman, P., and R. Maa.
1966. "Comparative Chadic: phonology and lexicon." *Journal of African Languages* 5 (3): 218-251.

Pia, J. Joseph.
1984. "Multiply-tiered vocalic inventories: an Afroasiatic trait." In J. Bynon (ed.), *Current Progress* (see Appleyard 1984), pp. 463-475.

Prasse, K.-G.
1975. "The reconstruction of proto-Berber short vowels." In J. and T. Bynon (ed.), *Hamito-Semitica*, pp. 215-228. The Hague, Paris: Mouton.

Sasse, H.-J.
1979. "The consonant phonemes of proto-East-Cushitic (PEC): a first approximation." *Afroasiatic Linguistics* 7, 1: 1-67.

Schuh, R. G.
1981. *A Dictionary of Ngizim.* Berkeley, Los Angeles: University of California Press.

Shryock, A. M.
1990. "Issues in Chadic classification: the Masa group." M.A. thesis, University of California at Los Angeles.

Steingass, F. J.
1978 (1884). *Arabic-English Dictionary.* New Delhi: Cosmo Publications. (Reprint of 1884 edition.)

Vycichl, W.
1983. *Dictionaire étymologique de la langue copte.* Leuven: Peeters.

1990. *La vocalisation de la langue egyptienne*, Vol. 1: *La phonetique* . Cairo: Institut Francais d'Archeologie Orientale.

Wedekind, K.
1985. "Why Bench' (Ethiopia) has five level tones today." In Pieper Stickel (ed.), *Studia Linguistica Diachronica et Synchronica*, pp.881-901. Berlin, New York, Amsterdam: Mouton de Gruyter.
1990. Gimo-Jan or Ben-Yem-Om: Benç̌-Yemsa phonemes, tones, and words." In R. Hayward (ed.), *Omotic Language Studies* (see above), pp. 68-184.

Zaborski, A.
1980. "Can Omotic be reclassified as West Cushitic?" In G. Goldberg (ed.), *Ethiopian Studies: Proceedings of the Sixth International Conference, Tel-Aviv, 14-17 April 1980* , pp. 525-530. Rotterdam: Balkema, 1986.

Index 1

Proto-Afroasiatic (Proto-Afrasian) Consonants

Index 2

Reconstructed Root Meanings

D

S

Other Volumes Available
University of California Publications in Linguistics

Vol. 75. James A. Matisoff. *The Grammar of Lahu*. ISBN 0-520-09467-0
Vol. 96. Brent D. Galloway. *A Grammar of Upriver Halkomelem*. ISBN 0-520-09619-3
Vol. 104. Haruo Aoki and Deward E. Walker, Jr. *Nez Perce Oral Narratives*. ISBN 0-520-09693-2
Vol. 107. Jon P. Dayley. *Tzutujil Grammar*. ISBN 0-520-09962-1
Vol. 111. James A. Matisoff. *The Dictionary of Lahu*. ISBN 0-520-09711-4
Vol. 112. David John Weber. *A Grammar of Huallaga (Huánuco) Quechua*. ISBN 0-520-09732-7
Vol. 113. Kathryn Klingebiel. *Noun + Verb Compounding in Western Romance*. ISBN 0-520-09729-7
Vol. 115. Jon P. Dayley. *Tümpisa (Panamint) Shoshone Grammar*. ISBN 0-520-09752-1
Vol. 116. Jon P. Dayley. *Tümpisa (Panamint) Shoshone Dictionary*. ISBN 0-520-09754-8
Vol. 118. Xiao-nan Susan Shen. *The Prosody of Mandarin Chinese*. ISBN 0-520-09750-5
Vol. 119. Maurice L. Zigmond, Curtis G. Booth, and Pamela Munro (ed. by Pamela Munro). *Kawaiisu: A Grammar and Dictionary with Texts*. ISBN 0-520-09747-5
Vol. 120. Thomas Edward Payne. *The Twins Stories: Participant Coding in Yagua Narrative*. ISBN 0-520-09774-2
Vol. 121. Derek Nurse and Thomas J. Hinnebusch. *Swahili and Sabaki: A Linguistic History*. ISBN 0-520-09775-0
Vol. 122. Haruo Aoki. *Nez Perce Dictionary*. ISBN 0-520-09763-7
Vol. 123. Mary Ellen Ryder. *Ordered Chaos: The Interpretation of Noun-Noun Compounds*. ISBN 0-520-09777-7
Vol. 124. Jean Gail Mulder. *Ergativity in Coast Tsimshian (Sm'algya̱x)*. ISBN 0-520-09788-2.
Vol. 125. Villiana Calac Hyde and Eric Elliott. *Yumáyk Yumáyk Long Ago*. ISBN 0-520-09791-2

University of California Press
Berkeley 94720

ISBN 0-520-09799-8